FREE Study Skills Videos/

MW00442077

Dear Customer,

Thank you for your purchase from Mometrix! We consider it an honor and a privilege that you have purchased our product and we want to ensure your satisfaction.

As part of our ongoing effort to meet the needs of test takers, we have developed a set of Study Skills Videos that we would like to give you for <u>FREE</u>. These videos cover our *best practices* for getting ready for your exam, from how to use our study materials to how to best prepare for the day of the test.

All that we ask is that you email us with feedback that would describe your experience so far with our product. Good, bad, or indifferent, we want to know what you think!

To get your FREE Study Skills Videos, you can use the **QR code** below, or send us an **email** at studyvideos@mometrix.com with *FREE VIDEOS* in the subject line and the following information in the body of the email:

- The name of the product you purchased.
- Your product rating on a scale of 1-5, with 5 being the highest rating.
- Your feedback. It can be long, short, or anything in between. We just want to know your impressions and experience so far with our product. (Good feedback might include how our study material met your needs and ways we might be able to make it even better. You could highlight features that you found helpful or features that you think we should add.)

If you have any questions or concerns, please don't hesitate to contact me directly.

Thanks again!

Sincerely,

Jay Willis
Vice President
jay.willis@mometrix.com
1-800-673-8175

SCAN HERE

Civil Service Exam

Study Guide 2024-2025

Test Prep Secrets for Police Officer, Firefighter, Postal, and More

400+ Practice Questions

150+ Online Video Tutorials

4th Edition

Copyright © 2024 by Mometrix Media LLC

All rights reserved. This product, or parts thereof, may not be reproduced, stored in a retrieval system, or transmitted in any form or by any means—electronic, mechanical, photocopy, recording, scanning, or other—except for brief quotations in critical reviews or articles, without the prior written permission of the publisher.

Written and edited by the Mometrix Civil Service Test Team

Printed in the United States of America

This paper meets the requirements of ANSI/NISO Z39.48-1992 (Permanence of Paper).

Mometrix offers volume discount pricing to institutions. For more information or a price quote, please contact our sales department at sales@mometrix.com or 888-248-1219.

Mometrix Media LLC is not affiliated with or endorsed by any official testing organization. All organizational and test names are trademarks of their respective owners.

Paperback
ISBN 13: 978-1-5167-2608-0
ISBN 10: 1-5167-2608-1

DEAR FUTURE EXAM SUCCESS STORY

First of all, **THANK YOU** for purchasing Mometrix study materials!

Second, congratulations! You are one of the few determined test-takers who are committed to doing whatever it takes to excel on your exam. **You have come to the right place.** We developed these study materials with one goal in mind: to deliver you the information you need in a format that's concise and easy to use.

In addition to optimizing your guide for the content of the test, we've outlined our recommended steps for breaking down the preparation process into small, attainable goals so you can make sure you stay on track.

We've also analyzed the entire test-taking process, identifying the most common pitfalls and showing how you can overcome them and be ready for any curveball the test throws you.

Standardized testing is one of the biggest obstacles on your road to success, which only increases the importance of doing well in the high-pressure, high-stakes environment of test day. Your results on this test could have a significant impact on your future, and this guide provides the information and practical advice to help you achieve your full potential on test day.

Your success is our success

We would love to hear from you! If you would like to share the story of your exam success or if you have any questions or comments in regard to our products, please contact us at **800-673-8175** or **support@mometrix.com**.

Thanks again for your business and we wish you continued success!

Sincerely,
The Mometrix Test Preparation Team

TABLE OF CONTENTS

Introduction

Thank you for purchasing this resource! You have made the choice to prepare yourself for a test that could have a huge impact on your future, and this guide is designed to help you be fully ready for test day. Obviously, it's important to have a solid understanding of the test material, but you also need to be prepared for the unique environment and stressors of the test, so that you can perform to the best of your abilities.

For this purpose, the first section that appears in this guide is the **Secret Keys**. We've devoted countless hours to meticulously researching what works and what doesn't, and we've boiled down our findings to the five most impactful steps you can take to improve your performance on the test. We start at the beginning with study planning and move through the preparation process, all the way to the testing strategies that will help you get the most out of what you know when you're finally sitting in front of the test.

We recommend that you start preparing for your test as far in advance as possible. However, if you've bought this guide as a last-minute study resource and only have a few days before your test, we recommend that you skip over the first two Secret Keys since they address a long-term study plan.

If you struggle with **test anxiety**, we strongly encourage you to check out our recommendations for how you can overcome it. Test anxiety is a formidable foe, but it can be beaten, and we want to make sure you have the tools you need to defeat it.

Copyright © Mometrix Media. You have been licensed one copy of this document for personal use only. Any other reproduction or redistribution is strictly prohibited. All rights reserved. This content is provided for test preparation purposes only and does not imply an endorsement by Mometrix of any particular political, scientific, or religious point of view.

Secret Key #1 – Plan Big, Study Small

There's a lot riding on your performance. If you want to ace this test, you're going to need to keep your skills sharp and the material fresh in your mind. You need a plan that lets you review everything you need to know while still fitting in your schedule. We'll break this strategy down into three categories.

Information Organization

Start with the information you already have: the official test outline. From this, you can make a complete list of all the concepts you need to cover before the test. Organize these concepts into groups that can be studied together, and create a list of any related vocabulary you need to learn so you can brush up on any difficult terms. You'll want to keep this vocabulary list handy once you actually start studying since you may need to add to it along the way.

Time Management

Once you have your set of study concepts, decide how to spread them out over the time you have left before the test. Break your study plan into small, clear goals so you have a manageable task for each day and know exactly what you're doing. Then just focus on one small step at a time. When you manage your time this way, you don't need to spend hours at a time studying. Studying a small block of content for a short period each day helps you retain information better and avoid stressing over how much you have left to do. You can relax knowing that you have a plan to cover everything in time. In order for this strategy to be effective though, you have to start studying early and stick to your schedule. Avoid the exhaustion and futility that comes from last-minute cramming!

Study Environment

The environment you study in has a big impact on your learning. Studying in a coffee shop, while probably more enjoyable, is not likely to be as fruitful as studying in a quiet room. It's important to keep distractions to a minimum. You're only planning to study for a short block of time, so make the most of it. Don't pause to check your phone or get up to find a snack. It's also important to **avoid multitasking**. Research has consistently shown that multitasking will make your studying dramatically less effective. Your study area should also be comfortable and well-lit so you don't have the distraction of straining your eyes or sitting on an uncomfortable chair.

 The time of day you study is also important. You want to be rested and alert. Don't wait until just before bedtime. Study when you'll be most likely to comprehend and remember. Even better, if you know what time of day your test will be, set that time aside for study. That way your brain will be used to working on that subject at that specific time and you'll have a better chance of recalling information.

Finally, it can be helpful to team up with others who are studying for the same test. Your actual studying should be done in as isolated an environment as possible, but the work of organizing the information and setting up the study plan can be divided up. In between study sessions, you can discuss with your teammates the concepts that you're all studying and quiz each other on the details. Just be sure that your teammates are as serious about the test as you are. If you find that your study time is being replaced with social time, you might need to find a new team.

Copyright © Mometrix Media. You have been licensed one copy of this document for personal use only. Any other reproduction or redistribution is strictly prohibited. All rights reserved. This content is provided for test preparation purposes only and does not imply an endorsement by Mometrix of any particular political, scientific, or religious point of view.

Secret Key #2 – Make Your Studying Count

You're devoting a lot of time and effort to preparing for this test, so you want to be absolutely certain it will pay off. This means doing more than just reading the content and hoping you can remember it on test day. It's important to make every minute of study count. There are two main areas you can focus on to make your studying count.

Retention

It doesn't matter how much time you study if you can't remember the material. You need to make sure you are retaining the concepts. To check your retention of the information you're learning, try recalling it at later times with minimal prompting. Try carrying around flashcards and glance at one or two from time to time or ask a friend who's also studying for the test to quiz you.

To enhance your retention, look for ways to put the information into practice so that you can apply it rather than simply recalling it. If you're using the information in practical ways, it will be much easier to remember. Similarly, it helps to solidify a concept in your mind if you're not only reading it to yourself but also explaining it to someone else. Ask a friend to let you teach them about a concept you're a little shaky on (or speak aloud to an imaginary audience if necessary). As you try to summarize, define, give examples, and answer your friend's questions, you'll understand the concepts better and they will stay with you longer. Finally, step back for a big picture view and ask yourself how each piece of information fits with the whole subject. When you link the different concepts together and see them working together as a whole, it's easier to remember the individual components.

Finally, practice showing your work on any multi-step problems, even if you're just studying. Writing out each step you take to solve a problem will help solidify the process in your mind, and you'll be more likely to remember it during the test.

Modality

Modality simply refers to the means or method by which you study. Choosing a study modality that fits your own individual learning style is crucial. No two people learn best in exactly the same way, so it's important to know your strengths and use them to your advantage.

For example, if you learn best by visualization, focus on visualizing a concept in your mind and draw an image or a diagram. Try color-coding your notes, illustrating them, or creating symbols that will trigger your mind to recall a learned concept. If you learn best by hearing or discussing information, find a study partner who learns the same way or read aloud to yourself. Think about how to put the information in your own words. Imagine that you are giving a lecture on the topic and record yourself so you can listen to it later.

For any learning style, flashcards can be helpful. Organize the information so you can take advantage of spare moments to review. Underline key words or phrases. Use different colors for different categories. Mnemonic devices (such as creating a short list in which every item starts with the same letter) can also help with retention. Find what works best for you and use it to store the information in your mind most effectively and easily.

3

Copyright © Mometrix Media. You have been licensed one copy of this document for personal use only. Any other reproduction or redistribution is strictly prohibited. All rights reserved. This content is provided for test preparation purposes only and does not imply an endorsement by Mometrix of any particular political, scientific, or religious point of view.

Secret Key #3 – Practice the Right Way

Your success on test day depends not only on how many hours you put into preparing, but also on whether you prepared the right way. It's good to check along the way to see if your studying is paying off. One of the most effective ways to do this is by taking practice tests to evaluate your progress. Practice tests are useful because they show exactly where you need to improve. Every time you take a practice test, pay special attention to these three groups of questions:

- The questions you got wrong
- The questions you had to guess on, even if you guessed right
- The questions you found difficult or slow to work through

This will show you exactly what your weak areas are, and where you need to devote more study time. Ask yourself why each of these questions gave you trouble. Was it because you didn't understand the material? Was it because you didn't remember the vocabulary? Do you need more repetitions on this type of question to build speed and confidence? Dig into those questions and figure out how you can strengthen your weak areas as you go back to review the material.

 Additionally, many practice tests have a section explaining the answer choices. It can be tempting to read the explanation and think that you now have a good understanding of the concept. However, an explanation likely only covers part of the question's broader context. Even if the explanation makes perfect sense, **go back and investigate** every concept related to the question until you're positive you have a thorough understanding.

As you go along, keep in mind that the practice test is just that: practice. Memorizing these questions and answers will not be very helpful on the actual test because it is unlikely to have any of the same exact questions. If you only know the right answers to the sample questions, you won't be prepared for the real thing. **Study the concepts** until you understand them fully, and then you'll be able to answer any question that shows up on the test.

It's important to wait on the practice tests until you're ready. If you take a test on your first day of study, you may be overwhelmed by the amount of material covered and how much you need to learn. Work up to it gradually.

On test day, you'll need to be prepared for answering questions, managing your time, and using the test-taking strategies you've learned. It's a lot to balance, like a mental marathon that will have a big impact on your future. Like training for a marathon, you'll need to start slowly and work your way up. When test day arrives, you'll be ready.

Start with the strategies you've read in the first two Secret Keys—plan your course and study in the way that works best for you. If you have time, consider using multiple study resources to get different approaches to the same concepts. It can be helpful to see difficult concepts from more than one angle. Then find a good source for practice tests. Many times, the test website will suggest potential study resources or provide sample tests.

Copyright © Mometrix Media. You have been licensed one copy of this document for personal use only. Any other reproduction or redistribution is strictly prohibited. All rights reserved.
This content is provided for test preparation purposes only and does not imply an endorsement by Mometrix of any particular political, scientific, or religious point of view.

Practice Test Strategy

If you're able to find at least three practice tests, we recommend this strategy:

UNTIMED AND OPEN-BOOK PRACTICE

Take the first test with no time constraints and with your notes and study guide handy. Take your time and focus on applying the strategies you've learned.

TIMED AND OPEN-BOOK PRACTICE

Take the second practice test open-book as well, but set a timer and practice pacing yourself to finish in time.

TIMED AND CLOSED-BOOK PRACTICE

Take any other practice tests as if it were test day. Set a timer and put away your study materials. Sit at a table or desk in a quiet room, imagine yourself at the testing center, and answer questions as quickly and accurately as possible.

Keep repeating timed and closed-book tests on a regular basis until you run out of practice tests or it's time for the actual test. Your mind will be ready for the schedule and stress of test day, and you'll be able to focus on recalling the material you've learned.

Copyright © Mometrix Media. You have been licensed one copy of this document for personal use only. Any other reproduction or redistribution is strictly prohibited. All rights reserved.
This content is provided for test preparation purposes only and does not imply an endorsement by Mometrix of any particular political, scientific, or religious point of view.

Secret Key #4 – Pace Yourself

Once you're fully prepared for the material on the test, your biggest challenge on test day will be managing your time. Just knowing that the clock is ticking can make you panic even if you have plenty of time left. Work on pacing yourself so you can build confidence against the time constraints of the exam. Pacing is a difficult skill to master, especially in a high-pressure environment, so **practice is vital**.

Set time expectations for your pace based on how much time is available. For example, if a section has 60 questions and the time limit is 30 minutes, you know you have to average 30 seconds or less per question in order to answer them all. Although 30 seconds is the hard limit, set 25 seconds per question as your goal, so you reserve extra time to spend on harder questions. When you budget extra time for the harder questions, you no longer have any reason to stress when those questions take longer to answer.

Don't let this time expectation distract you from working through the test at a calm, steady pace, but keep it in mind so you don't spend too much time on any one question. Recognize that taking extra time on one question you don't understand may keep you from answering two that you do understand later in the test. If your time limit for a question is up and you're still not sure of the answer, mark it and move on, and come back to it later if the time and the test format allow. If the testing format doesn't allow you to return to earlier questions, just make an educated guess; then put it out of your mind and move on.

On the easier questions, be careful not to rush. It may seem wise to hurry through them so you have more time for the challenging ones, but it's not worth missing one if you know the concept and just didn't take the time to read the question fully. Work efficiently but make sure you understand the question and have looked at all of the answer choices, since more than one may seem right at first.

Even if you're paying attention to the time, you may find yourself a little behind at some point. You should speed up to get back on track, but do so wisely. Don't panic; just take a few seconds less on each question until you're caught up. Don't guess without thinking, but do look through the answer choices and eliminate any you know are wrong. If you can get down to two choices, it is often worthwhile to guess from those. Once you've chosen an answer, move on and don't dwell on any that you skipped or had to hurry through. If a question was taking too long, chances are it was one of the harder ones, so you weren't as likely to get it right anyway.

On the other hand, if you find yourself getting ahead of schedule, it may be beneficial to slow down a little. The more quickly you work, the more likely you are to make a careless mistake that will affect your score. You've budgeted time for each question, so don't be afraid to spend that time. Practice an efficient but careful pace to get the most out of the time you have.

Copyright © Mometrix Media. You have been licensed one copy of this document for personal use only. Any other reproduction or redistribution is strictly prohibited. All rights reserved. This content is provided for test preparation purposes only and does not imply an endorsement by Mometrix of any particular political, scientific, or religious point of view.

Secret Key #5 – Have a Plan for Guessing

When you're taking the test, you may find yourself stuck on a question. Some of the answer choices seem better than others, but you don't see the one answer choice that is obviously correct. What do you do?

The scenario described above is very common, yet most test takers have not effectively prepared for it. Developing and practicing a plan for guessing may be one of the single most effective uses of your time as you get ready for the exam.

In developing your plan for guessing, there are three questions to address:

- When should you start the guessing process?
- How should you narrow down the choices?
- Which answer should you choose?

When to Start the Guessing Process

Unless your plan for guessing is to select C every time (which, despite its merits, is not what we recommend), you need to leave yourself enough time to apply your answer elimination strategies. Since you have a limited amount of time for each question, that means that if you're going to give yourself the best shot at guessing correctly, you have to decide quickly whether or not you will guess.

Of course, the best-case scenario is that you don't have to guess at all, so first, see if you can answer the question based on your knowledge of the subject and basic reasoning skills. Focus on the key words in the question and try to jog your memory of related topics. Give yourself a chance to bring the knowledge to mind, but once you realize that you don't have (or you can't access) the knowledge you need to answer the question, it's time to start the guessing process.

It's almost always better to start the guessing process too early than too late. It only takes a few seconds to remember something and answer the question from knowledge. Carefully eliminating wrong answer choices takes longer. Plus, going through the process of eliminating answer choices can actually help jog your memory.

Summary: Start the guessing process as soon as you decide that you can't answer the question based on your knowledge.

7

Copyright © Mometrix Media. You have been licensed one copy of this document for personal use only. Any other reproduction or redistribution is strictly prohibited. All rights reserved. This content is provided for test preparation purposes only and does not imply an endorsement by Mometrix of any particular political, scientific, or religious point of view.

How to Narrow Down the Choices

The next chapter in this book (**Test-Taking Strategies**) includes a wide range of strategies for how to approach questions and how to look for answer choices to eliminate. You will definitely want to read those carefully, practice them, and figure out which ones work best for you. Here though, we're going to address a mindset rather than a particular strategy.

Your odds of guessing an answer correctly depend on how many options you are choosing from.

Number of options left	5	4	3	2	1
Odds of guessing correctly	20%	25%	33%	50%	100%

You can see from this chart just how valuable it is to be able to eliminate incorrect answers and make an educated guess, but there are two things that many test takers do that cause them to miss out on the benefits of guessing:

- Accidentally eliminating the correct answer
- Selecting an answer based on an impression

We'll look at the first one here, and the second one in the next section.

To avoid accidentally eliminating the correct answer, we recommend a thought exercise called **the $5 challenge**. In this challenge, you only eliminate an answer choice from contention if you are willing to bet $5 on it being wrong. Why $5? Five dollars is a small but not insignificant amount of money. It's an amount you could afford to lose but wouldn't want to throw away. And while losing

$5 once might not hurt too much, doing it twenty times will set you back $100. In the same way, each small decision you make—eliminating a choice here, guessing on a question there—won't by itself impact your score very much, but when you put them all together, they can make a big difference. By holding each answer choice elimination decision to a higher standard, you can reduce the risk of accidentally eliminating the correct answer.

The $5 challenge can also be applied in a positive sense: If you are willing to bet $5 that an answer choice *is* correct, go ahead and mark it as correct.

Summary: Only eliminate an answer choice if you are willing to bet $5 that it is wrong.

Copyright © Mometrix Media. You have been licensed one copy of this document for personal use only. Any other reproduction or redistribution is strictly prohibited. All rights reserved.
This content is provided for test preparation purposes only and does not imply an endorsement by Mometrix of any particular political, scientific, or religious point of view.

Which Answer to Choose

You're taking the test. You've run into a hard question and decided you'll have to guess. You've eliminated all the answer choices you're willing to bet $5 on. Now you have to pick an answer. Why do we even need to talk about this? Why can't you just pick whichever one you feel like when the time comes?

The answer to these questions is that if you don't come into the test with a plan, you'll rely on your impression to select an answer choice, and if you do that, you risk falling into a trap. The test writers know that everyone who takes their test will be guessing on some of the questions, so they intentionally write wrong answer choices to seem plausible. You still have to pick an answer though, and if the wrong answer choices are designed to look right, how can you ever be sure that you're not falling for their trap? The best solution we've found to this dilemma is to take the decision out of your hands entirely. Here is the process we recommend:

Once you've eliminated any choices that you are confident (willing to bet $5) are wrong, select the first remaining choice as your answer.

Whether you choose to select the first remaining choice, the second, or the last, the important thing is that you use some preselected standard. Using this approach guarantees that you will not be enticed into selecting an answer choice that looks right, because you are not basing your decision on how the answer choices look.

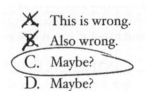

This is not meant to make you question your knowledge. Instead, it is to help you recognize the difference between your knowledge and your impressions. There's a huge difference between thinking an answer is right because of what you know, and thinking an answer is right because it looks or sounds like it should be right.

Summary: To ensure that your selection is appropriately random, make a predetermined selection from among all answer choices you have not eliminated.

Copyright © Mometrix Media. You have been licensed one copy of this document for personal use only. Any other reproduction or redistribution is strictly prohibited. All rights reserved.
This content is provided for test preparation purposes only and does not imply an endorsement by Mometrix of any particular political, scientific, or religious point of view.

Test-Taking Strategies

This section contains a list of test-taking strategies that you may find helpful as you work through the test. By taking what you know and applying logical thought, you can maximize your chances of answering any question correctly!

It is very important to realize that every question is different and every person is different: no single strategy will work on every question, and no single strategy will work for every person. That's why we've included all of them here, so you can try them out and determine which ones work best for different types of questions and which ones work best for you.

Question Strategies

☑ READ CAREFULLY

Read the question and the answer choices carefully. Don't miss the question because you misread the terms. You have plenty of time to read each question thoroughly and make sure you understand what is being asked. Yet a happy medium must be attained, so don't waste too much time. You must read carefully and efficiently.

☑ CONTEXTUAL CLUES

Look for contextual clues. If the question includes a word you are not familiar with, look at the immediate context for some indication of what the word might mean. Contextual clues can often give you all the information you need to decipher the meaning of an unfamiliar word. Even if you can't determine the meaning, you may be able to narrow down the possibilities enough to make a solid guess at the answer to the question.

☑ PREFIXES

If you're having trouble with a word in the question or answer choices, try dissecting it. Take advantage of every clue that the word might include. Prefixes can be a huge help. Usually, they allow you to determine a basic meaning. *Pre-* means before, *post-* means after, *pro-* is positive, *de-* is negative. From prefixes, you can get an idea of the general meaning of the word and try to put it into context.

☑ HEDGE WORDS

Watch out for critical hedge words, such as *likely, may, can, sometimes, often, almost, mostly, usually, generally, rarely,* and *sometimes*. Question writers insert these hedge phrases to cover every possibility. Often an answer choice will be wrong simply because it leaves no room for exception. Be on guard for answer choices that have definitive words such as *exactly* and *always*.

☑ SWITCHBACK WORDS

Stay alert for *switchbacks*. These are the words and phrases frequently used to alert you to shifts in thought. The most common switchback words are *but, although,* and *however*. Others include *nevertheless, on the other hand, even though, while, in spite of, despite,* and *regardless of*. Switchback words are important to catch because they can change the direction of the question or an answer choice.

Copyright © Mometrix Media. You have been licensed one copy of this document for personal use only. Any other reproduction or redistribution is strictly prohibited. All rights reserved. This content is provided for test preparation purposes only and does not imply an endorsement by Mometrix of any particular political, scientific, or religious point of view.

⊘ Face Value

When in doubt, use common sense. Accept the situation in the problem at face value. Don't read too much into it. These problems will not require you to make wild assumptions. If you have to go beyond creativity and warp time or space in order to have an answer choice fit the question, then you should move on and consider the other answer choices. These are normal problems rooted in reality. The applicable relationship or explanation may not be readily apparent, but it is there for you to figure out. Use your common sense to interpret anything that isn't clear.

Answer Choice Strategies

⊘ Answer Selection

The most thorough way to pick an answer choice is to identify and eliminate wrong answers until only one is left, then confirm it is the correct answer. Sometimes an answer choice may immediately seem right, but be careful. The test writers will usually put more than one reasonable answer choice on each question, so take a second to read all of them and make sure that the other choices are not equally obvious. As long as you have time left, it is better to read every answer choice than to pick the first one that looks right without checking the others.

⊘ Answer Choice Families

An answer choice family consists of two (in rare cases, three) answer choices that are very similar in construction and cannot all be true at the same time. If you see two answer choices that are direct opposites or parallels, one of them is usually the correct answer. For instance, if one answer choice says that quantity x increases and another either says that quantity x decreases (opposite) or says that quantity y increases (parallel), then those answer choices would fall into the same family. An answer choice that doesn't match the construction of the answer choice family is more likely to be incorrect. Most questions will not have answer choice families, but when they do appear, you should be prepared to recognize them.

⊘ Eliminate Answers

Eliminate answer choices as soon as you realize they are wrong, but make sure you consider all possibilities. If you are eliminating answer choices and realize that the last one you are left with is also wrong, don't panic. Start over and consider each choice again. There may be something you missed the first time that you will realize on the second pass.

⊘ Avoid Fact Traps

Don't be distracted by an answer choice that is factually true but doesn't answer the question. You are looking for the choice that answers the question. Stay focused on what the question is asking for so you don't accidentally pick an answer that is true but incorrect. Always go back to the question and make sure the answer choice you've selected actually answers the question and is not merely a true statement.

⊘ Extreme Statements

In general, you should avoid answers that put forth extreme actions as standard practice or proclaim controversial ideas as established fact. An answer choice that states the "process should be used in certain situations, if…" is much more likely to be correct than one that states the "process should be discontinued completely." The first is a calm rational statement and doesn't even make a definitive, uncompromising stance, using a hedge word *if* to provide wiggle room, whereas the second choice is far more extreme.

11

Copyright © Mometrix Media. You have been licensed one copy of this document for personal use only. Any other reproduction or redistribution is strictly prohibited. All rights reserved.
This content is provided for test preparation purposes only and does not imply an endorsement by Mometrix of any particular political, scientific, or religious point of view.

⊘ Benchmark

As you read through the answer choices and you come across one that seems to answer the question well, mentally select that answer choice. This is not your final answer, but it's the one that will help you evaluate the other answer choices. The one that you selected is your benchmark or standard for judging each of the other answer choices. Every other answer choice must be compared to your benchmark. That choice is correct until proven otherwise by another answer choice beating it. If you find a better answer, then that one becomes your new benchmark. Once you've decided that no other choice answers the question as well as your benchmark, you have your final answer.

⊘ Predict the Answer

Before you even start looking at the answer choices, it is often best to try to predict the answer. When you come up with the answer on your own, it is easier to avoid distractions and traps because you will know exactly what to look for. The right answer choice is unlikely to be word-for-word what you came up with, but it should be a close match. Even if you are confident that you have the right answer, you should still take the time to read each option before moving on.

General Strategies

⊘ Tough Questions

If you are stumped on a problem or it appears too hard or too difficult, don't waste time. Move on! Remember though, if you can quickly check for obviously incorrect answer choices, your chances of guessing correctly are greatly improved. Before you completely give up, at least try to knock out a couple of possible answers. Eliminate what you can and then guess at the remaining answer choices before moving on.

⊘ Check Your Work

Since you will probably not know every term listed and the answer to every question, it is important that you get credit for the ones that you do know. Don't miss any questions through careless mistakes. If at all possible, try to take a second to look back over your answer selection and make sure you've selected the correct answer choice and haven't made a costly careless mistake (such as marking an answer choice that you didn't mean to mark). This quick double check should more than pay for itself in caught mistakes for the time it costs.

⊘ Pace Yourself

It's easy to be overwhelmed when you're looking at a page full of questions; your mind is confused and full of random thoughts, and the clock is ticking down faster than you would like. Calm down and maintain the pace that you have set for yourself. Especially as you get down to the last few minutes of the test, don't let the small numbers on the clock make you panic. As long as you are on track by monitoring your pace, you are guaranteed to have time for each question.

⊘ Don't Rush

It is very easy to make errors when you are in a hurry. Maintaining a fast pace in answering questions is pointless if it makes you miss questions that you would have gotten right otherwise. Test writers like to include distracting information and wrong answers that seem right. Taking a little extra time to avoid careless mistakes can make all the difference in your test score. Find a pace that allows you to be confident in the answers that you select.

Copyright © Mometrix Media. You have been licensed one copy of this document for personal use only. Any other reproduction or redistribution is strictly prohibited. All rights reserved.
This content is provided for test preparation purposes only and does not imply an endorsement by Mometrix of any particular political, scientific, or religious point of view.

⊘ Keep Moving

Panicking will not help you pass the test, so do your best to stay calm and keep moving. Taking deep breaths and going through the answer elimination steps you practiced can help to break through a stress barrier and keep your pace.

Final Notes

The combination of a solid foundation of content knowledge and the confidence that comes from practicing your plan for applying that knowledge is the key to maximizing your performance on test day. As your foundation of content knowledge is built up and strengthened, you'll find that the strategies included in this chapter become more and more effective in helping you quickly sift through the distractions and traps of the test to isolate the correct answer.

Now that you're preparing to move forward into the test content chapters of this book, be sure to keep your goal in mind. As you read, think about how you will be able to apply this information on the test. If you've already seen sample questions for the test and you have an idea of the question format and style, try to come up with questions of your own that you can answer based on what you're reading. This will give you valuable practice applying your knowledge in the same ways you can expect to on test day.

Good luck and good studying!

Copyright © Mometrix Media. You have been licensed one copy of this document for personal use only. Any other reproduction or redistribution is strictly prohibited. All rights reserved.
This content is provided for test preparation purposes only and does not imply an endorsement by Mometrix of any particular political, scientific, or religious point of view.

Copyright © Mometrix Media. You have been licensed one copy of this document for personal use only. Any other reproduction or redistribution is strictly prohibited. All rights reserved. This content is provided for test preparation purposes only and does not imply an endorsement by Mometrix of any particular political, scientific, or religious point of view.

Civil Service Tests

WHAT ARE CIVIL SERVICE TESTS?

The term "civil service test" can be confusing, but essentially the phrase refers to a test one takes in order to qualify for a government job. These positions may be at the city, county, state, or federal level. Civil service jobs encompass a wide variety of occupations, in every field from administration to zoology. However, not every government job is a civil service job. For some government positions, a person must run for office and win an election. For others, a person must be appointed or recommended by someone in office, and in many cases he/she must be approved or confirmed by an official government agency or board before moving into the position.

Most government jobs, though, are filled through a regular hiring process. When a job opening comes up, it is made public, on government bulletin boards and websites and possibly in local newspapers. In most cases, the job listing will provide an idea of the salary or wage the job offers, and it will also list the minimum requirements a person must have to apply. If an exam is required as part of the application process, this information will also be included. These exams are also known as civil service tests.

You should know that not all civil service positions are referred to as civil service jobs. Sometimes these positions are simply known as "municipal jobs," "state jobs," "county employment," etc. No matter the title, all civil service jobs have two things in common—they are government jobs, and taking some sort of exam is part of the application process.

There are two broad categories of civil service exams—competitive and noncompetitive. On noncompetitive tests, everyone who achieves the minimum passing score or higher will be placed into a pool of people eligible to be hired, on an equal ranking. In other words, if you score a 95 on an exam that requires a passing score of 70, and the person next to you scores a 75, you will both be placed on the eligibility list on an equal footing. Your 95 won't give you an advantage over the person with the 75. On competitive exams, the opposite is true—people who score higher are ranked above those with lower scores. Those with the highest scores are first in line for the next step in the hiring process.

WHY DO WE HAVE CIVIL SERVICE TESTS?

Why do people applying for government jobs have to take a test? There are several good reasons for civil service exams. One of the main ones is to prevent "cronyism," or government officials using their power to give jobs to friends, family members, or anyone else they choose. Cronyism is bad because it's unfair; only people who know the right people have a chance to get a government job. It's also corrupt, because it often leads to hiring in exchange for bribes.

Another negative effect of cronyism is that jobs are staffed with people who aren't very qualified for the position (or even qualified at all). To have good government, it is imperative that only qualified people are hired for government jobs. Preventing cronyism is the reason the civil service exam system was originally developed in the United States.

Besides preventing cronyism and making sure that only qualified people are hired, civil service testing provides another valuable function for government agencies. Government jobs are highly sought after; in many cities it's not unusual to have thousands of applicants for a government job. By requiring people to achieve minimum scores on civil service tests, governments save countless

Copyright © Mometrix Media. You have been licensed one copy of this document for personal use only. Any other reproduction or redistribution is strictly prohibited. All rights reserved.
This content is provided for test preparation purposes only and does not imply an endorsement by Mometrix of any particular political, scientific, or religious point of view.

man-hours that would otherwise be spent reviewing resumes and interviewing people who turn out to be unqualified.

WHAT ARE CIVIL SERVICE TESTS LIKE?

Like the jobs they test for, civil service exams come in many different forms. Some exams are very job specific, designed and written to test for advanced levels of knowledge and skills in a particular area. Others are much broader, measuring a person's general skills and knowledge in subjects such as language, math, reading comprehension, writing, making decisions, etc. Most civil service exams fall into the latter category, and those are the tests this guide is focused on. Of course, if you're taking a more specialized exam, this guide can also be very helpful, because it's likely that some portion of the test will be on general subjects.

Even on the general knowledge exams, the degree of difficulty can vary widely. Reading comprehension portions, for example, can range from tests that simply measure a person's ability to understand basic, written information to exams that require the test taker to have a highly advanced vocabulary and to be able to make well-reasoned, logical inferences based on the text. Of course, no matter how hard the civil service test is, you can significantly improve your chances of achieving a high score by relying on this guide to help you prepare.

The test format will almost always be multiple-choice. This is because anywhere from dozens to thousands of people will take the same test, so government agencies need an exam that doesn't require each test form to be reviewed and scored by hand. Multiple-choice tests are easily scored, making the task easier, faster, and less expensive.

On the majority of civil service exams, there is only one answer for each question, but that's not always true, so you need to read the instructions carefully. On occasion the instructions will tell you to "select all that apply," which means there might be more than one correct answer.

On most tests, applicants will be told to select "the correct answer," which means that one answer will clearly stand out from the others as being the only correct one. However, some tests will require the test taker to select "the best answer," which does not mean the same thing. On these questions, one or two of the wrong answer choices will be close to being correct, or even partially correct, but they won't be quite as satisfactory as the correct answer. On these kinds of questions, you'll want to spend a bit more time weighing the choices before making your selection.

Another thing to keep in mind is that on most civil service exams, the test taker will have four answer choices to choose from, while a few tests will offer five answer choices. Those with five choices aren't necessarily harder than those with only four, so if you encounter one of the exams with five answer choices, there's no need to worry. Even on tests with only four answer choices, it's difficult for test designers to come up with four different answers that sound right. Usually at least one answer is clearly wrong to anyone who has any familiarity with the subject. On tests with five choices, there will usually be two answers that are obviously wrong. This won't always be the case, but most of the time, no matter how many answer choices each question has, there will only be two or three that are actually plausible.

Many civil service exams are taken the old-fashioned way, with pencil and paper, but a growing number are now taken on a computer. You don't need any special computer skills to take a general civil service test electronically, as you'll be given all the instructions you need at the test center. Of course, if the job you're applying for requires advanced computer skills, this may not be true. Be sure to read the test details carefully before applying to take any civil service exam.

Copyright © Mometrix Media. You have been licensed one copy of this document for personal use only. Any other reproduction or redistribution is strictly prohibited. All rights reserved. This content is provided for test preparation purposes only and does not imply an endorsement by Mometrix of any particular political, scientific, or religious point of view.

There are two kinds of computer-based exams. Most are simply electronic versions of the pencil and paper version, with no other differences. There's another kind, though, called computer adaptive tests, and there are major differences between these and the pencil and paper tests. On these exams, the first question you see is one of medium difficulty; test designers will make sure it's neither very easy nor very hard.

The next question you see will depend on your answer to the first question. If you answer incorrectly, you'll get an easier question. If you answer correctly, you'll get a harder question. (However, you won't know if you answered a question correctly or not.) This process continues for the entire test—correct answers lead to harder questions, while incorrect answers lead to easier questions. In other words, the computer adapts the test to your responses. Naturally, the harder questions count more when it comes to scoring the test.

HOW DO I TAKE A CIVIL SERVICE TEST?

How you'll go about taking a civil service exam depends on many factors. There are thousands of different civil service tests given every year in America at the federal, state, and local levels. They are given throughout the year and in hundreds of locations. Some are given only when the pool of people who are eligible to be hired drops below a certain point. Others are given on a regular basis, usually once or twice a year. You'll need to go online and look up the exact information for the positions you're interested in.

CIVIL SERVICE JOB SITES

Almost all civil service job openings are listed online now, usually on a page of the official site of the government entity. We haven't listed the official civil service webpage for every city and county government in the US in this guide, because this would take hundreds of pages. You can find the online list of civil service jobs, salaries, requirements, test dates, etc., in your area by simply going to a search engine and entering the phrase "government jobs" along with the name of the county or city you're interested in working for. If you don't have access to a computer, simply call or visit the county courthouse or municipal building to find out where you can view the information in person.

Keep in mind that there are federal jobs all over the country, not just in Washington, D.C. Also, if you live close to the border of another state, and you're willing to drive (or move) for the right job offer, you should consider taking civil service tests in that state, too. A few states require civil service employees to actually live in the state, but most do not. Also, some states break down job listings by region. In this case, make sure you're applying for jobs only in regions where you want to work.

Finally, if you're planning on applying for more than one job, in the same state or in different states, don't forget that civil service exams are not all alike. They can vary widely, job by job or state by state. Don't assume that if you're applying for a secretarial position in two states that the civil service exams will be identical. They might be quite similar, but they might be quite different, too. The same holds true if you're applying for two different maintenance positions in the same state—the tests could be exactly the same, but that's not necessarily the case. Always check the official job listings for more information about the required test.

Here are the websites for civil service jobs for all 50 states, the District of Columbia, and the federal government.

Federal Jobs   https://www.usajobs.gov/

Alabama   https://joblink.alabama.gov/ada/

Copyright © Mometrix Media. You have been licensed one copy of this document for personal use only. Any other reproduction or redistribution is strictly prohibited. All rights reserved.
This content is provided for test preparation purposes only and does not imply an endorsement by Mometrix of any particular political, scientific, or religious point of view.

Alaska	http://jobs.alaska.gov/statejobs.html
Arizona	http://www.hr.az.gov/AZStateJobs/
Arkansas	https://www.ark.org/arstatejobs/index.php
California	http://jobs.ca.gov/
Colorado	http://agency.governmentjobs.com/colorado/default.cfm
Connecticut	http://das.ct.gov/cr1.aspx?page=13
Delaware	http://delawarestatejobs.com/
District of Columbia	http://dchr.dc.gov/page/careers
Florida	https://peoplefirst.myflorida.com/peoplefirst
Georgia	http://team.georgia.gov/careers/
Hawaii	http://agency.governmentjobs.com/hawaii/default.cfm
Idaho	https://dhr.idaho.gov/JobSeekers/StateJobOpenings.html
Illinois	http://work.illinois.gov/
Indiana	http://www.in.gov/spd/2334.htm
Iowa	https://das.iowa.gov/human-resources/state-employment
Kansas	http://da.ks.gov/ps/aaa/recruitment/
Kentucky	https://careers.ky.gov/Pages/default.aspx
Louisiana	http://www.civilservice.louisiana.gov/
Maine	http://www.maine.gov/bhr/state_jobs/index.htm
Maryland	http://www.dbm.maryland.gov/jobseekers/Pages/JobSearch.aspx
Massachusetts	https://massanf.taleo.net/careersection/ex/joblist.ftl
Michigan	http://agency.governmentjobs.com/michigan/default.cfm
Minnesota	https://mn.gov/mmb/careers/search-for-jobs/
Mississippi	http://www.mspb.ms.gov/
Missouri	https://www.mo.gov/work/job-seekers/state-job-openings/
Montana	http://mt.gov/statejobs/default.mcpx
Nebraska	http://statejobs.nebraska.gov/
Nevada	http://nv.gov/employment/

Copyright © Mometrix Media. You have been licensed one copy of this document for personal use only. Any other reproduction or redistribution is strictly prohibited. All rights reserved.
This content is provided for test preparation purposes only and does not imply an endorsement by Mometrix of any particular political, scientific, or religious point of view.

New Hampshire	https://das.nh.gov/
New Jersey	http://www.state.nj.us/nj/employ/
New Mexico	http://www.spo.state.nm.us/
New York	http://www.labor.ny.gov/jobs/regional.shtm
North Carolina	http://www.osp.state.nc.us/jobs/
North Dakota	http://www.nd.gov/category.htm?id=95
Ohio	https://www.governmentjobs.com/careers/ohio
Oklahoma	http://www.ok.gov/opm/State_Jobs/
Oregon	http://www.oregon.gov/DAS/STJOBS/Pages/index.aspx
Pennsylvania	http://www.employment.pa.gov/Pages/jobopportunities.aspx
Rhode Island	http://www.dlt.ri.gov/jobsri/
South Carolina	http://www.jobs.sc.gov/OHR/OHR-jobs-portal-index.phtm
South Dakota	http://sd.gov/employment.aspx
Tennessee	https://www.tn.gov/hr/section/employment
Texas	http://www.twc.state.tx.us/jobseekers/job-search
Utah	https://agency.governmentjobs.com/utah/default.cfm
Vermont	http://humanresources.vermont.gov/
Virginia	http://jobs.virginia.gov/
Washington	http://www.careers.wa.gov/
West Virginia	http://www.personnel.wv.gov/job_seekers/Pages/default.aspx
Wisconsin	http://wisc.jobs/public/index.asp
Wyoming	http://wyoming.gov/

Copyright © Mometrix Media. You have been licensed one copy of this document for personal use only. Any other reproduction or redistribution is strictly prohibited. All rights reserved. This content is provided for test preparation purposes only and does not imply an endorsement by Mometrix of any particular political, scientific, or religious point of view.

Word Relationship Questions—Spelling and Vocabulary

In all civil service jobs, communication abilities are extremely important, whether the position is considered skilled or unskilled. If you're hired for a government job, there's a good chance that you'll be interacting with the public as part of the job. You'll also be required to communicate with colleagues and superiors frequently. Good communication skills will enable you to perform your job smoothly and efficiently, get along well with your coworkers and bosses, and create a positive impression on members of the public.

Whether spoken or written, words are at the heart of all communication, so having good verbal skills is essential. You'll need to be able to express yourself clearly as well as to easily grasp what a coworker or manager is trying to say. This is why questions that test your skill with words constitute such a big part of the civil service exam. They're on the test to weed out people who don't have the verbal skills necessary for success on the job.

You'll be tested on your spelling abilities. Why is good spelling important in this day and age when nearly all written communication is done on computers, and nearly all of them have spell checkers? Spelling skills are important because they demonstrate that you have good, basic intelligence and that you have done a fair amount of reading. Knowing how to spell correctly is one of the marks of a person with a well-rounded education. While it's true that there are some very smart people who are not very good spellers, these are the exception, not the rule. Generally speaking, smart people are good spellers, and vice versa.

Spell checkers are certainly very useful tools, but they weren't designed to eliminate the need for good spelling. Their purpose is to call the typist's attention to the occasional mistake that might be easily overlooked, not to replace the typist. Every time the spell checker flags a word, the typist has to click either *Replace* or *Ignore*, and that takes time. With one or two errors, it doesn't take very long, of course, but a person with poor spelling skills would use up a significant amount of time correcting mistakes, even with a spell checker. This would have a negative impact on productivity. Additionally, a spell checker won't catch a word that is spelled correctly but is the wrong one (such as to/too/two). Good spelling skills are very important in civil service jobs, and you should expect to see a lot of spelling questions on the exam.

You'll also be tested for vocabulary, which measures your knowledge of word meanings. Your vocabulary is simply the total of the words you recognize and understand. Keep in mind that if a word is in your vocabulary it doesn't necessarily mean that you hear, read, write, or speak that word on a regular basis. (The words you use on a regular basis are known as your working vocabulary.)

There are thousands of words we don't encounter regularly, but we still need to know the meaning of many of these. Many of the words you'll see on the vocabulary section of your civil service test will fall into this category —words most people don't use in everyday conversation with their families and friends, but that might come up from time to time on the job or while reading. It will be fairly easy to understand how knowing the meaning of these words is important for a civil service position. However, it is certain that you'll also run into some words on the exam that you are very unlikely to encounter on the job.

Copyright © Mometrix Media. You have been licensed one copy of this document for personal use only. Any other reproduction or redistribution is strictly prohibited. All rights reserved. This content is provided for test preparation purposes only and does not imply an endorsement by Mometrix of any particular political, scientific, or religious point of view.

So, if these words aren't going to come up in the course of your job duties, why are they on the civil service exam? They're on the test because they serve a very useful function for government agencies that use these exams as part of the hiring process. A person's vocabulary is a very good measuring stick of his/her overall knowledge and intelligence. With very few exceptions, an extensive vocabulary is a mark of someone who is very intelligent. This is only logical—the more words a person knows, the more reading he/she has done, and the more subjects and fields he/she is familiar with. Generally speaking, employers would prefer to hire people with above-average levels of knowledge and intelligence, and that's why you'll see unusual and rarely used vocabulary words on the exam.

Also, a person with a large vocabulary will generally be a more effective communicator. A person with a limited vocabulary will have a hard time understanding others and clearly expressing himself precisely because he doesn't know the meaning of a lot of words. There's no need to panic, though. You won't be required to possess the vocabulary of a Harvard professor in order to do well on the civil service exam. You will just need a vocabulary that's pretty good. If you don't think yours measures up, the practice questions in this guide can help remedy that.

Some of the vocabulary questions you'll see will simply show you a word, and then ask you to select the answer choice that is the correct meaning of the word. Here's an example:

1. Crevice is closest in meaning to:
   a.   a serving platter
   b.   a large hole
   c.   a narrow opening
   d.   the fringe on a drape

The basic vocabulary questions on the test you take might have a slightly different format. There may be three answer choices, or possibly five. Instead of standing alone, the word may be used in a sentence. The answer choices might have slightly longer definitions. However, there won't be any major differences, as this is the standard setup for a straightforward vocabulary question.

Spelling Primer

GENERAL SPELLING RULES
WORDS ENDING WITH A CONSONANT
Usually, the final consonant is **doubled** on a word before adding a suffix. This is the rule for single syllable words, words ending with one consonant, and multi-syllable words with the last syllable accented. The following are examples:

- *beg* becomes *begging* (single syllable)
- *shop* becomes *shopped* (single syllable)
- *add* becomes *adding* (already ends in double consonant, do not add another *d*)
- *deter* becomes *deterring* (multi-syllable, accent on last syllable)
- *regret* becomes *regrettable* (multi-syllable, accent on last syllable)
- *compost* becomes *composting* (do not add another *t* because the accent is on the first syllable)

Copyright © Mometrix Media. You have been licensed one copy of this document for personal use only. Any other reproduction or redistribution is strictly prohibited. All rights reserved.
This content is provided for test preparation purposes only and does not imply an endorsement by Mometrix of any particular political, scientific, or religious point of view.

WORDS ENDING WITH Y OR C

The general rule for words ending in *y* is to keep the *y* when adding a suffix if the **y is preceded by a vowel**. If the word **ends in a consonant and y** the *y* is changed to an *i* before the suffix is added (unless the suffix itself begins with *i*). The following are examples:

- *pay* becomes *paying* (keep the *y*)
- *bully* becomes *bullied* (change to *i*)
- *bully* becomes *bullying* (keep the *y* because the suffix is –*ing*)

If a word ends with *c* and the suffix begins with an *e, i,* or *y*, the letter *k* is usually added to the end of the word. The following are examples:

- panic becomes panicky
- mimic becomes mimicking

WORDS CONTAINING IE OR EI, AND/OR ENDING WITH E

Most words are spelled with an *i* before *e*, except when they follow the letter *c*, **or** sound like *a*. For example, the following words are spelled correctly according to these rules:

- piece, friend, believe (*i* before *e*)
- receive, ceiling, conceited (except after *c*)
- weight, neighborhood, veil (sounds like *a*)

To add a suffix to words ending with the letter *e*, first determine if the *e* is silent. If it is, the *e* will be kept if the added suffix begins with a consonant. If the suffix begins with a vowel, the *e* is dropped. The following are examples:

- *age* becomes *ageless* (keep the *e*)
- *age* becomes *aging* (drop the *e*)

An exception to this rule occurs when the word ends in *ce* or *ge* and the suffix *able* or *ous* is added; these words will retain the letter *e*. The following are examples:

- courage becomes courageous
- notice becomes noticeable

WORDS ENDING WITH ISE OR IZE

A small number of words end with *ise*. Most of the words in the English language with the same sound end in *ize*. The following are examples:

- advertise, advise, arise, chastise, circumcise, and comprise
- compromise, demise, despise, devise, disguise, enterprise, excise, and exercise
- franchise, improvise, incise, merchandise, premise, reprise, and revise
- supervise, surmise, surprise, and televise

Words that end with *ize* include the following:

- accessorize, agonize, authorize, and brutalize
- capitalize, caramelize, categorize, civilize, and demonize
- downsize, empathize, euthanize, idolize, and immunize

Copyright © Mometrix Media. You have been licensed one copy of this document for personal use only. Any other reproduction or redistribution is strictly prohibited. All rights reserved. This content is provided for test preparation purposes only and does not imply an endorsement by Mometrix of any particular political, scientific, or religious point of view.

- legalize, metabolize, mobilize, organize, and ostracize
- plagiarize, privatize, utilize, and visualize

(Note that some words may technically be spelled with *ise*, especially in British English, but it is more common to use *ize*. Examples include *symbolize/symbolise* and *baptize/baptise*.)

WORDS ENDING WITH CEED, SEDE, OR CEDE

There are only three words in the English language that end with *ceed*: *exceed, proceed,* and *succeed*. There is only one word in the English language that ends with *sede*: *supersede*. Most other words that sound like *sede* or *ceed* end with *cede*. The following are examples:

- concede, recede, and precede

WORDS ENDING IN ABLE OR IBLE

For words ending in *able* or *ible*, there are no hard and fast rules. The following are examples:

- adjustable, unbeatable, collectable, deliverable, and likeable
- edible, compatible, feasible, sensible, and credible

There are more words ending in *able* than *ible*; this is useful to know if guessing is necessary.

WORDS ENDING IN ANCE OR ENCE

The suffixes *ence, ency,* and *ent* are used in the following cases:

- the suffix is preceded by the letter *c* but sounds like *s* – *innocence*
- the suffix is preceded by the letter *g* but sounds like *j* – *intelligence, negligence*

The suffixes *ance, ancy,* and *ant* are used in the following cases:

- the suffix is preceded by the letter *c* but sounds like *k* – *significant, vacant*
- the suffix is preceded by the letter *g* with a hard sound – *elegant, extravagance*

If the suffix is preceded by other letters, there are no clear rules. For example: *finance, abundance,* and *assistance* use the letter *a*, while *decadence, competence,* and *excellence* use the letter *e*.

WORDS ENDING IN TION, SION, OR CIAN

Words ending in *tion, sion,* or *cian* all sound like *shun* or *zhun*. There are no rules for which ending is used for words. The following are examples:

- action, agitation, caution, fiction, nation, and motion
- admission, expression, mansion, permission, and television
- electrician, magician, musician, optician, and physician (note that these words tend to describe occupations)

WORDS WITH THE AI OR IA COMBINATION

When deciding if *ai* or *ia* is correct, the combination of *ai* usually sounds like one vowel sound, as in *Britain*, while the vowels in *ia* are pronounced separately, as in *guardian*. The following are examples:

- captain, certain, faint, hair, malaise, and praise (*ai* makes one sound)
- bacteria, beneficiary, diamond, humiliation, and nuptial (*ia* makes two sounds)

23

Copyright © Mometrix Media. You have been licensed one copy of this document for personal use only. Any other reproduction or redistribution is strictly prohibited. All rights reserved.
This content is provided for test preparation purposes only and does not imply an endorsement by Mometrix of any particular political, scientific, or religious point of view.

RULES FOR PLURALS
NOUNS ENDING IN CH, SH, S, X, OR Z

When a noun ends in the letters *ch, sh, s, x,* or *z,* an *es* instead of a singular *s* is added to the end of the word to make it plural. The following are examples:

- church becomes churches
- bush becomes bushes
- bass becomes basses
- mix becomes mixes
- buzz becomes buzzes

This is the rule with proper names as well; the Ross family would become the Rosses.

NOUNS ENDING IN Y OR AY/EY/IY/OY/UY

If a noun ends with a **consonant and y**, the plural is formed by replacing the *y* with *ies*. For example, *fly* becomes *flies* and *puppy* becomes *puppies*. If a noun ends with a **vowel and y**, the plural is formed by adding an *s*. For example, *alley* becomes *alleys* and *boy* becomes *boys*.

NOUNS ENDING IN F OR FE

Most nouns ending in *f* or *fe* are pluralized by replacing the *f* with *v* and adding *es*. The following are examples:

- knife becomes knives; self becomes selves; wolf becomes wolves.

An exception to this rule is the word *roof; roof* becomes *roofs.*

NOUNS ENDING IN O

Most nouns ending with a **consonant and o** are pluralized by adding *es*. The following are examples:

- hero becomes heroes; tornado becomes tornadoes; potato becomes potatoes

Most nouns ending with a **vowel and o** are pluralized by adding *s*. The following are examples:

- portfolio becomes portfolios; radio becomes radios; cameo becomes cameos.

An exception to these rules is seen with musical terms ending in *o*. These words are pluralized by adding *s* even if they end in a consonant and *o*. The following are examples: *soprano* becomes *sopranos; banjo* becomes *banjos; piano* becomes *pianos.*

LETTERS, NUMBERS, AND SYMBOLS

Letters and numbers become plural by adding an apostrophe and *s*. The following are examples:

- The *L's* are the people whose names begin with the letter *L*.
- They broke the teams down into groups of *3's*.
- The sorority girls were all *KD's*.

COMPOUND NOUNS

A **compound noun** is a noun that is made up of two or more words; they can be written with hyphens. For example, *mother-in-law* or *court-martial* are compound nouns. To make them plural,

Copyright © Mometrix Media. You have been licensed one copy of this document for personal use only. Any other reproduction or redistribution is strictly prohibited. All rights reserved. This content is provided for test preparation purposes only and does not imply an endorsement by Mometrix of any particular political, scientific, or religious point of view.

an *s* or *es* is added to the noun portion of the word. The following are examples: *mother-in-law* becomes *mothers-in-law; court-martial* becomes *courts-martial.*

EXCEPTIONS

Some words do not fall into any specific category for making the singular form plural. They are **irregular**. Certain words become plural by changing the vowels within the word. The following are examples:

- woman becomes women; goose becomes geese; foot becomes feet

Some words change in unusual ways in the plural form. The following are examples:

- mouse becomes mice; ox becomes oxen; person becomes people

Some words are the same in both the singular and plural forms. The following are examples:

- *Salmon, deer,* and *moose* are the same whether singular or plural.

COMMONLY MISSPELLED WORDS

accidentally	accommodate	accompanied	accompany
achieved	acknowledgment	across	address
aggravate	aisle	ancient	anxiety
apparently	appearance	arctic	argument
arrangement	attendance	auxiliary	awkward
bachelor	barbarian	beggar	beneficiary
biscuit	brilliant	business	cafeteria
calendar	campaign	candidate	ceiling
cemetery	changeable	changing	characteristic
chauffeur	colonel	column	commit
committee	comparative	compel	competent
competition	conceive	congratulations	conqueror
conscious	coolly	correspondent	courtesy
curiosity	cylinder	deceive	deference
deferred	definite	describe	desirable
desperate	develop	diphtheria	disappear
disappoint	disastrous	discipline	discussion
disease	dissatisfied	dissipate	drudgery
ecstasy	efficient	eighth	eligible
embarrass	emphasize	especially	exaggerate
exceed	exhaust	exhilaration	existence
explanation	extraordinary	familiar	fascinate
February	fiery	finally	forehead
foreign	foreigner	foremost	forfeit
ghost	glamorous	government	grammar
grateful	grief	grievous	handkerchief
harass	height	hoping	hurriedly
hygiene	hypocrisy	imminent	incidentally
incredible	independent	indigestible	inevitable
innocence	intelligible	intentionally	intercede
interest	irresistible	judgment	legitimate
liable	library	likelihood	literature

25

Copyright © Mometrix Media. You have been licensed one copy of this document for personal use only. Any other reproduction or redistribution is strictly prohibited. All rights reserved. This content is provided for test preparation purposes only and does not imply an endorsement by Mometrix of any particular political, scientific, or religious point of view.

maintenance	maneuver	manual	mathematics
mattress	miniature	mischievous	misspell
momentous	mortgage	neither	nickel
niece	ninety	noticeable	notoriety
obedience	obstacle	occasion	occurrence
omitted	operate	optimistic	organization
outrageous	pageant	pamphlet	parallel
parliament	permissible	perseverance	persuade
physically	physician	possess	possibly
practically	prairie	preceding	prejudice
prevalent	professor	pronunciation	pronouncement
propeller	protein	psychiatrist	psychology
quantity	questionnaire	rally	recede
receive	recognize	recommend	referral
referred	relieve	religious	resistance
restaurant	rhetoric	rhythm	ridiculous
sacrilegious	salary	scarcely	schedule
secretary	sentinel	separate	severely
sheriff	shriek	similar	soliloquy
sophomore	species	strenuous	studying
suffrage	supersede	suppress	surprise
symmetry	temperament	temperature	tendency
tournament	tragedy	transferred	truly
twelfth	tyranny	unanimous	unpleasant
usage	vacuum	valuable	vein
vengeance	vigilance	villain	Wednesday
weird	wholly		

Vocabulary Primer

WORD ROOTS AND PREFIXES AND SUFFIXES

AFFIXES

Affixes in the English language are morphemes that are added to words to create related but different words. Derivational affixes form new words based on and related to the original words. For example, the affix *–ness* added to the end of the adjective *happy* forms the noun *happiness*. Inflectional affixes form different grammatical versions of words. For example, the plural affix *–s* changes the singular noun *book* to the plural noun *books*, and the past tense affix *–ed* changes the present tense verb *look* to the past tense *looked.* Prefixes are affixes placed in front of words. For example, *heat* means to make hot; *preheat* means to heat in advance. Suffixes are affixes placed at the ends of words. The *happiness* example above contains the suffix *–ness.* Circumfixes add parts both before and after words, such as how *light* becomes *enlighten* with the prefix *en-* and the suffix *–en.* Interfixes create compound words via central affixes: *speed* and *meter* become *speedometer* via the interfix *–o–.*

> **Review Video: Affixes**
> Visit mometrix.com/academy and enter code: 782422

26

Copyright © Mometrix Media. You have been licensed one copy of this document for personal use only. Any other reproduction or redistribution is strictly prohibited. All rights reserved.
This content is provided for test preparation purposes only and does not imply an endorsement by Mometrix of any particular political, scientific, or religious point of view.

WORD ROOTS, PREFIXES, AND SUFFIXES TO HELP DETERMINE MEANINGS OF WORDS

Many English words were formed from combining multiple sources. For example, the Latin *habēre* means "to have," and the prefixes *in-* and *im-* mean a lack or prevention of something, as in *insufficient* and *imperfect*. Latin combined *in-* with *habēre* to form *inhibēre,* whose past participle was *inhibitus*. This is the origin of the English word *inhibit,* meaning to prevent from having. Hence by knowing the meanings of both the prefix and the root, one can decipher the word meaning. In Greek, the root *enkephalo-* refers to the brain. Many medical terms are based on this root, such as encephalitis and hydrocephalus. Understanding the prefix and suffix meanings (*-itis* means inflammation; *hydro-* means water) allows a person to deduce that encephalitis refers to brain inflammation and hydrocephalus refers to water (or other fluid) in the brain.

> **Review Video: <u>Determining Word Meanings</u>**
> Visit mometrix.com/academy and enter code: 894894

PREFIXES

Knowing common prefixes is helpful for all readers as they try to determining meanings or definitions of unfamiliar words. For example, a common word used when cooking is *preheat*. Knowing that *pre-* means in advance can also inform them that *presume* means to assume in advance, that *prejudice* means advance judgment, and that this understanding can be applied to many other words beginning with *pre-*. Knowing that the prefix *dis-* indicates opposition informs the meanings of words like *disbar, disagree, disestablish,* and many more. Knowing *dys-* means bad, impaired, abnormal, or difficult informs *dyslogistic, dysfunctional, dysphagia,* and *dysplasia.*

SUFFIXES

In English, certain suffixes generally indicate both that a word is a noun, and that the noun represents a state of being or quality. For example, *-ness* is commonly used to change an adjective into its noun form, as with *happy* and *happiness, nice* and *niceness,* and so on. The suffix *–tion* is commonly used to transform a verb into its noun form, as with *converse* and *conversation or move* and *motion.* Thus, if readers are unfamiliar with the second form of a word, knowing the meaning of the transforming suffix can help them determine meaning.

PREFIXES FOR NUMBERS

Prefix	Definition	Examples
bi-	two	bisect, biennial
mono-	one, single	monogamy, monologue
poly-	many	polymorphous, polygamous
semi-	half, partly	semicircle, semicolon
uni-	one	uniform, unity

27

Copyright © Mometrix Media. You have been licensed one copy of this document for personal use only. Any other reproduction or redistribution is strictly prohibited. All rights reserved. This content is provided for test preparation purposes only and does not imply an endorsement by Mometrix of any particular political, scientific, or religious point of view.

PREFIXES FOR TIME, DIRECTION, AND SPACE

Prefix	Definition	Examples
a-	in, on, of, up, to	abed, afoot
ab-	from, away, off	abdicate, abjure
ad-	to, toward	advance, adventure
ante-	before, previous	antecedent, antedate
anti-	against, opposing	antipathy, antidote
cata-	down, away, thoroughly	catastrophe, cataclysm
circum-	around	circumspect, circumference
com-	with, together, very	commotion, complicate
contra-	against, opposing	contradict, contravene
de-	from	depart
dia-	through, across, apart	diameter, diagnose
dis-	away, off, down, not	dissent, disappear
epi-	upon	epilogue
ex-	out	extract, excerpt
hypo-	under, beneath	hypodermic, hypothesis
inter-	among, between	intercede, interrupt
intra-	within	intramural, intrastate
ob-	against, opposing	objection
per-	through	perceive, permit
peri-	around	periscope, perimeter
post-	after, following	postpone, postscript
pre-	before, previous	prevent, preclude
pro-	forward, in place of	propel, pronoun
retro-	back, backward	retrospect, retrograde
sub-	under, beneath	subjugate, substitute
super-	above, extra	supersede, supernumerary
trans-	across, beyond, over	transact, transport
ultra-	beyond, excessively	ultramodern, ultrasonic

NEGATIVE PREFIXES

Prefix	Definition	Examples
a-	without, lacking	atheist, agnostic
in-	not, opposing	incapable, ineligible
non-	not	nonentity, nonsense
un-	not, reverse of	unhappy, unlock

Copyright © Mometrix Media. You have been licensed one copy of this document for personal use only. Any other reproduction or redistribution is strictly prohibited. All rights reserved.
This content is provided for test preparation purposes only and does not imply an endorsement by Mometrix of any particular political, scientific, or religious point of view.

Mometrix

EXTRA PREFIXES

Prefix	Definition	Examples
for-	away, off, from	forget, forswear
fore-	previous	foretell, forefathers
homo-	same, equal	homogenized, homonym
hyper-	excessive, over	hypercritical, hypertension
in-	in, into	intrude, invade
mal-	bad, poorly, not	malfunction, malpractice
mis-	bad, poorly, not	misspell, misfire
neo-	new	Neolithic, neoconservative
omni-	all, everywhere	omniscient, omnivore
ortho-	right, straight	orthogonal, orthodox
over-	above	overbearing, oversight
pan-	all, entire	panorama, pandemonium
para-	beside, beyond	parallel, paradox
re-	backward, again	revoke, recur
sym-	with, together	sympathy, symphony

Below is a list of common suffixes and their meanings:

ADJECTIVE SUFFIXES

Suffix	Definition	Examples
-able (-ible)	capable of being	tolerable, edible
-esque	in the style of, like	picturesque, grotesque
-ful	filled with, marked by	thankful, zestful
-ific	make, cause	terrific, beatific
-ish	suggesting, like	churlish, childish
-less	lacking, without	hopeless, countless
-ous	marked by, given to	religious, riotous

Copyright © Mometrix Media. You have been licensed one copy of this document for personal use only. Any other reproduction or redistribution is strictly prohibited. All rights reserved.
This content is provided for test preparation purposes only and does not imply an endorsement by Mometrix of any particular political, scientific, or religious point of view.

NOUN SUFFIXES

Suffix	Definition	Examples
-acy	state, condition	accuracy, privacy
-ance	act, condition, fact	acceptance, vigilance
-ard	one that does excessively	drunkard, sluggard
-ation	action, state, result	occupation, starvation
-dom	state, rank, condition	serfdom, wisdom
-er (-or)	office, action	teacher, elevator, honor
-ess	feminine	waitress, duchess
-hood	state, condition	manhood, statehood
-ion	action, result, state	union, fusion
-ism	act, manner, doctrine	barbarism, socialism
-ist	worker, follower	monopolist, socialist
-ity (-ty)	state, quality, condition	acidity, civility, twenty
-ment	result, action	Refreshment
-ness	quality, state	greatness, tallness
-ship	position	internship, statesmanship
-sion (-tion)	state, result	revision, expedition
-th	act, state, quality	warmth, width
-tude	quality, state, result	magnitude, fortitude

VERB SUFFIXES

Suffix	Definition	Examples
-ate	having, showing	separate, desolate
-en	cause to be, become	deepen, strengthen
-fy	make, cause to have	glorify, fortify
-ize	cause to be, treat with	sterilize, mechanize

NUANCE AND WORD MEANINGS

SYNONYMS AND ANTONYMS

When you understand how words relate to each other, you will discover more in a passage. This is explained by understanding **synonyms** (e.g., words that mean the same thing) and **antonyms** (e.g., words that mean the opposite of one another). As an example, *dry* and *arid* are synonyms, and *dry* and *wet* are antonyms.

There are many pairs of words in English that can be considered synonyms, despite having slightly different definitions. For instance, the words *friendly* and *collegial* can both be used to describe a warm interpersonal relationship, and one would be correct to call them synonyms. However, *collegial* (kin to *colleague*) is often used in reference to professional or academic relationships, and *friendly* has no such connotation.

If the difference between the two words is too great, then they should not be called synonyms. *Hot* and *warm* are not synonyms because their meanings are too distinct. A good way to determine whether two words are synonyms is to substitute one word for the other word and verify that the meaning of the sentence has not changed. Substituting *warm* for *hot* in a sentence would convey a different meaning. Although warm and hot may seem close in meaning, warm generally means that the temperature is moderate, and hot generally means that the temperature is excessively high.

Copyright © Mometrix Media. You have been licensed one copy of this document for personal use only. Any other reproduction or redistribution is strictly prohibited. All rights reserved.
This content is provided for test preparation purposes only and does not imply an endorsement by Mometrix of any particular political, scientific, or religious point of view.

Antonyms are words with opposite meanings. *Light* and *dark*, *up* and *down*, *right* and *left*, *good* and *bad*: these are all sets of antonyms. Be careful to distinguish between antonyms and pairs of words that are simply different. *Black* and *gray*, for instance, are not antonyms because gray is not the opposite of black. *Black* and *white*, on the other hand, are antonyms.

Not every word has an antonym. For instance, many nouns do not. What would be the antonym of *chair*? During your exam, the questions related to antonyms are more likely to concern adjectives. You will recall that adjectives are words that describe a noun. Some common adjectives include *purple*, *fast*, *skinny*, and *sweet*. From those four adjectives, *purple* is the item that lacks a group of obvious antonyms.

> **Review Video: <u>What Are Synonyms and Antonyms?</u>**
> Visit mometrix.com/academy and enter code: 105612

DENOTATIVE VS. CONNOTATIVE MEANING

The **denotative** meaning of a word is the literal meaning. The **connotative** meaning goes beyond the denotative meaning to include the emotional reaction that a word may invoke. The connotative meaning often takes the denotative meaning a step further due to associations the reader makes with the denotative meaning. Readers can differentiate between the denotative and connotative meanings by first recognizing how authors use each meaning. Most non-fiction, for example, is fact-based and authors do not use flowery, figurative language. The reader can assume that the writer is using the denotative meaning of words. In fiction, the author may use the connotative meaning. Readers can determine whether the author is using the denotative or connotative meaning of a word by implementing context clues.

> **Review Video: <u>Connotation and Denotation</u>**
> Visit mometrix.com/academy and enter code: 310092

NUANCES OF WORD MEANING RELATIVE TO CONNOTATION, DENOTATION, DICTION, AND USAGE

A word's denotation is simply its objective dictionary definition. However, its connotation refers to the subjective associations, often emotional, that specific words evoke in listeners and readers. Two or more words can have the same dictionary meaning, but very different connotations. Writers use diction (word choice) to convey various nuances of thought and emotion by selecting synonyms for other words that best communicate the associations they want to trigger for readers. For example, a car engine is naturally greasy; in this sense, "greasy" is a neutral term. But when a person's smile, appearance, or clothing is described as "greasy," it has a negative connotation. Some words have even gained additional or different meanings over time. For example, *awful* used to be used to describe things that evoked a sense of awe. When *awful* is separated into its root word, awe, and suffix, -ful, it can be understood to mean "full of awe." However, the word is now commonly used to describe things that evoke repulsion, terror, or another intense, negative reaction.

> **Review Video: <u>Word Usage in Sentences</u>**
> Visit mometrix.com/academy and enter code: 197863

USING CONTEXT TO DETERMINE MEANING
CONTEXT CLUES

Readers of all levels will encounter words that they have either never seen or have encountered only on a limited basis. The best way to define a word in **context** is to look for nearby words that can assist in revealing the meaning of the word. For instance, unfamiliar nouns are often accompanied by examples that provide a definition. Consider the following sentence: *Dave arrived*

Copyright © Mometrix Media. You have been licensed one copy of this document for personal use only. Any other reproduction or redistribution is strictly prohibited. All rights reserved. This content is provided for test preparation purposes only and does not imply an endorsement by Mometrix of any particular political, scientific, or religious point of view.

at the party in hilarious garb: a leopard-print shirt, buckskin trousers, and bright green sneakers. If a reader was unfamiliar with the meaning of garb, he or she could read the examples (i.e., a leopard-print shirt, buckskin trousers, and high heels) and quickly determine that the word means *clothing.* Examples will not always be this obvious. Consider this sentence: *Parsley, lemon, and flowers were just a few of the items he used as garnishes.* Here, the word *garnishes* is exemplified by parsley, lemon, and flowers. Readers who have eaten in a variety of restaurants will probably be able to identify a garnish as something used to decorate a plate.

> **Review Video: Reading Comprehension: Using Context Clues**
> Visit mometrix.com/academy and enter code: 613660

USING CONTRAST IN CONTEXT CLUES

In addition to looking at the context of a passage, readers can use contrast to define an unfamiliar word in context. In many sentences, the author will not describe the unfamiliar word directly; instead, he or she will describe the opposite of the unfamiliar word. Thus, you are provided with some information that will bring you closer to defining the word. Consider the following example: *Despite his intelligence, Hector's low brow and bad posture made him look obtuse.* The author writes that Hector's appearance does not convey intelligence. Therefore, *obtuse* must mean unintelligent. Here is another example: *Despite the horrible weather, we were beatific about our trip to Alaska.* The word *despite* indicates that the speaker's feelings were at odds with the weather. Since the weather is described as *horrible*, then *beatific* must mean something positive.

SUBSTITUTION TO FIND MEANING

In some cases, there will be very few contextual clues to help a reader define the meaning of an unfamiliar word. When this happens, one strategy that readers may employ is **substitution**. A good reader will brainstorm some possible synonyms for the given word, and he or she will substitute these words into the sentence. If the sentence and the surrounding passage continue to make sense, then the substitution has revealed at least some information about the unfamiliar word. Consider the sentence: *Frank's admonition rang in her ears as she climbed the mountain.* A reader unfamiliar with *admonition* might come up with some substitutions like *vow, promise, advice, complaint*, or *compliment*. All of these words make general sense of the sentence, though their meanings are diverse. However, this process has suggested that an admonition is some sort of message. The substitution strategy is rarely able to pinpoint a precise definition, but this process can be effective as a last resort.

Occasionally, you will be able to define an unfamiliar word by looking at the descriptive words in the context. Consider the following sentence: *Fred dragged the recalcitrant boy kicking and screaming up the stairs.* The words *dragged, kicking*, and *screaming* all suggest that the boy does not want to go up the stairs. The reader may assume that *recalcitrant* means something like unwilling or protesting. In this example, an unfamiliar adjective was identified.

Additionally, using description to define an unfamiliar noun is a common practice compared to unfamiliar adjectives, as in this sentence: *Don's wrinkled frown and constantly shaking fist identified him as a curmudgeon of the first order.* Don is described as having a *wrinkled frown and constantly shaking fist*, suggesting that a *curmudgeon* must be a grumpy person. Contrasts do not always provide detailed information about the unfamiliar word, but they at least give the reader some clues.

WORDS WITH MULTIPLE MEANINGS

When a word has more than one meaning, readers can have difficulty determining how the word is being used in a given sentence. For instance, the verb *cleave*, can mean either *join* or *separate.* When

Copyright © Mometrix Media. You have been licensed one copy of this document for personal use only. Any other reproduction or redistribution is strictly prohibited. All rights reserved.
This content is provided for test preparation purposes only and does not imply an endorsement by Mometrix of any particular political, scientific, or religious point of view.

readers come upon this word, they will have to select the definition that makes the most sense. Consider the following sentence: *Hermione's knife cleaved the bread cleanly.* Since a knife cannot join bread together, the word must indicate separation. A slightly more difficult example would be the sentence: *The birds cleaved to one another as they flew from the oak tree.* Immediately, the presence of the words *to one another* should suggest that in this sentence *cleave* is being used to mean *join.* Discovering the intent of a word with multiple meanings requires the same tricks as defining an unknown word: look for contextual clues and evaluate the substituted words.

CONTEXT CLUES TO HELP DETERMINE MEANINGS OF WORDS

If readers simply bypass unknown words, they can reach unclear conclusions about what they read. However, looking for the definition of every unfamiliar word in the dictionary can slow their reading progress. Moreover, the dictionary may list multiple definitions for a word, so readers must search the word's context for meaning. Hence context is important to new vocabulary regardless of reader methods. Four types of context clues are examples, definitions, descriptive words, and opposites. Authors may use a certain word, and then follow it with several different examples of what it describes. Sometimes authors actually supply a definition of a word they use, which is especially true in informational and technical texts. Authors may use descriptive words that elaborate upon a vocabulary word they just used. Authors may also use opposites with negation that help define meaning.

EXAMPLES AND DEFINITIONS

An author may use a word and then give examples that illustrate its meaning. Consider this text: "Teachers who do not know how to use sign language can help students who are deaf or hard of hearing understand certain instructions by using gestures instead, like pointing their fingers to indicate which direction to look or go; holding up a hand, palm outward, to indicate stopping; holding the hands flat, palms up, curling a finger toward oneself in a beckoning motion to indicate 'come here'; or curling all fingers toward oneself repeatedly to indicate 'come on', 'more', or 'continue.'" The author of this text has used the word "gestures" and then followed it with examples, so a reader unfamiliar with the word could deduce from the examples that "gestures" means "hand motions." Readers can find examples by looking for signal words "for example," "for instance," "like," "such as," and "e.g."

While readers sometimes have to look for definitions of unfamiliar words in a dictionary or do some work to determine a word's meaning from its surrounding context, at other times an author may make it easier for readers by defining certain words. For example, an author may write, "The company did not have sufficient capital, that is, available money, to continue operations." The author defined "capital" as "available money," and heralded the definition with the phrase "that is." Another way that authors supply word definitions is with appositives. Rather than being introduced by a signal phrase like "that is," "namely," or "meaning," an appositive comes after the vocabulary word it defines and is enclosed within two commas. For example, an author may write, "The Indians introduced the Pilgrims to pemmican, cakes they made of lean meat dried and mixed with fat, which proved greatly beneficial to keep settlers from starving while trapping." In this example, the appositive phrase following "pemmican" and preceding "which" defines the word "pemmican."

DESCRIPTIONS

When readers encounter a word they do not recognize in a text, the author may expand on that word to illustrate it better. While the author may do this to make the prose more picturesque and vivid, the reader can also take advantage of this description to provide context clues to the meaning of the unfamiliar word. For example, an author may write, "The man sitting next to me on the airplane was obese. His shirt stretched across his vast expanse of flesh, strained almost to bursting."

Copyright © Mometrix Media. You have been licensed one copy of this document for personal use only. Any other reproduction or redistribution is strictly prohibited. All rights reserved. This content is provided for test preparation purposes only and does not imply an endorsement by Mometrix of any particular political, scientific, or religious point of view.

The descriptive second sentence elaborates on and helps to define the previous sentence's word "obese" to mean extremely fat. A reader unfamiliar with the word "repugnant" can decipher its meaning through an author's accompanying description: "The way the child grimaced and shuddered as he swallowed the medicine showed that its taste was particularly repugnant."

<u>OPPOSITES</u>

Text authors sometimes introduce a contrasting or opposing idea before or after a concept they present. They may do this to emphasize or heighten the idea they present by contrasting it with something that is the reverse. However, readers can also use these context clues to understand familiar words. For example, an author may write, "Our conversation was not cheery. We sat and talked very solemnly about his experience and a number of similar events." The reader who is not familiar with the word "solemnly" can deduce by the author's preceding use of "not cheery" that "solemn" means the opposite of cheery or happy, so it must mean serious or sad. Or if someone writes, "Don't condemn his entire project because you couldn't find anything good to say about it," readers unfamiliar with "condemn" can understand from the sentence structure that it means the opposite of saying anything good, so it must mean reject, dismiss, or disapprove. "Entire" adds another context clue, meaning total or complete rejection.

SYNTAX TO DETERMINE PART OF SPEECH AND MEANINGS OF WORDS

Syntax refers to sentence structure and word order. Suppose that a reader encounters an unfamiliar word when reading a text. To illustrate, consider an invented word like "splunch." If this word is used in a sentence like "Please splunch that ball to me," the reader can assume from syntactic context that "splunch" is a verb. We would not use a noun, adjective, adverb, or preposition with the object "that ball," and the prepositional phrase "to me" further indicates "splunch" represents an action. However, in the sentence, "Please hand that splunch to me," the reader can assume that "splunch" is a noun. Demonstrative adjectives like "that" modify nouns. Also, we hand someone some*thing*—a thing being a noun; we do not hand someone a verb, adjective, or adverb. Some sentences contain further clues. For example, from the sentence, "The princess wore the glittering splunch on her head," the reader can deduce that it is a crown, tiara, or something similar from the syntactic context, without knowing the word.

SYNTAX TO INDICATE DIFFERENT MEANINGS OF SIMILAR SENTENCES

The syntax, or structure, of a sentence affords grammatical cues that aid readers in comprehending the meanings of words, phrases, and sentences in the texts that they read. Seemingly minor differences in how the words or phrases in a sentence are ordered can make major differences in meaning. For example, two sentences can use exactly the same words but have different meanings based on the word order:

- "The man with a broken arm sat in a chair."
- "The man sat in a chair with a broken arm."

While both sentences indicate that a man sat in a chair, differing syntax indicates whether the man's or chair's arm was broken.

> **Review Video: <u>What is Syntax?</u>**
> Visit mometrix.com/academy and enter code: 242280

DETERMINING MEANING OF PHRASES AND PARAGRAPHS

Like unknown words, the meanings of phrases, paragraphs, and entire works can also be difficult to discern. Each of these can be better understood with added context. However, for larger groups of

Copyright © Mometrix Media. You have been licensed one copy of this document for personal use only. Any other reproduction or redistribution is strictly prohibited. All rights reserved. This content is provided for test preparation purposes only and does not imply an endorsement by Mometrix of any particular political, scientific, or religious point of view.

words, more context is needed. Unclear phrases are similar to unclear words, and the same methods can be used to understand their meaning. However, it is also important to consider how the individual words in the phrase work together. Paragraphs are a bit more complicated. Just as words must be compared to other words in a sentence, paragraphs must be compared to other paragraphs in a composition or a section.

DETERMINING MEANING IN VARIOUS TYPES OF COMPOSITIONS

To understand the meaning of an entire composition, the type of composition must be considered. **Expository writing** is generally organized so that each paragraph focuses on explaining one idea, or part of an idea, and its relevance. **Persuasive writing** uses paragraphs for different purposes to organize the parts of the argument. **Unclear paragraphs** must be read in the context of the paragraphs around them for their meaning to be fully understood. The meaning of full texts can also be unclear at times. The purpose of composition is also important for understanding the meaning of a text. To quickly understand the broad meaning of a text, look to the introductory and concluding paragraphs. Fictional texts are different. Some fictional works have implicit meanings, but some do not. The target audience must be considered for understanding texts that do have an implicit meaning, as most children's fiction will clearly state any lessons or morals. For other fiction, the application of literary theories and criticism may be helpful for understanding the text.

RESOURCES FOR DETERMINING WORD MEANING AND USAGE

While these strategies are useful for determining the meaning of unknown words and phrases, sometimes additional resources are needed to properly use the terms in different contexts. Some words have multiple definitions, and some words are inappropriate in particular contexts or modes of writing. The following tools are helpful for understanding all meanings and proper uses for words and phrases.

- **Dictionaries** provide the meaning of a multitude of words in a language. Many dictionaries include additional information about each word, such as its etymology, its synonyms, or variations of the word.
- **Glossaries** are similar to dictionaries, as they provide the meanings of a variety of terms. However, while dictionaries typically feature an extensive list of words and comprise an entire publication, glossaries are often included at the end of a text and only include terms and definitions that are relevant to the text they follow.
- **Spell Checkers** are used to detect spelling errors in typed text. Some spell checkers may also detect the misuse of plural or singular nouns, verb tenses, or capitalization. While spell checkers are a helpful tool, they are not always reliable or attuned to the author's intent, so it is important to review the spell checker's suggestions before accepting them.
- **Style Manuals** are guidelines on the preferred punctuation, format, and grammar usage according to different fields or organizations. For example, the Associated Press Stylebook is a style guide often used for media writing. The guidelines within a style guide are not always applicable across different contexts and usages, as the guidelines often cover grammatical or formatting situations that are not objectively correct or incorrect.

Copyright © Mometrix Media. You have been licensed one copy of this document for personal use only. Any other reproduction or redistribution is strictly prohibited. All rights reserved.
This content is provided for test preparation purposes only and does not imply an endorsement by Mometrix of any particular political, scientific, or religious point of view.

Spelling Practice Test 1

Choose the correct spelling of the missing word.

1. John prefers _____ art to the classics.

- a. Contemporary
- b. Contemperary
- c. Contemparary
- d. Conteporary

2. Allen told Steve that he would give him the ____ version of the story when he had time.

- a. Unabridgged
- b. Unabriddged
- c. Unabbridged
- d. Unabridged

3. Lisa was known for having _____ relationships.

- a. Promiscous
- b. Promicuous
- c. Promiscuous
- d. Promicious

4. The new tax was passed for ____ the waterfront district.

- a. Revitallizing
- b. Revitalizzing
- c. Revitelizing
- d. Revitalizing

5. The increased _____ to the class fund allowed for an end-of-year party.

- a. Revenuee
- b. Revenue
- c. Revanue
- d. Revanuee

6. The teenager _____ some candy from the grocery store.

- a. Pillferred
- b. Pilferred
- c. Pillfered
- d. Pilfered

7. As he was from a small town, some of Dean's views were _____.

- a. Parochial
- b. Perochial
- c. Porochial
- d. Parochiel

36

Copyright © Mometrix Media. You have been licensed one copy of this document for personal use only. Any other reproduction or redistribution is strictly prohibited. All rights reserved. This content is provided for test preparation purposes only and does not imply an endorsement by Mometrix of any particular political, scientific, or religious point of view.

8. All of the students dreaded the quizzes the professor gave since he tested on ____ material.

   a. Obscere
   b. Obscore
   c. Obbscure
   d. Obscure

9. The judge sued the newspaper for ___.

   a. Libel
   b. Labal
   c. Lobel
   d. Libbel

10. Susan's ____ of darkness prevents her from leaving her house at night.

   a. Abhorance
   b. Abhorence
   c. Abhorrence
   d. Abhorrance

11. The girl was ___ when she found out her puppy was injured.

   a. Destraught
   b. Distaught
   c. Distraught
   d. Distrauht

12. The _____ crowd mourned the loss of their leader.

   a. Sember
   b. Somber
   c. Sombar
   d. Sombor

13. The ___ Southern girl was known for her polite behavior.

   a. Gentell
   b. Ganteel
   c. Genteal
   d. Genteel

14. The mother attempted to ____ her son with toys.

   a. Molifey
   b. Mollify
   c. Molify
   d. Mollifey

15. Some people accused John of thinking too much. He would sometimes ___ a subject for months at a time.

   a. Pondar
   b. Pondder
   c. Ponnder
   d. Ponder

Copyright © Mometrix Media. You have been licensed one copy of this document for personal use only. Any other reproduction or redistribution is strictly prohibited. All rights reserved.
This content is provided for test preparation purposes only and does not imply an endorsement by Mometrix of any particular political, scientific, or religious point of view.

16. The young artist had an _____ passion for watercolors.

    a. Unbradled
    b. Unbriddled
    c. Unbridled
    d. Unbridlled

17. The _____ kept the students cool while they sat outside studying.

    a. Zephyir
    b. Zepheyer
    c. Zepyr
    d. Zephyr

18. The pianist played his rendition of a _____.

    a. Sonata
    b. Sonatta
    c. Sonate
    d. Sonete

19. The entertainer had no _____ about performing in front of two thousand screaming fans.

    a. Qulams
    b. Quelms
    c. Qualms
    d. Qualmes

20. The _____ still enjoyed being around its mother but was growing more independent each day.

    a. Yearling
    b. Yeerling
    c. Yearlling
    d. Yearlinng

Copyright © Mometrix Media. You have been licensed one copy of this document for personal use only. Any other reproduction or redistribution is strictly prohibited. All rights reserved.
This content is provided for test preparation purposes only and does not imply an endorsement by Mometrix of any particular political, scientific, or religious point of view.

Spelling Practice Test 1 Answer Key

1. A: *Contemporary* is the correct spelling. It means up-to-date, modern, or new. In the sentence, a contrast is being drawn with "the classics," which are older pieces of art.

2. D: *Unabridged* is the correct spelling. It means unshortened, complete, or full length. As an example, long books are sometimes sold in "abridged" versions, meaning that they are edited and shortened. In the example sentence, Allen says he needs more time to give the story, suggesting that he means the full version.

3. C: *Promiscuous* is the correct spelling. This word is used to describe people who have casual romantic relationships with a number of different people. It has a generally negative connotation.

4. D: *Revitalizing* is the correct spelling. It means life-restoring or enlivening. It is apparent from the context of this sentence that the waterfront district has been moribund (depressed and dying) and that the government is attempting to stimulate the economy through taxation.

5. B: *Revenue* is the correct spelling. It is defined as money earned through economic activity. A general equation for profit is revenue minus expenses. The revenue earned by the class would make it possible for them to have a party at the end of the year.

6. D: *Pilfered* is the correct spelling. It means stolen. The teenager in the sentence is performing some petty shoplifting at the local store.

7. A: *Parochial* is the correct spelling. It means locally focused or innocent of the ways of the world. A parochial person is unsophisticated and perhaps naive. Being parochial is not necessarily negative, though the word is often used in a critical fashion. A person like Dean who grew up and continued to live in a small town might not take an interest in the outside world, and might therefore be considered parochial.

8. D: *Obscure* is the correct spelling. It means hard to find, uncommon, or rare. Many students have experienced the dread of taking tests from a teacher who includes not just the most important information, but also the random bits of knowledge that are easy to forget.

9. A: *Libel* is the correct spelling. A libel is a false or misleading statement that injures the reputation of another person or group. It is illegal to make or publish such statements.

10. C: *Abhorrence* is the correct spelling. It means hatred or distaste. This makes sense, as a hatred of darkness would prevent one from leaving the house at night.

11. C: *Distraught* is the correct spelling. This word means traumatized, violently emotional, or severely sad and angry. The injury of a pet could make a person distraught.

12. B: *Somber* is the correct spelling. This word means sad or mournful. A group whose leader has died would certainly be somber.

13. D: *Genteel* is the correct spelling. It means sophisticated, classy, or well-bred. Southern women are stereotyped as being demure, well-mannered, and classy, so genteel would be a good fit in this sentence.

Copyright © Mometrix Media. You have been licensed one copy of this document for personal use only. Any other reproduction or redistribution is strictly prohibited. All rights reserved.
This content is provided for test preparation purposes only and does not imply an endorsement by Mometrix of any particular political, scientific, or religious point of view.

14. B: *Mollify* is the correct spelling. To mollify someone is to diminish his/her anger and appease him/her. The parents of young children get a great deal of practice in mollifying their sons and daughters after fits and temper tantrums.

15. D: *Ponder* is the correct spelling. It means to think, meditate, or ruminate. In general, it is good to be a person who ponders, though excessive analysis and thinking can sometimes stand in the way of necessary action.

16. C: *Unbridled* is the correct spelling. It means unrestrained or excessive. A bridle is used to restrain a fast horse, so an unbridled horse will run fast and loose. The word's usage has expanded to include many things besides horses.

17. D: *Zephyr* is the correct spelling. This uncommon word means a west wind.

18. A: *Sonata* is the correct spelling. A sonata is a piece of music written for one or two instruments.

19. C: *Qualms* is the correct spelling. Qualms are reservations or doubts. An experienced performer might not feel any anxiety about performing, even before a very large crowd.

20. A: *Yearling* is the correct spelling. A yearling is a young horse or other animal. Although horses grow up faster than infant humans, a year-old horse might still be afraid to go out entirely on its own.

Copyright © Mometrix Media. You have been licensed one copy of this document for personal use only. Any other reproduction or redistribution is strictly prohibited. All rights reserved.
This content is provided for test preparation purposes only and does not imply an endorsement by Mometrix of any particular political, scientific, or religious point of view.

Spelling Practice Test 2

Each question gives three different spellings of a word. Two are incorrect and one is correct. Select the choice from each set of three that is spelled correctly.

1. A. separate   B. seperate   C. sepparate

2. A. nucular   B. nuclear   C. nuculear

3. A. fermiliar   B. farmiliar   C. familiar

4. A. sacrilegious   B. sacreligious   C. sacraligious

5. A. aggitated   B. agittated   C. agitated

6. A. orientated   B. oriented   C. oreinted

7. A. indispensible   B. indespensible   C. indispensable

8. A. similar   B. simular   C. similiar

9. A. atitude   B. attitude   C. atittude

10. A. abreviate   B. abbreviate   C. abreeviate

11. A. absorb   B. apsorb   C. abzorb

12. A. acumulate   B. acummulate   C. accumulate

13. A. airial   B. aireal   C. aerial

14. A. comedian   B. commedian   C. comedien

15. A. ashphalt   B. asphalt   C. aspalt

16. A. forcable   B. forcible   C. forceble

17. A. anicdote   B. antecdote   C. anecdote

18. A. flexible   B. flexable   C. flexiable

19. A. defendant   B. defendent   C. difendent

20. A. plainteff   B. plaintif   C. plaintiff

21. A. idiocincrasy   B. idiosyncrasy   C. idiosincracy

22. A. hazardous   B. hazerdous   C. hazzardous

23. A. horific   B. horrific   C. horriffic

24. A. hansome   B. handsom   C. handsome

25. A. liaison   B. liason   C. leiaison

Copyright © Mometrix Media. You have been licensed one copy of this document for personal use only. Any other reproduction or redistribution is strictly prohibited. All rights reserved. This content is provided for test preparation purposes only and does not imply an endorsement by Mometrix of any particular political, scientific, or religious point of view.

26. A. galexy   B. galaxy   C. gallaxy

27. A. attorneys   B. atorneys   C. attornys

28. A. asteriks   B. asterix   C. asterisk

29. A. equalibrium   B. equilibrum   C. equilibrium

30. A. brilliance   B. brillance   C. briliance

31. A. blanche   B. blanch   C. blance

32. A. ecstasy   B. extasy   C. ecstacy

33. A. deppreciate   B. depreciate   C. deappreciate

34. A. terpitude   B. turpittude   C. turpitude

35. A. oposite   B. opposite   C. opossite

36. A. tyrrany   B. tyrranny   C. tyranny

37. A. schism   B. scism   C. shism

38. A. scedule   B. shedule   C. schedule

39. A. incandescent   B. incandesent   C. incandecent

40. A. teriffic   B. terrific   C. terriffic

41. A. homogeneize   B. homogenize   C. homoginise

42. A. sieve   B. seive   C. sive

43. A. truely   B. truley   C. truly

44. A. sincerely   B. sincerly   C. sinceerly

45. A. transeint   B. transient   C. transhent

46. A. sedition   B. sidition   C. sadition

47. A. theives   B. thiefs   C. thieves

48. A. vengance   B. vengeance   C. vengence

49. A. nilon   B. nylon   C. nyllon

50. A. unnacceptable   B. unaceptible   C. unacceptable

51. A. deficit   B. defecit   C. defficit

52. A. disaproval   B. disapproval   C. dissaproval

53. A. diffidence   B. difidence   C. diffedince

Copyright © Mometrix Media. You have been licensed one copy of this document for personal use only. Any other reproduction or redistribution is strictly prohibited. All rights reserved.
This content is provided for test preparation purposes only and does not imply an endorsement by Mometrix of any particular political, scientific, or religious point of view.

54. A. picknicking   B. picnicing   C. picnicking

55. A. orregano   B. oreganno   C. oregano

56. A. batchelor   B. bachelor   C. bachler

57. A. indelible   B. indelable   C. indellible

58. A. dyurnal   B. diurnal   C. dayernal

59. A. impatience   B. impatiense   C. empatiance

60. A. parlament   B. parliment   C. parliament

Copyright © Mometrix Media. You have been licensed one copy of this document for personal use only. Any other reproduction or redistribution is strictly prohibited. All rights reserved.
This content is provided for test preparation purposes only and does not imply an endorsement by Mometrix of any particular political, scientific, or religious point of view.

Spelling Practice Test 2 Answer Key

1. A: separate
2. B: nuclear
3. C: familiar
4. A: sacrilegious
5. C: agitated
6. B: oriented
7. C: indispensable
8. A: similar
9. B: attitude
10. B: abbreviate
11. A: absorb
12. C: accumulate
13. C: aerial
14. A: comedian
15. B: asphalt
16. B: forcible
17. C: anecdote
18. A: flexible
19. A: defendant
20. C: plaintiff
21. B: idiosyncrasy
22. A: hazardous
23. B: horrific
24. C: handsome
25. A: liaison

26. B: galaxy
27. A: attorneys
28. C: asterisk
29. C: equilibrium
30. A: brilliance
31. B: blanch.
32. A: ecstasy
33. B: depreciate
34. C: turpitude
35. B: opposite
36. C: tyranny
37. A: schism
38. C: schedule
39. A: incandescent
40. B: terrific
41. B: homogenize
42. A: sieve
43. C: truly
44. A: sincerely
45. B: transient
46. A: sedition
47. C: thieves
48. B: vengeance
49. B: nylon
50. C: unacceptable

51. A: deficit
52. B: disapproval
53. A: diffidence
54. C: picnicking
55. C: oregano
56. B: bachelor
57. A: indelible
58. B: diurnal
59. A: impatience
60. C: parliament

44

Copyright © Mometrix Media. You have been licensed one copy of this document for personal use only. Any other reproduction or redistribution is strictly prohibited. All rights reserved. This content is provided for test preparation purposes only and does not imply an endorsement by Mometrix of any particular political, scientific, or religious point of view.

Vocabulary Practice Test 1

For each word, choose the answer that contains the word or phrase that is closest in meaning.

1. Elucidate

    a. to complain
    b. to escape
    c. to explain
    d. to extract

2. Accord

    a. plan
    b. agreement
    c. rope
    d. skill

3. Annual

    a. to declare void
    b. around Christmas time
    c. new
    d. yearly

4. Scarce

    a. rare
    b. plentiful
    c. odd
    d. ferocious

5. Convince

    a. to deceive
    b. to persuade
    c. to accuse
    d. to harass

6. Incite

    a. understanding
    b. to provoke
    c. to delay
    d. to remove

7. Invoke

    a. to create
    b. to appeal to
    c. to twist
    d. to reverse

Copyright © Mometrix Media. You have been licensed one copy of this document for personal use only. Any other reproduction or redistribution is strictly prohibited. All rights reserved.
This content is provided for test preparation purposes only and does not imply an endorsement by Mometrix of any particular political, scientific, or religious point of view.

8. Haughty

    a. arrogant

    b. confused

    c. mild

    d. very large

9. Dubious

    a. remarkable

    b. silent

    c. tricky

    d. questionable

10. Novel

    a. unusual

    b. ordinary

    c. popular

    d. boring

11. Bequeath

    a. to quiver

    b. to give

    c. under

    d. to take unlawfully

12. Disdain

    a. contempt

    b. concern

    c. fragility

    d. remorse

13. Compel

    a. to measure against

    b. to rethink

    c. to force

    d. to move fast

14. Illustrious

    a. generous

    b. celebrated

    c. expensive

    d. very ill

15. Mortify

    a. to refrigerate

    b. to apply

    c. to strengthen

    d. to embarrass

Copyright © Mometrix Media. You have been licensed one copy of this document for personal use only. Any other reproduction or redistribution is strictly prohibited. All rights reserved. This content is provided for test preparation purposes only and does not imply an endorsement by Mometrix of any particular political, scientific, or religious point of view.

16. Authorize
   a. to approve
   b. to seal by burning
   c. to make louder
   d. to steal

17. Penchant
   a. necklace
   b. wealthy
   c. accent
   d. tendency

18. Capitulate
   a. to reduce in size
   b. to repeat
   c. to agree to
   d. to surrender

19. Imbibe
   a. to drink
   b. to offer money to
   c. to include
   d. to follow behind

20. Bucolic
   a. deadly
   b. rural
   c. using very few words
   d. very overweight

21. Impetus
   a. lacking power
   b. regret
   c. shamelessness
   d. motivation

22. Prevail
   a. to fall ill
   b. to pay more than necessary
   c. to achieve victory
   d. to have foresight

23. podium
   a. small town
   b. insert worn in a shoe
   c. raised platform
   d. foot doctor

Copyright © Mometrix Media. You have been licensed one copy of this document for personal use only. Any other reproduction or redistribution is strictly prohibited. All rights reserved.
This content is provided for test preparation purposes only and does not imply an endorsement by Mometrix of any particular political, scientific, or religious point of view.

24. Blatant

    a. hidden
    b. obvious
    c. disgusting
    d. very old

25. Inflict

    a. to devise
    b. to demand
    c. to revolt
    d. to impose

Copyright © Mometrix Media. You have been licensed one copy of this document for personal use only. Any other reproduction or redistribution is strictly prohibited. All rights reserved.
This content is provided for test preparation purposes only and does not imply an endorsement by Mometrix of any particular political, scientific, or religious point of view.

Vocabulary Practice Test 1 Answer Key

1. C: to explain

2. B: agreement

3. D: yearly

4. A: rare

5. B: to persuade

6. B: to provoke

7. B: to appeal to

8. A: arrogant

9. D: questionable

10. A: unusual

11. B: to give

12. A: contempt

13. C: to force

14. B: celebrated

15. D: to embarrass

16. A: to approve

17. D: tendency

18. D: to surrender

19. A: to drink

20. B: rural

21. D: motivation

22. C: to achieve victory

23. C: raised platform

24. B: obvious

25. D: to impose

49

Copyright © Mometrix Media. You have been licensed one copy of this document for personal use only. Any other reproduction or redistribution is strictly prohibited. All rights reserved.
This content is provided for test preparation purposes only and does not imply an endorsement by Mometrix of any particular political, scientific, or religious point of view.

Vocabulary Practice Test 2

For each word, choose the answer that contains the word or phrase that is closest in meaning.

1. Universal
   a. everywhere
   b. high quality
   c. related to college
   d. poetry that doesn't rhyme

2. Morbid
   a. lacking excitement
   b. average
   c. horizontal
   d. related to death

3. Malicious
   a. spiteful
   b. good-tasting
   c. delicate
   d. intense

4. Quip
   a. a tool
   b. a medical device
   c. a joke
   d. a kind of flower

5. Subtle
   a. slight
   b. round
   c. plain
   d. outdated

6. Broach
   a. to remove
   b. to ban
   c. to bring up
   d. to twist

7. Aphorism
   a. fable
   b. funny story
   c. proverb
   d. cutting remark

Copyright © Mometrix Media. You have been licensed one copy of this document for personal use only. Any other reproduction or redistribution is strictly prohibited. All rights reserved.
This content is provided for test preparation purposes only and does not imply an endorsement by Mometrix of any particular political, scientific, or religious point of view.

8. Innocuous

   a. causing nausea
   b. harmless
   c. dangerous
   d. mysterious

9. Surreptitious

   a. sneaky
   b. very loud
   c. long and winding
   d. saying the same thing

10. Simulate

   a. to excite
   b. to pretend
   c. to connect
   d. to grow fast

11. Precede

   a. to continue
   b. to come after
   c. to come before
   d. to take place

12. Epitaph

   a. curse word
   b. false sounding apology
   c. inscription on a tombstone
   d. engraved invitation

13. Pretentious

   a. pompous
   b. very large
   c. faint-sounding
   d. round

14. Paradox

   a. a matching pair
   b. a contradiction
   c. a small star
   d. half a light-year

15. Superfluous

   a. gigantic
   b. awesome
   c. unnecessary
   d. filled with joy

Copyright © Mometrix Media. You have been licensed one copy of this document for personal use only. Any other reproduction or redistribution is strictly prohibited. All rights reserved.
This content is provided for test preparation purposes only and does not imply an endorsement by Mometrix of any particular political, scientific, or religious point of view.

16. Valid

- a. butler
- b. powerful
- c. fast
- d. legitimate

17. Jargon

- a. language
- b. container
- c. boundary
- d. painter's toolbox

18. Obstinate

- a. backwards
- b. friendly
- c. stubborn
- d. extremely ill

19. Eloquent

- a. equal on all sides
- b. persuasive
- c. of foreign birth
- d. bent

20. Clandestine

- a. shocking
- b. fatal
- c. wise
- d. secret

21. Colloquial

- a. taking place at college
- b. double-jointed
- c. informal
- d. regrettable

22. Conundrum

- a. maze
- b. short novel
- c. riddle
- d. tall tower

23. Placid

- a. drunk
- b. queasy
- c. perfectly round
- d. peaceful

Copyright © Mometrix Media. You have been licensed one copy of this document for personal use only. Any other reproduction or redistribution is strictly prohibited. All rights reserved.
This content is provided for test preparation purposes only and does not imply an endorsement by Mometrix of any particular political, scientific, or religious point of view.

24. haggle

 a. to dispute
 b. to shout
 c. to fray
 d. to swallow

25. taciturn

 a. polite
 b. rude
 c. quiet
 d. having many curves

Copyright © Mometrix Media. You have been licensed one copy of this document for personal use only. Any other reproduction or redistribution is strictly prohibited. All rights reserved.
This content is provided for test preparation purposes only and does not imply an endorsement by Mometrix of any particular political, scientific, or religious point of view.

Vocabulary Practice Test 2 Answer Key

1. A: everywhere

2. D: related to death

3. A: spiteful

4. C: a joke

5. A: slight

6. C: to bring up

7. C: proverb

8. B: harmless

9. A: sneaky

10. B: to pretend

11. C: to come before

12. C: inscription on a tombstone

13. A: pompous

14. B: a contradiction

15. C: unnecessary

16. D: legitimate

17. A: language

18. C: stubborn

19. B: persuasive

20. D: secret

21. C: informal

22. C: riddle

23. D: peaceful

24. A: to dispute

25. C: quiet

54

Copyright © Mometrix Media. You have been licensed one copy of this document for personal use only. Any other reproduction or redistribution is strictly prohibited. All rights reserved. This content is provided for test preparation purposes only and does not imply an endorsement by Mometrix of any particular political, scientific, or religious point of view.

Vocabulary Practice Test 3

For each word, choose the answer that contains the word or phrase that is closest in meaning.

1. Endorse
   a. to remove
   b. to give
   c. to approve
   d. to accelerate

2. Placate
   a. to fasten
   b. to go away
   c. to soothe
   d. to stare

3. Benevolent
   a. charitable
   b. evil
   c. confused
   d. sad

4. Covert
   a. fast
   b. terrible
   c. hidden
   d. go back

5. Larceny
   a. theft
   b. kindness
   c. humor
   d. resolve

6. Poignant
   a. foul-smelling
   b. deeply moving
   c. perfectly ripe
   d. very tasty

7. Aloof
   a. outgoing
   b. insane
   c. intelligent
   d. detached

Copyright © Mometrix Media. You have been licensed one copy of this document for personal use only. Any other reproduction or redistribution is strictly prohibited. All rights reserved.
This content is provided for test preparation purposes only and does not imply an endorsement by Mometrix of any particular political, scientific, or religious point of view.

8. Precedent

    a. something that happened before
    b. something that is happening right now
    c. something that will happen later
    d. something that will never happen

9. Profound

    a. involving money
    b. near-sighted
    c. deep
    d. circular driveway

10. Analogy

    a. tongue twister
    b. abbreviation from first letter of words
    c. cheap reproduction
    d. comparison

11. Mode

    a. connecting point
    b. tool
    c. manner
    d. dessert

12. Vehemently

    a. passionately
    b. weakly
    c. shabbily
    d. rudely

13. Potent

    a. a drink with magic properties
    b. powerful
    c. sharp-edged
    d. danger

14. Animosity

    a. possessing four legs
    b. hatred
    c. sheer joy
    d. confusion

15. Appease

    a. to turn suddenly
    b. to soothe
    c. to disappear
    d. to meet as a group

Copyright © Mometrix Media. You have been licensed one copy of this document for personal use only. Any other reproduction or redistribution is strictly prohibited. All rights reserved. This content is provided for test preparation purposes only and does not imply an endorsement by Mometrix of any particular political, scientific, or religious point of view.

16. Contrite

   a. brief

   b. twisted

   c. sorry

   d. skillful

17. Obsequious

   a. subservient

   b. bedridden

   c. famous

   d. cunning

18. Embezzle

   a. to steal

   b. to give a refund

   c. to keep a promise

   d. to stir

19. Facetious

   a. slightly overweight

   b. feeling faint

   c. two-faced

   d. humorous

20. Benign

   a. to speak ill of someone

   b. gentle

   c. donate

   d. equal to or less than

21. Largesse

   a. physical size

   b. a small island

   c. generosity

   d. a musical notation

22. Verify

   a. to enlarge

   b. to prove

   c. to copy

   d. to deny

23. Rejoinder

   a. something left over

   b. someone who quits and rejoins

   c. a carpenter's tool

   d. a witty reply

Copyright © Mometrix Media. You have been licensed one copy of this document for personal use only. Any other reproduction or redistribution is strictly prohibited. All rights reserved.
This content is provided for test preparation purposes only and does not imply an endorsement by Mometrix of any particular political, scientific, or religious point of view.

24. Tenant

    a. principle or belief
    b. person who rents a house
    c. stubborn
    d. high-strung

25. Solicit

    a. to ask for
    b. to refuse
    c. to arrest
    d. to convict

Copyright © Mometrix Media. You have been licensed one copy of this document for personal use only. Any other reproduction or redistribution is strictly prohibited. All rights reserved. This content is provided for test preparation purposes only and does not imply an endorsement by Mometrix of any particular political, scientific, or religious point of view.

Vocabulary Practice Test 3 Answer Key

1. C: to approve

2. C: to soothe

3. A: charitable

4. C: hidden

5. A: theft

6. B: deeply moving

7. D: detached

8. A: something that happened before

9. C: deep

10. D: comparison

11. C: manner

12. A: passionately

13: B: powerful

14. B: hatred

15. B: to soothe

16. C: sorry

17. A: subservient

18. A: to steal

19. D: humorous

20. B: gentle

21. C: generosity

22. B: to prove

23. D: a witty reply

24. B: person who rents a house

25. A: to ask for

Copyright © Mometrix Media. You have been licensed one copy of this document for personal use only. Any other reproduction or redistribution is strictly prohibited. All rights reserved.
This content is provided for test preparation purposes only and does not imply an endorsement by Mometrix of any particular political, scientific, or religious point of view.

Vocabulary Practice Test 4

For each word, choose the answer that contains the word or phrase that is closest in meaning.

1. Chronic
   a. painful
   b. bent
   c. colorful
   d. long-lasting

2. Coerce
   a. to lie
   b. to cheat
   c. to swerve
   d. to force

3. Abrasive
   a. extended
   b. coarse
   c. magical
   d. checkered

4. Precocious
   a. very cute
   b. adorable
   c. developing early
   d. devout

5. Candid
   a. hidden
   b. shocking
   c. deceitful
   d. honest

6. Wax
   a. to increase
   b. to decrease
   c. to become old
   d. to drop sharply

7. Fortuitous
   a. lucky
   b. heavy
   c. strongly reinforced
   d. well-protected

Copyright © Mometrix Media. You have been licensed one copy of this document for personal use only. Any other reproduction or redistribution is strictly prohibited. All rights reserved.
This content is provided for test preparation purposes only and does not imply an endorsement by Mometrix of any particular political, scientific, or religious point of view.

8. Deter

  a. to change one's driving route
  b. to prevent
  c. to cause
  d. to read between the lines

9. Minute

  a. unable to speak
  b. very tiny
  c. belonging to myself
  d. extremely fragile

10. Revert

  a. to turn upside down
  b. to return to a previous condition
  c. to regard as sacred
  d. to turn inside out

11. Hazardous

  a. healthy
  b. deep
  c. very funny
  d. dangerous

12. Proscribe

  a. to recommend
  b. to read
  c. to forbid
  d. to portray

13. Spurn

  a. to reject
  b. to start a fire
  c. to embrace
  d. to threaten

14. Condone

  a. to tie a ribbon
  b. to allow something
  c. to transfer something
  d. to eat in a hurry

15. Evade

  a. to capture
  b. to avoid
  c. to light up
  d. to expel someone from a group

Copyright © Mometrix Media. You have been licensed one copy of this document for personal use only. Any other reproduction or redistribution is strictly prohibited. All rights reserved.
This content is provided for test preparation purposes only and does not imply an endorsement by Mometrix of any particular political, scientific, or religious point of view.

16. Entice

    a. to frighten
    b. to dislike
    c. to attract
    d. to instigate

17. Contrived

    a. artificial
    b. curved
    d. out of breath
    d. very sorry

18. Deprived

    a. having no conscience
    b. unable to walk on one's own
    c. lacking something essential
    d. very disappointed

19. Hyperbole

    a. a distant star
    b. an animal that burrows
    c. exaggerated language
    d. the peak of a roof

20. Clamor

    a. to curdle
    b. to grab
    c. a tool used with anvil
    d. an uproar

21. Averse

    a. reluctant
    b. rhyming
    c. to move across
    d. divided into halves

22. Belligerent

    a. speaking two languages
    b. devout
    c. unfaithful
    d. hostile

23. Desist

    a. dead
    b. to fight against
    c. to stop
    d. to demand

Copyright © Mometrix Media. You have been licensed one copy of this document for personal use only. Any other reproduction or redistribution is strictly prohibited. All rights reserved.
This content is provided for test preparation purposes only and does not imply an endorsement by Mometrix of any particular political, scientific, or religious point of view.

24. Rotund

  a. round
  b. loud
  c. speaking smoothly
  d. insightful

25. Wrangle

  a. to deceive
  b. to argue
  c. to volunteer
  d. to hesitate

Copyright © Mometrix Media. You have been licensed one copy of this document for personal use only. Any other reproduction or redistribution is strictly prohibited. All rights reserved.
This content is provided for test preparation purposes only and does not imply an endorsement by Mometrix of any particular political, scientific, or religious point of view.

Vocabulary Practice Test 4 Answer Key

1. D: long lasting

2. D: to force

3. B: coarse

4. C: developing early

5. D: honest

6. A: to increase

7. A: lucky

8. B: to prevent

9. B: very tiny

10. B: to return to a previous condition

11. D: dangerous

12. C: to forbid

13. A: to reject

14. B: to allow something

15. B: to avoid

16. C: to attract

17. A: artificial

18. C: lacking something essential

19. C: exaggerated language

20. D: an uproar

21. A: reluctant

22. D: hostile

23. C: to stop

24. A: round

25. B: to argue

Copyright © Mometrix Media. You have been licensed one copy of this document for personal use only. Any other reproduction or redistribution is strictly prohibited. All rights reserved.
This content is provided for test preparation purposes only and does not imply an endorsement by Mometrix of any particular political, scientific, or religious point of view.

Analogies

Another kind of language question you might see is one asking you to draw an analogy, and this kind of question is different from the other kinds we've already discussed. Instead, you'll see something like this:

1. Mare : Foal
   a. Dog : Cat
   b. Dolphin : Tuna
   c. Shark : Whale
   d. Hen : Chick

You're looking for two words that have the same relationship as the two words in the question stem. Here's what a full analogy looks like:

Food: Plate :: Beverage : Glass

Here is what the analogy means:

Food is to plate as beverage is to glass.

In other words, a beverage has the same relationship to a glass as food has to a plate. In both cases, the second item is used to serve the first item.

In the example above, select the answer that contains two words with the same kind of relationship as *mare* and *foal*. While all the pairs in the answers have some similarities, only *d* contains the same relationship of an adult female and a young animal of the same species.

Don't let analogy questions intimidate you. Just think of them exactly as they are—another kind of vocabulary question. In fact, some will be nothing more than synonym/antonym questions. If you've never answered analogy questions before, they might seem tricky, but once you've gone through a few of our practice questions, you'll see they're really nothing to worry about.

Sometimes the analogy questions have a slightly different format. For example, you might see a question phrased like this:

Mare : Foal :: Hen :
   a. rooster
   b. duck
   c. chick
   d. goose

As you can see, completing these kinds of analogies isn't much different than the first format; in fact, this layout may be a bit easier since you're given more information to start with.

One thing to keep in mind is that the order of the words is extremely important. The two words in the correct answer must not only have the same relationship as the two words in the question stem, they must also be in the same order. Mare : Foal :: Hen : Chick is correct because a mare is an adult female horse and a foal is a young horse, while a hen is an adult female chicken and a chick is a young chicken. However, Chick : Hen would *not* be a correct answer, because even though both elements of the analogy are present, they are in reverse order, changing the relationship.

Copyright © Mometrix Media. You have been licensed one copy of this document for personal use only. Any other reproduction or redistribution is strictly prohibited. All rights reserved. This content is provided for test preparation purposes only and does not imply an endorsement by Mometrix of any particular political, scientific, or religious point of view.

Analogies can represent many different kinds of relationships. Here are some of the most common:

- Synonyms—question : query
- Antonyms—straight : meandering
- Whole/Part—finger : hand | foot : toe
- Classification/Kind/Category/Composition, etc.—owl : nocturnal | owl : bird | building : brick | red : color | apparel : shirt
- Single/Group—cow : herd | tree : forest
- Degree—big : huge | angry : furious | tired : exhausted | hot : warm
- Subject/Action—doctor : prescribe | attorney : defend
- Action/Subject—hit : ball | levy : tax
- Object/User—wrench : mechanic | conductor : baton
- Object/Place—flower : garden | office : desk
- Object/Action—pen : write | cut : knife
- Cause/Effect—virus : illness | practice : improvement | stress : anxiety
- Aspect—cheetah : fast | mansion : huge

These are some of the most common kinds of analogies found on civil service exams. There are others, but there's no need to cover every conceivable kind of analogy you might run into. Ninety percent of the analogies you'll see will fall into one of the above categories, and you should have no trouble spotting the relationship in any that don't. Use the practice questions in this guide, as they can help you tremendously if you're having any trouble in this area.

Copyright © Mometrix Media. You have been licensed one copy of this document for personal use only. Any other reproduction or redistribution is strictly prohibited. All rights reserved.
This content is provided for test preparation purposes only and does not imply an endorsement by Mometrix of any particular political, scientific, or religious point of view.

Analogies Practice Test 1

Directions: For each of the following questions, you will find three capitalized terms and, in parentheses, four answer choices designated a, b, c, and d. Select the one answer choice that best completes the analogy with the three capitalized terms. (To record your answers, circle your answer choice.)

1. CHASTISE : REPRIMAND :: IMPETUOUS : _____
    a. punish
    b. rash
    c. considered
    d. poor

2. TELE : DISTANT :: CIRCUM : _____
    a. through
    b. above
    c. within
    d. around

3. CHENEY: BUSH :: MONDALE : _____
    a. Clinton
    b. Carter
    c. Reagan
    d. Obama

4. LISSOM : GRACEFUL :: _____: OBSTREPEROUS
    a. hostile
    b. lithe
    c. determined
    d. unconditional

5. HUMERUS : ARM :: _____ : LEG
    a. ulna
    b. clavicle
    c. femur
    d. mandible

6. PRODUCT : _____ :: MULTIPLICATION : DIVISION
    a. quotient
    b. divisor
    c. integer
    d. dividend

7. SWEATER : _____ :: WEAR : EAT
    a. shirt
    b. top hat
    c. asparagus
    d. looks

Copyright © Mometrix Media. You have been licensed one copy of this document for personal use only. Any other reproduction or redistribution is strictly prohibited. All rights reserved. This content is provided for test preparation purposes only and does not imply an endorsement by Mometrix of any particular political, scientific, or religious point of view.

8. IMPECUNIOUS : MONEY :: _____ : FOOD

   a. famished
   b. nauseated
   c. distracted
   d. antagonistic

9. DENIGRATE : MALIGN :: DEMUR : _____

   a. protest
   b. defer
   c. slander
   d. benumb

10. POST : AFTER :: PERI : _____

   a. around
   b. completely
   c. before
   d. much

11. GOAT : NANNY :: PIG : _____

   a. shoat
   b. ewe
   c. cub
   d. sow

12. CACHE : RESERVE :: DEARTH : _____

   a. stockpile
   b. paucity
   c. cudgel
   d. dirge

13. DISCURSIVE : DIGRESSIVE :: SUCCINCT : _____

   a. long-winded
   b. pithy
   c. taciturn
   d. staccato

14. ARABLE : FARMABLE :: ASYLUM : _____

   a. refuge
   b. danger
   c. arid
   d. fertile

15. SATIRE : HUMOR :: BUREAU : _____

   a. bureaucracy
   b. furniture
   c. complaint
   d. bedroom

Copyright © Mometrix Media. You have been licensed one copy of this document for personal use only. Any other reproduction or redistribution is strictly prohibited. All rights reserved.
This content is provided for test preparation purposes only and does not imply an endorsement by Mometrix of any particular political, scientific, or religious point of view.

16. TITAN : GIANT :: PROGENITOR : _____

   a. forebear
   b. descendant
   c. miniature
   d. primeval

17. MYRIAD : STATIONARY :: FEW : _____

   a. peripatetic
   b. many
   c. several
   d. halted

18. ZENITH : NADIR :: _____ : DISOBEDIENT

   a. defiant
   b. apex
   c. grandiloquent
   d. tractable

19. MISSISSIPPI : UNITED STATES :: THAMES : _____

   a. France
   b. England
   c. Germany
   d. Belgium

20. MANSION : HOUSE :: _____ : BOTTLE

   a. flagon
   b. container
   c. vessel
   d. pot

21. DICTIONARY : DEFINITIONS :: THESAURUS : _____

   a. pronunciations
   b. synonyms
   c. explanations
   d. pronouns

22. BEES : HIVE :: CATTLE : _____

   a. swarm
   b. pod
   c. herd
   d. flock

23. DIRGE : LAMENT :: PURGE : _____

   a. elegy
   b. weeping
   c. cleanse
   d. limpid

Copyright © Mometrix Media. You have been licensed one copy of this document for personal use only. Any other reproduction or redistribution is strictly prohibited. All rights reserved.
This content is provided for test preparation purposes only and does not imply an endorsement by Mometrix of any particular political, scientific, or religious point of view.

24. **LATITUDE : LONGITUDE : PARALLEL : _____**

    a. strait
    b. meridian
    c. equator
    d. aquifer

25. **WIT : WAG :: INSOLENCE : _____**

    a. boor
    b. student
    c. teacher
    d. soldier

26. **PREVENTION : DETERRENCE :: INCITEMENT : _____**

    a. excitement
    b. provocation
    c. request
    d. disregard

27. **ARCH : SAUCY :: _____ : ENMITY**

    a. antipathy
    b. oval
    c. circular
    d. delectable

28. **NOISOME : _____ :: THUNDEROUS : DEAFENING**

    a. pleasant
    b. boisterous
    c. malodorous
    d. silent

29. **INFIDEL : UNBELIEVER :: _____ : OUTCAST**

    a. pariah
    b. apostate
    c. apostle
    d. disciple

30. **VALUE : WORTH :: MEASURE : _____**

    a. gauge
    b. allowance
    c. demerit
    d. insignificance

31. **DOLPHIN : POD :: GOOSE : _____**

    a. troup
    b. nest
    c. gaggle
    d. drove

Copyright © Mometrix Media. You have been licensed one copy of this document for personal use only. Any other reproduction or redistribution is strictly prohibited. All rights reserved. This content is provided for test preparation purposes only and does not imply an endorsement by Mometrix of any particular political, scientific, or religious point of view.

32. DISSEMINATE : SPREAD :: DEPRECATE : _____

a. disparage
b. demur
c. dispel
d. dissemble

33. EGO : CONSCIOUS :: _____ : UNCONSCIOUS

a. operant
b. id
c. identity
d. collective

34. MAL : _____ :: NEO : NEW

a. water
b. bad
c. change
d. hand

35. PEDOLOGY : CHILDREN :: ICHTHYOLOGY : _____

a. insects
b. fishes
c. ants
d. fungi

36. BLITHE : CAREFREE :: BRUSQUE : _____

a. curt
b. civil
c. urbane
d. courteous

37. SONNET : 14 :: HAIKU : _____

a. 3
b. 5.
c. 7
d. 9

38. WOLF : WOLVES :: PASSERBY : _____

a. passerby
b. passerbys
c. passersby
d. passersbys

39. CANDID : FRANK :: CAPITULATE : _____

a. repeat
b. surrender
c. burnish
d. chapter

Copyright © Mometrix Media. You have been licensed one copy of this document for personal use only. Any other reproduction or redistribution is strictly prohibited. All rights reserved. This content is provided for test preparation purposes only and does not imply an endorsement by Mometrix of any particular political, scientific, or religious point of view.

40. BEAR : DONKEY :: CUB : _____

    a. kid

    b. pup

    c. foal

    d. joey

41. MOLLUSK : SNAIL :: MARSUPIAL : _____

    a. koala

    b. mouse

    c. raccoon

    d. squirrel

42. DEARTH : PAUCITY :: COUNTENANCE : _____

    a. condone

    b. deny

    c. express

    d. cower

43. DEER : FAWN :: LION : _____

    a. kid

    b. cub

    c. cygnet

    d. shoat

44. LUCRE : PROFIT :: OFFICIOUS : _____

    a. bureaucratic

    b. meddling

    c. authoritarian

    d. legal

45. CARPE DIEM : SEIZE THE DAY :: PERSONA NON GRATA : _____

    a. ungrateful person

    b. unwelcome person

    c. absent person

    d. anonymous person

46. ALACRITY : LASSITUDE :: ANTIPATHY : _____

    a. dislike

    b. hatred

    c. sympathy

    d. beneficence

47. LOCK : PRIDE :: _____ : LIONS

    a. key

    b. permit

    c. collection

    d. hair

Copyright © Mometrix Media. You have been licensed one copy of this document for personal use only. Any other reproduction or redistribution is strictly prohibited. All rights reserved. This content is provided for test preparation purposes only and does not imply an endorsement by Mometrix of any particular political, scientific, or religious point of view.

48. ENERVATE : ENERGIZE :: ESPOUSE : _____

    a. oppose
    b. wed
    c. equine
    d. epistolary

49. CHERUB : CHERUBIM :: NEBULA : _____

    a. nebuli
    b. nebulae
    c. nebulus
    d. nebulous

50. DIATRIBE : DIALECT :: JEREMIAD : _____

    a. eject
    b. tirade
    c. mermaid
    d. idiom

51. SOPRANO : FEMALE :: _____ : MALE

    a. tenor
    b. alto
    c. bass
    d. contralto

52. GENUS : GENERA :: ALUMNUS : _____

    a. alumni
    b. alumna
    c. alumnae
    d. alum

53. HISS : OR :: ONOMATOPOEIA : _____

    a. preposition
    b. verb
    c. pronoun
    d. conjunction

54. PROSCRIBE : PRESCRIBE :: DENOUNCE : _____

    a. dictate
    b. repel
    c. invite
    d. dentition

55. EWE : _____ :: MARE : HORSE

    a. sheep
    b. goat
    c. lamb
    d. cow

Copyright © Mometrix Media. You have been licensed one copy of this document for personal use only. Any other reproduction or redistribution is strictly prohibited. All rights reserved. This content is provided for test preparation purposes only and does not imply an endorsement by Mometrix of any particular political, scientific, or religious point of view.

56. XCIV : 94 :: XXXVI : _____

    a. 106

    b. 136

    c. 134

    d. 36

57. INUNDATE : FLOOD :: JARGON : _____

    a. argot

    b. language

    c. precipitation

    d. overwhelm

58. 8 : 2 :: 64 : _____

    a. 2

    b. 4

    c. 8

    d. 12

59. HER : ME :: _____ : FIRST

    a. first

    b. second

    c. third

    d. fourth

60. SCORE: GROSS :: 20 : _____

    a. 1

    b. 5

    c. 15

    d. 144

Copyright © Mometrix Media. You have been licensed one copy of this document for personal use only. Any other reproduction or redistribution is strictly prohibited. All rights reserved.
This content is provided for test preparation purposes only and does not imply an endorsement by Mometrix of any particular political, scientific, or religious point of view.

Analogies Practice Test 1 Answers Key

1. B: Rash. Chastise and reprimand are synonyms. Rash is a synonym for impulsive.

2. D: Around. As the prefix tele- means distant, the prefix circa- means around.

3. B: Carter. As Cheney was US Vice President in President Bush's administration, so Mondale was in President Carter's administration.

4. A: Hostile. Lissom and graceful are synonyms. The answer choice synonym for obstreperous is hostile.

5. C: Femur. The humerus is a bone in the arm; the femur is a bone in the leg.

6. A: Quotient. A quotient is the result of division as a product is the result of multiplication.

7. C: Asparagus. One eats asparagus; one wears a sweater.

8. A: Famished. As a person who is impecunious needs money, so a person who is famished needs food.

9. A: Protest. Denigrate and malign are synonyms. The answer choice synonym for demur is protest.

10. A: Around. As the prefix post- means after, the prefix peri- means around.

11. D: Sow. A female goat is a nanny and a female pig is a sow.

12. B: Paucity. Cache and reserve are synonyms. The answer choice synonym for dearth is paucity.

13. B: Pithy. Discursive and digressive are synonyms. The answer choice synonym for succinct is pithy.

14. A: Refuge. Arable and farmable are synonyms. The answer choice synonym for asylum is refuge.

15. B: Furniture. Satire is a kind of humor and a bureau is a kind of furniture.

16. A: Forebear. Titan and Giant are synonyms. The answer choice synonym for progenitor is forebear.

17. A: Peripatetic. Myriad and few are antonyms. The answer choice antonym for stationary is peripatetic.

18. D: Tractable. Zenith and nadir are antonyms. The answer choice antonym for disobedient is tractable.

19. B: England. As the Mississippi is a river in the United States, so the Thames is a river in England.

20. A: Flagon. As a mansion is a large house, so a flagon is a large bottle.

21. B: Synonyms. As a dictionary is a collection of definitions, so a thesaurus is a collection of synonyms.

75

Copyright © Mometrix Media. You have been licensed one copy of this document for personal use only. Any other reproduction or redistribution is strictly prohibited. All rights reserved. This content is provided for test preparation purposes only and does not imply an endorsement by Mometrix of any particular political, scientific, or religious point of view.

22. C: Herd. A group of bees is called a hive, and a group of cattle is called a herd.

23. C: Cleanse. Dirge and lament are synonyms. The answer choice synonym for purge is cleanse.

24. B: Meridian. A parallel is a line of latitude, while a meridian is a ling of longitude.

25. A: Boor. A defining quality of a wag is wit, as a defining quality of a boor is insolence.

26. B: Provocation. Prevention and deterrence are synonyms. The answer choice synonym for incitement is provocation.

27. A: Antipathy. Arch and saucy are synonyms. The answer choice synonym for enmity is antipathy.

28. C: Malodorous. Thunderous and deafening are synonyms. The answer choice synonym for noisome is malodorous.

29. A: Pariah. As an unbeliever with respect to a particular religion is called an infidel, so an outcast is called a pariah (in Hindu castes).

30. A: Gauge. Value and worth are synonyms. The answer choice synonym for measure is gauge.

31. C: Gaggle. A group of dolphins is called a pod and a group of geese is called a gaggle.

32. A: Disparage. Disseminate and spread are synonyms. The answer choice synonym for deprecate is disparage.

33. B: Id. In Freudian theory the ego is the conscious component of the psyche and the id is the unconscious component of the psyche.

34. B: Bad. As the prefix neo- means new, the prefix mal- means bad.

35. B: Fishes. As pedology is the study of children, so ichthyology is the study of fishes.

36. A: Curt. Blithe and carefree are synonyms. The answer choice synonym for brusque is curt.

37. A: 3. In poetry, a sonnet has 14 lines and a haiku has 3 lines.

38. C: Passersby. The plural of wolf is wolves and the plural of passerby is passersby.

39. B: Surrender. Candid and frank are synonyms. The answer choice synonym for capitulate is surrender.

40. C: Foal. As a bear baby is called a cub, so a donkey baby is called a foal.

41. A: Koala. A snail is an example of a mollusk and a koala is an example of a marsupial.

42. A: Condone. Dearth and paucity are synonyms. The answer choice synonym for countenance is condone.

43. B: Cub. As a deer's offspring is called a fawn, so a lion's offspring is called a cub.

44. B: Meddling. Lucre and profit are synonyms. The answer choice synonym for officious is meddling.

Copyright © Mometrix Media. You have been licensed one copy of this document for personal use only. Any other reproduction or redistribution is strictly prohibited. All rights reserved.
This content is provided for test preparation purposes only and does not imply an endorsement by Mometrix of any particular political, scientific, or religious point of view.

45. B: Unwelcome person. As carpe diem means seize the day, so persona non grata means unwelcome person.

46. C: Sympathy. Alacrity and lassitude are antonyms. The answer choice antonym for antipathy is sympathy.

47. D: Hair. The collective noun for lions is a pride; the collective noun for hair is a lock.

48. A: Oppose. Enervate and energize are antonyms. The answer choice antonym for espouse is oppose.

49. B: Nebulae. As the plural of cherub is cherubim, so the plural of nebula is nebulae.

50. D: Idiom. Diatribe and jeremiad are synonyms. The answer choice synonym for dialect is idiom.

51. A: Tenor. As soprano is the highest female vocal range, tenor is the highest adult male vocal range.

52. A: Alumni. Alumni is the plural form of alumnus as genera is the plural form of genus.

53. D: Conjunction. Or is an example of a conjunction as hiss is an example of onomatopoeia.

54. A: Dictate. Proscribe and denounce are synonyms. The answer choice synonym for prescribe is dictate.

55. A: Sheep. A ewe is a female sheep as a mare is a female horse.

56. D: 36. As XCIV is the Roman numeral representation of 94, so XXXVI is the Roman numeral representation of 36.

57. A: Argot. Inundate and flood are synonyms. The answer choice synonym for jargon is argot.

58. B: 4. 8 squared is 64. 2 squared is 4.

59. C: Third. Her is a third-person pronoun and me is a first-person pronoun.

60. D: 144. As a score is 20, so a gross is 144.

Copyright © Mometrix Media. You have been licensed one copy of this document for personal use only. Any other reproduction or redistribution is strictly prohibited. All rights reserved.
This content is provided for test preparation purposes only and does not imply an endorsement by Mometrix of any particular political, scientific, or religious point of view.

Analogies Practice Test 2

Directions: For each of the following questions, you will find three capitalized terms and, in parentheses, four answer choices designated a, b, c, and d. Select the one answer choice that best completes the analogy with the three capitalized terms. To record your answers, circle your answer choice.

1. AUSPICIOUS : OMINOUS :: PARSIMONIOUS : _____
   a. spendthrift
   b. frugal
   c. licentious
   d. secular

2. ORATOR : ELOQUENCE :: PESSIMIST : _____
   a. fluency
   b. naysayer
   c. hopelessness
   d. thoughtfulness

3. CONTUMACIOUS : INSUBORDINATE :: DIATRIBE : _____
   a. obedient
   b. indirect
   c. suppress
   d. tirade

4. AD HOC: COMMITTEE :: _____ : FABRIC
   a. chenille
   b. extemporized
   c. composition
   d. propaganda

5. TWAIN : CLEMENS :: CARROLL : _____
   a. Dodgson
   b. squally
   c. Lewis
   d. thrice

6. COLORADO : CO :: MARYLAND : _____
   a. MA
   b. MD
   c. MR
   d. ML

7. INTER : BETWEEN :: TRANS : _____
   a. above
   b. without
   c. within
   d. across

78

Copyright © Mometrix Media. You have been licensed one copy of this document for personal use only. Any other reproduction or redistribution is strictly prohibited. All rights reserved.
This content is provided for test preparation purposes only and does not imply an endorsement by Mometrix of any particular political, scientific, or religious point of view.

8. PERSPICACIOUS : DENSE :: _____ : INSIPID

a. thrilling
b. boring
c. intuitive
d. uninspired

9. VERB : COLLATE :: PREPOSITION : _____

a. the
b. behind
c. used
d. perfectly

10. MEET : _____ :: SATE : APPETITE

a. need
b. whim
c. option
d. companion

11. CIRCLE : CIRCUMFERENCE :: OCTAGON : _____

a. area
b. perimeter
c. radius
d. width

12. _____ : RED :: KELLY : GREEN

a. king
b. tide
c. grace
d. crimson

13. BERET : _____ :: HAT : SHOE

a. alpine
b. balaclava
c. wingtip
d. bonnet

14. MANE : _____ :: CANE : KEN

a. knowledge
b. stick
c. hair
d. men

15. ABACUS : CALCULATOR :: MIMEOGRAPH : _____

a. fax machine
b. word processor
c. photocopier
d. telegraph

Copyright © Mometrix Media. You have been licensed one copy of this document for personal use only. Any other reproduction or redistribution is strictly prohibited. All rights reserved.
This content is provided for test preparation purposes only and does not imply an endorsement by Mometrix of any particular political, scientific, or religious point of view.

16. CLANDESTINE : SURREPTITIOUS :: COGENT : _____

   a. incoherent
   b. persuasive
   c. secretive
   d. officious

17. CRANIUM : HEAD :: _____ : ARM

   a. femur
   b. clavicle
   c. ulna
   d. sternum

18. ASHEN : WHITE :: _____ : RED

   a. octave
   b. sanguine
   c. ermine
   d. mauve

19. BELLICOSE : WAR :: BACCHANALIAN : _____

   a. party
   b. solitude
   c. outdoors
   d. luxury

20. SOBRIQUET : ALIAS :: STOLID : _____

   a. pseudonym
   b. solid
   c. impassive
   d. tourniquet

21. PANTS : WEAR :: CHAMPAGNE : _____

   a. eat
   b. dress
   c. drink
   d. applaud

22. COMPARATIVE : MORE :: SUPERLATIVE : _____

   a. some
   b. more
   c. all
   d. most

23. AXIS : ITALY :: ALLIES : _____

   a. Japan
   b. Germany
   c. England
   d. Spain

Copyright © Mometrix Media. You have been licensed one copy of this document for personal use only. Any other reproduction or redistribution is strictly prohibited. All rights reserved. This content is provided for test preparation purposes only and does not imply an endorsement by Mometrix of any particular political, scientific, or religious point of view.

24. NEPHOLOGY : PATHOLOGY :: _____ : DISEASES

a. Egypt
b. archaeology
c. parasites
d. clouds

25. ILK : ELK :: BIG : _____

a. moose
b. type
c. beg
d. enormous

26. HUSBAND : ECONOMIZE :: MARRY : _____

a. wife
b. save
c. spouse
d. unite

27. SEDATIVE : SLEEPINESS :: ALCOHOL : _____

a. intoxication
b. anger
c. thirst
d. solitude

28. BASS : MALE :: _____ : FEMALE

a. alto
b. contralto
c. soprano
d. tenor

29. ISOSCELES : SCALENE :: RECTANGLE : _____

a. circle
b. square
c. geometry
d. octagon

30. INVETERATE : HABITUAL :: QUOTIDIAN : _____

a. numerical
b. commonplace
c. absolute
d. vertebrate

31. SON-IN-LAW : SONS-IN-LAW :: THESIS : _____

a. thesi
b. theses
c. thesises
d. theseses

Copyright © Mometrix Media. You have been licensed one copy of this document for personal use only. Any other reproduction or redistribution is strictly prohibited. All rights reserved.
This content is provided for test preparation purposes only and does not imply an endorsement by Mometrix of any particular political, scientific, or religious point of view.

32. TABULA RASA : BLANK SLATE :: SUI GENERIS : _____

a. indispensible
b. appropriate
c. one of a kind
d. no contest

33. ARACHNOPHOBIA : SPIDERS :: _____ : HEIGHTS

a. acrophobia
b. agoraphobia
c. latiphobia
d. longiphobia

34. FRENETIC : _____ :: FEVERISH : GUILE

a. ingenuous
b. duplicity
c. toil
d. turmoil

35. GENUS : HOMO :: SPECIES : _____

a. sapiens
b. animalia
c. chordate
d. hominidae

36. DEBILITATE : INVIGORATE :: DIFFIDENT : _____

a. shy
b. energize
c. brash
d. similar

37. GROVEL : ASK :: DEMAND : _____

a. consider
b. ponder
c. request
d. refuse

38. CLOY : SATIATE :: DAUNTLESS : _____

a. needy
b. fearless
c. contentious
d. deleterious

39. EFFERVESCENT : LIVELY :: EFFETE : _____

a. fair
b. faithful
c. bubbly
d. exhausted

Copyright © Mometrix Media. You have been licensed one copy of this document for personal use only. Any other reproduction or redistribution is strictly prohibited. All rights reserved.
This content is provided for test preparation purposes only and does not imply an endorsement by Mometrix of any particular political, scientific, or religious point of view.

40. VENERATE : HONOR :: UNDULATE : _____

    a. obey

    b. withstand

    c. fluctuate

    d. ingratiate

41. RIPOSTE : RETORT :: MELANGE : _____

    a. question

    b. mixture

    c. request

    d. melody

42. HERETICAL : HETERODOX :: _____ : ILLICIT

    a. unlawful

    b. legitimate

    c. spoken

    d. illusory

43. KABUL : AFGHANISTAN :: _____ : CANADA

    a. Quebec

    b. Vancouver

    c. Ottawa

    d. Toronto

44. PERIODICAL : MAGAZINE :: OCCASIONAL : _____

    a. always

    b. novel

    c. intermittent

    d. never

45. NOUN : DEDICATION :: VERB : _____

    a. dedicate

    b. deed

    c. from

    d. decision

46. NIMBUS : CLOUD :: IGUANA : _____

    a. green

    b. hard

    c. lizard

    d. cirrus

47. ADAPT : ADEPT :: CHANGE : _____

    a. skilled

    b. changed

    c. changeable

    d. inapt

Copyright © Mometrix Media. You have been licensed one copy of this document for personal use only. Any other reproduction or redistribution is strictly prohibited. All rights reserved.
This content is provided for test preparation purposes only and does not imply an endorsement by Mometrix of any particular political, scientific, or religious point of view.

48. ALFRESCO : OUTDOORS :: DE RIGUEUR : _____

a. rigid
b. necessary
c. retaliatory
d. haughty

49. IMPASSIVE : EXPRESSIVE :: LOQUACIOUS : _____

a. taciturn
b. garrulous
c. aloof
d. permeable

50. 1/6 : 7/12 :: 6 : _____

a. 3
b. 7
c. 21
d. 30

51. AMERICAN REVOLUTION : BUNKER HILL :: AMERICAN CIVIL WAR : _____

a. Valley Forge
b. Antietam
c. Dunkirk
d. Marne

52. BEAR : _____ :: LION : LEONINE

a. ursine
b. bovine
c. porcine
d. ovine

53. MORSE : CODE :: BELL : _____

a. phonograph
b. telephone
c. fire engine
d. jingle

54. BLANDISH : BRANDISH :: CAJOLE : _____

a. wield
b. praise
c. Cajun
d. decline

55. BOVINE : COW :: EQUINE : _____

a. equality
b. horse
c. fox
d. vulture

Copyright © Mometrix Media. You have been licensed one copy of this document for personal use only. Any other reproduction or redistribution is strictly prohibited. All rights reserved.
This content is provided for test preparation purposes only and does not imply an endorsement by Mometrix of any particular political, scientific, or religious point of view.

56. BROACH : RAISE :: BROOCH : _____

 a. rise
 b. ornamental pin
 c. raisin
 d. stick

57. BUCOLIC : COUNTRY :: URBAN : _____

 a. village
 b. state
 c. city
 d. built-up

58. TREASON : TRAITOR :: MURDER : _____

 a. murderous
 b. autocrat
 c. brazen
 d. felon

59. AMELIORATE : BETTER :: ADULTERATE : _____

 a. impure
 b. mediocre
 c. ambulatory
 d. ambivalent

60. ADMIRE : ADORE :: DISLIKE : _____

 a. discomfit
 b. detest
 c. antipathy
 d. horror

Copyright © Mometrix Media. You have been licensed one copy of this document for personal use only. Any other reproduction or redistribution is strictly prohibited. All rights reserved. This content is provided for test preparation purposes only and does not imply an endorsement by Mometrix of any particular political, scientific, or religious point of view.

Analogies Practice Test 2 Answers Key

1. A: Spendthrift. Auspicious and ominous are antonyms. The answer choice antonym for parsimonious is spendthrift.

2. C: Hopelessness. A characteristic quality of an orator is eloquence; a characteristic quality of a pessimist is hopelessness.

3. D: Tirade. Contumacious and insubordinate are synonyms. The answer choice synonym for diatribe is tirade.

4. A: Chenille. As chenille is a type of fabric, so Ad Hoc is a type of committee.

5. A: Dodgson. The author Samuel Clemens used the pseudonym Mark Twain, as the author Charles Dodgson used the pseudonym Lewis Carroll.

6. B: MD. As the postal code for Colorado is CO, the postal code for Maryland is MD.

7. D: Across. As the prefix inter- means between, the prefix trans- means across.

8. A: Thrilling. Perspicacious and dense are antonyms. The answer choice antonym for insipid is thrilling.

9. B: Behind. Collate is an example of a verb; behind is an example of a preposition.

10. A: Need. To meet a need is to satisfy it, and to sate an appetite is to satisfy it.

11. B: Perimeter. As the circumference is the measurement of the outer boundary of a circle, the perimeter is the measurement of the outer boundary of an octagon.

12. D: Crimson. As kelly is a shade of green, so is crimson a shade of red.

13. C: Wingtip. A wingtip is a type of shoe as a beret is a type of hat.

14. D: Men. As mane rhymes with cane, so men rhymes with ken.

15. C: Photocopier. An abacus was an early technology that served some of the same functions as a calculator does today; similarly, a mimeograph was an early technology that served some of the same functions that a photocopier serves today.

16. B: Persuasive. Clandestine and surreptitious are synonyms. The answer choice synonym for cogent is persuasive.

17. C: Ulna. The cranium is in the head and the ulna is in the arm.

18. B: Sanguine. Ashen describes a color closest to white; sanguine describes a shade of red.

19. A: Party. Someone who is bellicose is drawn to war as someone who is bacchanalian is drawn to parties.

20. C: Impassive. Sobriquet and alias are synonyms. The answer choice synonym for stolid is impassive.

Copyright © Mometrix Media. You have been licensed one copy of this document for personal use only. Any other reproduction or redistribution is strictly prohibited. All rights reserved. This content is provided for test preparation purposes only and does not imply an endorsement by Mometrix of any particular political, scientific, or religious point of view.

21. C: Drink. As one drinks champagne, so one wears pants.

22. D: Most. More is the comparative form measuring quantity, and most is the superlative form.

23. C: England. England was one of the Allies during World War II as Italy was one of the Axis nations.

24. D: Clouds. Nephology is the study of clouds as pathology is the study of diseases.

25. C: Beg. If you replace the vowel in ilk with an e, you get elk. Similarly, if you replace the vowel in big with an e, you get beg.

26. D: Unite. Husband and economize are synonyms. The answer choice synonym for marry is unite.

27. A: Intoxication. As ingesting a sedative leads to sleepiness, so ingesting alcohol leads to intoxication.

28. B: Contralto. As bass is the lowest male vocal range, so contralto is the lowest female vocal range.

29. B: Square. Isosceles and scalene are both types of triangles, as rectangles and squares are both types of quadrilaterals.

30. B: Commonplace. Inveterate and habitual are synonyms. The answer choice synonym for quotidian is commonplace.

31. B: Theses. As the plural of son-in-law is sons-in-law, so the plural of thesis is theses.

32. C: One of a kind. As tabula rasa means a blank slate, so sui generis means one of a kind.

33. A: Acrophobia. As arachnophobia is the fear of spiders, so acrophobia is the fear of heights.

34. B: Duplicity. Frenetic and feverish are synonyms. The answer choice synonym for guile is duplicity.

35. A: Sapiens. Homo is an example of a genus, while sapiens is an example of a species.

36. C: Brash. Debilitate and invigorate are antonyms. The answer choice antonym for diffident is brash.

37. C: Request. Grovel is an extreme way to ask; demand is an extreme way to request.

38. B: Fearless. Cloy and satiate are synonyms. The answer choice synonym for dauntless is fearless.

39. D: Exhausted. Effervescent and lively are synonyms. The answer choice synonym for effete is exhausted.

40. C: Fluctuate. Venerate and honor are synonyms. The answer choice synonym for undulate is fluctuate.

41. B: Mixture. Riposte means retort and mélange means mixture.

Copyright © Mometrix Media. You have been licensed one copy of this document for personal use only. Any other reproduction or redistribution is strictly prohibited. All rights reserved. This content is provided for test preparation purposes only and does not imply an endorsement by Mometrix of any particular political, scientific, or religious point of view.

42. A: Unlawful. Heretical and heterodox are synonyms. The answer choice synonym for illicit is unlawful.

43. C: Ottawa. As Kabul is the capital of Afghanistan, so is Ottawa the capital of Canada.

44. C: Intermittent. Periodical and magazine are synonyms. The answer choice synonym for occasional is intermittent. Although periodical could also be a synonym for occasional, there is no synonym for magazine among the answer choices.

45. A: Dedicate. Dedication is a noun and dedicate is a verb.

46. C: Lizard. As a nimbus is a type of cloud, so an iguana is a type of lizard.

47. A: Skilled. As adapt means change, so adept means skilled.

48. B: Necessary. As al fresco means outdoors, so de rigueur means necessary.

49. A: Taciturn. Impassive and expressive are antonyms. The answer choice antonym for loquacious is taciturn.

50. C: 21. The fractions 1/6 and 7/12 have a ratio of 1 to 3.5 as do the integers 6 and 21. (Multiply 1/6 by 7/2 to get 7/12; multiply 6 by 7/2 to get 21.)

51. B: Antietam. Antietam was a major battle of the American Civil War as Bunker Hill was a major battle of the American Revolution.

52. A: Ursine. As leonine refers to lions, so ursine refers to bears.

53. B: Telephone. As Samuel Morse is known for his invention of Morse code, so Alexander Graham Bell is known for his invention of the telephone.

54. A: Wield. Blandish and cajole are synonyms. The answer choice synonym for brandish is wield.

55. B: Horse. As bovine refers to cows, so equine refers to horses.

56. B: Ornamental pin. Broach and raise are synonyms. The answer choice synonym for brooch is ornamental pin.

57. C: City. Bucolic is a term to describe the country as urban is a term to describe the city.

58. D: Felon. One who commits murder is a felon as one who commits treason is a traitor.

59. A: Impure. When something is ameliorated it is made better; when something is adulterated it is made impure.

60. B: Detest. To detest someone is to dislike him/her extremely, as to adore someone is to admire him/her extremely.

Copyright © Mometrix Media. You have been licensed one copy of this document for personal use only. Any other reproduction or redistribution is strictly prohibited. All rights reserved.
This content is provided for test preparation purposes only and does not imply an endorsement by Mometrix of any particular political, scientific, or religious point of view.

Reading Comprehension

There are many kinds of civil service jobs, but one thing they all have in common is reading. Every civil service job in existence requires at least some reading on a regular basis, even if it's only reading forms that need to be filled out, along with the occasional memo. Many jobs, however, will involve extensive, frequent reading. In fact, the amount of reading required in most civil service positions is substantial. That's why reading comprehension is one of the most important topics covered on most exams for these careers.

You'll need to be able to read at an acceptable speed while also being able to clearly understand what you've read. The ability to follow instructions is essential for civil service careers, and in most cases, you'll be given written instructions. Not all of them will be simple and clear cut. In many situations the directions (or any other written material you'll be working with) will require you to do one thing in one kind of situation, do something else in another situation, and take yet another action in a third scenario. It's likely that you'll be expected to make important decisions based on material you've read. A person who is always asking coworkers or supervisors for clarification of written orders and memos will not be a very productive employee. He/she will also be a drag on the productivity of others, which is not acceptable.

If reading is not your strong suit, you'll want to remedy that before sitting down and taking the civil service exam. Without strong reading comprehension skills, it's going to be virtually impossible to get a high enough score to qualify for a job. Even if a person manages to get hired despite poor reading skills, he'll find that it will be very difficult to succeed on the job, or even enjoy going to work. If you need improvement in this area, you'll want to start working on it right away. Improving your reading skills can be done, and you can achieve remarkable results if you're diligent and willing to work hard, but it takes time. It can't be accomplished overnight. This guide will give you knowledge you need to improve your reading comprehension and exercises to help measure your progress.

IMPORTANT SKILLS

TOPICS AND MAIN IDEAS

One of the most important skills in reading comprehension is the identification of topics and main ideas. There is a subtle difference between the two. The topic is the subject of a text, or what the text is about. The main idea, on the other hand, is the most important point being made by the author. The topic is usually expressed in a few words at the most, while the main idea often needs a full sentence to be completely defined. As an example, a short passage might have the topic of penguins and the main idea *Penguins are different from other birds in many ways.* In most nonfiction writing, the topic and the main idea will be stated directly, often in a sentence at the very beginning or end of the text. When being tested on an understanding of the author's topic, the reader can quickly *skim* the passage for the general idea, stopping to read only the first sentence of each paragraph. A paragraph's first sentence is often (though not always) the main topic sentence, and it gives you a summary of the content of the paragraph. However, there are cases in which the reader must figure out an unstated topic or main idea. In these instances, the student must read every sentence of the text and come up with an overarching idea that is supported by each of those sentences.

SUPPORTING DETAILS

While the main idea is the overall premise of a story, supporting details provide evidence and backing for the main point. In order to show that a main idea is correct, or valid, the author needs to

Copyright © Mometrix Media. You have been licensed one copy of this document for personal use only. Any other reproduction or redistribution is strictly prohibited. All rights reserved. This content is provided for test preparation purposes only and does not imply an endorsement by Mometrix of any particular political, scientific, or religious point of view.

add details that prove the point. All texts contain details, but they are only classified as supporting details when they serve to reinforce some larger point. Supporting details are most commonly found in informative and persuasive texts. In some cases, they will be clearly indicated with words like *for example* or *for instance*, or they will be enumerated with words like *first*, *second*, and *last*. However, they are not always indicated with special words. As a reader, it is important to consider whether the author's supporting details really back up the main point. Supporting details can be factual and correct but still not relevant to the author's point. Conversely, supporting details can seem pertinent but be ineffective because they are based on opinion or assertions that cannot be proven.

An example of a main idea is: "Giraffes live in the Serengeti of Africa." A supporting detail about giraffes could be: "A giraffe uses its long neck to reach twigs and leaves on trees." The main idea gives the general idea that the text is about giraffes. The supporting detail gives a specific fact about how the giraffes eat.

> **Review Video: Supporting Details**
> Visit mometrix.com/academy and enter code: 396297

THEME

As opposed to a main idea, themes are seldom expressed directly in a text, so they can be difficult to identify. A theme is an issue, idea, or question raised by the text. For instance, a theme of Shakespeare's *Hamlet* is indecision, as the title character explores his own psyche and the results of his failure to make bold choices. A great work of literature may have many themes, and the reader is justified in identifying any for which he or she can find support. One common characteristic of themes is that they raise more questions than they answer. In a good piece of fiction, the author is not always trying to convince the reader, but is instead trying to elevate the reader's perspective and encourage him to consider the themes more deeply. When reading, one can identify themes by constantly asking what general issues the text is addressing. A good way to evaluate an author's approach to a theme is to begin reading with a question in mind (for example, how does this text approach the theme of love?) and then look for textual evidence that addresses that question.

PURPOSES FOR WRITING
POSITION

In order to be an effective reader, one must pay attention to the author's position and purpose. Even texts that seem objective and impartial, like textbooks, have a position and bias. Readers need to take these into account when considering the author's message. When an author uses emotional language or clearly favors one side of an argument, his position is clear. However, the author's position may be evident not only in what he writes, but in what he doesn't write. For this reason, it is sometimes necessary to review other texts on the same topic in order to understand the author's position. If this is not possible, it may be useful to acquire a little background personal information about the author. When the only source of information is the text, however, the reader should look for language and argumentation that seems to indicate a particular stance on the subject.

> **Review Video: Author's Position**
> Visit mometrix.com/academy and enter code: 827954

PURPOSE

Identifying the purpose of an author is usually easier than identifying her position. In most cases, the author has no interest in hiding his or her purpose. A text that is meant to entertain, for instance, should be obviously written to please the reader. Most narratives, or stories, are written

Copyright © Mometrix Media. You have been licensed one copy of this document for personal use only. Any other reproduction or redistribution is strictly prohibited. All rights reserved. This content is provided for test preparation purposes only and does not imply an endorsement by Mometrix of any particular political, scientific, or religious point of view.

to entertain, though they may also inform or persuade. Informative texts are easy to identify as well. The most difficult purpose to identify is persuasion, because the author has an interest in making this purpose hard to detect. When a person knows that the author is trying to convince him, he is automatically more wary and skeptical of the argument. For this reason, persuasive texts often try to establish an entertaining tone, hoping to amuse the reader into agreement, or an informative tone, hoping to create an appearance of authority and objectivity.

An author's purpose is often evident in the organization of the text. For instance, if the text has headings and subheadings, if key terms are in bold, and if the author makes his main idea clear from the beginning, then the likely purpose of the text is to inform. If the author begins by making a claim and then makes various arguments to support that claim, the purpose is probably to persuade. If the author is telling a story, or is more interested in holding the attention of the reader than in making a particular point or delivering information, then his purpose is most likely to entertain. As a reader, it is best to judge an author on how well he accomplishes his purpose. In other words, it is not entirely fair to complain that a textbook is boring: if the text is clear and easy to understand, then the author has done his job. Similarly, a storyteller should not be judged too harshly for slightly altering a fact to fit his story, so long as he is able to entertain the reader.

PERSUASIVE ESSAY

The author's purpose for writing will affect both his writing style and the reader's response. In a persuasive essay, the author is attempting to change the reader's mind or convince him of something he did not believe previously. There are several identifying characteristics of persuasive writing. One is opinion presented as fact. When an author attempts to persuade the reader, he often presents his or her opinions as if they were fact. A reader must be on guard for statements that sound factual but cannot be subjected to research, observation, or experimentation. Another characteristic of persuasive writing is emotional language. An author will often try to play on the reader's emotion by appealing to his sympathy or sense of morality. When an author uses colorful or evocative language with the intent of arousing the reader's passions, it is likely that he is attempting to persuade. Finally, in many cases a persuasive text will give an unfair explanation of opposing positions, if these positions are mentioned at all.

INFORMATIVE TEXT

An informative text is written to educate and enlighten the reader. Informative texts are almost always nonfiction, and are rarely structured as a story. The intention of an informative text is to deliver information in the most comprehensible way possible, so the structure of the text is likely to be very clear. In an informative text, the thesis statement is often in the first sentence. The author may use descriptive language, but is likely to put more emphasis on clarity and precision. Informative essays do not typically appeal to the emotions. They often contain facts and figures, and rarely include the opinion of the author. Sometimes a persuasive essay can resemble an informative essay, especially if the author maintains an even tone and presents his or her views as if they were established fact.

> **Review Video: Informational Text**
> Visit mometrix.com/academy and enter code: 924964

ENTERTAINMENT

The success or failure of an author's intent to entertain is determined by the reader. Entertaining texts may be either fiction or nonfiction, and may describe real or imagined people, places, and events. Entertaining texts are often narratives, or stories. A text that is written to entertain is likely to contain colorful language that engages the imagination and the emotions. Such writing often

Copyright © Mometrix Media. You have been licensed one copy of this document for personal use only. Any other reproduction or redistribution is strictly prohibited. All rights reserved. This content is provided for test preparation purposes only and does not imply an endorsement by Mometrix of any particular political, scientific, or religious point of view.

features a great deal of figurative language, enlivening its subject matter with images and analogies. Though an entertaining text is not usually written to persuade or inform, it may accomplish both of these tasks. An entertaining text may appeal to the reader's emotions and cause him or her to think differently about a particular subject. In any case, entertaining texts tend to showcase the personality of the author more than other types of writing.

> **Review Video: Best Tips for Effectively Reading Fiction**
> Visit mometrix.com/academy and enter code: 391411

EXPRESSION OF FEELINGS

When an author intends to express feelings, he/she may use colorful and evocative language. An author may write emotionally for any number of reasons. Sometimes, emotional language is used to describe a personal situation of great pain or happiness. Sometimes an author is attempting to persuade the reader, and so will use emotion to stir up the passions. It can be easy to identify this kind of expression when the writer uses phrases like *I felt* and *I sense*. However, sometimes the author will simply describe feelings without introducing them. As a reader, it is important to recognize when an author is expressing emotion, and not to be overwhelmed by sympathy or passion. A reader should maintain some detachment so that he or she can still evaluate the strength of the author's argument or the quality of the writing.

DESCRIPTION

Most writing is descriptive in a sense because it describes events, ideas, or people to the reader. Some texts, however, are primarily concerned with description. A descriptive text focuses on a particular subject and attempts to depict it in a way that will be clear to the reader. Descriptive texts contain many adjectives and adverbs, words that give shades of meaning and create a more detailed mental picture for the reader. A descriptive text fails when it is unclear or vague to the reader. On the other hand, a descriptive text that compiles too much detail can be boring and overwhelming to the reader. A descriptive text will certainly be informative, and it may be persuasive and entertaining as well. Descriptive writing is challenging, but when it is done well, it can be enjoyable to read.

WRITING DEVICES
COMPARING AND CONTRASTING

Authors will use different stylistic and writing devices to make their meaning more clearly understood. One of those devices is comparison and contrast. When an author describes how two things are alike, he or she is comparing them. When the author describes the ways in which two things are different, he or she is contrasting them. The "compare and contrast" essay is one of the most common forms in nonfiction. It is often signaled with certain words: a comparison may be indicated with such words as *both*, *same*, *like*, *too*, and *as well*; while a contrast may be indicated by words like *but*, *however*, *on the other hand*, *instead*, and *yet*. Of course, comparisons and contrasts may be implicit without any such signaling language. Also, a single sentence may both compare and contrast. Consider the sentence *Brian and Sheila love ice cream, but Brian prefers vanilla and Sheila prefers strawberry*. In one sentence, the author has described both a similarity (love of ice cream) and a difference (favorite flavor).

> **Review Video: How to Compare and Contrast**
> Visit mometrix.com/academy and enter code: 171799

92

Copyright © Mometrix Media. You have been licensed one copy of this document for personal use only. Any other reproduction or redistribution is strictly prohibited. All rights reserved. This content is provided for test preparation purposes only and does not imply an endorsement by Mometrix of any particular political, scientific, or religious point of view.

CAUSE AND EFFECT

One of the most common text structures is cause and effect. A cause is an act or event that makes something happen, and an effect is what happens as a result. A cause-and-effect relationship is not always explicit, but there are some words that signal causality, such as *since, because*, and *as a result*. Consider the sentence *Because the sky was clear, Ron did not bring an umbrella*. The cause is the clear sky, and the effect is that Ron did not bring an umbrella. However, sometimes the cause-and-effect relationship will not be clearly noted. For instance, the sentence *He was late and missed the meeting* does not contain any signaling words, but it still contains a cause (he was late) and an effect (he missed the meeting). It is possible for a single cause to have multiple effects, or for a single effect to have multiple causes. Also, an effect can in turn be the cause of another effect in what is known as a cause-and-effect chain.

ANALOGY

Authors often use analogies to add meaning to the text. An analogy is a comparison of two things. The words in the analogy are connected by a certain, often undetermined relationship. Look at this analogy: moo is to cow as quack is to duck. This analogy compares the sound that a cow makes with the sound that a duck makes. Even if the word 'quack' was not given, one could deduce that it is the correct word to complete the analogy based on the relationship between the words 'moo' and 'cow.' Some common relationships for analogies include synonyms, antonyms, part to whole, definition, and actor to action.

POINT OF VIEW

Another element that impacts a text is the author's point of view. A text's point of view is the perspective from which it is told. An author always has a point of view even before drawing up a plot line. The author will know what events will take place, how he/she wants the characters to interact, and how the story will resolve. An author will also have an opinion on the topic, or series of events, that is presented in the story, based on his/her own prior experience and beliefs.

The two main points of view that authors use are first person and third person. If the narrator of the story is also the main character, or *protagonist*, the text is written in first person. In first person, the author writes with the word *I*. A third-person point of view is probably the most common. Using third person, authors refer to each character using the words *he* or *she*. In third-person omniscient, the narrator is not a character in the story and tells the story of all of the characters with the same insight.

TRANSITIONAL WORDS

A good writer uses transitional words and phrases to guide the reader through the text. You are no doubt familiar with the common transitions, though you may never have considered how they operate. Some transitional phrases (*after, before, during, in the middle of*) give information about time. Some indicate that an example is about to be given (*for example, in fact, for instance*). Writers use them to compare (*also, likewise*) and contrast (*however, but, yet*). Transitional words and phrases can suggest addition (*and, also, furthermore, moreover*) and logical relationships (*if, then, therefore, as a result, since*). Finally, transitional words and phrases can demarcate the steps in a process (*first, second, last*). You should incorporate transitional words and phrases to orient your reader and explain the structure of your composition.

TYPES OF PASSAGES

NARRATIVE

A narrative passage is a story, fiction or nonfiction. To be classified as a narrative, a text must have a few key elements. To begin with, it must have a plot. That is, it must describe a series of events. If it

Copyright © Mometrix Media. You have been licensed one copy of this document for personal use only. Any other reproduction or redistribution is strictly prohibited. All rights reserved. This content is provided for test preparation purposes only and does not imply an endorsement by Mometrix of any particular political, scientific, or religious point of view.

is a good narrative, these events will be interesting and emotionally engaging to the reader. A narrative also has characters. These could be people, animals, or even inanimate objects, so long as they participate in the plot. A narrative passage often contains figurative language, which is meant to stimulate the imagination of the reader by making comparisons and observations. A metaphor, which uses one thing to describe another, is a common piece of figurative language. *The moon was a frosty snowball* is an example of a metaphor: it is obviously untrue in the literal sense, but it paints a vivid image for the reader. Narratives often proceed in a clear sequence, but may not always do so.

EXPOSITORY

An expository passage aims to inform and enlighten the reader. It is nonfiction and usually centers around a simple, easily defined topic. Since the goal of exposition is to teach, it should be as clear as possible. It is common for an expository passage to contain helpful organizing words like *first*, *next*, *for example*, and *therefore*. These words keep the reader oriented in the text. Although expository passages do not need to feature creative, descriptive writing, they are often more effective when they do. For a reader, the challenge of expository passages is to maintain steady attention. Expository passages are not always on subjects in which a reader is naturally interested, and the writer is often more concerned with clarity and comprehensibility than with engaging the reader. For this reason, many expository passages seem dull. Taking notes is a good way to maintain focus when reading an expository passage.

> **Review Video: Expository Passages**
> Visit mometrix.com/academy and enter code: 256515

TECHNICAL

A technical passage describes a complex object or process. Technical writing is common in medical and technological fields, in which complicated mathematical, scientific, and engineering ideas need to be explained simply and clearly. To aid comprehension, a technical passage usually follows a very logical order. Technical passages typically have clear headings and subheadings, helping to keep the reader oriented in the text. It is also common to organize sections by numbers or letters. Many technical passages look more like an outline than a piece of prose. The amount of jargon or difficult vocabulary in a technical passage varies, depending on the intended audience. As much as possible, technical passages try to avoid language that the reader will have to research to understand the message. Of course, it is not always possible to avoid jargon.

> **Review Video: Technical Passages**
> Visit mometrix.com/academy and enter code: 478923

PERSUASIVE

A persuasive passage is meant to change the reader's mind or lead him/her into agreement with the author. The persuasive intent may be obvious, or it may be difficult to discern. In some cases, a persuasive passage will be indistinguishable from an informative passage: it will make an assertion and offer supporting details. However, a persuasive passage is more likely to make claims based on opinion and to appeal to the reader's emotions. Persuasive passages may not describe alternate positions or may display significant bias when they do. It may be clear that a persuasive passage is giving the author's viewpoint, or the passage may adopt a seemingly objective tone. A persuasive passage is successful if it can make a convincing argument and win the trust of the reader.

A persuasive essay will likely focus on one central argument, but it may make several smaller claims along the way. These are subordinate arguments with which the reader must agree if he or she is going to accept the central argument. The central argument is only as strong as the

94

Copyright © Mometrix Media. You have been licensed one copy of this document for personal use only. Any other reproduction or redistribution is strictly prohibited. All rights reserved. This content is provided for test preparation purposes only and does not imply an endorsement by Mometrix of any particular political, scientific, or religious point of view.

subordinate claims. These claims should be rooted in fact and observation, rather than subjective judgment. The best persuasive essays provide enough supporting detail to justify claims without overwhelming the reader. Remember that a fact must be susceptible to independent verification—it must be something the reader can confirm. Also, statistics are only effective when they take into account possible objections. For instance, a statistic on the number of foreclosed houses would only be useful if it was measured over a defined interval and in a defined area. Most readers are wary of statistics, because they are so often misleading. If possible, a persuasive essay should include references so that the reader can obtain more information. Of course, this means that the writer's accuracy and fairness may be judged by the inquiring reader, but giving references adds credence.

Opinions are formed by emotion as well as reason, and persuasive writers often appeal to the feelings of the reader. Although readers should always be skeptical of this technique, it is often used in a proper and ethical manner. For instance, many subjects have an obvious emotional component, and therefore cannot be fully covered without an appeal to the emotions. Consider an article on drunk driving: it makes sense to include specific examples that will alarm or sadden the reader. After all, drunk driving often has serious and tragic consequences. Emotional appeals are not appropriate, however, when they attempt to mislead the reader. For instance, in political advertisements it is common to emphasize the patriotism of the preferred candidate, because this will encourage the audience to link his/her own positive feelings about the country with his/her opinion of the candidate. However, these ads often falsely imply that the other candidate is unpatriotic. Another common and improper emotional appeal is the use of loaded language, such as referring to an avidly religious person as a "fanatic" or a passionate environmentalist as a "tree hugger." These terms introduce an emotional component that detracts from the argument.

RESPONDING TO LITERATURE

PREDICTION

When reading good literature, the reader is moved to engage actively in the text. One part of being an active reader involves making predictions. A prediction is a guess about what will happen next. Readers are constantly making predictions based on what they have read and what they already know. Consider the following sentence: *Staring at the computer screen in shock, Kim blindly reached for the brimming glass of water on the shelf beside her.* The sentence suggests that Kim is agitated and that she is not looking at the glass she is going to pick up, so a reader might predict that she is going to knock the glass over. Of course, not every prediction will be accurate: perhaps Kim will pick the glass up without incident. Nevertheless, the author has certainly created the expectation that the water might be spilled. Predictions are always subject to revision as the reader acquires more information.

> **Review Video: Predictive Reading**
> Visit mometrix.com/academy and enter code: 437248

Test-taking tip: To respond to questions requiring future predictions, the student's answers should be based on evidence of past or present behavior.

INFERENCE

Readers are often required to understand text that claims and suggests ideas without stating them directly. An inference is a piece of information that is implied but not written outright by the author. For instance, consider the following sentence: *Mark made more money that week than he had in the previous year.* From this sentence, the reader can infer that Mark either did not make much money in the previous year or made a great deal of money that week. Often, a reader can use information he or she already knows to make inferences. Take as an example the sentence *When his*

Copyright © Mometrix Media. You have been licensed one copy of this document for personal use only. Any other reproduction or redistribution is strictly prohibited. All rights reserved.
This content is provided for test preparation purposes only and does not imply an endorsement by Mometrix of any particular political, scientific, or religious point of view.

coffee arrived, he looked around the table for the silver cup. Many people know that cream is typically served in a silver cup, so using their own base of knowledge they can infer that the subject of this sentence takes his coffee with cream. Making inferences requires concentration, attention, and practice.

Test-taking tip: While being tested on his/her ability to make correct inferences, the student must look for contextual clues. An answer can be *true* but not *correct*. The contextual clues will help you choose the best answer out of the given choices. Understand the context in which a phrase is stated. When asked for the implied meaning of a statement made in the passage, the student should immediately locate the statement and read the context in which it was made. Also, look for an answer choice with a similar phrase to the statement in question.

SEQUENCE

A reader must be able to identify a text's sequence, or the order in which things happen. Often, and especially when the sequence is very important to the author, it is indicated with signal words like *first, then, next,* and *last.* However, sometimes a sequence is merely implied and must be noted by the reader. Consider the sentence *He walked in the front door and switched on the hall lamp.* Clearly, the man did not turn the lamp on before he walked in the door, so the implied sequence is that he first walked in the door and then turned on the lamp. Texts do not always proceed in an orderly sequence from first to last. Sometimes they begin at the end as a foreshadowing device and then start over at the beginning. As a reader, it can be useful to make brief notes to clarify the sequence.

> **Review Video: Sequence**
> Visit mometrix.com/academy and enter code: 489027
>
> **Review Video: Sequence of Events in a Story**
> Visit mometrix.com/academy and enter code: 807512

DRAWING CONCLUSIONS

In addition to inferring and predicting things about the text, the reader must often draw conclusions about the information he has read. When asked for a *conclusion*, look for critical "hedge" phrases such as *likely, may, can,* and *will often,* among others. When you are being tested on this knowledge, remember that question writers insert these hedge phrases to cover every possibility. Often an answer will be wrong simply because it leaves no room for exception. Extreme positive or negative answers (such as always, never, etc.) are usually not correct. The reader should not use any outside knowledge that is not gathered from the reading passage to answer the related questions. Correct answers can be drawn directly from the reading passage.

OPINIONS, FACTS, AND FALLACIES

Critical thinking skills are mastered through understanding various types of writing and the different purposes of authors. Every author writes for a purpose. Understanding that purpose, and how the author accomplishes a goal, will allow you to critique the writing and determine whether or not you agree with the conclusions.

FACT AND OPINION

Readers must always be conscious of the distinction between fact and opinion. A fact can be subjected to analysis and either proved or disproved. An opinion, on the other hand, is the author's personal feeling, which may not be proven by research, evidence, or argument. If the author writes that the distance from New York to Boston is about two hundred miles, he is stating a fact. But if he writes that New York is too crowded, then he is giving an opinion, because there is no objective

Copyright © Mometrix Media. You have been licensed one copy of this document for personal use only. Any other reproduction or redistribution is strictly prohibited. All rights reserved.
This content is provided for test preparation purposes only and does not imply an endorsement by Mometrix of any particular political, scientific, or religious point of view.

standard for overpopulation. An opinion may be indicated by words like *believe, think,* or *feel.* Also, an opinion may be supported by facts. For instance, the author might give the population density of New York as a reason for why it is overcrowded. An opinion supported by fact tends to be more convincing. When authors support their opinions with other opinions, the reader is unlikely to be persuaded.

The author should present facts from reliable sources. An opinion is what the author thinks about a given topic. An opinion is not common knowledge or proven by expert sources, but it is information that the author believes and wants the reader to consider. To distinguish between fact and opinion, a reader needs to examine the type of source, what information backs up a claim, and whether or not the author may be motivated to convey a certain point of view. For example, if a panel of scientists has conducted multiple studies on the effectiveness of taking a certain vitamin, the results are more likely to be factual than if a company selling the vitamin claims that it can produce positive effects. The company is motivated to sell its product, while the scientists are examining it more objectively. If the author uses phrases such as "I think," the statement is an opinion.

In their attempt to persuade, writers often make mistakes in their thinking patterns and writing choices. It's important to understand these so you can make an informed decision. Every author has a point of view, but when he/she ignores reasonable counterarguments or distorts opposing viewpoints, this is demonstrating a bias. A bias is evident when the author is unfair or inaccurate in his or her presentation. Bias may be intentional or unintentional, but it should always alert the reader to question the argument. It should be noted that a biased author may still be correct. However, the author will be correct in spite of her bias, not because of it. A stereotype is like a bias, except that it is specifically applied to a group or place. Stereotyping is considered to be particularly abhorrent because it promotes negative generalizations about people. Many people are familiar with the negative stereotypes of certain ethnic, religious, and cultural groups. Readers should be very wary of authors who stereotype. These faulty assumptions typically reveal the author's ignorance and lack of curiosity or objectivity.

Sometimes, authors will appeal to the reader's emotion in an attempt to persuade or distract the reader from the argument's weakness. For instance, the author may try to inspire the reader's pity by delivering a heart-rending story. An author also might use the bandwagon approach, suggesting that his/her opinion is correct because it is held by the majority. Some authors resort to name-calling, in which insults and harsh words are delivered to the opponent in an attempt to distract. In advertising, a common appeal is the testimonial, in which a famous person endorses a product. Of course, the fact that a celebrity likes something should not really matter to the reader. These and other emotional appeals are usually evidence of poor reasoning and a weak argument.

LOGICAL FALLACIES

Certain *logical fallacies* are frequent in writing. A logical fallacy is a failure of reasoning. As a reader, it is important to recognize logical fallacies, because they diminish the value of the author's message. The four most common logical fallacies in writing are the false analogy, circular reasoning, false dichotomy, and overgeneralization. In a false analogy, the author suggests that two things are similar, when in fact they are different. This fallacy is often committed when the author is attempting to convince the reader that something unknown is like something relatively familiar. The author takes advantage of the reader's ignorance to make this false comparison. One example might be the following statement: *Failing to tip a waitress is like stealing money out of somebody's wallet.* Of course, failing to tip is very rude, especially when the service has been good, but people are not arrested for failing to tip as they would be for stealing money from a wallet. To compare stingy diners with thieves is a false analogy.

Copyright © Mometrix Media. You have been licensed one copy of this document for personal use only. Any other reproduction or redistribution is strictly prohibited. All rights reserved.
This content is provided for test preparation purposes only and does not imply an endorsement by Mometrix of any particular political, scientific, or religious point of view.

Circular reasoning is one of the more difficult logical fallacies to identify, because it is typically hidden behind dense language and complicated sentences. Reasoning is described as circular when it offers no support for assertions other than restating them in different words. Put another way, a circular argument uses itself as evidence of truth. A simple example of circular argument is when a person uses a word to define itself, such as saying *Niceness is the state of being nice.* If the reader does not know what *nice* means, then this definition will not be very useful. In a text, circular reasoning is usually more complex. For instance, an author might say, *Poverty is a problem for society because it creates trouble for people throughout the community.* It is redundant to say that poverty is a problem because it creates trouble. When an author engages in circular reasoning, it is often because he or she has not fully thought through the argument, or cannot come up with any legitimate justifications.

One of the most common logical fallacies is the false dichotomy, in which the author creates an artificial sense that there are only two possible alternatives in a situation. This fallacy is common when the author has an agenda and wants to give the impression that his/her view is the only sensible one. A false dichotomy has the effect of limiting the reader's options and imagination. An example is the statement *You need to go to the party with me, or you'll just be bored at home.* The speaker suggests that the only other possibility besides being at the party is being bored at home. This is not true, as it is possible to be entertained at home or to go somewhere other than the party. Readers should always be wary of the false dichotomy—when an author limits the alternatives, it is always wise to ask whether his argument valid.

Overgeneralization is a logical fallacy in which the author makes a claim so broad that it cannot be proved or disproved. In most cases, overgeneralization occurs when the author wants to create an illusion of authority, or when he/she is using sensational language to sway the reader's opinion. For instance, in the sentence *Everybody knows that she is a terrible teacher*, the author makes an assumption that cannot really be believed. The author is attempting to create the illusion of consensus when none actually exists. It may be that most people have a negative view of the teacher, but to say that *everybody* feels that way is an exaggeration. When a reader spots overgeneralization, she should become skeptical about the argument, because an author will often try to hide a weak or unsupported assertion behind authoritative language.

Two other types of logical fallacies are slippery slope arguments and hasty generalizations. In a slippery slope argument, the author says that if something happens, a certain result is guaranteed, even though this may not be true. For example, studying hard does not mean you are going to ace a test. Hasty generalization means drawing a conclusion too early, without finishing analysis of the argument's details. Writers of persuasive texts often use these techniques because they are very effective. In order to identify logical fallacies, readers need to read carefully and ask questions as they read. Thinking critically means not taking everything at face value. Readers need to critically evaluate an author's argument to make sure that the logic is sound.

ORGANIZATION OF TEXT

The way a text is organized can help the reader understand more clearly the author's intent and conclusions. There are various ways to organize a text, and each has its own purposes and uses.

PRESENTING A PROBLEM

Some nonfiction texts are organized to present a problem followed by a solution. In this type of text, it is common for the problem to be explained before the solution is offered. In some cases, as when the problem is well known, the solution may be briefly introduced at the beginning. The entire passage may focus on the solution, and the problem will be referenced only occasionally. Some texts

Copyright © Mometrix Media. You have been licensed one copy of this document for personal use only. Any other reproduction or redistribution is strictly prohibited. All rights reserved. This content is provided for test preparation purposes only and does not imply an endorsement by Mometrix of any particular political, scientific, or religious point of view.

outline multiple solutions to a problem, leaving the reader to choose among them. If the author has an interest in or allegiance to one solution, he may fail to mention or may inaccurately describe other solutions. Readers should be careful of the author's agenda when reading a problem-solution text. Only by understanding the author's point of view and interests can one properly judge the proposed solution.

CHRONOLOGICAL ORDER

An author needs to organize information logically so the reader can follow it and locate information within the text. Two common organizational structures are cause and effect and chronological order. When using chronological order, the author presents information in the order that it happened. For example, biographies are written in chronological order; the subject's birth and childhood are presented first, followed by adult life, and finally the events leading up to death.

CAUSE AND EFFECT

In cause and effect, an author presents an event that causes something else to happen. For example, if one were to go to bed very late, he/she would be tired the next day. The cause is going to bed late, with the effect of being tired the next day.

It can be tricky to identify the cause-and-effect relationships in a text, but there are a few ways to approach this task. These relationships are often signaled with certain terms. When an author uses words like *because*, *since*, *in order*, and *so*, she is likely describing a cause-and-effect relationship. Consider the sentence, "He called her because he needed the homework." This is a simple causal relationship, in which the cause was his need for the homework and the effect was his phone call. Not all cause-and-effect relationships are marked in this way, however. Consider the sentences, "He called her. He needed the homework." When the cause-and-effect relationship is not indicated with a keyword, it can be discovered by asking why something happened. Why did he call? The answer is in the next sentence—he needed the homework.

Persuasive essays, in which an author tries to make a convincing argument and change the reader's mind, usually include cause-and-effect relationships. However, these relationships should not always be taken at face value. An author frequently assumes a cause or takes an effect for granted. To read a persuasive essay effectively, one needs to judge the cause-and-effect relationships the author is presenting. For instance, an author could write the following: "The parking deck has been unprofitable because people prefer to ride their bikes." The relationship is clear: the cause is that people prefer to ride their bikes, and the effect is that the parking deck has been unprofitable. However, a reader should consider whether this argument is conclusive. There could be other reasons for the failure of the parking deck: a down economy, excessive fees, etc. Too often, authors present causal relationships as if they are fact rather than opinion. Readers should be on the alert for these dubious claims.

COMPARISON AND CONTRAST

Thinking critically about ideas and conclusions can seem like a daunting task. One way to make it easier is to understand the basic elements of ideas and writing techniques. Looking at the way different ideas relate to each other is a good way for the reader to begin his/her analysis. For instance, an author may write about two opposing ideas. Analyzing these is known as contrast. Contrast is often marred by the author's obvious partiality to one of the ideas. A discerning reader will be put off by an author who does not "fight fairly." In an analysis of opposing ideas, both ideas should be presented in their clearest and most reasonable terms. If the author does prefer a side, he/she should avoid indicating this preference with pejorative language. An analysis of opposing ideas should proceed through the major differences point by point, with a full explanation of each

Copyright © Mometrix Media. You have been licensed one copy of this document for personal use only. Any other reproduction or redistribution is strictly prohibited. All rights reserved.
This content is provided for test preparation purposes only and does not imply an endorsement by Mometrix of any particular political, scientific, or religious point of view.

side. For instance, in an analysis of capitalism and communism, it would be important to outline each side's view on labor, markets, prices, personal responsibility, etc. It would be less effective to describe the theory of communism and then explain how capitalism has thrived in the West. An analysis of opposing views should present each side in the same manner.

Many texts follow the compare-and-contrast model, exploring the similarities and differences between two ideas or things. Analysis of the similarities is called comparison. In order for a comparison to work, the author must place the ideas or things in an equivalent structure. That is, the author must present the ideas in the same way. Imagine an author wanted to show the similarities between cricket and baseball. He/she could do this by summarizing the equipment and rules for each game. It would be incorrect to summarize the equipment of cricket and then tell the history of baseball, since this would make it impossible for the reader to see the similarities. It is perhaps too obvious to say that an analysis of similar ideas should emphasize the similarities. Of course, the author should also include differences. Often, these small differences will only reinforce the more general similarity.

DRAWING CONCLUSIONS
IDENTIFYING THE LOGICAL CONCLUSION

An author should have a clear purpose in mind while writing. Especially when reading informational texts, it is important to understand the logical conclusion of the author's ideas. Identifying this logical conclusion can help the reader understand whether he/she agrees with the writer or not. It is much like making an inference: it requires the reader to combine the information given by the text with what he already knows to make a supportable assertion. If a passage is written well, the conclusion should be obvious even when it is unstated. If the author intends the reader to draw a certain conclusion, then all argumentation and detail should lead toward it. One way to approach the task of drawing conclusions is to make brief notes of all the author's points. When these are arranged on paper, they may clarify the logical conclusion. Another way to approach conclusions is to consider whether the author's reasoning raises any pertinent questions. Sometimes it is possible to draw multiple conclusions from a passage, and on occasion these were never intended by the author. It is essential, however, that these conclusions be supported directly by the text.

> **Review Video: How to Support a Conclusion**
> Visit mometrix.com/academy and enter code: 281653

TEXT EVIDENCE

The term *text evidence* refers to information that supports a main point or points in a story and can guide the reader to a conclusion. Information used as text evidence is precise, descriptive, and factual. A main point is often followed by supporting details that provide evidence to back up a claim. For example, a story may include the claim that winter occurs during opposite months in the Northern and Southern hemispheres. Text evidence based on this claim may include countries where winter occurs in opposite months, along with the reasons (the tilt of the earth as it rotates around the sun).

> **Review Video: Textual Evidence**
> Visit mometrix.com/academy and enter code: 486236

Readers interpret text and respond in a number of ways. Using textual support helps defend your response or interpretation because it roots your thinking in the text. You are interpreting based on information in the text and not simply your own ideas. When crafting a response, look for

Copyright © Mometrix Media. You have been licensed one copy of this document for personal use only. Any other reproduction or redistribution is strictly prohibited. All rights reserved. This content is provided for test preparation purposes only and does not imply an endorsement by Mometrix of any particular political, scientific, or religious point of view.

important quotes and details from the text to bolster your argument. If you are writing about a character's personality trait, for example, use details from the text to show how the character displayed this trait. You can also include statistics and facts from a nonfiction text to strengthen your response. For example, instead of writing, "A lot of people use cell phones," use statistics to provide a specific number. This strengthens your argument because it is more precise.

CREDIBILITY

The text used to support an argument can be the argument's downfall if it is not credible. A text is credible, or believable, when the author is knowledgeable and objective, or unbiased. The author's motivations for writing play a critical role in determining the credibility of the text and must be evaluated when assessing that credibility. The author's motives should be simply to disseminate information. The purpose of the text should be to inform or describe, not to persuade. When an author writes a persuasive text, his/her motivation is to convince the reader to do what he/she wants. The extent of the author's knowledge and motivation must be evaluated when assessing the credibility of a text. Reports written about the ozone layer by an environmental scientist and a hairdresser will have a different level of credibility.

> **Review Video: Author Credibility**
> Visit mometrix.com/academy and enter code: 827257

RESPONSE TO TEXT

After determining your own opinion and evaluating the credibility of your supporting text, it is sometimes necessary to communicate your ideas and findings to others. When writing a response to a text, it is important to use elements of the text to support your assertion or defend your position. Using supporting evidence from the text strengthens the argument because it shows that you read the original piece in depth and based your response on the details and facts within that text. Elements of text that can be used in a response include: facts, details, statistics, and direct quotations. When writing a response, one must indicate which information comes from the original text and then base the discussion, argument, or defense around this information.

DIRECTLY STATED INFORMATION

A reader should constantly draw conclusions from the text. Sometimes conclusions are implied from written information, and other times the information is stated directly within the passage. It is always stronger to draw conclusions from information stated within a passage, rather than from mere implications. At times an author may provide some information and then describe a counterargument. The reader should be alert for direct statements that are subsequently rejected or weakened by the author and should always read the entire passage before drawing conclusions. Many readers are trained to expect the author's conclusions at either the beginning or the end of the passage, but many texts do not adhere to this format.

IMPLICATIONS

Drawing conclusions from information implied within a passage requires the reader's confidence. Implications are things the author does not state directly, but that can be assumed based on what the author does say. For instance, consider the following simple passage: "I stepped outside and opened my umbrella. By the time I got to work, the cuffs of my pants were soaked." The author never states that it is raining, but this fact is clearly implied. Conclusions based on implication must be well supported by the text. In order to draw a solid conclusion, a reader should have multiple pieces of evidence, or, if he only has one, must be assured that there is no other possible explanation than his conclusion. A good reader will be able to draw many conclusions from information implied by the text, which enriches the reading experience considerably.

Copyright © Mometrix Media. You have been licensed one copy of this document for personal use only. Any other reproduction or redistribution is strictly prohibited. All rights reserved. This content is provided for test preparation purposes only and does not imply an endorsement by Mometrix of any particular political, scientific, or religious point of view.

OUTLINING

As an aid to drawing conclusions, the reader should be adept at outlining the information contained in the passage; an effective outline will reveal the structure of the passage, and will lead to solid conclusions. An effective outline will have a title referencing the basic subject of the text, though it need not repeat the main idea. In most outlines, the main idea is the first major section. It will establish each major idea of the passage as the head of a category. The most common outline format indicates the main ideas of the passage with Roman numerals. None of the Roman numerals will designate minor details or secondary ideas. Moreover, all supporting ideas and details should be placed in the appropriate section on the outline. An outline does not need to include every detail listed in the text, but it should feature all that are central to the argument or message. Each details should be listed under the appropriate main idea.

> **Review Video: Outlining as an Aid to Drawing Conclusions**
> Visit mometrix.com/academy and enter code: 584445

SUMMARY

It is also helpful to summarize the information in paragraph or passage format. This process is similar to creating an effective outline. To begin with, a summary should accurately define the main idea of the passage, though it does not need to explain it in exhaustive detail. It should continue by laying out the most important supporting details or arguments from the passage. All significant supporting details should be included, but no irrelevant or insignificant details. Also, the summary must accurately report these details. Too often, the desire for brevity in a summary leads to the sacrifice of clarity or veracity. Summaries are often difficult to read, because they omit all the graceful language, descriptions, and asides that distinguish great writing. However, if the summary is effective, it should contain the same message as the original text.

> **Review Video: Summarizing Text**
> Visit mometrix.com/academy and enter code: 172903

PARAPHRASING

Paraphrasing is another method the reader can use to aid comprehension. When paraphrasing, one rephrases what the author has written in his/her own words, "translating" the author's message and including as many details as possible.

INFORMATIONAL SOURCES

Informational sources may come in short forms like memos and articles or longer forms like books, magazines, and journals. These longer sources of information each have their own way of organizing information, but there are some similarities that the reader should be aware of.

TABLE OF CONTENTS

Most books, magazines, and journals have a table of contents at the beginning. This helps the reader find the different parts of the book. The table of contents is usually found a page or two after the title page in a book, and on the first few pages of a magazine. However, many magazines now place the table of contents in the midst of advertisements, because they know readers will have to look at the ads as they search for the table. The standard orientation for a table of contents has the sections of the book listed along the left side, with the initial page number for each along the right. It is common in a book for the prefatory material (preface, introduction, etc.) to be numbered with Roman numerals. The contents are always listed in order from the beginning of the book to the end.

Copyright © Mometrix Media. You have been licensed one copy of this document for personal use only. Any other reproduction or redistribution is strictly prohibited. All rights reserved.
This content is provided for test preparation purposes only and does not imply an endorsement by Mometrix of any particular political, scientific, or religious point of view.

INDEX

A nonfiction book also typically has an index at the end so that the reader can easily find information on particular topics. An index lists the topics in alphabetical order. The names of people are listed with the last name first. For example, *Adams, John* would come before *Washington, George*. To the right of the entry, the relevant page numbers are listed. When a topic is mentioned over several pages, the index will often connect these pages with a dash. For instance, if the subject is mentioned from pages 35 to 42 and again on 53, then the index entry will be labeled as *35–42, 53*. Some entries will have subsets, which are listed below the main entry, indented slightly, and placed in alphabetical order. This is common for subjects that are discussed frequently in the book. For instance, in a book about Elizabethan drama, William Shakespeare will likely be an important topic. Beneath Shakespeare's name in the index, there might be listings for *death of, dramatic works of, life of*, etc. These more specific entries help the reader refine his search.

HEADINGS AND SUBHEADINGS

Many informative texts, especially textbooks, use headings and subheadings for organization. Headings and subheadings are typically printed in larger and bolder fonts (or all capitals), and are often in a different color than the main body of the text. Headings may be larger than subheadings. Also, headings and subheadings are not always complete sentences. A heading announces the topic that will be addressed in the text below. Headings are meant to alert the reader to what is about to come. Subheadings announce the topics of smaller sections within the entire section indicated by the heading. For instance, the heading of a section in a science textbook might be *AMPHIBIANS*, and within that section might be subheadings for *Frogs, Salamanders*, and *Newts*. Readers should always pay close attention to headings and subheadings, because they prime the brain for the information that is about to be delivered, and because they make it easy to go back and find particular details in a long text.

REFERENCE MATERIALS

DICTIONARIES

Knowledge of reference materials such as dictionaries, encyclopedias, and manuals is vital for any reader. Dictionaries contain a multitude of information about words. A standard dictionary entry begins with a pronunciation guide for the word. The entry will also give the word's part of speech (noun, verb, adjective, etc.). A good dictionary will also include the word's etymology, or origin, including the language from which it is derived and its meaning in that language.

Dictionary entries are in alphabetical order. Many words have more than one definition, in which case the definitions will be numbered. Also, if a word can be used as different parts of speech, its various definitions may be separated. A sample entry might look like this:

WELL: (adverb) 1. in a good way (noun) 1. a hole drilled into the earth

The correct definition of a word will vary depending on how it is used in a sentence. When looking up a word found while reading, the best way to determine the relevant definition is to substitute the dictionary's definitions for the word in the text, and select the definition that seems most appropriate.

ENCYCLOPEDIAS

Encyclopedias used to be the best source for general information on a range of common subjects. Many people took pride in owning a set of encyclopedias, which were often written by top researchers. Now, encyclopedias largely exist online. Although they no longer have a preeminent place in general scholarship, these digital encyclopedias now often feature audio and video clips. A

103

Copyright © Mometrix Media. You have been licensed one copy of this document for personal use only. Any other reproduction or redistribution is strictly prohibited. All rights reserved.
This content is provided for test preparation purposes only and does not imply an endorsement by Mometrix of any particular political, scientific, or religious point of view.

good encyclopedia remains the best place to obtain basic information about a well-known topic. There are also specialty encyclopedias that cover more obscure or expert information. For instance, medical encyclopedias contain the detail and sophistication required by doctors. For a regular person researching a subject like ostriches, Pennsylvania, or the Crimean War, a basic encyclopedia is a good source.

THESAURUS

A thesaurus is a reference book that gives synonyms of words. Unlike a dictionary, a thesaurus does not give definitions, only lists of synonyms. A thesaurus can be helpful in finding the meaning of an unfamiliar word when reading. If the meaning of a synonym is known, then the meaning of the unfamiliar word can be inferred. A thesaurus is also helpful when writing. Using a thesaurus helps authors to vary their word choice.

DATABASE

A database is an informational source with a different format than a publication or a memo. It is a system for storing and organizing large amounts of information. As personal computers have become more common and accessible, databases have become ever more present. The standard layout of a database is a grid, with labels along the left side and top. The horizontal rows and vertical columns that make up the grid are usually numbered or lettered, so that a particular square within the database might be referenced as A3 or G5. Databases are good for storing information that can be expressed succinctly. They are most commonly used to store numerical data but can also be used to store the answers to yes/no questions and other brief data points. Information that is ambiguous (multiple possible meanings) or difficult to express in a few words is not appropriate for a database.

CONTEXT

Often, a reader will come across a word he/she does not recognize. It is important to be able to identify a word's definition from its context. This means defining a word based on the words around it and the way it is used in a sentence. Consider the following sentence: *The elderly scholar spent his evenings hunched over arcane texts that few other people even knew existed.* The adjective *arcane* is uncommon, but the reader can obtain significant information about it based on its use here. Because few other people know of the texts' existence, the reader can assume that arcane texts must be rare and only of interest to a few people. Because they are being read by an elderly scholar, the reader can assume that they focus on difficult academic subjects. Sometimes, words can even be defined by process of elimination. Consider the following sentence: *Ron's fealty to his parents was not shared by Karen, who disobeyed their every command.* Because someone who disobeys is not demonstrating *fealty*, the word can be inferred to mean obedience or respect.

PRIMARY SOURCES

When conducting research, it is important to use reputable primary sources. A primary source is the documentary evidence closest to the subject being studied. For instance, the primary sources for an essay about penguins would be photographs and recordings of the birds, as well as accounts of people who have studied penguins in person. A secondary source would be a review of a movie about penguins or a book outlining the observations made by others. A primary source should be credible and, if it is on a subject that is still being explored, recent. One way to assess the credibility of a work is to see how often it is mentioned in other books and articles on the same subject. By reading the works cited and bibliography sections of other books, one can get a sense of the acknowledged authorities in the field.

Copyright © Mometrix Media. You have been licensed one copy of this document for personal use only. Any other reproduction or redistribution is strictly prohibited. All rights reserved. This content is provided for test preparation purposes only and does not imply an endorsement by Mometrix of any particular political, scientific, or religious point of view.

INTERNET

The Internet was once considered an unreliable place to find sources for an essay or article, but its credibility has improved greatly over the years. Still, students need to exercise caution when researching online. The best sources are those affiliated with established institutions, like universities, public libraries, and think tanks. Most newspapers are available online, and many of them allow the public to browse their archives. Magazines frequently offer similar services. When obtaining information from an unknown website, however, one must exercise considerably more caution. A website can be considered trustworthy if it is referenced by other reputable sites. Also, credible sites tend to be properly maintained and frequently updated. A site is easier to trust when the author provides some information about him or herself, including some credentials that indicate expertise in the subject matter.

ORGANIZING AND UNDERSTANDING GRAPHIC INFORMATION

Two of the most common ways to organize ideas from a text, paraphrasing and summarizing, are verbal organizational methods. Graphic organizers are also useful in arranging ideas from a text. A graphic organizer is a way to simplify information and take only key points from the text. A graphic organizer such as a timeline may have an event listed for a corresponding date on the timeline, whereas an outline may have an event listed under a key point that occurs in the text. Each reader needs to create the type of graphic organizer that works the best for him or her—the method that will best aid in recalling information from a story. Examples include a *spider-map*, which takes a main idea from the story and places it in a bubble, with supporting points branching off the main idea, an *outline*, useful for diagramming the main and supporting points of the entire story, and a *Venn diagram*, which classifies information as separate or overlapping.

> **Review Video: Graphic Organizers**
> Visit mometrix.com/academy and enter code: 665513

Authors can also use these graphic organizers to enliven their presentation or text, but this may be counterproductive if the graphics are confusing or misleading. A graph should strip the author's message down to the essentials. It should have a clear title and should be in the appropriate format. Authors may elect to use tables, line or bar graphs, or pie charts to illustrate their message. Each of these formats is correct for different types of data. The graphic should be large enough to read and should be divided into appropriate categories. For instance, if the text discusses the differences between federal spending on the military and on the space program, a pie chart or a bar graph would be the most effective choices. The pie chart could show each type of spending as a portion of total federal spending, while the bar graph would be better for directly comparing the amounts of money spent on these two programs.

In most cases, the work of interpreting information presented in graphs, tables, charts, and diagrams is done for the reader. The author usually makes clear his or her reasons for presenting a certain set of data in such a way. However, an effective reader will avoid taking the author's claims for granted. Before considering the information presented in the graphic, the reader should consider whether the author has chosen the correct format for presentation, or whether the author has omitted variables or other information that might undermine his case. Interpreting the graphic itself is essentially an exercise in spotting trends. On a graph, for instance, the reader should be alert for how one variable responds to a change in the other. If education level increases, for example, does income increase as well? The same can be done for a table. Readers should be alert for values that break or exaggerate a trend; these may be meaningless outliers or indicators of a change in conditions.

Copyright © Mometrix Media. You have been licensed one copy of this document for personal use only. Any other reproduction or redistribution is strictly prohibited. All rights reserved. This content is provided for test preparation purposes only and does not imply an endorsement by Mometrix of any particular political, scientific, or religious point of view.

When a reader is required to draw conclusions from the information presented in graphs, tables, charts, or diagrams, it is important to limit these conclusions to the terms of the graphic itself. In other words, the reader should avoid extrapolating from the data to make claims that are not supportable. As an example, consider a graph that compares the price of eggs to the demand. If the price and demand rise and fall together, a reader would be justified in saying that the demand for eggs and the price are tied together. However, this simple graph does not indicate which of these variables causes the other, so the reader would not be justified in concluding that the price of eggs raises or lowers the demand, as demand could be tied to a multitude of other factors not included in the chart.

TABLES AND CHARTS

TABLES

Tables are presented in a standard format so they will be easy to read and understand. A title is at the top, a short phrase indicating the information the table or graph intends to convey. The title of a table could be something like "Average Income for Various Education Levels" or "Price of Milk Compared to Demand." A table is composed of information laid out in vertical columns and horizontal rows. Typically, each column will have a label. If "Average Income for Various Education Levels" was placed in a table format, the two columns could be labeled "Education Level" and "Average Income." Each location on the table is called a cell, which holds a piece of information. Cells are defined by their column and row (e.g., second column, fifth row).

GRAPHS

Like a table, a graph typically has a title at the top. This title may simply state the identities of the two axes: e.g., "Income vs. Education." However, the title may also be something more descriptive, like "A comparison of average income with level of education." In any case, bar and line graphs are laid out along two perpendicular lines, or axes. The vertical axis is called the y-axis, and the horizontal axis is called the x-axis. It is typical for the x-axis to be the independent variable and the y-axis to be the dependent variable. The independent variable is the one manipulated by the researcher or creator of the graph. In the above example, the independent variable would be "level of education," since the maker of the graph will define these values (high school, college, master's degree, etc.). The dependent value is not controlled by the researcher.

When selecting a graph format, it is important to consider the intention and the structure of the presentation. A bar graph is appropriate for displaying the relations between a series of distinct quantities that are on the same scale. For instance, if one wanted to display the amount of money spent on groceries during the months of a year, a bar graph would be appropriate. The vertical axis would represent values of money, and the horizontal axis would identify each month. A line graph also requires data expressed in common units, but it is better for demonstrating the general trend in that data. If the grocery expenses were plotted on a line graph instead of a bar graph, there would be more emphasis on whether the amount of money spent rose or fell over the course of the year. Whereas a bar graph is good for showing the relationships between the different values plotted, the line graph is good for showing whether the values tended to increase, decrease, or remain stable.

LINE GRAPH

A line graph is typically used for measuring trends over time. It is set up along a vertical and horizontal axis. The variables being measured are listed along the left and bottom sides of the axes. Points are then plotted along the graph to correspond with their values for each variable. For instance, imagine a line graph measuring a person's income for each month of the year. If the person earned $1500 in January, there would be a point directly above January and directly to the right of $1500. Once all of the lines are plotted, they are connected with a line from left to right. This

Copyright © Mometrix Media. You have been licensed one copy of this document for personal use only. Any other reproduction or redistribution is strictly prohibited. All rights reserved.
This content is provided for test preparation purposes only and does not imply an endorsement by Mometrix of any particular political, scientific, or religious point of view.

line provides a nice visual illustration of the general trends. For instance, if the line sloped up, it would indicate that the person's income had increased over the course of the year.

BAR GRAPH

The bar graph is one of the most common visual representations of information. Bar graphs are used to illustrate sets of numerical data. The graph has a vertical axis, along which numbers are listed, and a horizontal axis, along which categories, words, or some other indicators are placed. An example of a bar graph is a depiction of the respective heights of famous basketball players: the vertical axis would contain numbers ranging from five to eight feet, and the horizontal axis would contain the names of the players. The length of the bar above the player's name would illustrate his height, lining up with the number listed along the left side. In this representation, then, it would be easy to see that Yao Ming is taller than Michael Jordan, because Yao's bar would be higher.

PIE CHART

A pie chart, also known as a circle graph, is useful for depicting how a single unit or category is divided. The standard pie chart is a circle divided into wedges. Each of these wedges is proportional in size to its part of the whole. Consider a pie chart representing a student's budget. If the student spends half her money on rent, then the pie chart will represent that amount with a line through the center of the pie. If she spends a quarter of her money on food, there will be a line extending from the edge of the circle to the center at a right angle to the line depicting rent. This illustration would make it clear that the student spends twice as much money on rent as she does on food. The pie chart is only appropriate for showing how a whole is divided, not for demonstrating the relationships between parts of different wholes. For example, it would not be helpful to use a pie chart to compare the respective amounts of state and federal spending devoted to infrastructure, since these values are only meaningful in the context of the entire budget.

DETERMINING WORD MEANING

An understanding of the basics of language is helpful, and often vital, to understanding what you read. *Structural analysis* refers to looking at the parts of a word and breaking it down into its different components to determine the meaning. By learning the meanings of word fundamentals, you can decipher the meaning of words that may not yet be in your vocabulary. Parts of a word include prefixes, suffixes, and the root word. Prefixes are common letter combinations at the beginning of words, while suffixes are common letter combinations at the end. The main part of the word is known as the root. Visually, it would look like this: prefix + root word + suffix. Look first at the individual meanings of the root word, prefix and/or suffix. Use knowledge of the meaning(s) of the prefix and/or suffix to see what information it adds to the root. Even if the meaning of the root is unknown, one can use knowledge of the prefix and/or suffix to determine an approximate meaning of the word. For example, if one sees the word *uninspired* and does not know what it means, they can use the knowledge that *un-* means 'not' to know that the full word means "not inspired." Understanding the common prefixes and suffixes can illuminate at least part of the meaning of an unfamiliar word.

Below is a list of common prefixes and their meanings:

Prefix	Definition	Examples
a-	in, on, of, up, to	abed, afoot
a-	without, lacking	atheist, agnostic
ab-	from, away, off	abdicate, abjure
ad-	to, toward	advance

Copyright © Mometrix Media. You have been licensed one copy of this document for personal use only. Any other reproduction or redistribution is strictly prohibited. All rights reserved.
This content is provided for test preparation purposes only and does not imply an endorsement by Mometrix of any particular political, scientific, or religious point of view.

Prefix	Definition	Examples
am-	friend, love	amicable, amatory
ante-	before, previous	antecedent, antedate
anti-	against, opposing	antipathy, antidote
auto-	self	autonomy, autobiography
belli-	war, warlike	bellicose
bene-	well, good	benefit, benefactor
bi-	two	bisect, biennial
bio-	life	biology, biosphere
cata-	down, away, thoroughly	catastrophe, cataclysm
chron-	time	chronometer, chronology
circum-	around	circumspect, circumference
com-	with, together, very	commotion, complicate
contra-	against, opposing	contradict, contravene
cred-	belief, trust	credible, credit
de-	from	depart
dem-	people	demographics, democracy
dia-	through, across, apart	diameter, diagnose
dis-	away, off, down, not	dissent, disappear
epi-	upon	epilogue
equi-	equal, equally	equivalent
ex-	out	extract
for-	away, off, from	forget, forswear
fore-	before, previous	foretell, forefathers
homo-	same, equal	homogenized
hyper-	excessive, over	hypercritical, hypertension
hypo-	under, beneath	hypodermic, hypothesis
in-	in, into	intrude, invade
in-	not, opposing	incapable, ineligible
inter-	among, between	intercede, interrupt
intra-	within	intramural, intrastate
magn-	large	magnitude, magnify
mal-	bad, poorly, not	malfunction
micr-	small	microbe, microscope
mis-	bad, poorly, not	misspell, misfire
mono-	one, single	monogamy, monologue
mort-	die, death	mortality, mortuary
neo-	new	neolithic, neoconservative
non-	not	nonentity, nonsense
ob-	against, opposing	objection
omni-	all, everywhere	omniscient
ortho-	right, straight	orthogonal, orthodox
over-	above	overbearing
pan-	all, entire	panorama, pandemonium

Copyright © Mometrix Media. You have been licensed one copy of this document for personal use only. Any other reproduction or redistribution is strictly prohibited. All rights reserved.
This content is provided for test preparation purposes only and does not imply an endorsement by Mometrix of any particular political, scientific, or religious point of view.

Prefix	Definition	Examples
para-	beside, beyond	parallel, paradox
per-	through	perceive, permit
peri-	around	periscope, perimeter
phil-	love, like	philosophy, philanthropic
poly-	many	polymorphous, polygamous
post-	after, following	postpone, postscript
pre-	before, previous	prevent, preclude
prim-	first, early	primitive, primary
pro-	forward, in place of	propel, pronoun
re-	back, backward, again	revoke, recur
retro-	back, backward	retrospect, retrograde
semi-	half, partly	semicircle, semicolon
sub-	under, beneath	subjugate, substitute
super-	above, extra	supersede, supernumerary
sym-	with, together	sympathy, symphony
trans-	across, beyond, over	transact, transport
ultra-	beyond, excessively	ultramodern, ultrasonic, ultraviolet
un-	not, reverse of	unhappy, unlock
uni-	one	uniform, unity
vis-	to see	visage, visible

Below is a list of common suffixes and their meanings:

Suffix	Definition	Examples
-able	able to, likely	capable, tolerable
-age	process, state, rank	passage, bondage
-ance	act, condition, fact	acceptance, vigilance
-arch	to rule	monarch, oligarch
-ard	one that does excessively	drunkard, wizard
-ate	having, showing	separate, desolate
-ation	action, state, result	occupation, starvation
-cy	state, condition	accuracy, captaincy
-dom	state, rank, condition	serfdom, wisdom
-en	cause to be, become	deepen, strengthen
-er	one who does	teacher, lawyer
-esce	become, grow, continue	convalesce, acquiesce
-esque	in the style of, like	picturesque, grotesque
-ess	feminine	waitress, lioness
-fic	making, causing	terrific, beatific
-ful	full of, marked by	thankful, beautiful
-fy	make, cause, cause to have	glorify, fortify
-hood	state, condition	manhood, statehood
-ible	able, likely, fit	edible, possible, divisible
-ion	action, result, state	union, fusion

Copyright © Mometrix Media. You have been licensed one copy of this document for personal use only. Any other reproduction or redistribution is strictly prohibited. All rights reserved.
This content is provided for test preparation purposes only and does not imply an endorsement by Mometrix of any particular political, scientific, or religious point of view.

Suffix	Definition	Examples
-ish	suggesting, like	churlish, childish
-ism	act, manner, doctrine	barbarism, socialism
-ist	doer, believer	monopolist, socialist
-ition	action, state, result	sedition, expedition
-ity	state, quality, condition	acidity, civility
-ize	make, cause to be, treat with	sterilize, mechanize, criticize
-less	lacking, without	hopeless, countless
-like	like, similar	childlike, dreamlike
-logue	type of written/spoken language	prologue, monologue
-ly	like, of the nature of	friendly, positively
-ment	means, result, action	refreshment, disappointment
-ness	quality, state	greatness, tallness
-or	doer, office, action	juror, elevator, honor
-ous	marked by, given to	religious, riotous
-ship	the art or skill of	statesmanship
-some	apt to, showing	tiresome, lonesome
-th	act, state, quality	warmth, width
-tude	quality, state, result	magnitude, fortitude
-ty	quality, state	enmity, activity
-ward	in the direction of	backward, homeward

The more words a person is exposed to, the greater his/her vocabulary will become. By reading on a regular basis, a person can see words in context in a variety of different ways. Based on experience, a person can recall how a word was used in the past and apply that knowledge to a new context. For example, a person may have seen the word *gull* used to mean a bird that is found near the seashore. However, a *gull* can also be a person who is easily tricked. If the word is used in context in reference to a character, the reader can recognize that the character is being called a bird that is not seen as extremely intelligent. What a reader knows about a word can be useful when making comparisons or figuring out the meaning of a new use of a word, as in figurative language, idioms, analogies, and multiple-meaning words.

DENOTATIVE AND CONNOTATIVE MEANING

When defining words in a text, words often have a meaning that is more than the dictionary definition. The denotative meaning of a word is the literal meaning. The connotative meaning goes beyond the denotative meaning to include the emotional reaction a word may invoke, due to associations the reader makes with the denotative meaning. The reader can differentiate between the denotative and connotative meanings by first recognizing when authors use each meaning. Most nonfiction, for example, is fact-based, and the authors typically do not use flowery, figurative language. The reader can assume that the writer is using the denotative, or literal, meaning of words. In fiction, on the other hand, the author may be using the connotative meaning, as connotation is one form of figurative language. The reader should use context clues to determine whether the author is using the denotative or connotative meaning of a word.

CONTEXT

Readers of all levels encounter words with which they are somewhat unfamiliar. The best way to define a word in context is to look for nearby words for clues. For instance, unfamiliar nouns are often accompanied by examples that furnish a definition. Consider the following sentence: "Dave

Copyright © Mometrix Media. You have been licensed one copy of this document for personal use only. Any other reproduction or redistribution is strictly prohibited. All rights reserved.
This content is provided for test preparation purposes only and does not imply an endorsement by Mometrix of any particular political, scientific, or religious point of view.

arrived at the party in hilarious garb: a leopard-print shirt, buckskin trousers, and high heels." If a reader was unfamiliar with the meaning of garb, he could read the examples and quickly determine that the word means "clothing." Examples will not always be this obvious. For instance, consider this sentence: "Parsley, lemon, and flowers were just a few of items he used as garnishes." Here, the possibly unfamiliar word *garnishes* is exemplified by parsley, lemon, and flowers. Readers who have eaten in a variety of restaurants can identify a garnish as something used to decorate a plate.

It is sometimes possible to define an unfamiliar word by looking at the descriptive words in context. Consider the following sentence: "Fred dragged the recalcitrant boy kicking and screaming up the stairs." *Dragged*, *kicking*, and *screaming* all suggest that the boy does not want to go up the stairs. The reader may assume that *recalcitrant* means something like unwilling or protesting. In that example, an unfamiliar adjective was identified. It is perhaps more typical to use description to define an unfamiliar noun, as in this sentence: "Don's wrinkled frown and constantly shaking fist identified him as a curmudgeon of the first order." Don is described as having a "wrinkled frown and constantly shaking fist," suggesting that a *curmudgeon* must be a grumpy old man. Context does not always provide detailed information about the unfamiliar word, but can at least give the reader some clues.

Contrasts

In addition to looking at the context of a passage, readers can often use contrasts to define an unfamiliar word in context. In many sentences, the author will not describe the unfamiliar word directly, but will instead describe the opposite of the unfamiliar word. Of course, this provides information about the word the reader needs to define. Consider the following example: "Despite his intelligence, Hector's low brow and bad posture made him look obtuse." The author suggests that Hector's appearance was opposite to his actual intelligence. Therefore, *obtuse* must mean unintelligent or stupid. Here is another example: "Despite the horrible weather, we were beatific about our trip to Alaska." The word *despite* indicates that the speaker's feelings were at odds with the weather. Since the weather is described as "horrible," *beatific* must mean something pleasant.

Substitution

In some cases, there will be very few contextual clues to help a reader define an unfamiliar word. When this happens, one useful strategy is substitution. A good reader can brainstorm possible synonyms for the given word, and then substitute these words into the sentence. If the sentence and the surrounding passage continue to make sense, the substitution has revealed at least some information about the unfamiliar word. Consider the sentence, "Frank's admonition rang in her ears as she climbed the mountain." A reader unfamiliar with *admonition* might come up with some substitutions like "vow," "promise," "advice," "complaint," or "compliment." All of these words make general sense of the sentence, though their meanings are diverse. The process has suggested, however, that an admonition is some sort of message. The substitution strategy is rarely able to pinpoint a precise definition, but can be effective as a last resort.

Multiple Meaning Words

When a word has more than one meaning, it can be tricky to determine its meaning in a given sentence. Consider the verb *cleave*, which can mean either "join" or "separate." When a reader comes upon this word, he/she must select the definition that makes the most sense. So, take as an example the following sentence: "The birds cleaved together as they flew from the oak tree." Immediately, the presence of the word *together* should suggest that in this sentence *cleave* is being used to mean "*join*." A slightly more difficult example is "Hermione's knife cleaved the bread cleanly." It doesn't make sense for a knife to join bread together, so the word must be meant to

111

Copyright © Mometrix Media. You have been licensed one copy of this document for personal use only. Any other reproduction or redistribution is strictly prohibited. All rights reserved.
This content is provided for test preparation purposes only and does not imply an endorsement by Mometrix of any particular political, scientific, or religious point of view.

indicate separation. Discovering the meaning of a word with multiple meanings requires the same tricks as defining an unknown word: looking for contextual clues and evaluating substituted words.

LITERARY DEVICES
SYNONYMS AND ANTONYMS

Understanding how words relate to each other can often add meaning to a passage. This is explained by understanding synonyms (words that mean the same thing) and antonyms (words that mean the opposite). As an example, *dry* and *arid* are synonyms, and *dry* and *wet* are antonyms. There are many pairs of words that can be considered synonyms, despite having slightly different definitions. For instance, the words *friendly* and *collegial* can both be used to describe a warm interpersonal relationship, so it would be correct to call them synonyms. However, *collegial* (kin to *colleague*) is more often used in reference to professional or academic relationships, while *friendly* has no such connotation. Nevertheless, it would be appropriate to call these words synonyms. If the difference between the two words is too great, however, they may not be called synonyms. *Hot* and *warm* are not synonyms, for instance, because their meanings are too distinct. A good way to determine whether two words are synonyms is to substitute one for the other and see if the sentence means the same thing. Substituting *warm* for *hot* in a sentence would convey a different meaning.

Antonyms are opposites. *Light* and *dark*, *up* and *down*, *right* and *left*, *good* and *bad*: these are all sets of antonyms. It is important to distinguish between antonyms and pairs of words that are simply different. *Black* and *gray*, for instance, are not antonyms because gray is not the opposite of black. *Black* and *white*, on the other hand, are antonyms. Not every word has an antonym. Nouns in particular do not often have antonyms, as there is no "opposite" for humans, places, objects, etc. On a standardized test, the questions related to antonyms are more likely to concern adjectives, which describe nouns. Some common adjectives include *red*, *fast*, *skinny*, and *sweet*. Of these four examples, only *red* lacks a group of obvious antonyms.

> **Review Video: What Are Synonyms and Antonyms?**
> Visit mometrix.com/academy and enter code: 105612

FIGURATIVE LANGUAGE

Authors use many types of language devices to convey their meaning in a more descriptive or interesting way. Understanding these concepts will help you understand what you read. These devices are called *figurative language*—language that goes beyond the literal meaning of the words. Descriptive language that evokes imagery in the reader's mind is one type of figurative language. Exaggeration and comparison are other types. Similes and metaphors are types of comparison, commonly found in poetry. An example of figurative language (a simile in this case) is: "The child howled like a coyote when her mother told her to pick up the toys." In this example, the child's howling is compared to that of a coyote. Figurative language is descriptive in nature and helps the reader understand the sound being made in this sentence.

ALLITERATION

Alliteration is a stylistic device, or literary technique, in which successive words (more strictly, stressed syllables) begin with the same sound or letter. Alliteration is a frequent tool in poetry but it is also common in prose, particularly to highlight short phrases. An example of alliteration could be "thundering through the thickets," in which the initial th sound is used in four consecutive words. Especially in poetry, it contributes to euphony of the passage, lending it a musical air. It may act to humorous effect. Alliteration draws attention to itself, which may be a good or a bad thing. Authors should be conscious of the character of the sound to be repeated. In the above example, a

112

Copyright © Mometrix Media. You have been licensed one copy of this document for personal use only. Any other reproduction or redistribution is strictly prohibited. All rights reserved. This content is provided for test preparation purposes only and does not imply an endorsement by Mometrix of any particular political, scientific, or religious point of view.

th sound is somewhat difficult to make quickly in four consecutive words, so the phrase conveys a little of the difficulty of moving through tall grass. If the author is indeed trying to suggest this difficulty, then the alliteration is a success. Consider, however, the description of eyes as "glassy globes of glitter." This is definitely alliteration, since the initial *gl* sound is used three times. However, one might question whether this awkward sound is appropriate for a description of pretty eyes. The phrase is not especially pleasant to the ear, and therefore is probably not effective as alliteration. Related to alliteration are *assonance*, the repetition of vowel sounds, and *consonance*, the repetition of consonant sounds.

FIGURE OF SPEECH

A figure of speech, sometimes termed a rhetorical figure or device, or elocution, is a word or phrase that departs from straightforward, literal language. Figures of speech are often used and crafted for emphasis, freshness of expression, or clarity. However, clarity may also suffer if figures of speech are overused or wrongly used, so caution is needed.

As an example of the figurative use of a word, consider the sentence, "I am going to crown you." It may mean:

- I am going to place a literal crown on your head.
- I am going to symbolically exalt you to the place of kingship.
- I am going to punch you in the head with my clenched fist.
- I am going to put a second checker on top of your checker to signify that it has become a king.

METAPHOR

A metaphor is a type of figurative language in which the writer equates one thing with a different thing. In the sentence "The bird was an arrow arcing through the sky," the arrow is serving as a metaphor for the bird. The point of a metaphor is to encourage the reader to think about the thing being described in a different way. Using this example, we are being asked to envision the bird's flight as similar to the arc of an arrow, so we will imagine it to be swift and bending. Metaphors are a way for the author to describe without being direct and obvious. Metaphors are a more lyrical and suggestive way of providing information. Note that the thing to which a metaphor refers will not always be mentioned explicitly by the author. For instance, consider the following description of a forest in winter: "Swaying skeletons reached for the sky and groaned as the wind blew through them." The author is clearly using *skeletons* as a metaphor for leafless trees. This metaphor creates a spooky tone while inspiring the reader's imagination.

> **Review Video: Metaphors in Writing**
> Visit mometrix.com/academy and enter code: 133295

METONYMY

Metonymy is referring to one thing in terms of another, closely related thing. This is similar to metaphor, but there is less distance between the description and the thing being described. An example of metonymy is referring to the news media as the "press," although the press is the device by which newspapers are printed. Metonymy is a way of referring to something without having to repeat its name constantly. Synecdoche, on the other hand, is referring to a whole by one of its parts. An example of synecdoche would be calling a police officer a "badge." Synecdoche, like metonymy, is a handy way of reference without having to overuse certain words. It also allows the writer to emphasize aspects of the thing being described. For instance, referring to businessmen as "suits" suggests professionalism, conformity, and drabness.

Copyright © Mometrix Media. You have been licensed one copy of this document for personal use only. Any other reproduction or redistribution is strictly prohibited. All rights reserved.
This content is provided for test preparation purposes only and does not imply an endorsement by Mometrix of any particular political, scientific, or religious point of view.

HYPERBOLE

Hyperbole is overstatement for effect. The following sentence is an example of hyperbole: *He jumped ten feet in the air when he heard the good news*. Obviously, no person has the ability to jump ten feet in the air. The author hyperbolizes not because he believes the statement will be taken literally, but because the exaggeration conveys the extremity of emotion. Consider how much less colorful the sentence would be if the author simply said, "He jumped when he heard the good news." Hyperbole can be ineffective if the author does not exaggerate enough. For instance, if the author wrote, "He jumped two feet in the air when he heard the good news," the reader might not be sure whether this is actually true or just hyperbole. In many situations this distinction will not really matter. However, an author should avoid confusing or vague hyperbole when he needs to maintain credibility or authority with readers.

UNDERSTATEMENT

Understatement is the opposite of hyperbole. This device discounts or downplays something. Think about someone who climbs Mount Everest. Then, they say that the journey was *a little stroll*. As with other types of figurative language, understatement has a range of uses. The device may show self-defeat or modesty as in the Mount Everest example. However, some may think of understatement as false modesty (i.e., an attempt to bring attention to you or a situation). For example, a woman is praised on her diamond engagement ring. The woman says, *Oh, this little thing?* Her understatement might be heard as stuck-up or unfeeling.

> **Review Video: Hyperbole and Understatement**
> Visit mometrix.com/academy and enter code: 308470

SIMILE AND METAPHOR

A simile is a figurative expression similar to a metaphor, though it requires the use of a distancing word like *like* or *as*. Some examples are "The sun was like an orange," "eager as a beaver," and "nimble as a mountain goat." Because a simile includes *like* or a*s*, it creates a little space between the description and the thing being described. If an author says that a house was "like a shoebox," the tone is slightly different than if the author said that the house *was* a shoebox. In a simile, the author indicates an awareness that the description is not the same thing as the thing being described. In a metaphor, there is no such distinction, even though one may safely assume that the author is aware of it. This is a subtle difference, but authors will alternately use metaphors and similes depending on their intended tone.

> **Review Video: Similes**
> Visit mometrix.com/academy and enter code: 642949

PERSONIFICATION

Another type of figurative language is personification. This is the description of the nonhuman as if it were human. Literally, the word means the process of making something into a person. There is a wide range of approaches to personification, from common expressions like "whispering wind" to full novels like *Animal Farm* (George Orwell), in which the Bolshevik Revolution is reenacted by farmyard animals. The general intent of personification is to describe things in a manner that will be comprehensible to readers. When an author states that a tree "groans" in the wind, he/she of course does not mean that the tree is emitting a low, pained sound from its mouth. Instead, he/she means that the tree is making a noise similar to a human groan. This personification establishes a

Copyright © Mometrix Media. You have been licensed one copy of this document for personal use only. Any other reproduction or redistribution is strictly prohibited. All rights reserved. This content is provided for test preparation purposes only and does not imply an endorsement by Mometrix of any particular political, scientific, or religious point of view.

tone of sadness or suffering. A different tone would be established if the author said the tree was "swaying" or "dancing."

> **Review Video: Personification**
> Visit mometrix.com/academy and enter code: 260066

IRONY

Irony is a statement that suggests its opposite—an author or character says one thing but means another. For example, imagine a man walks in his front door, covered in mud and in tattered clothes. His wife asks him, "How was your day?" and he says "Great!" As in this example, irony often depends on information the reader obtains elsewhere. There is a fine distinction between irony and sarcasm. Irony is any statement in which the literal meaning is opposite from the intended meaning, while sarcasm is a statement of this type that is also insulting to the person at whom it is directed. A sarcastic statement suggests that the other person is stupid enough to believe an obviously false statement is true, while irony is a bit more subtle.

> **Review Video: What is Irony?**
> Visit mometrix.com/academy and enter code: 374204

Copyright © Mometrix Media. You have been licensed one copy of this document for personal use only. Any other reproduction or redistribution is strictly prohibited. All rights reserved. This content is provided for test preparation purposes only and does not imply an endorsement by Mometrix of any particular political, scientific, or religious point of view.

Reading Comprehension Practice Test

Directions: Each passage in the reading section is followed by several questions. Choose the best answer from the choices given.

Questions 1 to 3 refer to the following passage:

Alexander the Great died in Babylon at the age of 32 in 323 BC. He had been sick and febrile for two weeks prior to his death. Much speculation exists regarding his cause of death. Poisoning, assassination, and a number of infectious diseases have been posited. An incident mentioned by Plutarch may provide a significant clue. Shortly before his illness, as Alexander entered the city of Babylon, he was met by a flock of ravens. The birds behaved strangely, and many came to die at his feet. The strange behavior of these birds, taken as an ill omen at the time, is similar to the illness and death of birds observed in the United States in the weeks preceding the identification of the first human cases of the West Nile virus. This information suggests that Alexander the Great may have died of encephalitis caused by the West Nile virus.

1. The main purpose of this passage is to

    a. describe the symptoms of West Nile virus encephalitis.
    b. describe an incident involving birds and Alexander the Great.
    c. propose a cause for the death of Alexander the Great.
    d. connect Alexander the Great and Plutarch.

2. In the passage above, "posited" is synonymous with

    a. proposed.
    b. implicated.
    c. amplified.
    d. infected.

3. The author believes that the illness and death of birds observed in the United States indicated that the birds in Babylon

    a. were an ill omen.
    b. were ravens.
    c. were mentioned by Plutarch.
    d. were infected by the encephalitis virus.

Copyright © Mometrix Media. You have been licensed one copy of this document for personal use only. Any other reproduction or redistribution is strictly prohibited. All rights reserved.
This content is provided for test preparation purposes only and does not imply an endorsement by Mometrix of any particular political, scientific, or religious point of view.

Questions 4 to 7 refer to the following passage:

The invalidation of the Ptolemaic model of the solar system is owed chiefly to Nicolaus Copernicus, a Polish astronomer who lived from the late-15th century to the mid-16th century. An early Renaissance man, Copernicus studied a wide range of subjects encompassing mathematics, astronomy, medicine, and law. He studied at the University of Krakow and later at the University of Bologna. While in Italy, his investigations led him to question the widely held belief of the time that the sun and planets revolved around the earth.

In Copernicus' time, people believed that the earth was motionless and fixed at the center of the universe. This model had originated with the Greek astronomer Ptolemy 1,000 years earlier and was supported strongly by the Catholic Church. Copernicus, a church canon himself, challenged the Ptolemaic theory. In its place, he proposed a heliocentric or sun-centered astronomic model. From his observations, made with the naked eye, Copernicus concluded that all the planets—including the earth— revolved around the sun. He also measured the earth's daily axial rotation and proposed this motion as the cause of the apparent movement of heavenly bodies. Working before the advent of the telescope, Copernicus could not prove his theories. He died in 1543.

4. Which of the following sentences best states the main premise of this passage?
   a. Copernicus was an astronomer who followed in the footsteps of Ptolemy.
   b. Copernicus challenged the contemporary astronomic model of his day.
   c. Copernicus developed theories that could not be proven.
   d. Copernicus was a bishop in the Catholic Church.

5. The passage implies that Copernicus could not prove his theories because
   a. they were wrong.
   b. they were opposed by the Catholic Church.
   c. he had no telescope.
   d. he was too busy with his work in law and medicine.

6. In the passage above, the word "heliocentric" means
   a. with the naked eye.
   b. a motionless earth.
   c. revolutionary.
   d. with the sun at the center.

7. This passage is best labeled a
   a. cause and effect essay.
   b. persuasive essay.
   c. process analysis essay.
   d. description essay.

Copyright © Mometrix Media. You have been licensed one copy of this document for personal use only. Any other reproduction or redistribution is strictly prohibited. All rights reserved.
This content is provided for test preparation purposes only and does not imply an endorsement by Mometrix of any particular political, scientific, or religious point of view.

Questions 8 to 11 refer to the following passage:

Some wine aficionados prize the flavor of oak, usually imparted to the beverage through aging in wooden barrels. An alternative process, aging in metal casks with macerated wood chips, provides a stronger wood flavor in less time and therefore is less expensive. To test consumer preferences for wines processed in this manner, a survey of 618 people living in several East Coast cities was conducted early last year. Participants took a blind taste test of three samples of Oregon Pinot Noir. One sample was aged using macerated wood chips, one sample was aged under oak, and a third sample (the control) was aged in a metal tank. A questionnaire then asked subjects to rate the wines and asked a variety of other questions aimed at categorizing the subjects' consumption habits.

Although a variety of factors influenced wine preference, the test exposed a pattern concerning a preference for strongly wood-flavored wines. A large proportion of those persons interviewed (45%) did not care for the tannic wines. However, a sizable minority of 25% especially liked them very much, and preferred the tannic wines to the other samples. Younger consumers particularly fell into this category. Connoisseurs reported greater appreciation for wines aged "under oak," or in normal oak barrels.

Many high-quality wines today are aged under oak. Nonetheless, this process is time consuming; as a result, it makes wines more expensive. This survey demonstrated that price is very important in the buying decision, especially for people without extensive knowledge regarding wine. Many consumers are more concerned with price differences than with subtle differences in flavor. This trend defines a market segment that might be well served by wines aged with wood chips.

8. The main purpose of this passage is to describe

    a.   the process of aging wine with wood chips.
    b.   consumer preferences in wines.
    c.   the importance of price in wine marketing.
    d.   a survey that tested consumer preferences.

9. The word "macerated" is closest in meaning to

    a.   reduced.
    b.   liquefied.
    c.   persecuted.
    d.   facilitated.

10. According to the passage, what percentage of respondents did not like oak-flavored wines?

    a.   75%
    b.   55%
    c.   45%
    d.   25%

Copyright © Mometrix Media. You have been licensed one copy of this document for personal use only. Any other reproduction or redistribution is strictly prohibited. All rights reserved.
This content is provided for test preparation purposes only and does not imply an endorsement by Mometrix of any particular political, scientific, or religious point of view.

11. Which of the following statements best explains the advantage of using wood chips to make wine?

    a. It is an inexpensive way of making wines that appeal to young people.
    b. It is an inexpensive way of making wines that appeal to connoisseurs.
    c. It is a faster way to make expensive wines.
    d. It makes wines that are indistinguishable from those produced by more expensive processes.

Questions 12 to 14 refer to the following passage:

> The loss of barrier islands through erosion poses a serious challenge to many communities along the Atlantic and Gulf Coasts. Along with marshes and wetlands, these islands protect coastal towns from major storms. In the past seventy years, Louisiana alone has lost almost 2,000 square miles of coastal land to hurricanes and flooding. More than 100 square miles of wetlands protecting the city of New Orleans were wiped out by a single storm, Hurricane Katrina. Due to this exposure of coastal communities, recent hurricane seasons have proven the most expensive on record: annual losses since 2005 have been estimated in the hundreds of billions of dollars. This unfortunate trend is likely to continue, since meteorological research shows that the Atlantic basin is in an active storm period that could continue for decades.

12. Which of the following statements offers a supporting argument for the passage's claim that many coastal islands are eroding?

    a. Recent hurricane seasons have been expensive.
    b. The Atlantic Basin is entering an active period.
    c. Louisiana has lost 2,000 square miles of coastal land.
    d. Barrier islands are the first line of defense against coastal storms.

13. The passage describes recent hurricane seasons as the most expensive on record. Which of the following statements gives the implied reason for this increased expense?

    a. Hurricane Katrina was an extremely violent storm.
    b. Valuable buildings were destroyed in New Orleans.
    c. The Atlantic Basin is entering an active period.
    d. Destruction of barrier islands and coastal wetlands has left the mainland exposed.

14. Which of the following choices represents the best label for this passage?

    a. definition essay
    b. cause/effect essay
    c. comparison essay
    d. persuasive essay

Copyright © Mometrix Media. You have been licensed one copy of this document for personal use only. Any other reproduction or redistribution is strictly prohibited. All rights reserved. This content is provided for test preparation purposes only and does not imply an endorsement by Mometrix of any particular political, scientific, or religious point of view.

Questions 15 and 16 refer to the following passage:

Intercity passenger rail is widely used in Europe and Japan. In the United States, it could potentially provide significant benefits to society by complementing other heavily used modes of transportation. Potential benefits include controlling increases in air and highway congestion, stemming pollution caused by aircraft and automobiles, reducing fuel consumption and energy dependency, and increasing passenger safety. Rail transport can compete in markets comprised of nearby cities as well as along routes that parallel heavily traveled highway or air corridors.

15. This passage is best described as one that

    a. advocates implementation of a passenger rail system.

    b. describes passenger rail systems.

    c. points out advantages and disadvantages of passenger rail systems.

    d. narrates a trip on a passenger rail system.

16. The author sees intercity passenger rail as

    a. a replacement for other forms of travel such as air or highway.

    b. an alternative form of travel suited to all intercity routes in the United States.

    c. lacking any advantages over currently popular forms of travel.

    d. capable of augmenting currently available forms of travel in selected markets.

Question 17 refers to the following passage:

Absurdity is required for progress. It is absurd to try to change the world.

17. In this passage,

    a. the first sentence explains the second sentence.

    b. the second sentence explains the first sentence.

    c. neither sentence is a consequence of the other sentence.

    d. the two sentences comprise a circular argument.

Questions 18 to 22 refer to the following passage:

Magnesium is an important nutrient that supports immune system functioning and helps protect the body against cardiovascular diseases. Symptoms of magnesium deficiency often go unrecognized, but concern is growing that many people may not have sufficient body stores of this metal. Surveys show that most Americans do not receive the minimum daily requirement of magnesium in their diets.

Magnesium is absorbed from foods by the intestines, before the circulatory system transports it to the body's tissues. Less than half of ingested magnesium is normally taken up in this way. Health issues affecting the digestive tract may impair magnesium absorption. For example, gastrointestinal disorders such as Crohn's disease can limit magnesium uptake. The kidneys normally limit urinary excretion of magnesium, a function that can help make up for low dietary intake. However, alcohol abuse and certain medications can affect this balance and thereby lead to magnesium depletion.

Symptoms of magnesium deficiency include vomiting, fatigue, and loss of appetite. More severe cases can include symptoms such as muscular cramps, seizures, and

Copyright © Mometrix Media. You have been licensed one copy of this document for personal use only. Any other reproduction or redistribution is strictly prohibited. All rights reserved.
This content is provided for test preparation purposes only and does not imply an endorsement by Mometrix of any particular political, scientific, or religious point of view.

coronary abnormalities. Magnesium insufficiency also can affect the body's ability to absorb other cations, including calcium and potassium, and can lead to other health complications. Good sources of dietary magnesium include leafy green vegetables, potatoes, nuts, and seeds.

18. Which of the following statements is true?

a. People with magnesium deficiency may exhibit fatigue and loss of appetite.
b. People with magnesium deficiencies are often asymptomatic.
c. Severe magnesium deficiency may lead to Crohn's disease.
d. Magnesium is not absorbed by the digestive tract.

19. Which of the following labels best describes the previous passage?

a. comparison essay
b. definition essay
c. cause and effect essay
d. persuasive essay

20. Which of the following describes the intestine's normal absorption of magnesium?

a. inefficient.
b. very efficient except when disease is present.
c. rarely observed among the populations of developing countries.
d. enhanced by eating leafy green vegetables.

21. According to the passage, alcohol abuse can lead to which of the following problems?

a. poor magnesium absorption.
b. an impairment of kidney function.
c. compromise of the immune system.
d. gastrointestinal disorders.

22. The word "cation" is closest in meaning to:

a. element
b. nutrient similar to magnesium
c. symptom of deficiency
d. nutritional supplement

Questions 23 and 24 refer to the following passage:

Students may take classes in a wide variety of subjects for fun or self-improvement. Some classes provide students with training in useful life skills such as cooking or personal finance. Other classes provide instruction for recreational purposes, with topics such as photography, pottery, or painting. Classes may be large or small, or may involve one-on-one instruction in subjects like singing or playing a musical instrument. Classes taught by self-enrichment teachers seldom lead to a degree, and attendance in these classes is voluntary. Although often taught in nonacademic settings, topics may include academic subjects such as literature, foreign languages, and history. Despite their informal nature, these courses can provide students with useful, work-related skills such as knowledge of computers or foreign languages; these skills can make students more attractive to potential employers.

Copyright © Mometrix Media. You have been licensed one copy of this document for personal use only. Any other reproduction or redistribution is strictly prohibited. All rights reserved.
This content is provided for test preparation purposes only and does not imply an endorsement by Mometrix of any particular political, scientific, or religious point of view.

23. Which of the following statements represents the central idea of this passage?
   a. Self-improvement classes teach work-related skills.
   b. Attendance is voluntary for self-improvement classes.
   c. Many different kinds of self-improvement classes are available.
   d. Cooking is one type of self-improvement classes.

24. Which of the following statements is true?
   a. All self-improvement classes offer training in recreational subject areas.
   b. Self-improvement classes usually are taught in non-academic settings.
   c. Some informal classes teach useful work-related skills.
   d. In order to learn a foreign language, a student must enroll in a formal, degree-granting program.

Questions 25 and 26 refer to the following passage:

> The makeup she applied, although intended to display her pulchritude, instead revealed her narcissism.

25. In the context of this sentence, the word "pulchritude" means
   a. beauty
   b. dexterity
   c. skill
   d. sense of color

26. A synonym for the word "narcissism," as used in the text, is
   a. superiority
   b. respect
   c. conceitedness
   d. timidity

Questions 27 to 30 refer to the following passage:

> The selection of trees for planting in urban areas poses severe challenges due to soil adversities and space restrictions both above and belowground. Restricted spaces, especially in "downtown" situations or in densely built neighborhoods, make selecting, planting, and managing trees in urban areas difficult. Urban sites pose adversities that severely constrain the palette of suitable trees. As a result, an urgent need exists to find tough, small species of trees for urban spaces. Dwarf forms of native species have not been utilized greatly, and some foreign species may prove to be appropriate.

27. Which of the following is NOT identified by the passage as a problem encountered when planting trees in urban sites?
   a. poor soil
   b. air pollution
   c. limited room for root development
   d. restricted space

Copyright © Mometrix Media. You have been licensed one copy of this document for personal use only. Any other reproduction or redistribution is strictly prohibited. All rights reserved. This content is provided for test preparation purposes only and does not imply an endorsement by Mometrix of any particular political, scientific, or religious point of view.

28. In the context of this passage, the word "palette" means

   a. a board used by painters for mixing colors.
   b. choice.
   c. wooden platform.
   d. repertoire.

29. In the last sentence, which of the following statements does the author imply regarding dwarf forms of native species, which have not been greatly utilized?

   a. They are too small.
   b. They are ill-suited to urban sites.
   c. They would do better in foreign locations.
   d. They would do well in urban sites.

30. This passage is best described as a

   a. problem/solution essay.
   b. cause/effect essay.
   c. persuasive essay.
   d. narration essay.

Questions 31 to 33 refer to the following passage:

A new way to circumvent the cost and limitations of long distance telephone is called Voice over Internet Protocol, or VoIP. VoIP sends digital information over the Internet to the person you are calling. The information may come from your phone or your computer, and may comprise both voice and video signal if you have a camera. Companies that specialize in such technology as well as some traditional phone companies offer VoIP services. Some services require that you call from a computer augmented by special software, a microphone, speakers, and a sound card. Other services allow you to call from any regular phone without special equipment.

31. The word "circumvent" is closest in meaning to

   a. reduce.
   b. magnify.
   c. elude.
   d. camouflage.

32. Which of the following is required to take advantage of VoIP services?

   a. a camera
   b. a telephone
   c. special software
   d. none of the above

33. The information in the passage best supports which of the following statements?

   a. Voice over Internet Protocol services are available in most telephone markets.
   b. Voice over Internet Protocol services digitally encode voice and visual information.
   c. Voice over Internet Protocol services provide higher quality signals than traditional telephone services.
   d. Voice over Internet Protocol services must be purchased from companies that specialize in the technology.

Copyright © Mometrix Media. You have been licensed one copy of this document for personal use only. Any other reproduction or redistribution is strictly prohibited. All rights reserved.
This content is provided for test preparation purposes only and does not imply an endorsement by Mometrix of any particular political, scientific, or religious point of view.

Questions 34 to 37 refer to the following passage:

The provision of this bill that prevents any nonprofit recipient of a housing grant from conducting voter registration is an outrageous, undemocratic amendment that imposes restrictions on promoting the most fundamental of our civil liberties, the right to vote. This provision forbids any nonprofits from even applying for a grant if they have encouraged voting in the recent past. Restricting the prerogatives of nonprofits in this way is a violation of the first amendment rights of these organizations. There is absolutely no justification for preventing the efforts of nonprofit organizations to encourage civic activities such as voting.

34. This passage is best described as a

a. problem/solution essay.
b. cause/effect essay.
c. persuasive essay.
d. narration essay.

35. The word "prerogative" is closest in meaning to

a. privilege.
b. funding.
c. restriction.
d. ability.

36. What is the author's tone?

a. entertaining
b. angry
c. informative
d. apologetic

37. What is the author's main argument against the provision?

a. It will prevent voting.
b. It is unconstitutional.
c. It will prevent nonprofit organizations from receiving funding.
d. It is unjustified.

Questions 38 to 40 refer to the following passage:

Women have made significant contributions to patent literature in fields as diverse as domestic technology and biomedicine. A woman was involved in the design of the first computer: Lady Ada Lovelace worked with Charles Babbage to build the "difference engine," a device that could add and subtract. More recently, Gertrude Elion won the 1988 Nobel Prize in Medicine for her invention of a leukemia treatment based on immunosuppressants. She holds numerous medical patents. In addition, women have served as leading members of teams developing surgical methods and all the current AIDS drugs.

Copyright © Mometrix Media. You have been licensed one copy of this document for personal use only. Any other reproduction or redistribution is strictly prohibited. All rights reserved. This content is provided for test preparation purposes only and does not imply an endorsement by Mometrix of any particular political, scientific, or religious point of view.

38. The "difference engine" was

a. domestic technology.
b. a device used in biomedicine.
c. a computer.
d. invented by Gertrude Elion.

39. The structure of this paragraph is best described as

a. topic sentence and analysis
b. topic sentence and consequences
c. introductory sentence followed by causes and reasons
d. topic sentence followed by examples

40. The passage implies that

a. women are more productive inventors than men.
b. many surgical methods are patented.
c. women's contributions to the patent literature have been underappreciated.
d. Gertrud Elion did not deserve the Nobel Prize.

Copyright © Mometrix Media. You have been licensed one copy of this document for personal use only. Any other reproduction or redistribution is strictly prohibited. All rights reserved.
This content is provided for test preparation purposes only and does not imply an endorsement by Mometrix of any particular political, scientific, or religious point of view.

Reading Comprehension Answers Key

1. C: Although the passage does describe some of the symptoms of encephalitis caused by the West Nile virus as well as the incident in which the birds died at Alexander's feet; these descriptions are incidental to the paragraph's main purpose. The main idea of the paragraph is that Alexander may have died of encephalitis.

2. A: The third sentence, in which this word appears, reviews a number of possible, suggested, or proposed causes for Alexander's death. The author then recounts the incident of the ravens as evidence for a different cause of death.

3. D: The author's thesis holds that the birds contracted the encephalitis virus first and that it led to their death. The virus then spread to the human population, leading to the outbreak of West Nile encephalitis. The author suggests that this train of events occurred both in ancient Babylon and in the modern United States.

4. B: The passage describes how Copernicus made observations that contradicted the prevailing view of astronomy, which had been held since the time of Ptolemy. The Ptolemaic theory asserted that the sun and other planets revolved around the earth. The passage states that Copernicus came to question the Ptolemaic theory and challenged it.

5. C: The second paragraph in the passage states that Copernicus made his observations with the naked eye. The penultimate sentence states that he worked before the advent of the telescope and that he could not prove his theories. The paragraph implies that a telescope would have made this proof possible.

6. D: The third sentence of the second paragraph states that Copernicus put forward the principles of a "heliocentric or sun-centered astronomy," in which the sun was at the center of rotation of the orbiting planets.

7. D: The essay describes the history of Copernicus and his astronomical observations, telling the reader about his life and contrasting his astronomical observations to those previously made by the ancient Greeks. It does not seek to persuade or to promote a particular point of view. It does not describe or analyze a process or describe any cause-and-effect relationships.

8. D: Although the passage describes various methods of aging wine in the presence of oak as well as consumer price sensitivity, the passage's main purpose is to describe the results of a survey conducted in order to examine consumer preferences. The passage describes the number of people surveyed, the types of questions asked, and the results of the survey.

9. A: To macerate is to break into smaller parts, typically by steeping in a liquid. In this case, the process produces small wood chips with a large surface area that flavors the wine more efficiently than the interior surface of the barrels used traditionally.

10. C: The second paragraph states that 45% of those persons interviewed rejected tannic wines. Tannic wines are those flavored by tannins, components of oak bark. The meaning of the term can be inferred from the phrasing of the second paragraph, in which the 25% who strongly favored the wood-flavored wines are contrasted to those who categorically disliked the tannic wines.

11. A: The second paragraph states that young wine lovers, especially, fell into the 25% who preferred the wood-chip produced wines. The first paragraph states that the process is faster and

126

Copyright © Mometrix Media. You have been licensed one copy of this document for personal use only. Any other reproduction or redistribution is strictly prohibited. All rights reserved.
This content is provided for test preparation purposes only and does not imply an endorsement by Mometrix of any particular political, scientific, or religious point of view.

therefore less expensive. Additionally, the last paragraph indicates that price sensitivity among consumers is an advantage for wines made with wood chips, from which one may infer that the process is less expensive.

12. C: The loss of coastal wetlands in Louisiana is an example of coastal island erosion caused by hurricanes, and so supports the statement. The other choices are also statements that appear in the passage, but they do not provide direct support for the claim that many coastal islands are eroding.

13. D: The passage describes the loss of these coastal barrier lands to erosion. The fifth sentence then states, "the result is that recent hurricane seasons have been the most expensive on record." This establishes the cause-and-effect between barrier island erosion and monetary losses due to great storms.

14. B: The essay does not make comparisons or seek to define or persuade. Instead, this passage describes the role of coastal wetlands, gives examples of recent losses of these lands, and concludes that these factors result in a substantial economic loss due to recent storms.

15. A: By pointing out only the benefits of a passenger rail system, the author attempts to make the case for the implementation of such a system in the United States. The author does not offer a description of the equipment or procedures used by such a system, but instead enumerates its advantages.

16. D: The author states that rail can complement other heavily used forms of transportation, including heavily traveled corridors between cities within close distances.

17. B: The logic of the passage holds that 1) trying to change the world is absurd; 2) progress changes the world; and therefore, 3) absurdity is required for progress.

18. A: The third paragraph indicates that symptoms of magnesium deficiency often include vomiting, fatigue, and loss of appetite.

19. C: The passage describes both the causes of magnesium deficiency (dietary shortage or poor uptake exacerbated by gastrointestinal disorders) and its results (reduced functioning of the immune system and lessened resistance to cardiovascular disease).

20. A: The second paragraph informs that less than half of ingested magnesium is absorbed under normal circumstances.

21. B: According to the second paragraph, the kidneys usually limit magnesium excretion in the urine, but alcohol abuse and/or certain medications may affect this function. Impairment of this kidney function may lead to magnesium depletion. The passage does not state that magnesium uptake—a function of the intestines—is affected by alcohol.

22. B: The final paragraph indicates that magnesium deficiency can affect the absorption of "other cations," implying that magnesium itself is also a cation. The examples given, calcium and potassium, are also nutrients.

23. C: The passage explores the wide variety of self-improvement classes offered. As such, it touches upon the variety of content and subject matter, different venues in which the classes may be taught, and the range of enrollment sizes that may be encountered.

Copyright © Mometrix Media. You have been licensed one copy of this document for personal use only. Any other reproduction or redistribution is strictly prohibited. All rights reserved.
This content is provided for test preparation purposes only and does not imply an endorsement by Mometrix of any particular political, scientific, or religious point of view.

24. C: The passage points out that some of the subjects taught in informal courses may prove useful in the workplace and may make the student more desirable to potential employers. This includes topics such as computer science and foreign languages.

25. A: Pulchritude means "beauty," and in this case refers to the method of putting on makeup to enhance natural beauty.

26. C: The word "narcissism" comes from the name of the Greek god Narcissus, who was so attractive that he enjoyed gazing at his reflection in a pond. Narcissism refers to excessive fascination with oneself, one's appearance, etc.

27. B: The first sentence identifies poor soil as a problem in the first sentence ("soil adversities"). The second sentence points to restricted space, both above and belowground (the latter restricting root development). Although air pollution also may affect the growth of urban trees, the passage does not mention this factor.

28. D: The word, derived from the board used by painters during the Renaissance, refers to the variety of techniques or materials available in any art. The third sentence of the passage informs us that this range is limited by the adverse conditions in urban sites. Note that the word refers to the range of available trees, and not to the choice made among them, so Choice B is incorrect.

29. D: Since space restriction is one of the major problems encountered in planting trees in urban sites, the author implies that dwarf trees—since they are small—would prove successful in this cramped environment.

30. A: The essay first poses a problem—namely, the difficulty of growing trees in urban environments due to poor soil and limited space. The author then suggests two solutions to this problem: dwarf trees, which are small and require limited space, and foreign species, which are less well known and may include some particularly hardy examples.

31. C: To "circumvent" means to get around an obstacle or problem or to find a way to avoid it. To "elude" has the same meaning. The problem in this case is one of high cost, and circumventing it leads to a reduction in that cost, as in Choice A. Nevertheless, Choice C is the closest in meaning.

32. D: Although certain circumstances might require each of the choices, the article makes a point of enumerating the variety of providers available and that different equipment configurations will work with different services. This includes computer-based and telephone-based services.

33. B: The second sentence defines VoIP as something that uses the internet to send digital information. The third sentence specifies that this information may comprise both voice and video signals. Although digital VoIP signals may be of higher quality than other technologies and may be available in most markets, the passage does not make these points.

34. C: The passage is an argument against a legislative proposal. Its purpose is to persuade legislators or voters to reject the proposal or the provision it discusses. The tone of the passage is contentious and opinionated, not objective like narrative writing. It does not attempt to present an opposing point of view or an analysis, as would befit cause/effect or problem/solution writing.

35. A: A prerogative is a right or privilege, in this case the right to conduct voter registration activities.

Copyright © Mometrix Media. You have been licensed one copy of this document for personal use only. Any other reproduction or redistribution is strictly prohibited. All rights reserved. This content is provided for test preparation purposes only and does not imply an endorsement by Mometrix of any particular political, scientific, or religious point of view.

36. B: The author plainly is not attempting to entertain. The use of words such as "outrageous," "undemocratic," and "absolutely" imparts a strongly emotional tone to the passage, which can be described as antagonistic, irate, or angry.

37. B: In the third sentence, the author argues that the provision violates the first amendment of the Constitution. Although the passage also claims such a provision as unjustified, this claim offers not so much an argument as a rhetorical flourish.

38. C: The introductory phrase of the second sentence, "A woman was involved in the design of the first computer:" ends with a colon, indicating that an example will follow. Thus, the difference engine described in the following clause is an example of a computer. The difference engine is described further in the passage as a device that could add and subtract, which is a function of a computer.

39. D: The first sentence introduces the topic, the contributions made to the patent literature by women. The remainder of the paragraph is dedicated to giving examples of these contributions, beginning with Lady Lovelace two centuries ago and continuing through present day contributions to biomedicine. The passage does not describe any causes or effects, so the passage cannot be considered an analysis.

40. B: The thrust of the paragraph asserts that women have registered many patents. The final sentence informs us that women have led teams that developed surgical methods. Although not stated explicitly, the paragraph implies that these methods have been patented.

Copyright © Mometrix Media. You have been licensed one copy of this document for personal use only. Any other reproduction or redistribution is strictly prohibited. All rights reserved.
This content is provided for test preparation purposes only and does not imply an endorsement by Mometrix of any particular political, scientific, or religious point of view.

Mathematics

In the high tech world we live in, it might seem that having good math ability is no longer very important. After all, when does a person have to mentally perform even the easiest math operation anymore? It seems that any time you need to deal with math, the work has already been done for you, or you simply have to push a few buttons on a computer, smart phone, or—if you're really old-fashioned—on an actual calculator.

It's true that there has been quite a revolution when it comes to how we do math even in the last 10–20 years. As hard as it may be to believe today, when small, portable calculators first came on the American market around 1970, they cost about $300 (about $1800 in today's dollars!) and performed only the four basic functions—addition, subtraction, division, and multiplication. Very few people could afford to own one, and most people still used pencil and paper to solve math problems. Now you can buy a better calculator for about a dollar at most discount stores.

If you're like the average person, though, it's been a long time since you used an actual handheld calculator, let alone pencil and paper, to solve any math problems. You use your phone or computer to do math on the rare occasions when it comes up. When those first portable calculators came out, many people predicted that one day in the not too distant future math knowledge would become superfluous for the average person. It might seem as if their prediction came true.

Yet while math may have become superfluous in the day-to-day lives of most people, math abilities are still essential for success in life. We may use different tools to perform our "figuring" these days, but it's still vital to know how to do the operations ourselves. A person with a well-rounded education should be able to perform all but the most complicated math operations either mentally or with pencil and paper.

This is why civil service exams have math questions. An office worker shouldn't need to stop and open up the computer's calculator function every time he needs to add, subtract, multiply or divide. He/she should be able to do basic math mentally. So, in order to do well on your civil service exam, you'll need to make sure your math knowledge and skills are in good shape. If you've been out of school for several years, your skills might have gotten a little rusty, and you may not be as familiar with some of the more advanced or less frequently used concepts as you once were.

In this chapter you'll find a thorough refresher course in math to get you up to speed quickly. It starts with the basics and then builds on that foundation all the way through algebra and geometry. (Yes, you may very well encounter basic algebra or geometry questions, or both, on the civil service test.) Even if you struggled with math in school, you'll find all the information you need to master the math portion of the civil service exam in this chapter. Take your time and go at your own pace, and use the practice test at the end as a diagnostic tool to measure your readiness for the exam.

Numbers and Operations

CLASSIFICATIONS OF NUMBERS

Numbers are the basic building blocks of mathematics. Specific features of numbers are identified by the following terms:

Integer – any positive or negative whole number, including zero. Integers do not include fractions $\left(\frac{1}{3}\right)$, decimals (0.56), or mixed numbers $\left(7\frac{3}{4}\right)$.

130

Copyright © Mometrix Media. You have been licensed one copy of this document for personal use only. Any other reproduction or redistribution is strictly prohibited. All rights reserved. This content is provided for test preparation purposes only and does not imply an endorsement by Mometrix of any particular political, scientific, or religious point of view.

Prime number – any whole number greater than 1 that has only two factors, itself and 1; that is, a number that can be divided evenly only by 1 and itself.

Composite number – any whole number greater than 1 that has more than two different factors; in other words, any whole number that is not a prime number. For example: The composite number 8 has the factors of 1, 2, 4, and 8.

Even number – any integer that can be divided by 2 without leaving a remainder. For example: 2, 4, 6, 8, and so on.

Odd number – any integer that cannot be divided evenly by 2. For example: 3, 5, 7, 9, and so on.

Decimal number – any number that uses a decimal point to show the part of the number that is less than one. Example: 1.234.

Decimal point – a symbol used to separate the ones place from the tenths place in decimals or dollars from cents in currency.

Decimal place – the position of a number to the right of the decimal point. In the decimal 0.123, the 1 is in the first place to the right of the decimal point, indicating tenths; the 2 is in the second place, indicating hundredths; and the 3 is in the third place, indicating thousandths.

The **decimal**, or base 10, system is a number system that uses ten different digits (0, 1, 2, 3, 4, 5, 6, 7, 8, 9). An example of a number system that uses something other than ten digits is the **binary**, or base 2, number system, used by computers, which uses only the numbers 0 and 1. It is thought that the decimal system originated because people had only their 10 fingers for counting.

Rational numbers include all integers, decimals, and fractions. Any terminating or repeating decimal number is a rational number.

Irrational numbers cannot be written as fractions or decimals because the number of decimal places is infinite and there is no recurring pattern of digits within the number. For example, pi (π) begins with 3.141592 and continues without terminating or repeating, so pi is an irrational number.

Real numbers are the set of all rational and irrational numbers.

> **Review Video: <u>Classification of Numbers</u>**
> Visit mometrix.com/academy and enter code: 461071
>
> **Review Video: <u>Prime and Composite Numbers</u>**
> Visit mometrix.com/academy and enter code: 565581

NUMBERS IN WORD FORM AND PLACE VALUE

When writing numbers out in word form or translating word form to numbers, it is essential to understand how a place value system works. In the decimal or base-10 system, each digit of a number represents how many of the corresponding place value—a specific factor of 10—are contained in the number being represented. To make reading numbers easier, every three digits to

Copyright © Mometrix Media. You have been licensed one copy of this document for personal use only. Any other reproduction or redistribution is strictly prohibited. All rights reserved.
This content is provided for test preparation purposes only and does not imply an endorsement by Mometrix of any particular political, scientific, or religious point of view.

the left of the decimal place is preceded by a comma. The following table demonstrates some of the place values:

Power of 10	10^3	10^2	10^1	10^0	10^{-1}	10^{-2}	10^{-3}
Value	1,000	100	10	1	0.1	0.01	0.001
Place	thousands	hundreds	tens	ones	tenths	hundredths	thousandths

For example, consider the number 4,546.09, which can be separated into each place value like this:

4: thousands
5: hundreds
4: tens
6: ones
0: tenths
9: hundredths

This number in word form would be *four thousand five hundred forty-six and nine hundredths*.

Review Video: Place Value
Visit mometrix.com/academy and enter code: 205433

The term **rational** means that the number can be expressed as a ratio or fraction. That is, a number, r, is rational if and only if it can be represented by a fraction $\frac{a}{b}$ where a and b are integers and b does not equal 0. The set of rational numbers includes integers and decimals. If there is no finite way to represent a value with a fraction of integers, then the number is **irrational**. Common examples of irrational numbers include: $\sqrt{5}$, $\left(1 + \sqrt{2}\right)$, and π.

Review Video: Rational and Irrational Numbers
Visit mometrix.com/academy and enter code: 280645

Review Video: Ordering Rational Numbers
Visit mometrix.com/academy and enter code: 419578

A number line is a graph to see the distance between numbers. Basically, this graph shows the relationship between numbers. So a number line may have a point for zero and may show negative numbers on the left side of the line. Any positive numbers are placed on the right side of the line. For example, consider the points labeled on the following number line:

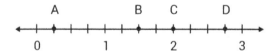

Copyright © Mometrix Media. You have been licensed one copy of this document for personal use only. Any other reproduction or redistribution is strictly prohibited. All rights reserved.
This content is provided for test preparation purposes only and does not imply an endorsement by Mometrix of any particular political, scientific, or religious point of view.

We can use the dashed lines on the number line to identify each point. Each dashed line between two whole numbers is $\frac{1}{4}$. The line halfway between two numbers is $\frac{1}{2}$.

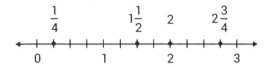

Review Video: The Number Line
Visit mometrix.com/academy and enter code: 816439

Rounding is reducing the digits in a number while still trying to keep the value similar. The result will be less accurate but in a simpler form and easier to use. Whole numbers can be rounded to the nearest ten, hundred, or thousand.

When you are asked to estimate the solution to a problem, you will need to provide only an approximate figure or **estimation** for your answer. In this situation, you will need to round each number in the calculation to the level indicated (nearest hundred, nearest thousand, etc.) or to a level that makes sense for the numbers involved. When estimating a sum **all numbers must be rounded to the same level**. You cannot round one number to the nearest thousand while rounding another to the nearest hundred.

Review Video: Rounding and Estimation
Visit mometrix.com/academy and enter code: 126243

A precursor to working with negative numbers is understanding what **absolute values** are. A number's absolute value is simply the distance away from zero a number is on the number line. The absolute value of a number is always positive and is written $|x|$. For example, the absolute value of 3, written as $|3|$, is 3 because the distance between 0 and 3 on a number line is three units. Likewise, the absolute value of –3, written as $|-3|$, is 3 because the distance between 0 and –3 on a number line is three units. So $|3| = |-3|$.

Review Video: Absolute Value
Visit mometrix.com/academy and enter code: 314669

An **operation** is simply a mathematical process that takes some value(s) as input(s) and produces an output. Elementary operations are often written in the following form: *value operation value*. For instance, in the expression $1 + 2$ the values are 1 and 2 and the operation is addition. Performing the operation gives the output of 3. In this way we can say that $1 + 2$ and 3 are equal, or $1 + 2 = 3$.

ADDITION

Addition increases the value of one quantity by the value of another quantity (both called **addends**). Example: $2 + 4 = 6$ or $8 + 9 = 17$. The result is called the **sum**. With addition, the order does not matter, $4 + 2 = 2 + 4$.

Copyright © Mometrix Media. You have been licensed one copy of this document for personal use only. Any other reproduction or redistribution is strictly prohibited. All rights reserved.
This content is provided for test preparation purposes only and does not imply an endorsement by Mometrix of any particular political, scientific, or religious point of view.

When adding signed numbers, if the signs are the same simply add the absolute values of the addends and apply the original sign to the sum. For example, $(+4) + (+8) = +12$ and $(-4) + (-8) = -12$. When the original signs are different, take the absolute values of the addends and subtract the smaller value from the larger value, then apply the original sign of the larger value to the difference. Example: $(+4) + (-8) = -4$ and $(-4) + (+8) = +4$.

SUBTRACTION

Subtraction is the opposite operation to addition; it decreases the value of one quantity (the **minuend**) by the value of another quantity (the **subtrahend**). For example, $6 - 4 = 2$ or $17 - 8 = 9$. The result is called the **difference**. Note that with subtraction, the order does matter, $6 - 4 \neq 4 - 6$.

For subtracting signed numbers, change the sign of the subtrahend and then follow the same rules used for addition. Example: $(+4) - (+8) = (+4) + (-8) = -4$

MULTIPLICATION

Multiplication can be thought of as repeated addition. One number (the **multiplier**) indicates how many times to add the other number (the **multiplicand**) to itself. Example: $3 \times 2 = 2 + 2 + 2 = 6$. With multiplication, the order does not matter, $2 \times 3 = 3 \times 2$ or $3 + 3 = 2 + 2 + 2$, either way the result (the **product**) is the same.

If the signs are the same, the product is positive when multiplying signed numbers. Example: $(+4) \times (+8) = +32$ and $(-4) \times (-8) = +32$. If the signs are opposite, the product is negative. Example: $(+4) \times (-8) = -32$ and $(-4) \times (+8) = -32$. When more than two factors are multiplied together, the sign of the product is determined by how many negative factors are present. If there are an odd number of negative factors then the product is negative, whereas an even number of negative factors indicates a positive product. Example: $(+4) \times (-8) \times (-2) = +64$ and $(-4) \times (-8) \times (-2) = -64$.

DIVISION

Division is the opposite operation to multiplication; one number (the **divisor**) tells us how many parts to divide the other number (the **dividend**) into. The result of division is called the **quotient**. Example: $20 \div 4 = 5$. If 20 is split into 4 equal parts, each part is 5. With division, the order of the numbers does matter, $20 \div 4 \neq 4 \div 20$.

The rules for dividing signed numbers are similar to multiplying signed numbers. If the dividend and divisor have the same sign, the quotient is positive. If the dividend and divisor have opposite signs, the quotient is negative. Example: $(-4) \div (+8) = -0.5$.

> **Review Video: Mathematical Operations**
> Visit mometrix.com/academy and enter code: 208095

PARENTHESES

Parentheses are used to designate which operations should be done first when there are multiple operations. Example: $4 - (2 + 1) = 1$; the parentheses tell us that we must add 2 and 1, and then subtract the sum from 4, rather than subtracting 2 from 4 and then adding 1 (this would give us an answer of 3).

> **Review Video: Mathematical Parentheses**
> Visit mometrix.com/academy and enter code: 978600

134

Copyright © Mometrix Media. You have been licensed one copy of this document for personal use only. Any other reproduction or redistribution is strictly prohibited. All rights reserved. This content is provided for test preparation purposes only and does not imply an endorsement by Mometrix of any particular political, scientific, or religious point of view.

EXPONENTS

An **exponent** is a superscript number placed next to another number at the top right. It indicates how many times the base number is to be multiplied by itself. Exponents provide a shorthand way to write what would be a longer mathematical expression, Example: $2^4 = 2 \times 2 \times 2 \times 2$. A number with an exponent of 2 is said to be "squared," while a number with an exponent of 3 is said to be "cubed." The value of a number raised to an exponent is called its power. So 8^4 is read as "8 to the 4th power," or "8 raised to the power of 4."

> **Review Video: What is an Exponent?**
> Visit mometrix.com/academy and enter code: 600998

ROOTS

A **root**, such as a square root, is another way of writing a fractional exponent. Instead of using a superscript, roots use the radical symbol ($\sqrt{}$) to indicate the operation. A radical will have a number underneath the bar, and may sometimes have a number in the upper left: $\sqrt[n]{a}$, read as "the nth root of a." The relationship between radical notation and exponent notation can be described by this equation:

$$\sqrt[n]{a} = a^{\frac{1}{n}}$$

The two special cases of $n = 2$ and $n = 3$ are called square roots and cube roots. If there is no number to the upper left, the radical is understood to be a square root ($n = 2$). Nearly all of the roots you encounter will be square roots. A square root is the same as a number raised to the one-half power. When we say that a is the square root of b ($a = \sqrt{b}$), we mean that a multiplied by itself equals b: ($a \times a = b$).

A **perfect square** is a number that has an integer for its square root. There are 10 perfect squares from 1 to 100: 1, 4, 9, 16, 25, 36, 49, 64, 81, 100 (the squares of integers 1 through 10).

> **Review Video: Roots**
> Visit mometrix.com/academy and enter code: 795655
>
> **Review Video: Perfect Squares and Square Roots**
> Visit mometrix.com/academy and enter code: 648063

WORD PROBLEMS AND MATHEMATICAL SYMBOLS

When working on word problems, you must be able to translate verbal expressions or "math words" into math symbols. This chart contains several "math words" and their appropriate symbols:

Phrase	Symbol
equal, is, was, will be, has, costs, gets to, is the same as, becomes	$=$
times, of, multiplied by, product of, twice, doubles, halves, triples	$\times$
divided by, per, ratio of/to, out of	$\div$
plus, added to, sum, combined, and, more than, totals of	$+$
subtracted from, less than, decreased by, minus, difference between	$-$
what, how much, original value, how many, a number, a variable	x, n, etc.

EXAMPLES OF TRANSLATED MATHEMATICAL PHRASES

- The phrase four more than twice a number can be written algebraically as $2x + 4$.

Copyright © Mometrix Media. You have been licensed one copy of this document for personal use only. Any other reproduction or redistribution is strictly prohibited. All rights reserved.
This content is provided for test preparation purposes only and does not imply an endorsement by Mometrix of any particular political, scientific, or religious point of view.

- The phrase half a number decreased by six can be written algebraically as $\frac{1}{2}x - 6$.
- The phrase the sum of a number and the product of five and that number can be written algebraically as $x + 5x$.
- You may see a test question that says, "Olivia is constructing a bookcase from seven boards. Two of them are for vertical supports and five are for shelves. The height of the bookcase is twice the width of the bookcase. If the seven boards total 36 feet in length, what will be the height of Olivia's bookcase?" You would need to make a sketch and then create the equation to determine the width of the shelves. The height can be represented as double the width. (If x represents the width of the shelves in feet, then the height of the bookcase is $2x$. Since the seven boards total 36 feet, $2x + 2x + x + x + x + x + x = 36$ or $9x = 36$; $x = 4$. The height is twice the width, or 8 feet.)

A great way to make use of some of the features built into the decimal system would be regrouping when attempting longform subtraction operations. When subtracting within a place value, sometimes the minuend is smaller than the subtrahend, **regrouping** enables you to 'borrow' a unit from a place value to the left in order to get a positive difference. For example, consider subtracting 189 from 525 with regrouping.

First, set up the subtraction problem in vertical form:

$$
\begin{array}{r}
525 \\
-\ 189 \\
\hline
\end{array}
$$

Notice that the numbers in the ones and tens columns of 525 are smaller than the numbers in the ones and tens columns of 189. This means you will need to use regrouping to perform subtraction:

$$
\begin{array}{ccc}
5 & 2 & 5 \\
-\ 1 & 8 & 9 \\
\hline
\end{array}
$$

To subtract 9 from 5 in the ones column you will need to borrow from the 2 in the tens columns:

$$
\begin{array}{ccc}
5 & 1 & 15 \\
-\ 1 & 8 & 9 \\
\hline
& & 6 \\
\end{array}
$$

Next, to subtract 8 from 1 in the tens column you will need to borrow from the 5 in the hundreds column:

$$
\begin{array}{ccc}
4 & 11 & 15 \\
-\ 1 & 8 & 9 \\
\hline
& 3 & 6 \\
\end{array}
$$

Last, subtract the 1 from the 4 in the hundreds column:

$$
\begin{array}{ccc}
4 & 11 & 15 \\
-\ 1 & 8 & 9 \\
\hline
3 & 3 & 6 \\
\end{array}
$$

> **Review Video: Subtracting Large Numbers**
> Visit mometrix.com/academy and enter code: 603350

Copyright © Mometrix Media. You have been licensed one copy of this document for personal use only. Any other reproduction or redistribution is strictly prohibited. All rights reserved. This content is provided for test preparation purposes only and does not imply an endorsement by Mometrix of any particular political, scientific, or religious point of view.

The **order of operations** is a set of rules that dictates the order in which we must perform each operation in an expression so that we will evaluate it accurately. If we have an expression that includes multiple different operations, the order of operations tells us which operations to do first. The most common mnemonic for the order of operations is **PEMDAS**, or "Please Excuse My Dear Aunt Sally." PEMDAS stands for parentheses, exponents, multiplication, division, addition, and subtraction. It is important to understand that multiplication and division have equal precedence, as do addition and subtraction, so those pairs of operations are simply worked from left to right in order.

For example, evaluating the expression $5 + 20 \div 4 \times (2 + 3)^2 - 6$ using the correct order of operations would be done like this:

- **P:** Perform the operations inside the parentheses: $(2 + 3) = 5$
- **E:** Simplify the exponents: $(5)^2 = 5 \times 5 = 25$
   - The expression now looks like this: $5 + 20 \div 4 \times 25 - 6$
- **MD:** Perform multiplication and division from left to right: $20 \div 4 = 5$; then $5 \times 25 = 125$
   - The expression now looks like this: $5 + 125 - 6$
- **AS:** Perform addition and subtraction from left to right: $5 + 125 = 130$; then $130 - 6 = 124$

> **Review Video: Order of Operations**
> Visit mometrix.com/academy and enter code: 259675

The properties of exponents are as follows:

Property	Description
$a^1 = a$	Any number to the power of 1 is equal to itself
$1^n = 1$	The number 1 raised to any power is equal to 1
$a^0 = 1$	Any number raised to the power of 0 is equal to 1
$a^n \times a^m = a^{n+m}$	Add exponents to multiply powers of the same base number
$a^n \div a^m = a^{n-m}$	Subtract exponents to divide powers of the same base number
$(a^n)^m = a^{n \times m}$	When a power is raised to a power, the exponents are multiplied
$(a \times b)^n = a^n \times b^n$ $(a \div b)^n = a^n \div b^n$	Multiplication and division operations inside parentheses can be raised to a power. This is the same as each term being raised to that power.
$a^{-n} = \dfrac{1}{a^n}$	A negative exponent is the same as the reciprocal of a positive exponent

Note that exponents do not have to be integers. Fractional or decimal exponents follow all the rules above as well. Example: $5^{\frac{1}{4}} \times 5^{\frac{3}{4}} = 5^{\frac{1}{4}+\frac{3}{4}} = 5^1 = 5$.

> **Review Video: Properties of Exponents**
> Visit mometrix.com/academy and enter code: 532558

Scientific notation is a way of writing large numbers in a shorter form. The form $a \times 10^n$ is used in scientific notation, where a is greater than or equal to 1 but less than 10, and n is the number of places the decimal must move to get from the original number to a. Example: The number 230,400,000 is cumbersome to write. To write the value in scientific notation, place a decimal point between the first and second numbers, and include all digits through the last non-zero digit

Copyright © Mometrix Media. You have been licensed one copy of this document for personal use only. Any other reproduction or redistribution is strictly prohibited. All rights reserved. This content is provided for test preparation purposes only and does not imply an endorsement by Mometrix of any particular political, scientific, or religious point of view.

($a = 2.304$). To find the appropriate power of 10, count the number of places the decimal point had to move ($n = 8$). The number is positive if the decimal moved to the left, and negative if it moved to the right. We can then write 230,400,000 as 2.304×10^8. If we look instead at the number 0.00002304, we have the same value for a, but this time the decimal moved 5 places to the right ($n = -5$). Thus, 0.00002304 can be written as 2.304×10^{-5}. Using this notation makes it simple to compare very large or very small numbers. By comparing exponents, it is easy to see that 3.28×10^4 is smaller than 1.51×10^5, because 4 is less than 5.

Review Video: Scientific Notation
Visit mometrix.com/academy and enter code: 976454

FACTORS AND GREATEST COMMON FACTOR

Factors are numbers that are multiplied together to obtain a **product**. For example, in the equation $2 \times 3 = 6$, the numbers 2 and 3 are factors. A **prime number** has only two factors (1 and itself), but other numbers can have many factors.

A **common factor** is a number that divides exactly into two or more other numbers. For example, the factors of 12 are 1, 2, 3, 4, 6, and 12, while the factors of 15 are 1, 3, 5, and 15. The common factors of 12 and 15 are 1 and 3.

A **prime factor** is also a prime number. Therefore, the prime factors of 12 are 2 and 3. For 15, the prime factors are 3 and 5.

The **greatest common factor** (GCF) is the largest number that is a factor of two or more numbers. For example, the factors of 15 are 1, 3, 5, and 15; the factors of 35 are 1, 5, 7, and 35. Therefore, the greatest common factor of 15 and 35 is 5.

Review Video: Factors
Visit mometrix.com/academy and enter code: 920086

Review Video: Prime Numbers and Factorization
Visit mometrix.com/academy and enter code: 760669

Review Video: Greatest Common Factor and Least Common Multiple
Visit mometrix.com/academy and enter code: 838699

MULTIPLES AND LEAST COMMON MULTIPLE

Often listed out in multiplication tables, **multiples** are integer increments of a given factor. In other words, dividing a multiple by the factor will result in an integer. For example, the multiples of 7 include: $1 \times 7 = 7, 2 \times 7 = 14, 3 \times 7 = 21, 4 \times 7 = 28, 5 \times 7 = 35$. Dividing 7, 14, 21, 28, or 35 by 7 will result in the integers 1, 2, 3, 4, and 5, respectively.

The least common multiple (**LCM**) is the smallest number that is a multiple of two or more numbers. For example, the multiples of 3 include 3, 6, 9, 12, 15, etc.; the multiples of 5 include 5, 10, 15, 20, etc. Therefore, the least common multiple of 3 and 5 is 15.

Review Video: Multiples
Visit mometrix.com/academy and enter code: 626738

Copyright © Mometrix Media. You have been licensed one copy of this document for personal use only. Any other reproduction or redistribution is strictly prohibited. All rights reserved. This content is provided for test preparation purposes only and does not imply an endorsement by Mometrix of any particular political, scientific, or religious point of view.

FRACTIONS

A **fraction** is a number that is expressed as one integer written above another integer, with a dividing line between them $\left(\frac{x}{y}\right)$. It represents the **quotient** of the two numbers "x divided by y." It can also be thought of as x out of y equal parts.

The top number of a fraction is called the **numerator**, and it represents the number of parts under consideration. The 1 in $\frac{1}{4}$ means that 1 part out of the whole is being considered in the calculation. The bottom number of a fraction is called the **denominator**, and it represents the total number of equal parts. The 4 in $\frac{1}{4}$ means that the whole consists of 4 equal parts. A fraction cannot have a denominator of zero; this is referred to as "*undefined.*"

Fractions can be manipulated, without changing the value of the fraction, by multiplying or dividing (but not adding or subtracting) both the numerator and denominator by the same number. If you divide both numbers by a common factor, you are **reducing** or simplifying the fraction. Two fractions that have the same value but are expressed differently are known as **equivalent fractions**. For example, $\frac{2}{10}, \frac{3}{15}, \frac{4}{20}$, and $\frac{5}{25}$ are all equivalent fractions. They can also all be reduced or simplified to $\frac{1}{5}$.

When two fractions are manipulated so that they have the same denominator, this is known as finding a **common denominator**. The number chosen to be that common denominator should be the least common multiple of the two original denominators. Example: $\frac{3}{4}$ and $\frac{5}{6}$; the least common multiple of 4 and 6 is 12. Manipulating to achieve the common denominator: $\frac{3}{4} = \frac{9}{12}$; $\frac{5}{6} = \frac{10}{12}$.

> **Review Video: Overview of Fractions**
> Visit mometrix.com/academy and enter code: 262335

PROPER FRACTIONS AND MIXED NUMBERS

A fraction whose denominator is greater than its numerator is known as a **proper fraction**, while a fraction whose numerator is greater than its denominator is known as an **improper fraction**. Proper fractions have values *less than one* and improper fractions have values *greater than one.*

A **mixed number** is a number that contains both an integer and a fraction. Any improper fraction can be rewritten as a mixed number. Example: $\frac{8}{3} = \frac{6}{3} + \frac{2}{3} = 2 + \frac{2}{3} = 2\frac{2}{3}$. Similarly, any mixed number can be rewritten as an improper fraction. Example: $1\frac{3}{5} = 1 + \frac{3}{5} = \frac{5}{5} + \frac{3}{5} = \frac{8}{5}$.

> **Review Video: Proper and Improper Fractions and Mixed Numbers**
> Visit mometrix.com/academy and enter code: 211077

Copyright © Mometrix Media. You have been licensed one copy of this document for personal use only. Any other reproduction or redistribution is strictly prohibited. All rights reserved. This content is provided for test preparation purposes only and does not imply an endorsement by Mometrix of any particular political, scientific, or religious point of view.

ADDING AND SUBTRACTING FRACTIONS

If two fractions have a common denominator, they can be added or subtracted simply by adding or subtracting the two numerators and retaining the same denominator. If the two fractions do not already have the same denominator, one or both of them must be manipulated to achieve a common denominator before they can be added or subtracted. Example: $\frac{1}{2} + \frac{1}{4} = \frac{2}{4} + \frac{1}{4} = \frac{3}{4}$.

> **Review Video: Adding and Subtracting Fractions**
> Visit mometrix.com/academy and enter code: 378080

MULTIPLYING FRACTIONS

Two fractions can be multiplied by multiplying the two numerators to find the new numerator and the two denominators to find the new denominator. Example: $\frac{1}{3} \times \frac{2}{3} = \frac{1 \times 2}{3 \times 3} = \frac{2}{9}$.

DIVIDING FRACTIONS

Two fractions can be divided by flipping the numerator and denominator of the second fraction and then proceeding as though it were a multiplication problem. Example: $\frac{2}{3} \div \frac{3}{4} = \frac{2}{3} \times \frac{4}{3} = \frac{8}{9}$.

> **Review Video: Multiplying and Dividing Fractions**
> Visit mometrix.com/academy and enter code: 473632

MULTIPLYING A MIXED NUMBER BY A WHOLE NUMBER OR A DECIMAL

When multiplying a mixed number by something, it is usually best to convert it to an improper fraction first. Additionally, if the multiplicand is a decimal, it is most often simplest to convert it to a fraction. For instance, to multiply $4\frac{3}{8}$ by 3.5, begin by rewriting each quantity as a whole number plus a proper fraction. Remember, a mixed number is a fraction added to a whole number and a decimal is a representation of the sum of fractions, specifically tenths, hundredths, thousandths, and so on:

$$4\frac{3}{8} \times 3.5 = \left(4 + \frac{3}{8}\right) \times \left(3 + \frac{1}{2}\right)$$

Next, the quantities being added need to be expressed with the same denominator. This is achieved by multiplying and dividing the whole number by the denominator of the fraction. Recall that a whole number is equivalent to that number divided by 1:

$$= \left(\frac{4}{1} \times \frac{8}{8} + \frac{3}{8}\right) \times \left(\frac{3}{1} \times \frac{2}{2} + \frac{1}{2}\right)$$

When multiplying fractions, remember to multiply the numerators and denominators separately:

$$= \left(\frac{4 \times 8}{1 \times 8} + \frac{3}{8}\right) \times \left(\frac{3 \times 2}{1 \times 2} + \frac{1}{2}\right)$$

$$= \left(\frac{32}{8} + \frac{3}{8}\right) \times \left(\frac{6}{2} + \frac{1}{2}\right)$$

Now that the fractions have the same denominators, they can be added:

$$= \frac{35}{8} \times \frac{7}{2}$$

Copyright © Mometrix Media. You have been licensed one copy of this document for personal use only. Any other reproduction or redistribution is strictly prohibited. All rights reserved. This content is provided for test preparation purposes only and does not imply an endorsement by Mometrix of any particular political, scientific, or religious point of view.

Finally, perform the last multiplication and then simplify:

$$= \frac{35 \times 7}{8 \times 2} = \frac{245}{16} = \frac{240}{16} + \frac{5}{16} = 15\frac{5}{16}$$

COMPARING FRACTIONS

It is important to master the ability to compare and order fractions. This skill is relevant to many real-world scenarios. For example, carpenters often compare fractional construction nail lengths when preparing for a project, and bakers often compare fractional measurements to have the correct ratio of ingredients. There are three commonly used strategies when comparing fractions. These strategies are referred to as the common denominator approach, the decimal approach, and the cross-multiplication approach.

USING A COMMON DENOMINATOR TO COMPARE FRACTIONS

The fractions $\frac{2}{3}$ and $\frac{4}{7}$ have different denominators. $\frac{2}{3}$ has a denominator of 3, and $\frac{4}{7}$ has a denominator of 7. In order to precisely compare these two fractions, it is necessary to use a common denominator. A common denominator is a common multiple that is shared by both denominators. In this case, the denominators 3 and 7 share a multiple of 21. In general, it is most efficient to select the least common multiple for the two denominators.

Rewrite each fraction with the common denominator of 21. Then, calculate the new numerators as illustrated below.

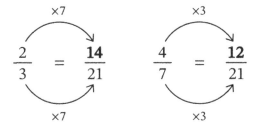

For $\frac{2}{3}$, multiply the numerator and denominator by 7. The result is $\frac{14}{21}$.

For $\frac{4}{7}$, multiply the numerator and denominator by 3. The result is $\frac{12}{21}$.

Now that both fractions have a denominator of 21, the fractions can accurately be compared by comparing the numerators. Since 14 is greater than 12, the fraction $\frac{14}{21}$ is greater than $\frac{12}{21}$. This means that $\frac{2}{3}$ is greater than $\frac{4}{7}$.

USING DECIMALS TO COMPARE FRACTIONS

Sometimes decimal values are easier to compare than fraction values. For example, $\frac{5}{8}$ is equivalent to 0.625 and $\frac{3}{5}$ is equivalent to 0.6. This means that the comparison of $\frac{5}{8}$ and $\frac{3}{5}$ can be determined by comparing the decimals 0.625 and 0.6. When both decimal values are extended to the thousandths place, they become 0.625 and 0.600, respectively. It becomes clear that 0.625 is greater than 0.600 because 625 thousandths is greater than 600 thousandths. In other words, $\frac{5}{8}$ is greater than $\frac{3}{5}$ because 0.625 is greater than 0.6.

Copyright © Mometrix Media. You have been licensed one copy of this document for personal use only. Any other reproduction or redistribution is strictly prohibited. All rights reserved.
This content is provided for test preparation purposes only and does not imply an endorsement by Mometrix of any particular political, scientific, or religious point of view.

USING CROSS-MULTIPLICATION TO COMPARE FRACTIONS

Cross-multiplication is an efficient strategy for comparing fractions. This is a shortcut for the common denominator strategy. Start by writing each fraction next to one another. Multiply the numerator of the fraction on the left by the denominator of the fraction on the right. Write down the result next to the fraction on the left. Now multiply the numerator of the fraction on the right by the denominator of the fraction on the left. Write down the result next to the fraction on the right. Compare both products. The fraction with the larger result is the larger fraction.

Consider the fractions $\frac{4}{7}$ and $\frac{5}{9}$.

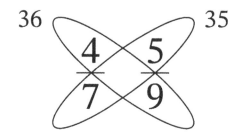

36 is greater than 35. Therefore, $\frac{4}{7}$ is greater than $\frac{5}{9}$.

DECIMALS

Decimals are one way to represent parts of a whole. Using the place value system, each digit to the right of a decimal point denotes the number of units of a corresponding *negative* power of ten. For example, consider the decimal 0.24. We can use a model to represent the decimal. Since a dime is worth one-tenth of a dollar and a penny is worth one-hundredth of a dollar, one possible model to represent this fraction is to have 2 dimes representing the 2 in the tenths place and 4 pennies representing the 4 in the hundredths place:

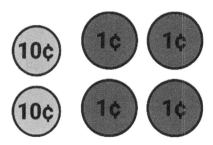

To write the decimal as a fraction, put the decimal in the numerator with 1 in the denominator. Multiply the numerator and denominator by tens until there are no more decimal places. Then simplify the fraction to lowest terms. For example, converting 0.24 to a fraction:

$$0.24 = \frac{0.24}{1} = \frac{0.24 \times 100}{1 \times 100} = \frac{24}{100} = \frac{6}{25}$$

> **Review Video: Decimals**
> Visit mometrix.com/academy and enter code: 837268

OPERATIONS WITH DECIMALS
ADDING AND SUBTRACTING DECIMALS

When adding and subtracting decimals, the decimal points must always be aligned. Adding decimals is just like adding regular whole numbers. Example: $4.5 + 2.0 = 6.5$.

Copyright © Mometrix Media. You have been licensed one copy of this document for personal use only. Any other reproduction or redistribution is strictly prohibited. All rights reserved.
This content is provided for test preparation purposes only and does not imply an endorsement by Mometrix of any particular political, scientific, or religious point of view.

If the problem-solver does not properly align the decimal points, an incorrect answer of 4.7 may result. An easy way to add decimals is to align all of the decimal points in a vertical column visually. This will allow you to see exactly where the decimal should be placed in the final answer. Begin adding from right to left. Add each column in turn, making sure to carry the number to the left if a column adds up to more than 9. The same rules apply to the subtraction of decimals.

> **Review Video: <u>Adding and Subtracting Decimals</u>**
> Visit mometrix.com/academy and enter code: 381101

Multiplying Decimals

A simple multiplication problem has two components: a **multiplicand** and a **multiplier**. When multiplying decimals, work as though the numbers were whole rather than decimals. Once the final product is calculated, count the number of places to the right of the decimal in both the multiplicand and the multiplier. Then, count that number of places from the right of the product and place the decimal in that position.

For example, 12.3×2.56 has a total of three places to the right of the respective decimals. Multiply 123×256 to get 31,488. Now, beginning on the right, count three places to the left and insert the decimal. The final product will be 31.488.

> **Review Video: <u>How to Multiply Decimals</u>**
> Visit mometrix.com/academy and enter code: 731574

Dividing Decimals

Every division problem has a **divisor** and a **dividend**. The dividend is the number that is being divided. In the problem $14 \div 7$, 14 is the dividend and 7 is the divisor. In a division problem with decimals, the divisor must be converted into a whole number. Begin by moving the decimal in the divisor to the right until a whole number is created. Next, move the decimal in the dividend the same number of spaces to the right. For example, 4.9 into 24.5 would become 49 into 245. The decimal was moved one space to the right to create a whole number in the divisor, and then the same was done for the dividend. Once the whole numbers are created, the problem is carried out normally: $245 \div 49 = 5$.

> **Review Video: <u>Dividing Decimals</u>**
> Visit mometrix.com/academy and enter code: 560690
>
> **Review Video: <u>Dividing Decimals by Whole Numbers</u>**
> Visit mometrix.com/academy and enter code: 535669

Percentages

Percentages can be thought of as fractions that are based on a whole of 100; that is, one whole is equal to 100%. The word **percent** means "per hundred." Percentage problems are often presented in three main ways:

- Find what percentage of some number another number is.
  - Example: What percentage of 40 is 8?
- Find what number is some percentage of a given number.
  - Example: What number is 20% of 40?

143

Copyright © Mometrix Media. You have been licensed one copy of this document for personal use only. Any other reproduction or redistribution is strictly prohibited. All rights reserved. This content is provided for test preparation purposes only and does not imply an endorsement by Mometrix of any particular political, scientific, or religious point of view.

- Find what number another number is a given percentage of.
  - Example: What number is 8 20% of?

There are three components in each of these cases: a **whole** (W), a **part** (P), and a **percentage** (%). These are related by the equation: $P = W \times \%$. This can easily be rearranged into other forms that may suit different questions better: $\% = \frac{P}{W}$ and $W = \frac{P}{\%}$. Percentage problems are often also word problems. As such, a large part of solving them is figuring out which quantities are what. For example, consider the following word problem:

In a school cafeteria, 7 students choose pizza, 9 choose hamburgers, and 4 choose tacos. What percentage of student choose tacos?

To find the whole, you must first add all of the parts: $7 + 9 + 4 = 20$. The percentage can then be found by dividing the part by the whole $\left(\% = \frac{P}{W}\right)$: $\frac{4}{20} = \frac{20}{100} = 20\%$.

> **Review Video: Computation with Percentages**
> Visit mometrix.com/academy and enter code: 693099

CONVERTING BETWEEN PERCENTAGES, FRACTIONS, AND DECIMALS

Converting decimals to percentages and percentages to decimals is as simple as moving the decimal point. To *convert from a decimal to a percentage*, move the decimal point **two places to the right**. To *convert from a percentage to a decimal*, move it **two places to the left**. It may be helpful to remember that the percentage number will always be larger than the equivalent decimal number. Example:

$$0.23 = 23\% \quad 5.34 = 534\% \quad 0.007 = 0.7\%$$
$$700\% = 7.00 \quad 86\% = 0.86 \quad 0.15\% = 0.0015$$

To convert a fraction to a decimal, simply divide the numerator by the denominator in the fraction. To convert a decimal to a fraction, put the decimal in the numerator with 1 in the denominator. Multiply the numerator and denominator by tens until there are no more decimal places. Then simplify the fraction to lowest terms. For example, converting 0.24 to a fraction:

$$0.24 = \frac{0.24}{1} = \frac{0.24 \times 100}{1 \times 100} = \frac{24}{100} = \frac{6}{25}$$

Fractions can be converted to a percentage by finding equivalent fractions with a denominator of 100. Example:

$$\frac{7}{10} = \frac{70}{100} = 70\% \quad \frac{1}{4} = \frac{25}{100} = 25\%$$

To convert a percentage to a fraction, divide the percentage number by 100 and reduce the fraction to its simplest possible terms. Example:

$$60\% = \frac{60}{100} = \frac{3}{5} \quad 96\% = \frac{96}{100} = \frac{24}{25}$$

> **Review Video: Converting Fractions to Percentages and Decimals**
> Visit mometrix.com/academy and enter code: 306233

Copyright © Mometrix Media. You have been licensed one copy of this document for personal use only. Any other reproduction or redistribution is strictly prohibited. All rights reserved. This content is provided for test preparation purposes only and does not imply an endorsement by Mometrix of any particular political, scientific, or religious point of view.

> **Review Video: <u>Converting Percentages to Decimals and Fractions</u>**
> Visit mometrix.com/academy and enter code: 287297
>
> **Review Video: <u>Converting Decimals to Fractions and Percentages</u>**
> Visit mometrix.com/academy and enter code: 986765
>
> **Review Video: <u>Converting Decimals, Improper Fractions, and Mixed Numbers</u>**
> Visit mometrix.com/academy and enter code: 696924

Algebra

PROPORTIONS

A proportion is a relationship between two quantities that dictates how one changes when the other changes. A **direct proportion** describes a relationship in which a quantity increases by a set amount for every increase in the other quantity, or decreases by that same amount for every decrease in the other quantity. Example: Assuming a constant driving speed, the time required for a car trip increases as the distance of the trip increases. The distance to be traveled and the time required to travel are directly proportional.

An **inverse proportion** is a relationship in which an increase in one quantity is accompanied by a decrease in the other, or vice versa. Example: the time required for a car trip decreases as the speed increases and increases as the speed decreases, so the time required is inversely proportional to the speed of the car.

> **Review Video: <u>Proportions</u>**
> Visit mometrix.com/academy and enter code: 505355

RATIOS

A **ratio** is a comparison of two quantities in a particular order. Example: If there are 14 computers in a lab, and the class has 20 students, there is a student to computer ratio of 20 to 14, commonly written as 20: 14. Ratios are normally reduced to their smallest whole number representation, so 20: 14 would be reduced to 10: 7 by dividing both sides by 2.

> **Review Video: <u>Ratios</u>**
> Visit mometrix.com/academy and enter code: 996914

CONSTANT OF PROPORTIONALITY

When two quantities have a proportional relationship, there exists a **constant of proportionality** between the quantities. The product of this constant and one of the quantities is equal to the other quantity. For example, if one lemon costs $0.25, two lemons cost $0.50, and three lemons cost $0.75, there is a proportional relationship between the total cost of lemons and the number of lemons purchased. The constant of proportionality is the **unit price**, namely $0.25/lemon. Notice that the total price of lemons, t, can be found by multiplying the unit price of lemons, p, and the number of lemons, n: $t = pn$.

Copyright © Mometrix Media. You have been licensed one copy of this document for personal use only. Any other reproduction or redistribution is strictly prohibited. All rights reserved.
This content is provided for test preparation purposes only and does not imply an endorsement by Mometrix of any particular political, scientific, or religious point of view.

WORK/UNIT RATE

Unit rate expresses a quantity of one thing in terms of one unit of another. For example, if you travel 30 miles every two hours, a unit rate expresses this comparison in terms of one hour: in one hour you travel 15 miles, so your unit rate is 15 miles per hour. Other examples are how much one ounce of food costs (price per ounce) or figuring out how much one egg costs out of the dozen (price per 1 egg, instead of price per 12 eggs). The denominator of a unit rate is always 1. Unit rates are used to compare different situations to solve problems. For example, to make sure you get the best deal when deciding which kind of soda to buy, you can find the unit rate of each. If soda #1 costs $1.50 for a 1-liter bottle, and soda #2 costs $2.75 for a 2-liter bottle, it would be a better deal to buy soda #2, because its unit rate is only $1.375 per 1-liter, which is cheaper than soda #1. Unit rates can also help determine the length of time a given event will take. For example, if you can paint 2 rooms in 4.5 hours, you can determine how long it will take you to paint 5 rooms by solving for the unit rate per room and then multiplying that by 5.

> **Review Video: Rates and Unit Rates**
> Visit mometrix.com/academy and enter code: 185363

TERMS AND COEFFICIENTS

Mathematical expressions consist of a combination of one or more values arranged in terms that are added together. As such, an expression could be just a single number, including zero. A **variable term** is the product of a real number, also called a **coefficient**, and one or more variables, each of which may be raised to an exponent. Expressions may also include numbers without a variable, called **constants** or **constant terms**. The expression $6s^2$, for example, is a single term where the coefficient is the real number 6 and the variable term is s^2. Note that if a term is written as simply a variable to some exponent, like t^2, then the coefficient is 1, because $t^2 = 1t^2$.

LINEAR EXPRESSIONS

A **single variable linear expression** is the sum of a single variable term, where the variable has no exponent, and a constant, which may be zero. For instance, the expression $2w + 7$ has $2w$ as the variable term and 7 as the constant term. It is important to realize that terms are separated by addition or subtraction. Since an expression is a sum of terms, expressions such as $5x - 3$ can be written as $5x + (-3)$ to emphasize that the constant term is negative. A real-world example of a single variable linear expression is the perimeter of a square, four times the side length, often expressed: $4s$.

In general, a **linear expression** is the sum of any number of variable terms so long as none of the variables have an exponent. For example, $3m + 8n - \frac{1}{4}p + 5.5q - 1$ is a linear expression, but $3y^3$ is not. In the same way, the expression for the perimeter of a general triangle, the sum of the side lengths $(a + b + c)$ is considered to be linear, but the expression for the area of a square, the side length squared (s^2) is not.

On a graph with two points, (x_1, y_1) and (x_2, y_2), the **slope** is found with the formula $m = \frac{y_2 - y_1}{x_2 - x_1}$; where $x_1 \neq x_2$ and m stands for slope. If the value of the slope is **positive**, the line has an *upward direction* from left to right. If the value of the slope is **negative**, the line has a *downward direction* from left to right. Consider the following example:

Copyright © Mometrix Media. You have been licensed one copy of this document for personal use only. Any other reproduction or redistribution is strictly prohibited. All rights reserved. This content is provided for test preparation purposes only and does not imply an endorsement by Mometrix of any particular political, scientific, or religious point of view.

A new book goes on sale in bookstores and online stores. In the first month, 5,000 copies of the book are sold. Over time, the book continues to grow in popularity. The data for the number of copies sold is in the table below.

# of Months on Sale	1	2	3	4	5
# of Copies Sold (In Thousands)	5	10	15	20	25

So, the number of copies that are sold and the time that the book is on sale is a proportional relationship. In this example, an equation can be used to show the data: $y = 5x$, where x is the number of months that the book is on sale. Also, y is the number of copies sold. So, the slope of the corresponding line is $\frac{\text{rise}}{\text{run}} = \frac{5}{1} = 5$.

> **Review Video: Finding the Slope of a Line**
> Visit mometrix.com/academy and enter code: 766664

Equations that can be written as $ax + b = 0$, where $a \neq 0$, are referred to as **one variable linear equations**. A solution to such an equation is called a **root**. In the case where we have the equation $5x + 10 = 0$, if we solve for x we get a solution of $x = -2$. In other words, the root of the equation is –2. This is found by first subtracting 10 from both sides, which gives $5x = -10$. Next, simply divide both sides by the coefficient of the variable, in this case 5, to get $x = -2$. This can be checked by plugging –2 back into the original equation $(5)(-2) + 10 = -10 + 10 = 0$.

The **solution set** is the set of all solutions of an equation. In our example, the solution set would simply be –2. If there were more solutions (there usually are in multivariable equations) then they would also be included in the solution set. When an equation has no true solutions, it is referred to as an **empty set**. Equations with identical solution sets are **equivalent equations**. An **identity** is a term whose value or determinant is equal to 1.

Linear equations can be written many ways. Below is a list of some forms linear equations can take:

- **Standard Form**: $Ax + By = C$; the slope is $\frac{-A}{B}$ and the y-intercept is $\frac{C}{B}$
- **Slope Intercept Form**: $y = mx + b$, where m is the slope and b is the y-intercept
- **Point-Slope Form**: $y - y_1 = m(x - x_1)$, where m is the slope and (x_1, y_1) is a point on the line
- **Two-Point Form**: $\frac{y - y_1}{x - x_1} = \frac{y_2 - y_1}{x_2 - x_1}$, where (x_1, y_1) and (x_2, y_2) are two points on the given line
- **Intercept Form**: $\frac{x}{x_1} + \frac{y}{y_1} = 1$, where $(x_1, 0)$ is the point at which a line intersects the x-axis, and $(0, y_1)$ is the point at which the same line intersects the y-axis

> **Review Video: Slope-Intercept and Point-Slope Forms**
> Visit mometrix.com/academy and enter code: 113216
>
> **Review Video: Linear Equations Basics**
> Visit mometrix.com/academy and enter code: 793005

SOLVING ONE-VARIABLE LINEAR EQUATIONS

Multiply all terms by the lowest common denominator to eliminate any fractions. Look for addition or subtraction to undo so you can isolate the variable on one side of the equal sign. Divide both

Copyright © Mometrix Media. You have been licensed one copy of this document for personal use only. Any other reproduction or redistribution is strictly prohibited. All rights reserved. This content is provided for test preparation purposes only and does not imply an endorsement by Mometrix of any particular political, scientific, or religious point of view.

sides by the coefficient of the variable. When you have a value for the variable, substitute this value into the original equation to make sure you have a true equation. Consider the following example:

Kim's savings are represented by the table below. Represent her savings, using an equation.

X (Months)	Y (Total Savings)
2	$1,300
5	$2,050
9	$3,050
11	$3,550
16	$4,800

The table shows a function with a constant rate of change, or slope, of 250. Given the points on the table, the slopes can be calculated as $\frac{(2,050-1300)}{(5-2)}$, $\frac{(3,050-2,050)}{(9-5)}$, $\frac{(3,550-3,050)}{(11-9)}$, and $\frac{(4,800-3,550)}{(16-11)}$, each of which equals 250. Thus, the table shows a constant rate of change, indicating a linear function. The slope-intercept form of a linear equation is written as $y = mx + b$, where m represents the slope and b represents the y-intercept. Substituting the slope into this form gives $y = 250x + b$. Substituting corresponding x- and y-values from any point into this equation will give the y-intercept, or b. Using the point, (2, 1,300), gives $1,300 = 250(2) + b$, which simplifies as $b = 800$. Thus, her savings may be represented by the equation, $y = 250x + 800$.

RULES FOR MANIPULATING EQUATIONS
LIKE TERMS

Like terms are terms in an equation that have the same variable, regardless of whether or not they also have the same coefficient. This includes terms that *lack* a variable; all constants (i.e., numbers without variables) are considered like terms. If the equation involves terms with a variable raised to different powers, the like terms are those that have the variable raised to the same power.

For example, consider the equation $x^2 + 3x + 2 = 2x^2 + x - 7 + 2x$. In this equation, 2 and –7 are like terms; they are both constants. $3x$, x, and $2x$ are like terms, they all include the variable x raised to the first power. x^2 and $2x^2$ are like terms, they both include the variable x, raised to the second power. $2x$ and $2x^2$ are not like terms; although they both involve the variable x, the variable is not raised to the same power in both terms. The fact that they have the same coefficient, 2, is not relevant.

> **Review Video: Rules for Manipulating Equations**
> Visit mometrix.com/academy and enter code: 838871

CARRYING OUT THE SAME OPERATION ON BOTH SIDES OF AN EQUATION

When solving an equation, the general procedure is to carry out a series of operations on both sides of an equation, choosing operations that will tend to simplify the equation when doing so. The reason why the same operation must be carried out on both sides of the equation is because that leaves the meaning of the equation unchanged, and yields a result that is equivalent to the original equation. This would not be the case if we carried out an operation on one side of an equation and not the other. Consider what an equation means: it is a statement that two values or expressions are equal. If we carry out the same operation on both sides of the equation—add 3 to both sides, for example—then the two sides of the equation are changed in the same way, and so remain equal. If

148

Copyright © Mometrix Media. You have been licensed one copy of this document for personal use only. Any other reproduction or redistribution is strictly prohibited. All rights reserved. This content is provided for test preparation purposes only and does not imply an endorsement by Mometrix of any particular political, scientific, or religious point of view.

we do that to only one side of the equation—add 3 to one side but not the other—then that wouldn't be true; if we change one side of the equation but not the other then the two sides are no longer equal.

ADVANTAGE OF COMBINING LIKE TERMS

Combining like terms refers to adding or subtracting like terms—terms with the same variable—and therefore reducing sets of like terms to a single term. The main advantage of doing this is that it simplifies the equation. Often, combining like terms can be done as the first step in solving an equation, though it can also be done later, such as after distributing terms in a product.

For example, consider the equation $2(x + 3) + 3(2 + x + 3) = -4$. The 2 and the 3 in the second set of parentheses are like terms, and we can combine them, yielding $2(x + 3) + 3(x + 5) = -4$. Now we can carry out the multiplications implied by the parentheses, distributing the outer 2 and 3 accordingly: $2x + 6 + 3x + 15 = -4$. The $2x$ and the $3x$ are like terms, and we can add them together: $5x + 6 + 15 = -4$. Now, the constants 6, 15, and –4 are also like terms, and we can combine them as well: subtracting 6 and 15 from both sides of the equation, we get $5x = -4 - 6 - 15$, or $5x = -25$, which simplifies further to $x = -5$.

> **Review Video: Solving Equations by Combining Like Terms**
> Visit mometrix.com/academy and enter code: 668506

CANCELING TERMS ON OPPOSITE SIDES OF AN EQUATION

Two terms on opposite sides of an equation can be canceled if and only if they *exactly* match each other. They must have the same variable raised to the same power and the same coefficient. For example, in the equation $3x + 2x^2 + 6 = 2x^2 - 6$, $2x^2$ appears on both sides of the equation and can be canceled, leaving $3x + 6 = -6$. The 6 on each side of the equation *cannot* be canceled, because it is added on one side of the equation and subtracted on the other. While they cannot be canceled, however, the 6 and –6 are like terms and can be combined, yielding $3x = -12$, which simplifies further to $x = -4$.

It's also important to note that the terms to be canceled must be independent terms and cannot be part of a larger term. For example, consider the equation $2(x + 6) = 3(x + 4) + 1$. We cannot cancel the x's, because even though they match each other they are part of the larger terms $2(x + 6)$ and $3(x + 4)$. We must first distribute the 2 and 3, yielding $2x + 12 = 3x + 12 + 1$. Now we see that the terms with the x's do not match, but the 12s do, and can be canceled, leaving $2x = 3x + 1$, which simplifies to $x = -1$.

PROCESS FOR MANIPULATING EQUATIONS

ISOLATING VARIABLES

To **isolate a variable** means to manipulate the equation so that the variable appears by itself on one side of the equation, and does not appear at all on the other side. Generally, an equation or inequality is considered to be solved once the variable is isolated and the other side of the equation or inequality is simplified as much as possible. In the case of a two-variable equation or inequality, only one variable needs to be isolated; it will not usually be possible to simultaneously isolate both variables.

For a linear equation—an equation in which the variable only appears raised to the first power—isolating a variable can be done by first moving all the terms with the variable to one side of the equation and all other terms to the other side. (*Moving* a term really means adding the inverse of the term to both sides; when a term is *moved* to the other side of the equation its sign is flipped.)

Copyright © Mometrix Media. You have been licensed one copy of this document for personal use only. Any other reproduction or redistribution is strictly prohibited. All rights reserved.
This content is provided for test preparation purposes only and does not imply an endorsement by Mometrix of any particular political, scientific, or religious point of view.

Then combine like terms on each side. Finally, divide both sides by the coefficient of the variable, if applicable. The steps need not necessarily be done in this order, but this order will always work.

Review Video: Solving One-Step Equations
Visit mometrix.com/academy and enter code: 777004

EQUATIONS WITH MORE THAN ONE SOLUTION

Some types of non-linear equations, such as equations involving squares of variables, may have more than one solution. For example, the equation $x^2 = 4$ has two solutions: 2 and –2. Equations with absolute values can also have multiple solutions: $|x| = 1$ has the solutions $x = 1$ and $x = -1$.

It is also possible for a linear equation to have more than one solution, but only if the equation is true regardless of the value of the variable. In this case, the equation is considered to have infinitely many solutions, because any possible value of the variable is a solution. We know a linear equation has infinitely many solutions if when we combine like terms the variables cancel, leaving a true statement. For example, consider the equation $2(3x + 5) = x + 5(x + 2)$. Distributing, we get $6x + 10 = x + 5x + 10$; combining like terms gives $6x + 10 = 6x + 10$, and the $6x$-terms cancel to leave $10 = 10$. This is clearly true, so the original equation is true for any value of x. We could also have canceled the 10s leaving $0 = 0$, but again this is clearly true—in general if both sides of the equation match exactly, it has infinitely many solutions.

EQUATIONS WITH NO SOLUTION

Some types of non-linear equations, such as equations involving squares of variables, may have no solution. For example, the equation $x^2 = -2$ has no solutions in the real numbers, because the square of any real number must be positive. Similarly, $|x| = -1$ has no solution, because the absolute value of a number is always positive.

It is also possible for an equation to have no solution even if does not involve any powers greater than one, absolute values, or other special functions. For example, the equation $2(x + 3) + x = 3x$ has no solution. We can see that if we try to solve it: first we distribute, leaving $2x + 6 + x = 3x$. But now if we try to combine all the terms with the variable, we find that they cancel: we have $3x$ on the left and $3x$ on the right, canceling to leave us with $6 = 0$. This is clearly false. In general, whenever the variable terms in an equation cancel leaving different constants on both sides, it means that the equation has no solution. (If we are left with the *same* constant on both sides, the equation has infinitely many solutions instead.)

FEATURES OF EQUATIONS THAT REQUIRE SPECIAL TREATMENT
LINEAR EQUATIONS

A linear equation is an equation in which variables only appear by themselves: not multiplied together, not with exponents other than one, and not inside absolute value signs or any other functions. For example, the equation $x + 1 - 3x = 5 - x$ is a linear equation; while x appears multiple times, it never appears with an exponent other than one, or inside any function. The two-variable equation $2x - 3y = 5 + 2x$ is also a linear equation. In contrast, the equation $x^2 - 5 = 3x$ is *not* a linear equation, because it involves the term x^2. $\sqrt{x} = 5$ is not a linear equation, because it involves a square root. $(x - 1)^2 = 4$ is not a linear equation because even though there's no exponent on the x directly, it appears as part of an expression that is squared. The two-variable equation $x + xy - y = 5$ is not a linear equation because it includes the term xy, where two variables are multiplied together.

Copyright © Mometrix Media. You have been licensed one copy of this document for personal use only. Any other reproduction or redistribution is strictly prohibited. All rights reserved.
This content is provided for test preparation purposes only and does not imply an endorsement by Mometrix of any particular political, scientific, or religious point of view.

Linear equations can always be solved (or shown to have no solution) by combining like terms and performing simple operations on both sides of the equation. Some non-linear equations can be solved by similar methods, but others may require more advanced methods of solution, if they can be solved analytically at all.

SOLVING EQUATIONS INVOLVING ROOTS

In an equation involving roots, the first step is to isolate the term with the root, if possible, and then raise both sides of the equation to the appropriate power to eliminate it. Consider an example equation, $2\sqrt{x+1} - 1 = 3$. In this case, begin by adding 1 to both sides, yielding $2\sqrt{x+1} = 4$, and then dividing both sides by 2, yielding $\sqrt{x+1} = 2$. Now square both sides, yielding $x + 1 = 4$. Finally, subtracting 1 from both sides yields $x = 3$.

Squaring both sides of an equation may, however, yield a spurious solution—a solution to the squared equation that is *not* a solution of the original equation. It's therefore necessary to plug the solution back into the original equation to make sure it works. In this case, it does: $2\sqrt{3+1} - 1 = 2\sqrt{4} - 1 = 2(2) - 1 = 4 - 1 = 3$.

The same procedure applies for other roots as well. For example, given the equation $3 + \sqrt[3]{2x} = 5$, we can first subtract 3 from both sides, yielding $\sqrt[3]{2x} = 2$ and isolating the root. Raising both sides to the third power yields $2x = 2^3$; i.e., $2x = 8$. We can now divide both sides by 2 to get $x = 4$.

> **Review Video: Solving Equations Involving Roots**
> Visit mometrix.com/academy and enter code: 297670

SOLVING EQUATIONS WITH EXPONENTS

To solve an equation involving an exponent, the first step is to isolate the variable with the exponent. We can then take the appropriate root of both sides to eliminate the exponent. For instance, for the equation $2x^3 + 17 = 5x^3 - 7$, we can subtract $5x^3$ from both sides to get $-3x^3 + 17 = -7$, and then subtract 17 from both sides to get $-3x^3 = -24$. Finally, we can divide both sides by –3 to get $x^3 = 8$. Finally, we can take the cube root of both sides to get $x = \sqrt[3]{8} = 2$.

One important but often overlooked point is that equations with an exponent greater than 1 may have more than one answer. The solution to $x^2 = 9$ isn't simply $x = 3$; it's $x = \pm 3$ (that is, $x = 3$ or $x = -3$). For a slightly more complicated example, consider the equation $(x - 1)^2 - 1 = 3$. Adding 1 to both sides yields $(x - 1)^2 = 4$; taking the square root of both sides yields $x - 1 = 2$. We can then add 1 to both sides to get $x = 3$. However, there's a second solution. We also have the possibility that $x - 1 = -2$, in which case $x = -1$. Both $x = 3$ and $x = -1$ are valid solutions, as can be verified by substituting them both into the original equation.

> **Review Video: Solving Equations with Exponents**
> Visit mometrix.com/academy and enter code: 514557

SOLVING EQUATIONS WITH ABSOLUTE VALUES

When solving an equation with an absolute value, the first step is to isolate the absolute value term. We then consider two possibilities: when the expression inside the absolute value is positive or when it is negative. In the former case, the expression in the absolute value equals the expression on the other side of the equation; in the latter, it equals the additive inverse of that expression—the expression times negative one. We consider each case separately and finally check for spurious solutions.

Copyright © Mometrix Media. You have been licensed one copy of this document for personal use only. Any other reproduction or redistribution is strictly prohibited. All rights reserved. This content is provided for test preparation purposes only and does not imply an endorsement by Mometrix of any particular political, scientific, or religious point of view.

For instance, consider solving $|2x - 1| + x = 5$ for x. We can first isolate the absolute value by moving the x to the other side: $|2x - 1| = -x + 5$. Now, we have two possibilities. First, that $2x - 1$ is positive, and hence $2x - 1 = -x + 5$. Rearranging and combining like terms yields $3x = 6$, and hence $x = 2$. The other possibility is that $2x - 1$ is negative, and hence $2x - 1 = -(-x + 5) = x - 5$. In this case, rearranging and combining like terms yields $x = -4$. Substituting $x = 2$ and $x = -4$ back into the original equation, we see that they are both valid solutions.

Note that the absolute value of a sum or difference applies to the sum or difference as a whole, not to the individual terms; in general, $|2x - 1|$ is not equal to $|2x + 1|$ or to $|2x| - 1$.

SPURIOUS SOLUTIONS

A **spurious solution** may arise when we square both sides of an equation as a step in solving it or under certain other operations on the equation. It is a solution to the squared or otherwise modified equation that is *not* a solution of the original equation. To identify a spurious solution, it's useful when you solve an equation involving roots or absolute values to plug the solution back into the original equation to make sure it's valid.

CHOOSING WHICH VARIABLE TO ISOLATE IN TWO-VARIABLE EQUATIONS

Similar to methods for a one-variable equation, solving a two-variable equation involves isolating a variable: manipulating the equation so that a variable appears by itself on one side of the equation, and not at all on the other side. However, in a two-variable equation, you will usually only be able to isolate one of the variables; the other variable may appear on the other side along with constant terms, or with exponents or other functions.

Often one variable will be much more easily isolated than the other, and therefore that's the variable you should choose. If one variable appears with various exponents, and the other is only raised to the first power, the latter variable is the one to isolate: given the equation $a^2 + 2b = a^3 + b + 3$, the b only appears to the first power, whereas a appears squared and cubed, so b is the variable that can be solved for: combining like terms and isolating the b on the left side of the equation, we get $b = a^3 - a^2 + 3$. If both variables are equally easy to isolate, then it's best to isolate the dependent variable, if one is defined; if the two variables are x and y, the convention is that y is the dependent variable.

> **Review Video: Solving Equations with Variables on Both Sides**
> Visit mometrix.com/academy and enter code: 402497

FINDING AN UNKNOWN IN EQUIVALENT EXPRESSIONS

It is often necessary to apply information given about a rate or proportion to a new scenario. For example, if you know that Jedha can run a marathon (26.2 miles) in 3 hours, how long would it take her to run 10 miles at the same pace? Start by setting up equivalent expressions:

$$\frac{26.2 \text{ mi}}{3 \text{ hr}} = \frac{10 \text{ mi}}{x \text{ hr}}$$

Now, cross multiply and solve for x:

$$26.2x = 30$$
$$x = \frac{30}{26.2} = \frac{15}{13.1}$$
$$x \approx 1.15 \text{ hrs } or \text{ 1 hr 9 min}$$

Copyright © Mometrix Media. You have been licensed one copy of this document for personal use only. Any other reproduction or redistribution is strictly prohibited. All rights reserved. This content is provided for test preparation purposes only and does not imply an endorsement by Mometrix of any particular political, scientific, or religious point of view.

So, at this pace, Jedha could run 10 miles in about 1.15 hours or about 1 hour and 9 minutes.

Review Video: Cross Multiplying Fractions
Visit mometrix.com/academy and enter code: 893904

GRAPHICAL SOLUTIONS TO EQUATIONS

When equations are shown graphically, they are usually shown on a **Cartesian coordinate plane**. The Cartesian coordinate plane consists of two number lines placed perpendicular to each other and intersecting at the zero point, also known as the origin. The horizontal number line is known as the x-axis, with positive values to the right of the origin, and negative values to the left of the origin. The vertical number line is known as the y-axis, with positive values above the origin, and negative values below the origin. Any point on the plane can be identified by an ordered pair in the form (x, y), called coordinates. The x-value of the coordinate is called the abscissa, and the y-value of the coordinate is called the ordinate. The two number lines divide the plane into **four quadrants**: I, II, III, and IV.

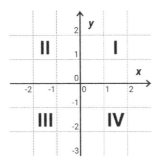

Note that in quadrant I $x > 0$ and $y > 0$, in quadrant II $x < 0$ and $y > 0$, in quadrant III $x < 0$ and $y < 0$, and in quadrant IV $x > 0$ and $y < 0$.

Recall that if the value of the slope of a line is positive, the line slopes upward from left to right. If the value of the slope is negative, the line slopes downward from left to right. If the y-coordinates are the same for two points on a line, the slope is 0 and the line is a **horizontal line**. If the x-coordinates are the same for two points on a line, there is no slope and the line is a **vertical line**. Two or more lines that have equivalent slopes are **parallel lines**. **Perpendicular lines** have slopes that are negative reciprocals of each other, such as $\frac{a}{b}$ and $\frac{-b}{a}$.

Review Video: Cartesian Coordinate Plane and Graphing
Visit mometrix.com/academy and enter code: 115173

GRAPHING EQUATIONS IN TWO VARIABLES

One way of graphing an equation in two variables is to plot enough points to get an idea for its shape and then draw the appropriate curve through those points. A point can be plotted by substituting in a value for one variable and solving for the other. If the equation is linear, we only need two points and can then draw a straight line between them.

For example, consider the equation $y = 2x - 1$. This is a linear equation—both variables only appear raised to the first power—so we only need two points. When $x = 0$, $y = 2(0) - 1 = -1$.

Copyright © Mometrix Media. You have been licensed one copy of this document for personal use only. Any other reproduction or redistribution is strictly prohibited. All rights reserved. This content is provided for test preparation purposes only and does not imply an endorsement by Mometrix of any particular political, scientific, or religious point of view.

When $x = 2$, $y = 2(2) - 1 = 3$. We can therefore choose the points $(0, -1)$ and $(2, 3)$, and draw a line between them:

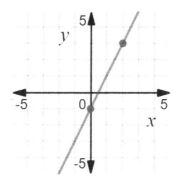

WORKING WITH INEQUALITIES

Commonly in algebra and other upper-level fields of math you find yourself working with mathematical expressions that do not equal each other. The statement comparing such expressions with symbols such as $<$ (less than) or $>$ (greater than) is called an *inequality*. An example of an inequality is $7x > 5$. To solve for x, simply divide both sides by 7 and the solution is shown to be $x > \frac{5}{7}$. Graphs of the solution set of inequalities are represented on a number line. Open circles are used to show that an expression approaches a number but is never quite equal to that number.

> **Review Video: Solving Multi-Step Inequalities**
> Visit mometrix.com/academy and enter code: 347842
>
> **Review Video: Solving Inequalities Using All 4 Basic Operations**
> Visit mometrix.com/academy and enter code: 401111

Conditional inequalities are those with certain values for the variable that will make the condition true and other values for the variable where the condition will be false. **Absolute inequalities** can have any real number as the value for the variable to make the condition true, while there is no real number value for the variable that will make the condition false. Solving inequalities is done by following the same rules for solving equations with the exception that when multiplying or dividing by a negative number the direction of the inequality sign must be flipped or reversed. **Double inequalities** are situations where two inequality statements apply to the same variable expression. Example: $-c < ax + b < c$.

> **Review Video: Conditional and Absolute Inequalities**
> Visit mometrix.com/academy and enter code: 980164

DETERMINING SOLUTIONS TO INEQUALITIES

To determine whether a coordinate is a solution of an inequality, you can substitute the values of the coordinate into the inequality, simplify, and check whether the resulting statement holds true. For instance, to determine whether $(-2,4)$ is a solution of the inequality $y \geq -2x + 3$, substitute the values into the inequality, $4 \geq -2(-2) + 3$. Simplify the right side of the inequality and the result is $4 \geq 7$, which is a false statement. Therefore, the coordinate is not a solution of the inequality. You can also use this method to determine which part of the graph of an inequality is

Copyright © Mometrix Media. You have been licensed one copy of this document for personal use only. Any other reproduction or redistribution is strictly prohibited. All rights reserved.
This content is provided for test preparation purposes only and does not imply an endorsement by Mometrix of any particular political, scientific, or religious point of view.

shaded. The graph of $y \geq -2x + 3$ includes the solid line $y = -2x + 3$ and, since it excludes the point $(-2,4)$ to the left of the line, it is shaded to the right of the line.

Review Video: <u>Graphing Linear Inequalities</u>
Visit mometrix.com/academy and enter code: 439421

FLIPPING INEQUALITY SIGNS

When given an inequality, we can always turn the entire inequality around, swapping the two sides of the inequality and changing the inequality sign. For instance, $x + 2 > 2x - 3$ is equivalent to $2x - 3 < x + 2$. Aside from that, normally the inequality does not change if we carry out the same operation on both sides of the inequality. There is, however, one principal exception: if we *multiply* or *divide* both sides of the inequality by a *negative number*, the inequality is flipped. For example, if we take the inequality $-2x < 6$ and divide both sides by -2, the inequality flips and we are left with $x > -3$. This *only* applies to multiplication and division, and only with negative numbers. Multiplying or dividing both sides by a positive number, or adding or subtracting any number regardless of sign, does not flip the inequality. Another special case that flips the inequality sign is when reciprocals are used. For instance, $3 > 2$ but the relation of the reciprocals is $\frac{1}{2} < \frac{1}{3}$.

COMPOUND INEQUALITIES

A **compound inequality** is an equality that consists of two inequalities combined with *and* or *or*. The two components of a proper compound inequality must be of opposite type: that is, one must be greater than (or greater than or equal to), the other less than (or less than or equal to). For instance, "$x + 1 < 2$ or $x + 1 > 3$" is a compound inequality, as is "$2x \geq 4$ and $2x \leq 6$." An *and* inequality can be written more compactly by having one inequality on each side of the common part: "$2x \geq 1$ and $2x \leq 6$," can also be written as $1 \leq 2x \leq 6$.

In order for the compound inequality to be meaningful, the two parts of an *and* inequality must overlap; otherwise, no numbers satisfy the inequality. On the other hand, if the two parts of an *or* inequality overlap, then *all* numbers satisfy the inequality and as such the inequality is usually not meaningful.

Solving a compound inequality requires solving each part separately. For example, given the compound inequality "$x + 1 < 2$ or $x + 1 > 3$," the first inequality, $x + 1 < 2$, reduces to $x < 1$, and the second part, $x + 1 > 3$, reduces to $x > 2$, so the whole compound inequality can be written as "$x < 1$ or $x > 2$." Similarly, $1 \leq 2x \leq 6$ can be solved by dividing each term by 2, yielding $\frac{1}{2} \leq x \leq 3$.

Review Video: <u>Compound Inequalities</u>
Visit mometrix.com/academy and enter code: 786318

SOLVING INEQUALITIES INVOLVING ABSOLUTE VALUES

To solve an inequality involving an absolute value, first isolate the term with the absolute value. Then proceed to treat the two cases separately as with an absolute value equation, but flipping the inequality in the case where the expression in the absolute value is negative (since that essentially involves multiplying both sides by -1.) The two cases are then combined into a compound inequality; if the absolute value is on the greater side of the inequality, then it is an *or* compound inequality, if on the lesser side, then it's an *and*.

Consider the inequality $2 + |x - 1| \geq 3$. We can isolate the absolute value term by subtracting 2 from both sides: $|x - 1| \geq 1$. Now, we're left with the two cases $x - 1 \geq 1$ or $x - 1 \leq -1$: note that in the latter, negative case, the inequality is flipped. $x - 1 \geq 1$ reduces to $x \geq 2$, and $x - 1 \leq -1$

155

Copyright © Mometrix Media. You have been licensed one copy of this document for personal use only. Any other reproduction or redistribution is strictly prohibited. All rights reserved. This content is provided for test preparation purposes only and does not imply an endorsement by Mometrix of any particular political, scientific, or religious point of view.

reduces to $x \leq 0$. Since in the inequality $|x - 1| \geq 1$ the absolute value is on the greater side, the two cases combine into an *or* compound inequality, so the final, solved inequality is "$x \leq 0$ or $x \geq 2$."

> **Review Video: <u>Solving Absolute Value Inequalities</u>**
> Visit mometrix.com/academy and enter code: 997008

SOLVING INEQUALITIES INVOLVING SQUARE ROOTS

Solving an inequality with a square root involves two parts. First, we solve the inequality as if it were an equation, isolating the square root and then squaring both sides of the equation. Second, we restrict the solution to the set of values of x for which the value inside the square root sign is non-negative.

For example, in the inequality, $\sqrt{x - 2} + 1 < 5$, we can isolate the square root by subtracting 1 from both sides, yielding $\sqrt{x - 2} < 4$. Squaring both sides of the inequality yields $x - 2 < 16$, so $x < 18$. Since we can't take the square root of a negative number, we also require the part inside the square root to be non-negative. In this case, that means $x - 2 \geq 0$. Adding 2 to both sides of the inequality yields $x \geq 2$. Our final answer is a compound inequality combining the two simple inequalities: $x \geq 2$ and $x < 18$, or $2 \leq x < 18$.

Note that we only get a compound inequality if the two simple inequalities are in opposite directions; otherwise, we take the one that is more restrictive.

The same technique can be used for other even roots, such as fourth roots. It is *not*, however, used for cube roots or other odd roots—negative numbers *do* have cube roots, so the condition that the quantity inside the root sign cannot be negative does not apply.

> **Review Video: <u>Solving Inequalities Involving Square Roots</u>**
> Visit mometrix.com/academy and enter code: 800288

SPECIAL CIRCUMSTANCES

Sometimes an inequality involving an absolute value or an even exponent is true for all values of x, and we don't need to do any further work to solve it. This is true if the inequality, once the absolute value or exponent term is isolated, says that term is greater than a negative number (or greater than or equal to zero). Since an absolute value or a number raised to an even exponent is *always* non-negative, this inequality is always true.

GRAPHICAL SOLUTIONS TO INEQUALITIES
GRAPHING SIMPLE INEQUALITIES

To graph a simple inequality, we first mark on the number line the value that signifies the end point of the inequality. If the inequality is strict (involves a less than or greater than), we use a hollow circle; if it is not strict (less than or equal to or greater than or equal to), we use a solid circle. We then fill in the part of the number line that satisfies the inequality: to the left of the marked point for less than (or less than or equal to), to the right for greater than (or greater than or equal to).

For example, we would graph the inequality $x < 5$ by putting a hollow circle at 5 and filling in the part of the line to the left:

Copyright © Mometrix Media. You have been licensed one copy of this document for personal use only. Any other reproduction or redistribution is strictly prohibited. All rights reserved.
This content is provided for test preparation purposes only and does not imply an endorsement by Mometrix of any particular political, scientific, or religious point of view.

GRAPHING COMPOUND INEQUALITIES

To graph a compound inequality, we fill in both parts of the inequality for an *or* inequality, or the overlap between them for an *and* inequality. More specifically, we start by plotting the endpoints of each inequality on the number line. For an *or* inequality, we then fill in the appropriate side of the line for each inequality. Typically, the two component inequalities do not overlap, which means the shaded part is *outside* the two points. For an *and* inequality, we instead fill in the part of the line that meets both inequalities.

For the inequality "$x \leq -3$ or $x > 4$," we first put a solid circle at –3 and a hollow circle at 4. We then fill the parts of the line *outside* these circles:

GRAPHING INEQUALITIES INCLUDING ABSOLUTE VALUES

An inequality with an absolute value can be converted to a compound inequality. To graph the inequality, first convert it to a compound inequality, and then graph that normally. If the absolute value is on the greater side of the inequality, we end up with an *or* inequality; we plot the endpoints of the inequality on the number line and fill in the part of the line *outside* those points. If the absolute value is on the smaller side of the inequality, we end up with an *and* inequality; we plot the endpoints of the inequality on the number line and fill in the part of the line *between* those points.

For example, the inequality $|x + 1| \geq 4$ can be rewritten as $x \geq 3$ or $x \leq -5$. We place solid circles at the points 3 and –5 and fill in the part of the line *outside* them:

GRAPHING INEQUALITIES IN TWO VARIABLES

To graph an inequality in two variables, we first graph the border of the inequality. This means graphing the equation that we get if we replace the inequality sign with an equals sign. If the inequality is strict ($>$ or $<$), we graph the border with a dashed or dotted line; if it is not strict ($\geq$ or $\leq$), we use a solid line. We can then test any point not on the border to see if it satisfies the inequality. If it does, we shade in that side of the border; if not, we shade in the other side. As an example, consider $y > 2x + 2$. To graph this inequality, we first graph the border, $y = 2x + 2$. Since it is a strict inequality, we use a dashed line. Then, we choose a test point. This can be any point not on the border; in this case, we will choose the origin, (0,0). (This makes the calculation easy and is generally a good choice unless the border passes through the origin.) Putting this into the original

Copyright © Mometrix Media. You have been licensed one copy of this document for personal use only. Any other reproduction or redistribution is strictly prohibited. All rights reserved.
This content is provided for test preparation purposes only and does not imply an endorsement by Mometrix of any particular political, scientific, or religious point of view.

inequality, we get $0 > 2(0) + 2$, i.e., $0 > 2$. This is *not* true, so we shade in the side of the border that does *not* include the point (0,0):

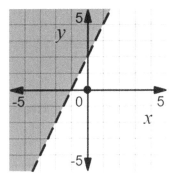

GRAPHING COMPOUND INEQUALITIES IN TWO VARIABLES

One way to graph a compound inequality in two variables is to first graph each of the component inequalities. For an *and* inequality, we then shade in only the parts where the two graphs overlap; for an *or* inequality, we shade in any region that pertains to either of the individual inequalities.

Consider the graph of "$y \geq x - 1$ and $y \leq -x$":

We first shade in the individual inequalities:

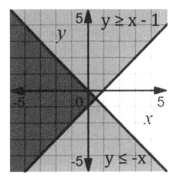

Now, since the compound inequality has an *and*, we only leave shaded the overlap—the part that pertains to *both* inequalities:

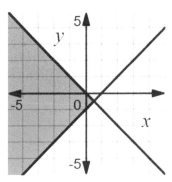

Copyright © Mometrix Media. You have been licensed one copy of this document for personal use only. Any other reproduction or redistribution is strictly prohibited. All rights reserved. This content is provided for test preparation purposes only and does not imply an endorsement by Mometrix of any particular political, scientific, or religious point of view.

If instead the inequality had been "$y \geq x - 1$ or $y \leq -x$," our final graph would involve the *total* shaded area:

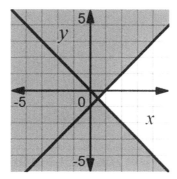

Review Video: Graphing Solutions to Inequalities
Visit mometrix.com/academy and enter code: 391281

SOLVING SYSTEMS OF EQUATIONS

A **system of equations** is a set of simultaneous equations that all use the same variables. A solution to a system of equations must be true for each equation in the system. **Consistent systems** are those with at least one solution. **Inconsistent systems** are systems of equations that have no solution.

Review Video: Solving Systems of Linear Equations
Visit mometrix.com/academy and enter code: 746745

SUBSTITUTION

To solve a system of linear equations by **substitution**, start with the easier equation and solve for one of the variables. Express this variable in terms of the other variable. Substitute this expression in the other equation and solve for the other variable. The solution should be expressed in the form (x, y). Substitute the values into both of the original equations to check your answer. Consider the following system of equations:

$$x + 6y = 15$$
$$3x - 12y = 18$$

Solving the first equation for x: $x = 15 - 6y$

Substitute this value in place of x in the second equation, and solve for y:

$$3(15 - 6y) - 12y = 18$$
$$45 - 18y - 12y = 18$$
$$30y = 27$$
$$y = \frac{27}{30} = \frac{9}{10} = 0.9$$

Copyright © Mometrix Media. You have been licensed one copy of this document for personal use only. Any other reproduction or redistribution is strictly prohibited. All rights reserved.
This content is provided for test preparation purposes only and does not imply an endorsement by Mometrix of any particular political, scientific, or religious point of view.

Plug this value for y back into the first equation to solve for x:

$$x = 15 - 6(0.9) = 15 - 5.4 = 9.6$$

Check both equations if you have time:

$$9.6 + 6(0.9) = 15 \qquad\qquad 3(9.6) - 12(0.9) = 18$$
$$9.6 + 5.4 = 15 \qquad\qquad 28.8 - 10.8 = 18$$
$$15 = 15 \qquad\qquad\qquad\qquad 18 = 18$$

Therefore, the solution is $(9.6, 0.9)$.

Review Video: The Substitution Method
Visit mometrix.com/academy and enter code: 565151

Review Video: Substitution and Elimination
Visit mometrix.com/academy and enter code: 958611

ELIMINATION

To solve a system of equations using **elimination**, begin by rewriting both equations in standard form $Ax + By = C$. Check to see if the coefficients of one pair of like variables add to zero. If not, multiply one or both of the equations by a non-zero number to make one set of like variables add to zero. Add the two equations to solve for one of the variables. Substitute this value into one of the original equations to solve for the other variable. Check your work by substituting into the other equation. Now, let's look at solving the following system using the elimination method:

$$5x + 6y = 4$$
$$x + 2y = 4$$

If we multiply the second equation by -3, we can eliminate the y-terms:

$$5x + 6y = 4$$
$$-3x - 6y = -12$$

Add the equations together and solve for x:

$$2x = -8$$
$$x = \frac{-8}{2} = -4$$

Plug the value for x back in to either of the original equations and solve for y:

$$-4 + 2y = 4$$
$$y = \frac{4+4}{2} = 4$$

Check both equations if you have time:

$$5(-4) + 6(4) = 4 \qquad\qquad -4 + 2(4) = 4$$
$$-20 + 24 = 4 \qquad\qquad -4 + 8 = 4$$
$$4 = 4 \qquad\qquad\qquad 4 = 4$$

Copyright © Mometrix Media. You have been licensed one copy of this document for personal use only. Any other reproduction or redistribution is strictly prohibited. All rights reserved. This content is provided for test preparation purposes only and does not imply an endorsement by Mometrix of any particular political, scientific, or religious point of view.

Therefore, the solution is $(-4,4)$.

Review Video: The Elimination Method
Visit mometrix.com/academy and enter code: 449121

GRAPHICALLY

To solve a system of linear equations **graphically**, plot both equations on the same graph. The solution of the equations is the point where both lines cross. If the lines do not cross (are parallel), then there is **no solution**.

For example, consider the following system of equations:

$$y = 2x + 7$$
$$y = -x + 1$$

Since these equations are given in slope-intercept form, they are easy to graph; the y-intercepts of the lines are $(0,7)$ and $(0,1)$. The respective slopes are 2 and –1, thus the graphs look like this:

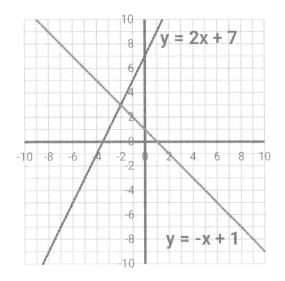

The two lines intersect at the point $(-2,3)$, thus this is the solution to the system of equations.

Solving a system graphically is generally only practical if both coordinates of the solution are integers; otherwise the intersection will lie between gridlines on the graph and the coordinates will be difficult or impossible to determine exactly. It also helps if, as in this example, the equations are in slope-intercept form or some other form that makes them easy to graph. Otherwise, another method of solution (by substitution or elimination) is likely to be more useful.

Review Video: Solving Systems by Graphing
Visit mometrix.com/academy and enter code: 634812

SOLVING SYSTEMS OF EQUATIONS USING THE TRACE FEATURE

Using the trace feature on a calculator requires that you rewrite each equation, isolating the y-variable on one side of the equal sign. Enter both equations in the graphing calculator and plot the graphs simultaneously. Use the trace cursor to find where the two lines cross. Use the zoom feature if necessary to obtain more accurate results. Always check your answer by substituting into the

Copyright © Mometrix Media. You have been licensed one copy of this document for personal use only. Any other reproduction or redistribution is strictly prohibited. All rights reserved.
This content is provided for test preparation purposes only and does not imply an endorsement by Mometrix of any particular political, scientific, or religious point of view.

original equations. The trace method is likely to be less accurate than other methods due to the resolution of graphing calculators but is a useful tool to provide an approximate answer.

MONOMIALS AND POLYNOMIALS

A **monomial** is a single constant, variable, or product of constants and variables, such as 7, x, $2x$, or $x^3 y$. There will never be addition or subtraction symbols in a monomial. Like monomials have like variables, but they may have different coefficients. **Polynomials** are algebraic expressions that use addition and subtraction to combine two or more monomials. Two terms make a **binomial**, three terms make a **trinomial**, etc. The **degree of a monomial** is the sum of the exponents of the variables. The **degree of a polynomial** is the highest degree of any individual term.

> **Review Video: Polynomials**
> Visit mometrix.com/academy and enter code: 305005

SIMPLIFYING POLYNOMIALS

Simplifying polynomials requires combining like terms. The like terms in a polynomial expression are those that have the same variable raised to the same power. It is often helpful to connect the like terms with arrows or lines in order to separate them from the other monomials. Once you have determined the like terms, you can rearrange the polynomial by placing them together. Remember to include the sign that is in front of each term. Once the like terms are placed together, you can apply each operation and simplify. When adding and subtracting polynomials, only add and subtract the **coefficient**, or the number part; the variable and exponent stay the same.

> **Review Video: Adding and Subtracting Polynomials**
> Visit mometrix.com/academy and enter code: 124088

THE FOIL METHOD

In general, multiplying polynomials is done by multiplying each term in one polynomial by each term in the other and adding the results. In the specific case for multiplying binomials, there is a useful acronym, FOIL, that can help you make sure to cover each combination of terms. The **FOIL method** for $(Ax + By)(Cx + Dy)$ would be:

F Multiply the *first* terms of each binomial $(\overset{first}{\overbrace{Ax}} + By)(\overset{first}{\overbrace{Cx}} + Dy)$ ACx^2

O Multiply the *outer* terms $(\overset{outer}{\overbrace{Ax}} + By)(Cx + \overset{outer}{\overbrace{Dy}})$ $ADxy$

I Multiply the *inner* terms $(Ax + \overset{inner}{\overbrace{By}})(\overset{inner}{\overbrace{Cx}} + Dy)$ $BCxy$

L Multiply the *last* terms of each binomial $(Ax + \overset{last}{\overbrace{By}})(Cx + \overset{last}{\overbrace{Dy}})$ BDy^2

Then, add up the result of each and combine like terms: $ACx^2 + (AD + BC)xy + BDy^2$.

For example, using the FOIL method on binomials $(x + 2)$ and $(x - 3)$:

$$\text{First:} \quad (\boxed{x} + 2)(\boxed{x} + (-3)) \;\rightarrow\; (x)(x) = x^2$$
$$\text{Outer:} \quad (\boxed{x} + 2)(x + \boxed{(-3)}) \;\rightarrow\; (x)(-3) = -3x$$
$$\text{Inner:} \quad (x + \boxed{2})(\boxed{x} + (-3)) \;\rightarrow\; (2)(x) = 2x$$
$$\text{Last:} \quad (x + \boxed{2})(x + \boxed{(-3)}) \;\rightarrow\; (2)(-3) = -6$$

Copyright © Mometrix Media. You have been licensed one copy of this document for personal use only. Any other reproduction or redistribution is strictly prohibited. All rights reserved.
This content is provided for test preparation purposes only and does not imply an endorsement by Mometrix of any particular political, scientific, or religious point of view.

This results in: $(x^2) + (-3x) + (2x) + (-6)$

Combine like terms: $x^2 + (-3 + 2)x + (-6) = x^2 - x - 6$

Review Video: <u>Multiplying Terms Using the FOIL Method</u>
Visit mometrix.com/academy and enter code: 854792

DIVIDING POLYNOMIALS

Use long division to divide a polynomial by either a monomial or another polynomial of equal or lesser degree.

When **dividing by a monomial**, divide each term of the polynomial by the monomial.

When **dividing by a polynomial**, begin by arranging the terms of each polynomial in order of one variable. You may arrange in ascending or descending order, but be consistent with both polynomials. To get the first term of the quotient, divide the first term of the dividend by the first term of the divisor. Multiply the first term of the quotient by the entire divisor and subtract that product from the dividend. Repeat for the second and successive terms until you either get a remainder of zero or a remainder whose degree is less than the degree of the divisor. If the quotient has a remainder, write the answer as a mixed expression in the form:

$$\text{quotient} + \frac{\text{remainder}}{\text{divisor}}$$

For example, we can evaluate the following expression in the same way as long division:

$$\frac{x^3 - 3x^2 - 2x + 5}{x - 5}$$

$$
\begin{array}{r}
x^2 + 2x + 8 \\
x - 5 \overline{\smash{\big)}\ x^3 - 3x^2 - 2x + 5} \\
\underline{-(x^3 - 5x^2)} \\
2x^2 - 2x \\
\underline{-(2x^2 - 10x)} \\
8x + 5 \\
\underline{-(8x - 40)} \\
45
\end{array}
$$

$$\frac{x^3 - 3x^2 - 2x + 5}{x - 5} = x^2 + 2x + 8 + \frac{45}{x - 5}$$

When **factoring** a polynomial, first check for a common monomial factor, that is, look to see if each coefficient has a common factor or if each term has an x in it. If the factor is a trinomial but not a perfect trinomial square, look for a factorable form, such as one of these:

$$x^2 + (a + b)x + ab = (x + a)(x + b)$$
$$(ac)x^2 + (ad + bc)x + bd = (ax + b)(cx + d)$$

For factors with four terms, look for groups to factor. Once you have found the factors, write the original polynomial as the product of all the factors. Make sure all of the polynomial factors are

163

Copyright © Mometrix Media. You have been licensed one copy of this document for personal use only. Any other reproduction or redistribution is strictly prohibited. All rights reserved.
This content is provided for test preparation purposes only and does not imply an endorsement by Mometrix of any particular political, scientific, or religious point of view.

prime. Monomial factors may be *prime* or *composite*. Check your work by multiplying the factors to make sure you get the original polynomial.

Below are patterns of some special products to remember to help make factoring easier:

- Perfect trinomial squares: $x^2 + 2xy + y^2 = (x + y)^2$ or $x^2 - 2xy + y^2 = (x - y)^2$
- Difference between two squares: $x^2 - y^2 = (x + y)(x - y)$
- Sum of two cubes: $x^3 + y^3 = (x + y)(x^2 - xy + y^2)$
  - Note: the second factor is *not* the same as a perfect trinomial square, so do not try to factor it further.
- Difference between two cubes: $x^3 - y^3 = (x - y)(x^2 + xy + y^2)$
  - Again, the second factor is *not* the same as a perfect trinomial square.
- Perfect cubes: $x^3 + 3x^2y + 3xy^2 + y^3 = (x + y)^3$ and $x^3 - 3x^2y + 3xy^2 - y^3 = (x - y)^3$

Rational expressions are fractions with polynomials in both the numerator and the denominator; the value of the polynomial in the denominator cannot be equal to zero. Be sure to keep track of values that make the denominator of the original expression zero as the final result inherits the same restrictions. For example, a denominator of $x - 3$ indicates that the expression is not defined when $x = 3$ and, as such, regardless of any operations done to the expression, it remains undefined there.

To **add or subtract** rational expressions, first find the common denominator, then rewrite each fraction as an equivalent fraction with the common denominator. Finally, add or subtract the numerators to get the numerator of the answer, and keep the common denominator as the denominator of the answer.

When **multiplying** rational expressions, factor each polynomial and cancel like factors (a factor which appears in both the numerator and the denominator). Then, multiply all remaining factors in the numerator to get the numerator of the product, and multiply the remaining factors in the denominator to get the denominator of the product. Remember: cancel entire factors, not individual terms.

To **divide** rational expressions, take the reciprocal of the divisor (the rational expression you are dividing by) and multiply by the dividend.

> **Review Video: Rational Expressions**
> Visit mometrix.com/academy and enter code: 415183

SIMPLIFYING RATIONAL EXPRESSIONS

To simplify a rational expression, factor the numerator and denominator completely. Factors that are the same and appear in the numerator and denominator have a ratio of 1. For example, look at the following expression:

$$\frac{x - 1}{1 - x^2}$$

Copyright © Mometrix Media. You have been licensed one copy of this document for personal use only. Any other reproduction or redistribution is strictly prohibited. All rights reserved.
This content is provided for test preparation purposes only and does not imply an endorsement by Mometrix of any particular political, scientific, or religious point of view.

The denominator, $(1 - x^2)$, is a difference of squares. It can be factored as $(1 - x)(1 + x)$. The factor $1 - x$ and the numerator $x - 1$ are opposites and have a ratio of –1. Rewrite the numerator as $-1(1 - x)$. So, the rational expression can be simplified as follows:

$$\frac{x - 1}{1 - x^2} = \frac{-1(1 - x)}{(1 - x)(1 + x)} = \frac{-1}{1 + x}$$

Note that since the original expression is only defined for $x \neq \{-1, 1\}$, the simplified expression has the same restrictions.

> **Review Video: Reducing Rational Expressions**
> Visit mometrix.com/academy and enter code: 788868

SOLVING QUADRATIC EQUATIONS

Quadratic equations are a special set of trinomials of the form $y = ax^2 + bx + c$ that occur commonly in math and real-world applications. The **roots** of a quadratic equation are the solutions that satisfy the equation when $y = 0$; in other words, where the graph touches the x-axis. There are several ways to determine these solutions including using the quadratic formula, factoring, completing the square, and graphing the function.

> **Review Video: Quadratic Equations Overview**
> Visit mometrix.com/academy and enter code: 476276
>
> **Review Video: Solutions of a Quadratic Equation on a Graph**
> Visit mometrix.com/academy and enter code: 328231

QUADRATIC FORMULA

The **quadratic formula** is used to solve quadratic equations when other methods are more difficult. To use the quadratic formula to solve a quadratic equation, begin by rewriting the equation in standard form $ax^2 + bx + c = 0$, where a, b, and c are coefficients. Once you have identified the values of the coefficients, substitute those values into the quadratic formula

$$x = \frac{-b \pm \sqrt{b^2 - 4ac}}{2a}$$

Evaluate the equation and simplify the expression. Again, check each root by substituting into the original equation. In the quadratic formula, the portion of the formula under the radical ($b^2 - 4ac$) is called the **discriminant**. If the discriminant is zero, there is only one root: $-\frac{b}{2a}$. If the discriminant is positive, there are two different real roots. If the discriminant is negative, there are no real roots; you will instead find complex roots. Often these solutions don't make sense in context and are ignored.

> **Review Video: Using the Quadratic Formula**
> Visit mometrix.com/academy and enter code: 163102

FACTORING

To solve a quadratic equation by factoring, begin by rewriting the equation in standard form, $x^2 + bx + c = 0$. Remember that the goal of factoring is to find numbers f and g such that $(x + f)(x + g) = x^2 + (f + g)x + fg$, in other words $(f + g) = b$ and $fg = c$. This can be a really

Copyright © Mometrix Media. You have been licensed one copy of this document for personal use only. Any other reproduction or redistribution is strictly prohibited. All rights reserved.
This content is provided for test preparation purposes only and does not imply an endorsement by Mometrix of any particular political, scientific, or religious point of view.

useful method when b and c are integers. Determine the factors of c and look for pairs that could sum to b.

For example, consider finding the roots of $x^2 + 6x - 16 = 0$. The factors of -16 include, -4 and 4, -8 and 2, -2 and 8, -1 and 16, and 1 and -16. The factors that sum to 6 are -2 and 8. Write these factors as the product of two binomials, $0 = (x - 2)(x + 8)$. Finally, since these binomials multiply together to equal zero, set them each equal to zero and solve each for x. This results in $x - 2 = 0$, which simplifies to $x = 2$ and $x + 8 = 0$, which simplifies to $x = -8$. Therefore, the roots of the equation are 2 and -8.

> **Review Video: Factoring Quadratic Equations**
> Visit mometrix.com/academy and enter code: 336566

COMPLETING THE SQUARE

One way to find the roots of a quadratic equation is to find a way to manipulate it such that it follows the form of a perfect square $(x^2 + 2px + p^2)$ by adding and subtracting a constant. This process is called **completing the square**. In other words, if you are given a quadratic that is not a perfect square, $x^2 + bx + c = 0$, you can find a constant d that could be added in to make it a perfect square:

$$x^2 + bx + c + (d - d) = 0; \{\text{Let } b = 2p \text{ and } c + d = p^2\}$$

then:

$$x^2 + 2px + p^2 - d = 0 \text{ and } d = \frac{b^2}{4} - c$$

Once you have completed the square you can find the roots of the resulting equation:

$$x^2 + 2px + p^2 - d = 0$$
$$(x + p)^2 = d$$
$$x + p = \pm\sqrt{d}$$
$$x = -p \pm \sqrt{d}$$

It is worth noting that substituting the original expressions into this solution gives the same result as the quadratic formula where $a = 1$:

$$x = -p \pm \sqrt{d} = -\frac{b}{2} \pm \sqrt{\frac{b^2}{4} - c} = -\frac{b}{2} \pm \frac{\sqrt{b^2 - 4c}}{2} = \frac{-b \pm \sqrt{b^2 - 4c}}{2}$$

Copyright © Mometrix Media. You have been licensed one copy of this document for personal use only. Any other reproduction or redistribution is strictly prohibited. All rights reserved. This content is provided for test preparation purposes only and does not imply an endorsement by Mometrix of any particular political, scientific, or religious point of view.

Completing the square can be seen as arranging block representations of each of the terms to be as close to a square as possible and then filling in the gaps. For example, consider the quadratic expression $x^2 + 6x + 2$:

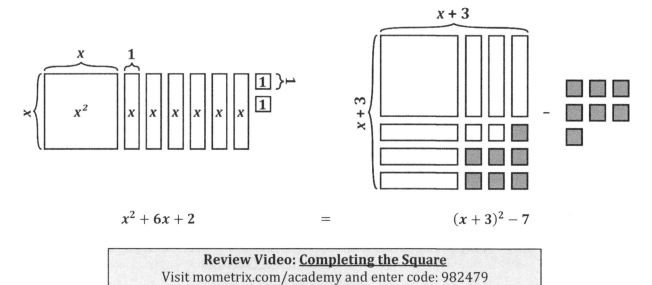

$$x^2 + 6x + 2 \qquad = \qquad (x + 3)^2 - 7$$

> **Review Video: Completing the Square**
> Visit mometrix.com/academy and enter code: 982479

USING GIVEN ROOTS TO FIND QUADRATIC EQUATION

One way to find the roots of a quadratic equation is to factor the equation and use the **zero product property**, setting each factor of the equation equal to zero to find the corresponding root. We can use this technique in reverse to find an equation given its roots. Each root corresponds to a linear equation which in turn corresponds to a factor of the quadratic equation.

For example, we can find a quadratic equation whose roots are $x = 2$ and $x = -1$. The root $x = 2$ corresponds to the equation $x - 2 = 0$, and the root $x = -1$ corresponds to the equation $x + 1 = 0$.

These two equations correspond to the factors $(x - 2)$ and $(x + 1)$, from which we can derive the equation $(x - 2)(x + 1) = 0$, or $x^2 - x - 2 = 0$.

Any integer multiple of this entire equation will also yield the same roots, as the integer will simply cancel out when the equation is factored. For example, $2x^2 - 2x - 4 = 0$ factors as $2(x - 2)(x + 1) = 0$.

FUNCTION AND RELATION

When expressing functional relationships, the **variables** x and y are typically used. These values are often written as the **coordinates** (x, y). The x-value is the independent variable and the y-value is the dependent variable. A **relation** is a set of data in which there is not a unique y-value for each x-value in the dataset. This means that there can be two of the same x-values assigned to different y-values. A relation is simply a relationship between the x- and y-values in each coordinate but does not apply to the relationship between the values of x and y in the data set. A **function** is a relation where one quantity depends on the other. For example, the amount of money that you make depends on the number of hours that you work. In a function, each x-value in the data set has one unique y-value because the y-value depends on the x-value.

Copyright © Mometrix Media. You have been licensed one copy of this document for personal use only. Any other reproduction or redistribution is strictly prohibited. All rights reserved.
This content is provided for test preparation purposes only and does not imply an endorsement by Mometrix of any particular political, scientific, or religious point of view.

FUNCTIONS

A function has exactly one value of **output variable** (dependent variable) for each value of the **input variable** (independent variable). The set of all values for the input variable (here assumed to be x) is the domain of the function, and the set of all corresponding values of the output variable (here assumed to be y) is the range of the function. When looking at a graph of an equation, the easiest way to determine if the equation is a function or not is to conduct the vertical line test. If a vertical line drawn through any value of x crosses the graph in more than one place, the equation is not a function.

DETERMINING A FUNCTION

You can determine whether an equation is a **function** by substituting different values into the equation for x. You can display and organize these numbers in a data table. A **data table** contains the values for x and y, which you can also list as coordinates. In order for a function to exist, the table cannot contain any repeating x-values that correspond with different y-values. If each x-coordinate has a unique y-coordinate, the table contains a function. However, there can be repeating y-values that correspond with different x-values. An example of this is when the function contains an exponent. Example: if $x^2 = y$, $2^2 = 4$, and $(-2)^2 = 4$.

> **Review Video: Definition of a Function**
> Visit mometrix.com/academy and enter code: 784611

FINDING THE DOMAIN AND RANGE OF A FUNCTION

The **domain** of a function $f(x)$ is the set of all input values for which the function is defined. The **range** of a function $f(x)$ is the set of all possible output values of the function—that is, of every possible value of $f(x)$, for any value of x in the function's domain. For a function expressed in a table, every input-output pair is given explicitly. To find the domain, we just list all the x-values and to find the range, we just list all the values of $f(x)$. Consider the following example:

x	−1	4	2	1	0	3	8	6
$f(x)$	3	0	3	−1	−1	2	4	6

In this case, the domain would be $\{-1, 4, 2, 1, 0, 3, 8, 6\}$ or, putting them in ascending order, $\{-1, 0, 1, 2, 3, 4, 6, 8\}$. (Putting the values in ascending order isn't strictly necessary, but generally makes the set easier to read.) The range would be $\{3, 0, 3, -1, -1, 2, 4, 6\}$. Note that some of these values appear more than once. This is entirely permissible for a function; while each value of x must be matched to a unique value of $f(x)$, the converse is not true. We don't need to list each value more than once, so eliminating duplicates, the range is $\{3, 0, -1, 2, 4, 6\}$, or, putting them in ascending order, $\{-1, 0, 2, 3, 4, 6\}$.

Note that by definition of a function, no input value can be matched to more than one output value. It is good to double-check to make sure that the data given follows this and is therefore actually a function.

> **Review Video: Domain and Range**
> Visit mometrix.com/academy and enter code: 778133
>
> **Review Video: Domain and Range of Quadratic Functions**
> Visit mometrix.com/academy and enter code: 331768

Copyright © Mometrix Media. You have been licensed one copy of this document for personal use only. Any other reproduction or redistribution is strictly prohibited. All rights reserved. This content is provided for test preparation purposes only and does not imply an endorsement by Mometrix of any particular political, scientific, or religious point of view.

WRITING A FUNCTION RULE USING A TABLE

If given a set of data, place the corresponding x- and y-values into a table and analyze the relationship between them. Consider what you can do to each x-value to obtain the corresponding y-value. Try adding or subtracting different numbers to and from x and then try multiplying or dividing different numbers to and from x. If none of these **operations** give you the y-value, try combining the operations. Once you find a rule that works for one pair, make sure to try it with each additional set of ordered pairs in the table. If the same operation or combination of operations satisfies each set of coordinates, then the table contains a function. The rule is then used to write the equation of the function in "$y = f(x)$" form.

DIRECT AND INVERSE VARIATIONS OF VARIABLES

Variables that vary directly are those that either both increase at the same rate or both decrease at the same rate. For example, in the functions $y = kx$ or $y = kx^n$, where k and n are positive, the value of y increases as the value of x increases and decreases as the value of x decreases.

Variables that vary inversely are those where one increases while the other decreases. For example, in the functions $y = \frac{k}{x}$ or $y = \frac{k}{x^n}$ where k and n are positive, the value of y increases as the value of x decreases and decreases as the value of x increases.

In both cases, k is the constant of variation.

PROPERTIES OF FUNCTIONS

There are many different ways to classify functions based on their structure or behavior. Important features of functions include:

- **End behavior**: the behavior of the function at extreme values ($f(x)$ as $x \to \pm\infty$)
- **y-intercept**: the value of the function at $f(0)$
- **Roots**: the values of x where the function equals zero ($f(x) = 0$)
- **Extrema**: minimum or maximum values of the function or where the function changes direction ($f(x) \geq k$ or $f(x) \leq k$)

CLASSIFICATION OF FUNCTIONS

An **invertible function** is defined as a function, $f(x)$, for which there is another function, $f^{-1}(x)$, such that $f^{-1}(f(x)) = x$. For example, if $f(x) = 3x - 2$ the inverse function, $f^{-1}(x)$, can be found:

$$x = 3(f^{-1}(x)) - 2$$
$$\frac{x+2}{3} = f^{-1}(x)$$

$$f^{-1}(f(x)) = \frac{3x - 2 + 2}{3}$$
$$= \frac{3x}{3}$$
$$= x$$

Note that $f^{-1}(x)$ is a valid function over all values of x.

In a **one-to-one function**, each value of x has exactly one value for y on the coordinate plane (this is the definition of a function) and each value of y has exactly one value for x. While the vertical line test will determine if a graph is that of a function, the horizontal line test will determine if a function is a one-to-one function. If a horizontal line drawn at any value of y intersects the graph in more than one place, the graph is not that of a one-to-one function. Do not make the mistake of using the horizontal line test exclusively in determining if a graph is that of a one-to-one function. A one-to-

Copyright © Mometrix Media. You have been licensed one copy of this document for personal use only. Any other reproduction or redistribution is strictly prohibited. All rights reserved. This content is provided for test preparation purposes only and does not imply an endorsement by Mometrix of any particular political, scientific, or religious point of view.

one function must pass both the vertical line test and the horizontal line test. As such, one-to-one functions are invertible functions.

A **many-to-one function** is a function whereby the relation is a function, but the inverse of the function is not a function. In other words, each element in the domain is mapped to one and only one element in the range. However, one or more elements in the range may be mapped to the same element in the domain. A graph of a many-to-one function would pass the vertical line test, but not the horizontal line test. This is why many-to-one functions are not invertible.

A **monotone function** is a function whose graph either constantly increases or constantly decreases. Examples include the functions $f(x) = x$, $f(x) = -x$, or $f(x) = x^3$.

An **even function** has a graph that is symmetric with respect to the y-axis and satisfies the equation $f(x) = f(-x)$. Examples include the functions $f(x) = x^2$ and $f(x) = ax^n$, where a is any real number and n is a positive even integer.

An **odd function** has a graph that is symmetric with respect to the origin and satisfies the equation $f(x) = -f(-x)$. Examples include the functions $f(x) = x^3$ and $f(x) = ax^n$, where a is any real number and n is a positive odd integer.

> **Review Video: Even and Odd Functions**
> Visit mometrix.com/academy and enter code: 278985

Constant functions are given by the equation $f(x) = b$, where b is a real number. There is no independent variable present in the equation, so the function has a constant value for all x. The graph of a constant function is a horizontal line of slope 0 that is positioned b units from the x-axis. If b is positive, the line is above the x-axis; if b is negative, the line is below the x-axis.

Identity functions are identified by the equation $f(x) = x$, where every value of the function is equal to its corresponding value of x. The only zero is the point (0,0). The graph is a line with a slope of 1.

In **linear functions**, the value of the function changes in direct proportion to x. The rate of change, represented by the slope on its graph, is constant throughout. The standard form of a linear equation is $ax + cy = d$, where a, c, and d are real numbers. As a function, this equation is commonly in the form $y = mx + b$ or $f(x) = mx + b$ where $m = -\frac{a}{c}$ and $b = \frac{d}{c}$. This is known as the slope-intercept form, because the coefficients give the slope of the graphed function (m) and its y-intercept (b). Solve the equation $mx + b = 0$ for x to get $x = -\frac{b}{m}$, which is the only zero of the function. The domain and range are both the set of all real numbers.

> **Review Video: Graphing Linear Functions**
> Visit mometrix.com/academy and enter code: 699478

Algebraic functions are those that exclusively use polynomials and roots. These would include polynomial functions, rational functions, square root functions, and all combinations of these functions, such as polynomials as the radicand. These combinations may be joined by addition, subtraction, multiplication, or division, but may not include variables as exponents.

> **Review Video: Common Functions**
> Visit mometrix.com/academy and enter code: 629798

Copyright © Mometrix Media. You have been licensed one copy of this document for personal use only. Any other reproduction or redistribution is strictly prohibited. All rights reserved.
This content is provided for test preparation purposes only and does not imply an endorsement by Mometrix of any particular political, scientific, or religious point of view.

ABSOLUTE VALUE FUNCTIONS

An **absolute value function** is in the format $f(x) = |ax + b|$. Like other functions, the domain is the set of all real numbers. However, because absolute value indicates positive numbers, the range is limited to positive real numbers. To find the zero of an absolute value function, set the portion inside the absolute value sign equal to zero and solve for x. An absolute value function is also known as a piecewise function because it must be solved in pieces—one for if the value inside the absolute value sign is positive, and one for if the value is negative. The function can be expressed as:

$$f(x) = \begin{cases} ax + b & \text{if } ax + b \geq 0 \\ -(ax + b) & \text{if } ax + b < 0 \end{cases}$$

This will allow for an accurate statement of the range. The graph of an example absolute value function, $f(x) = |2x - 1|$, is below:

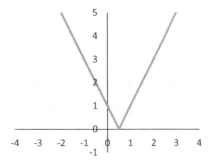

PIECEWISE FUNCTIONS

A **piecewise function** is a function that has different definitions on two or more different intervals. The following, for instance, is one example of a piecewise-defined function:

$$f(x) = \begin{cases} x^2, & x < 0 \\ x, & 0 \leq x \leq 2 \\ (x - 2)^2, & x > 2 \end{cases}$$

To graph this function, you would simply graph each part separately in the appropriate domain. The final graph would look like this:

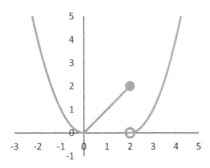

Note the filled and hollow dots at the discontinuity at $x = 2$. This is important to show which side of the graph that point corresponds to. Because $f(x) = x$ on the closed interval $0 \leq x \leq 2$, $f(2) = 2$. The point $(2, 2)$ is therefore marked with a filled circle, and the point $(2, 0)$, which is the endpoint of

171

Copyright © Mometrix Media. You have been licensed one copy of this document for personal use only. Any other reproduction or redistribution is strictly prohibited. All rights reserved. This content is provided for test preparation purposes only and does not imply an endorsement by Mometrix of any particular political, scientific, or religious point of view.

the rightmost $(x - 2)^2$ part of the graph but *not actually part of the function*, is marked with a hollow dot to indicate this.

Review Video: Piecewise Functions
Visit mometrix.com/academy and enter code: 707921

QUADRATIC FUNCTIONS

A **quadratic function** is a function in the form $y = ax^2 + bx + c$, where a does not equal 0. While a linear function forms a line, a quadratic function forms a **parabola**, which is a u-shaped figure that either opens upward or downward. A parabola that opens upward is said to be a **positive quadratic function,** and a parabola that opens downward is said to be a **negative quadratic function**. The shape of a parabola can differ, depending on the values of a, b, and c. All parabolas contain a **vertex**, which is the highest possible point, the **maximum**, or the lowest possible point, the **minimum**. This is the point where the graph begins moving in the opposite direction. A quadratic function can have zero, one, or two solutions, and therefore zero, one, or two x-intercepts. Recall that the x-intercepts are referred to as the zeros, or roots, of a function. A quadratic function will have only one y-intercept. Understanding the basic components of a quadratic function can give you an idea of the shape of its graph.

Example graph of a positive quadratic function, $x^2 + 2x - 3$:

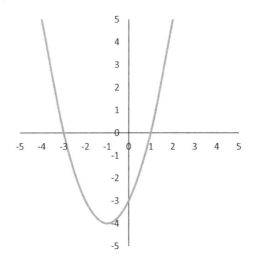

POLYNOMIAL FUNCTIONS

A **polynomial function** is a function with multiple terms and multiple powers of x, such as:

$$f(x) = a_n x^n + a_{n-1} x^{n-1} + a_{n-2} x^{n-2} + \cdots + a_1 x + a_0$$

where n is a non-negative integer that is the highest exponent in the polynomial and $a_n \neq 0$. The domain of a polynomial function is the set of all real numbers. If the greatest exponent in the polynomial is even, the polynomial is said to be of even degree and the range is the set of real numbers that satisfy the function. If the greatest exponent in the polynomial is odd, the polynomial is said to be odd and the range, like the domain, is the set of all real numbers.

RATIONAL FUNCTIONS

A **rational function** is a function that can be constructed as a ratio of two polynomial expressions: $f(x) = \frac{p(x)}{q(x)}$, where $p(x)$ and $q(x)$ are both polynomial expressions and $q(x) \neq 0$. The domain is the

Copyright © Mometrix Media. You have been licensed one copy of this document for personal use only. Any other reproduction or redistribution is strictly prohibited. All rights reserved.
This content is provided for test preparation purposes only and does not imply an endorsement by Mometrix of any particular political, scientific, or religious point of view.

set of all real numbers, except any values for which $q(x) = 0$. The range is the set of real numbers that satisfies the function when the domain is applied. When you graph a rational function, you will have vertical asymptotes wherever $q(x) = 0$. If the polynomial in the numerator is of lesser degree than the polynomial in the denominator, the x-axis will also be a horizontal asymptote. If the numerator and denominator have equal degrees, there will be a horizontal asymptote not on the x-axis. If the degree of the numerator is exactly one greater than the degree of the denominator, the graph will have an oblique, or diagonal, asymptote. The asymptote will be along the line $y = \frac{p_n}{q_{n-1}} x + \frac{p_{n-1}}{q_{n-1}}$, where p_n and q_{n-1} are the coefficients of the highest degree terms in their respective polynomials.

SQUARE ROOT FUNCTIONS

A **square root function** is a function that contains a radical and is in the format $f(x) = \sqrt{ax + b}$. The domain is the set of all real numbers that yields a positive radicand or a radicand equal to zero. Because square root values are assumed to be positive unless otherwise identified, the range is all real numbers from zero to infinity. To find the zero of a square root function, set the radicand equal to zero and solve for x. The graph of a square root function is always to the right of the zero and always above the x-axis.

Example graph of a square root function, $f(x) = \sqrt{2x + 1}$:

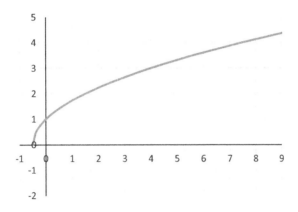

Measurement and Geometry

METRIC MEASUREMENT PREFIXES

Giga-	One billion	1 *giga*watt is one billion watts
Mega-	One million	1 *mega*hertz is one million hertz
Kilo-	One thousand	1 *kilo*gram is one thousand grams
Deci-	One-tenth	1 *deci*meter is one-tenth of a meter
Centi-	One-hundredth	1 *centi*meter is one-hundredth of a meter
Milli-	One-thousandth	1 *milli*liter is one-thousandth of a liter
Micro-	One-millionth	1 *micro*gram is one-millionth of a gram

> **Review Video: Metric System Conversion - How the Metric System Works**
> Visit mometrix.com/academy and enter code: 163709

Copyright © Mometrix Media. You have been licensed one copy of this document for personal use only. Any other reproduction or redistribution is strictly prohibited. All rights reserved.
This content is provided for test preparation purposes only and does not imply an endorsement by Mometrix of any particular political, scientific, or religious point of view.

MEASUREMENT CONVERSION

When converting between units, the goal is to maintain the same meaning but change the way it is displayed. In order to go from a larger unit to a smaller unit, multiply the number of the known amount by the equivalent amount. When going from a smaller unit to a larger unit, divide the number of the known amount by the equivalent amount.

For complicated conversions, it may be helpful to set up conversion fractions. In these fractions, one fraction is the **conversion factor**. The other fraction has the unknown amount in the numerator. So, the known value is placed in the denominator. Sometimes, the second fraction has the known value from the problem in the numerator and the unknown in the denominator. Multiply the two fractions to get the converted measurement. Note that since the numerator and the denominator of the factor are equivalent, the value of the fraction is 1. That is why we can say that the result in the new units is equal to the result in the old units even though they have different numbers.

It can often be necessary to chain known conversion factors together. As an example, consider converting 512 square inches to square meters. We know that there are 2.54 centimeters in an inch and 100 centimeters in a meter, and we know we will need to square each of these factors to achieve the conversion we are looking for.

$$\frac{512 \text{ in}^2}{1} \times \left(\frac{2.54 \text{ cm}}{1 \text{ in}}\right)^2 \times \left(\frac{1 \text{ m}}{100 \text{ cm}}\right)^2 = \frac{512 \text{ in}^2}{1} \times \left(\frac{6.4516 \text{ cm}^2}{1 \text{ in}^2}\right) \times \left(\frac{1 \text{ m}^2}{10,000 \text{ cm}^2}\right) = 0.330 \text{ m}^2$$

> **Review Video: Measurement Conversions**
> Visit mometrix.com/academy and enter code: 316703

COMMON UNITS AND EQUIVALENTS
METRIC EQUIVALENTS

1000 µg (microgram)	1 mg
1000 mg (milligram)	1 g
1000 g (gram)	1 kg
1000 kg (kilogram)	1 metric ton
1000 mL (milliliter)	1 L
1000 µm (micrometer)	1 mm
1000 mm (millimeter)	1 m
100 cm (centimeter)	1 m
1000 m (meter)	1 km

DISTANCE AND AREA MEASUREMENT

Unit	Abbreviation	US equivalent	Metric equivalent
Inch	in	1 inch	2.54 centimeters
Foot	ft	12 inches	0.305 meters
Yard	yd	3 feet	0.914 meters
Mile	mi	5280 feet	1.609 kilometers
Acre	ac	4840 square yards	0.405 hectares
Square Mile	sq. mi. or mi.^{2}	640 acres	2.590 square kilometers

Copyright © Mometrix Media. You have been licensed one copy of this document for personal use only. Any other reproduction or redistribution is strictly prohibited. All rights reserved.
This content is provided for test preparation purposes only and does not imply an endorsement by Mometrix of any particular political, scientific, or religious point of view.

CAPACITY MEASUREMENTS

Unit	Abbreviation	US equivalent	Metric equivalent
Fluid Ounce	fl oz	8 fluid drams	29.573 milliliters
Cup	c	8 fluid ounces	0.237 liter
Pint	pt.	16 fluid ounces	0.473 liter
Quart	qt.	2 pints	0.946 liter
Gallon	gal.	4 quarts	3.785 liters
Teaspoon	t or tsp.	1 fluid dram	5 milliliters
Tablespoon	T or tbsp.	4 fluid drams	15 or 16 milliliters
Cubic Centimeter	cc or cm^3	0.271 drams	1 milliliter

WEIGHT MEASUREMENTS

Unit	Abbreviation	US equivalent	Metric equivalent
Ounce	oz	16 drams	28.35 grams
Pound	lb	16 ounces	453.6 grams
Ton	tn.	2,000 pounds	907.2 kilograms

VOLUME AND WEIGHT MEASUREMENT CLARIFICATIONS

Always be careful when using ounces and fluid ounces. They are not equivalent.

$$1 \text{ pint} = 16 \text{ fluid ounces} \qquad 1 \text{ fluid ounce} \neq 1 \text{ ounce}$$
$$1 \text{ pound} = 16 \text{ ounces} \qquad 1 \text{ pint} \neq 1 \text{ pound}$$

Having one pint of something does not mean you have one pound of it. In the same way, just because something weighs one pound does not mean that its volume is one pint.

In the United States, the word "ton" by itself refers to a short ton or a net ton. Do not confuse this with a long ton (also called a gross ton) or a metric ton (also spelled *tonne*), which have different measurement equivalents.

$$1 \text{ US ton} = 2000 \text{ pounds} \qquad \neq \qquad 1 \text{ metric ton} = 1000 \text{ kilograms}$$

POINTS AND LINES

A **point** is a fixed location in space, has no size or dimensions, and is commonly represented by a dot. A **line** is a set of points that extends infinitely in two opposite directions. It has length, but no width or depth. A line can be defined by any two distinct points that it contains. A **line segment** is a portion of a line that has definite endpoints. A **ray** is a portion of a line that extends from a single point on that line in one direction along the line. It has a definite beginning, but no ending.

Point   Line   Segment   Ray

INTERACTIONS BETWEEN LINES

Intersecting lines are lines that have exactly one point in common. **Concurrent lines** are multiple lines that intersect at a single point. **Perpendicular lines** are lines that intersect at right angles. They are represented by the symbol ⊥. The shortest distance from a line to a point not on the line is a perpendicular segment from the point to the line. **Parallel lines** are lines in the same plane that

Copyright © Mometrix Media. You have been licensed one copy of this document for personal use only. Any other reproduction or redistribution is strictly prohibited. All rights reserved.
This content is provided for test preparation purposes only and does not imply an endorsement by Mometrix of any particular political, scientific, or religious point of view.

have no points in common and never meet. It is possible for lines to be in different planes, have no points in common, and never meet, but they are not parallel because they are in different planes.

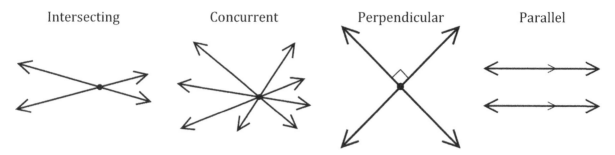

Review Video: Parallel and Perpendicular Lines
Visit mometrix.com/academy and enter code: 815923

A **transversal** is a line that intersects at least two other lines, which may or may not be parallel to one another. A transversal that intersects parallel lines is a common occurrence in geometry. A **bisector** is a line or line segment that divides another line segment into two equal lengths. A **perpendicular bisector** of a line segment is composed of points that are equidistant from the endpoints of the segment it is dividing.

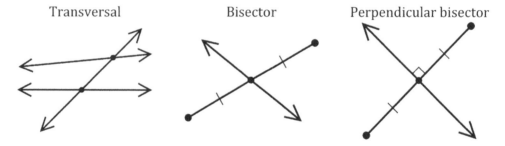

The **projection of a point on a line** is the point at which a perpendicular line drawn from the given point to the given line intersects the line. This is also the shortest distance from the given point to the line. The **projection of a segment on a line** is a segment whose endpoints are the points formed when perpendicular lines are drawn from the endpoints of the given segment to the given line. This is similar to the length a diagonal line appears to be when viewed from above.

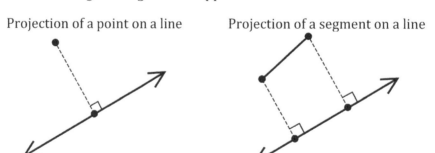

PLANES

A **plane** is a two-dimensional flat surface defined by three non-collinear points. A plane extends an infinite distance in all directions in those two dimensions. It contains an infinite number of points, parallel lines and segments, intersecting lines and segments, as well as parallel or intersecting rays.

Copyright © Mometrix Media. You have been licensed one copy of this document for personal use only. Any other reproduction or redistribution is strictly prohibited. All rights reserved.
This content is provided for test preparation purposes only and does not imply an endorsement by Mometrix of any particular political, scientific, or religious point of view.

A plane will never contain a three-dimensional figure or skew lines, which are lines that don't intersect and are not parallel. Two given planes are either parallel or they intersect at a line. A plane may intersect a circular conic surface to form **conic sections**, such as a parabola, hyperbola, circle or ellipse.

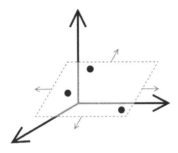

Review Video: **Lines and Planes**
Visit mometrix.com/academy and enter code: 554267

ANGLES AND VERTICES

An **angle** is formed when two lines or line segments meet at a common point. It may be a common starting point for a pair of segments or rays, or it may be the intersection of lines. Angles are represented by the symbol ∠.

The **vertex** is the point at which two segments or rays meet to form an angle. If the angle is formed by intersecting rays, lines, and/or line segments, the vertex is the point at which four angles are formed. The pairs of angles opposite one another are called vertical angles, and their measures are equal.

- An **acute** angle is an angle with a degree measure less than 90°.
- A **right** angle is an angle with a degree measure of exactly 90°.
- An **obtuse** angle is an angle with a degree measure greater than 90° but less than 180°.
- A **straight angle** is an angle with a degree measure of exactly 180°. This is also a semicircle.
- A **reflex angle** is an angle with a degree measure greater than 180° but less than 360°.
- A **full angle** is an angle with a degree measure of exactly 360°. This is also a circle.

Review Video: **Angles**
Visit mometrix.com/academy and enter code: 264624

RELATIONSHIPS BETWEEN ANGLES

Two angles whose sum is exactly 90° are said to be **complementary**. The two angles may or may not be adjacent. In a right triangle, the two acute angles are complementary.

Two angles whose sum is exactly 180° are said to be **supplementary**. The two angles may or may not be adjacent. Two intersecting lines always form two pairs of supplementary angles. Adjacent supplementary angles will always form a straight line.

Copyright © Mometrix Media. You have been licensed one copy of this document for personal use only. Any other reproduction or redistribution is strictly prohibited. All rights reserved. This content is provided for test preparation purposes only and does not imply an endorsement by Mometrix of any particular political, scientific, or religious point of view.

Two angles that have the same vertex and share a side are said to be **adjacent**. Vertical angles are not adjacent because they share a vertex but no common side.

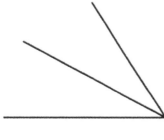

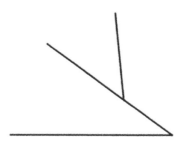

Adjacent
Share vertex and side

Not adjacent
Share part of a side, but not vertex

When two parallel lines are cut by a transversal, the angles that are between the two parallel lines are **interior angles**. In the diagram below, angles 3, 4, 5, and 6 are interior angles.

When two parallel lines are cut by a transversal, the angles that are outside the parallel lines are **exterior angles**. In the diagram below, angles 1, 2, 7, and 8 are exterior angles.

When two parallel lines are cut by a transversal, the angles that are in the same position relative to the transversal and a parallel line are **corresponding angles**. The diagram below has four pairs of corresponding angles: angles 1 and 5, angles 2 and 6, angles 3 and 7, and angles 4 and 8. Corresponding angles formed by parallel lines are congruent.

When two parallel lines are cut by a transversal, the two interior angles that are on opposite sides of the transversal are called **alternate interior angles**. In the diagram below, there are two pairs of alternate interior angles: angles 3 and 6, and angles 4 and 5. Alternate interior angles formed by parallel lines are congruent.

When two parallel lines are cut by a transversal, the two exterior angles that are on opposite sides of the transversal are called **alternate exterior angles**.

In the diagram below, there are two pairs of alternate exterior angles: angles 1 and 8, and angles 2 and 7. Alternate exterior angles formed by parallel lines are congruent.

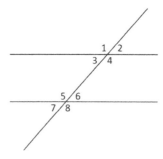

When two lines intersect, four angles are formed. The non-adjacent angles at this vertex are called vertical angles. Vertical angles are congruent. In the diagram, $\angle ABD \cong \angle CBE$ and $\angle ABC \cong \angle DBE$.

Copyright © Mometrix Media. You have been licensed one copy of this document for personal use only. Any other reproduction or redistribution is strictly prohibited. All rights reserved.
This content is provided for test preparation purposes only and does not imply an endorsement by Mometrix of any particular political, scientific, or religious point of view.

The other pairs of angles, ($\angle ABC$, $\angle CBE$) and ($\angle ABD$, $\angle DBE$), are supplementary, meaning the pairs sum to 180°.

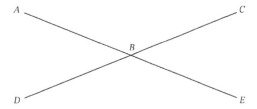

A **polygon** is a closed, two-dimensional figure with three or more straight line segments called **sides**. The point at which two sides of a polygon intersect is called the **vertex**. In a polygon, the number of sides is always equal to the number of vertices. A polygon with all sides congruent and all angles equal is called a **regular polygon**. Common polygons are:

$$\begin{aligned}
\text{Triangle} &= 3 \text{ sides} \\
\text{Quadrilateral} &= 4 \text{ sides} \\
\text{Pentagon} &= 5 \text{ sides} \\
\text{Hexagon} &= 6 \text{ sides} \\
\text{Heptagon} &= 7 \text{ sides} \\
\text{Octagon} &= 8 \text{ sides} \\
\text{Nonagon} &= 9 \text{ sides} \\
\text{Decagon} &= 10 \text{ sides} \\
\text{Dodecagon} &= 12 \text{ sides}
\end{aligned}$$

More generally, an n-gon is a polygon that has n angles and n sides.

> **Review Video: Intro to Polygons**
> Visit mometrix.com/academy and enter code: 271869

The sum of the interior angles of an n-sided polygon is $(n - 2) \times 180°$. For example, in a triangle $n = 3$. So the sum of the interior angles is $(3 - 2) \times 180° = 180°$. In a quadrilateral, $n = 4$, and the sum of the angles is $(4 - 2) \times 180° = 360°$.

> **Review Video: Sum of Interior Angles**
> Visit mometrix.com/academy and enter code: 984991

CONVEX AND CONCAVE POLYGONS

A **convex polygon** is a polygon whose diagonals all lie within the interior of the polygon. A **concave polygon** is a polygon with a least one diagonal that is outside the polygon. In the diagram below,

Copyright © Mometrix Media. You have been licensed one copy of this document for personal use only. Any other reproduction or redistribution is strictly prohibited. All rights reserved. This content is provided for test preparation purposes only and does not imply an endorsement by Mometrix of any particular political, scientific, or religious point of view.

quadrilateral *ABCD* is concave because diagonal $\overline{AC}$ lies outside the polygon and quadrilateral *EFGH* is convex because both diagonals lie inside the polygon.

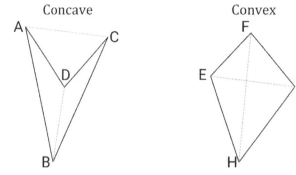

Congruent figures are geometric figures that have the same size and shape. All corresponding angles are equal, and all corresponding sides are equal. Congruence is indicated by the symbol ≅.

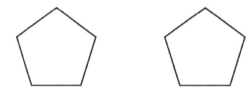

Congruent polygons

Similar figures are geometric figures that have the same shape, but do not necessarily have the same size. All corresponding angles are equal, and all corresponding sides are proportional, but they do not have to be equal. It is indicated by the symbol ~.

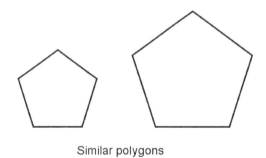

Similar polygons

Note that all congruent figures are also similar, but not all similar figures are congruent.

> **Review Video: Congruent Shapes**
> Visit mometrix.com/academy and enter code: 492281

Copyright © Mometrix Media. You have been licensed one copy of this document for personal use only. Any other reproduction or redistribution is strictly prohibited. All rights reserved.
This content is provided for test preparation purposes only and does not imply an endorsement by Mometrix of any particular political, scientific, or religious point of view.

A line that divides a figure or object into congruent parts is called a **line of symmetry**. An object may have no lines of symmetry, one line of symmetry, or multiple (i.e., more than one) lines of symmetry.

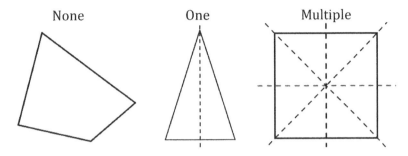

Review Video: Symmetry
Visit mometrix.com/academy and enter code: 528106

A triangle is a three-sided figure with the sum of its interior angles being 180°. The **perimeter of any triangle** is found by summing the three side lengths; $P = a + b + c$. For an equilateral triangle, this is the same as $P = 3a$, where a is any side length, since all three sides are the same length.

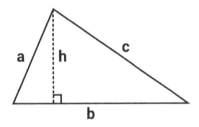

Review Video: Proof that a Triangle is 180 Degrees
Visit mometrix.com/academy and enter code: 687591

Review Video: Area and Perimeter of a Triangle
Visit mometrix.com/academy and enter code: 853779

The **area of any triangle** can be found by taking half the product of one side length referred to as the base, often given the variable b and the perpendicular distance from that side to the opposite vertex called the altitude or height and given the variable h. In equation form that is $A = \frac{1}{2}bh$. Another formula that works for any triangle is $A = \sqrt{s(s-a)(s-b)(s-c)}$, where s is the semiperimeter: $\frac{a+b+c}{2}$, and a, b, and c are the lengths of the three sides. Special cases include isosceles triangles, $A = \frac{1}{2}b\sqrt{a^2 - \frac{b^2}{4}}$, where b is the unique side and a is the length of one of the two congruent sides, and equilateral triangles, $A = \frac{\sqrt{3}}{4}a^2$, where a is the length of a side.

Review Video: Area of Any Triangle
Visit mometrix.com/academy and enter code: 138510

Copyright © Mometrix Media. You have been licensed one copy of this document for personal use only. Any other reproduction or redistribution is strictly prohibited. All rights reserved.
This content is provided for test preparation purposes only and does not imply an endorsement by Mometrix of any particular political, scientific, or religious point of view.

PARTS OF A TRIANGLE

An **altitude** of a triangle is a line segment drawn from one vertex perpendicular to the opposite side. In the diagram that follows, $\overline{BE}$, $\overline{AD}$, and $\overline{CF}$ are altitudes. The length of an altitude is also called the height of the triangle. The three altitudes in a triangle are always concurrent. The point of concurrency of the altitudes of a triangle, O, is called the **orthocenter**. Note that in an obtuse triangle, the orthocenter will be outside the triangle, and in a right triangle, the orthocenter is the vertex of the right angle.

A **median** of a triangle is a line segment drawn from one vertex to the midpoint of the opposite side. In the diagram that follows, $\overline{BH}$, $\overline{AG}$, and $\overline{CI}$ are medians. This is not the same as the altitude, except the altitude to the base of an isosceles triangle and all three altitudes of an equilateral triangle. The point of concurrency of the medians of a triangle, T, is called the **centroid**. This is the same point as the orthocenter only in an equilateral triangle. Unlike the orthocenter, the centroid is always inside the triangle. The centroid can also be considered the exact center of the triangle. Any shape triangle can be perfectly balanced on a tip placed at the centroid. The centroid is also the point that is two-thirds the distance from the vertex to the opposite side.

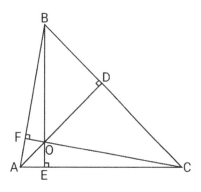 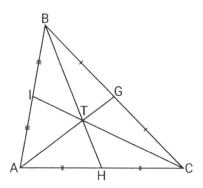

> **Review Video: Centroid, Incenter, Circumcenter, and Orthocenter**
> Visit mometrix.com/academy and enter code: 598260

CLASSIFICATIONS OF TRIANGLES

A **scalene triangle** is a triangle with no congruent sides. A scalene triangle will also have three angles of different measures. The angle with the largest measure is opposite the longest side, and the angle with the smallest measure is opposite the shortest side. An **acute triangle** is a triangle whose three angles are all less than 90°. If two of the angles are equal, the acute triangle is also an **isosceles triangle**. An isosceles triangle will also have two congruent angles opposite the two congruent sides. If the three angles are all equal, the acute triangle is also an **equilateral triangle**. An equilateral triangle will also have three congruent angles, each 60°. All equilateral triangles are also acute triangles. An **obtuse triangle** is a triangle with exactly one angle greater than 90°. The other two angles may or may not be equal. If the two remaining angles are equal, the obtuse triangle is also an isosceles triangle. A **right triangle** is a triangle with exactly one angle equal to 90°. All right triangles follow the Pythagorean theorem. A right triangle can never be acute or obtuse.

Copyright © Mometrix Media. You have been licensed one copy of this document for personal use only. Any other reproduction or redistribution is strictly prohibited. All rights reserved. This content is provided for test preparation purposes only and does not imply an endorsement by Mometrix of any particular political, scientific, or religious point of view.

Mometrix

The table below illustrates how each descriptor places a different restriction on the triangle:

Sides \ Angles	Acute: All angles < 90°	Obtuse: One angle > 90°	Right: One angle = 90°
Scalene: No equal side lengths	$90° > \angle a > \angle b > \angle c$ $x > y > z$	$\angle a > 90° > \angle b > \angle c$ $x > y > z$	$90° = \angle a > \angle b > \angle c$ $x > y > z$
Isosceles: Two equal side lengths	$90° > \angle a, \angle b, or \angle c$ $\angle b = \angle c, \qquad y = z$	$\angle a > 90° > \angle b = \angle c$ $x > y = z$	$\angle a = 90°$ $\angle b = \angle c = 45°$ $x > y = z$
Equilateral: Three equal side lengths	$60° = \angle a = \angle b = \angle c$ $x = y = z$		

Review Video: Introduction to Types of Triangles
Visit mometrix.com/academy and enter code: 511711

GENERAL RULES FOR TRIANGLES

The **triangle inequality theorem** states that the sum of the measures of any two sides of a triangle is always greater than the measure of the third side. If the sum of the measures of two sides were equal to the third side, a triangle would be impossible because the two sides would lie flat across the third side and there would be no vertex. If the sum of the measures of two of the sides was less than the third side, a closed figure would be impossible because the two shortest sides would never meet. In other words, for a triangle with sides lengths A, B, and C: $A + B > C$, $B + C > A$, and $A + C > B$.

The sum of the measures of the interior angles of a triangle is always 180°. Therefore, a triangle can never have more than one angle greater than or equal to 90°.

Copyright © Mometrix Media. You have been licensed one copy of this document for personal use only. Any other reproduction or redistribution is strictly prohibited. All rights reserved. This content is provided for test preparation purposes only and does not imply an endorsement by Mometrix of any particular political, scientific, or religious point of view.

In any triangle, the angles opposite congruent sides are congruent, and the sides opposite congruent angles are congruent. The largest angle is always opposite the longest side, and the smallest angle is always opposite the shortest side.

The line segment that joins the midpoints of any two sides of a triangle is always parallel to the third side and exactly half the length of the third side.

> **Review Video: General Rules (Triangle Inequality Theorem)**
> Visit mometrix.com/academy and enter code: 166488

SIMILARITY AND CONGRUENCE RULES

Similar triangles are triangles whose corresponding angles are equal and whose corresponding sides are proportional. Represented by AAA. Similar triangles whose corresponding sides are congruent are also congruent triangles.

Triangles can be shown to be **congruent** in 5 ways:

- **SSS**: Three sides of one triangle are congruent to the three corresponding sides of the second triangle.
- **SAS**: Two sides and the included angle (the angle formed by those two sides) of one triangle are congruent to the corresponding two sides and included angle of the second triangle.
- **ASA**: Two angles and the included side (the side that joins the two angles) of one triangle are congruent to the corresponding two angles and included side of the second triangle.
- **AAS**: Two angles and a non-included side of one triangle are congruent to the corresponding two angles and non-included side of the second triangle.
- **HL**: The hypotenuse and leg of one right triangle are congruent to the corresponding hypotenuse and leg of the second right triangle.

> **Review Video: Similar Triangles**
> Visit mometrix.com/academy and enter code: 398538

ROTATION

A **rotation** is a transformation that turns a figure around a point called the **center of rotation**, which can lie anywhere in the plane. If a line is drawn from a point on a figure to the center of rotation, and another line is drawn from the center to the rotated image of that point, the angle between the two lines is the **angle of rotation**. The vertex of the angle of rotation is the center of rotation.

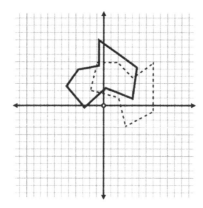

Copyright © Mometrix Media. You have been licensed one copy of this document for personal use only. Any other reproduction or redistribution is strictly prohibited. All rights reserved.
This content is provided for test preparation purposes only and does not imply an endorsement by Mometrix of any particular political, scientific, or religious point of view.

Review Video: <u>Rotation</u>
Visit mometrix.com/academy and enter code: 602600

TRANSLATION AND DILATION

A **translation** is a transformation which slides a figure from one position in the plane to another position in the plane. The original figure and the translated figure have the same size, shape, and orientation. A **dilation** is a transformation which proportionally stretches or shrinks a figure by a **scale factor**. The dilated image is the same shape and orientation as the original image but a different size. A polygon and its dilated image are similar.

Translation

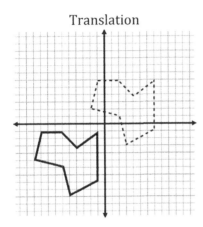

Dilation

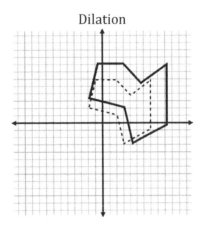

Review Video: <u>Translation</u>
Visit mometrix.com/academy and enter code: 718628

Review Video: <u>Dilation</u>
Visit mometrix.com/academy and enter code: 471630

A **reflection of a figure over a line** (a "flip") creates a congruent image that is the same distance from the line as the original figure but on the opposite side. The **line of reflection** is the perpendicular bisector of any line segment drawn from a point on the original figure to its reflected image (unless the point and its reflected image happen to be the same point, which happens when a figure is reflected over one of its own sides). A **reflection of a figure over a point** (an inversion) in two dimensions is the same as the rotation of the figure 180° about that point. The image of the figure is congruent to the original figure. The **point of reflection** is the midpoint of a line segment

Copyright © Mometrix Media. You have been licensed one copy of this document for personal use only. Any other reproduction or redistribution is strictly prohibited. All rights reserved.
This content is provided for test preparation purposes only and does not imply an endorsement by Mometrix of any particular political, scientific, or religious point of view.

which connects a point in the figure to its image (unless the point and its reflected image happen to be the same point, which happens when a figure is reflected in one of its own points).

Reflection of a figure over a line

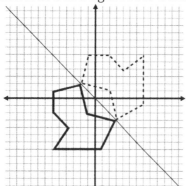

Reflection of a figure over a point

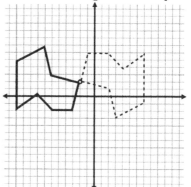

Review Video: Reflection
Visit mometrix.com/academy and enter code: 955068

The side of a triangle opposite the right angle is called the **hypotenuse**. The other two sides are called the legs. The Pythagorean theorem states a relationship among the legs and hypotenuse of a right triangle: $(a^2 + b^2 = c^2)$, where a and b are the lengths of the legs of a right triangle, and c is the length of the hypotenuse. Note that this formula will only work with right triangles.

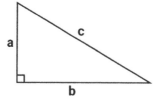

Review Video: Pythagorean Theorem
Visit mometrix.com/academy and enter code: 906576

In the diagram below, angle C is the right angle, and side c is the hypotenuse. Side a is the side opposite to angle A and side b is the side opposite to angle B. Using ratios of side lengths as a means to calculate the sine, cosine, and tangent of an acute angle only works for right triangles.

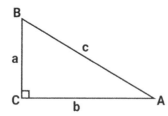

$$\sin A = \frac{\text{opposite side}}{\text{hypotenuse}} = \frac{a}{c}$$

$$\csc A = \frac{1}{\sin A} = \frac{\text{hypotenuse}}{\text{opposite side}} = \frac{c}{a}$$

$$\cos A = \frac{\text{adjacent side}}{\text{hypotenuse}} = \frac{b}{c}$$

$$\sec A = \frac{1}{\cos A} = \frac{\text{hypotenuse}}{\text{adjacent side}} = \frac{c}{b}$$

$$\tan A = \frac{\text{opposite side}}{\text{adjacent side}} = \frac{a}{b}$$

$$\cot A = \frac{1}{\tan A} = \frac{\text{adjacent side}}{\text{opposite side}} = \frac{b}{a}$$

Copyright © Mometrix Media. You have been licensed one copy of this document for personal use only. Any other reproduction or redistribution is strictly prohibited. All rights reserved. This content is provided for test preparation purposes only and does not imply an endorsement by Mometrix of any particular political, scientific, or religious point of view.

LAWS OF SINES AND COSINES

The **law of sines** states that $\frac{\sin A}{a} = \frac{\sin B}{b} = \frac{\sin C}{c}$, where A, B, and C are the angles of a triangle, and a, b, and c are the sides opposite their respective angles. This formula will work with all triangles, not just right triangles.

The **law of cosines** is given by the formula $c^2 = a^2 + b^2 - 2ab(\cos C)$, where a, b, and c are the sides of a triangle, and C is the angle opposite side c. This is a generalized form of the Pythagorean theorem that can be used on any triangle.

> **Review Video: Upper Level Trig: Law of Sines**
> Visit mometrix.com/academy and enter code: 206844
>
> **Review Video: Upper Level Trig: Law of Cosines**
> Visit mometrix.com/academy and enter code: 158911

A **quadrilateral** is a closed two-dimensional geometric figure that has four straight sides. The sum of the interior angles of any quadrilateral is 360°.

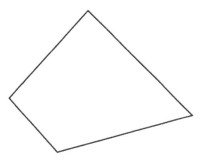

> **Review Video: Diagonals of Parallelograms, Rectangles, and Rhombi**
> Visit mometrix.com/academy and enter code: 320040

KITE

A **kite** is a quadrilateral with two pairs of adjacent sides that are congruent. A result of this is perpendicular diagonals. A kite can be concave or convex and has one line of symmetry.

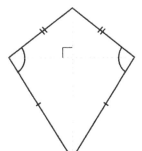
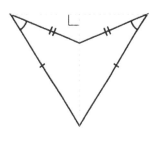

Copyright © Mometrix Media. You have been licensed one copy of this document for personal use only. Any other reproduction or redistribution is strictly prohibited. All rights reserved.
This content is provided for test preparation purposes only and does not imply an endorsement by Mometrix of any particular political, scientific, or religious point of view.

TRAPEZOID

Trapezoid: A trapezoid is defined as a quadrilateral that has at least one pair of parallel sides. There are no rules for the second pair of sides. So, there are no rules for the diagonals and no lines of symmetry for a trapezoid.

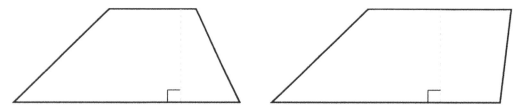

The **area of a trapezoid** is found by the formula $A = \frac{1}{2}h(b_1 + b_2)$, where h is the height (segment joining and perpendicular to the parallel bases), and b_1 and b_2 are the two parallel sides (bases). Do not use one of the other two sides as the height unless that side is also perpendicular to the parallel bases.

The **perimeter of a trapezoid** is found by the formula $P = a + b_1 + c + b_2$, where a, b_1, c, and b_2 are the four sides of the trapezoid.

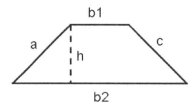

> **Review Video: <u>Area and Perimeter of a Trapezoid</u>**
> Visit mometrix.com/academy and enter code: 587523

Isosceles trapezoid: A trapezoid with equal base angles. This gives rise to other properties including: the two nonparallel sides have the same length, the two non-base angles are also equal, and there is one line of symmetry through the midpoints of the parallel sides.

PARALLELOGRAM

A **parallelogram** is a quadrilateral that has two pairs of opposite parallel sides. As such it is a special type of trapezoid. The sides that are parallel are also congruent. The opposite interior angles are always congruent, and the consecutive interior angles are supplementary. The diagonals of a parallelogram divide each other. Each diagonal divides the parallelogram into two congruent

Copyright © Mometrix Media. You have been licensed one copy of this document for personal use only. Any other reproduction or redistribution is strictly prohibited. All rights reserved. This content is provided for test preparation purposes only and does not imply an endorsement by Mometrix of any particular political, scientific, or religious point of view.

triangles. A parallelogram has no line of symmetry, but does have 180-degree rotational symmetry about the midpoint.

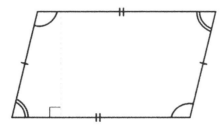

The **area of a parallelogram** is found by the formula $A = bh$, where b is the length of the base, and h is the height. Note that the base and height correspond to the length and width in a rectangle, so this formula would apply to rectangles as well. Do not confuse the height of a parallelogram with the length of the second side. The two are only the same measure in the case of a rectangle.

The **perimeter of a parallelogram** is found by the formula $P = 2a + 2b$ or $P = 2(a + b)$, where a and b are the lengths of the two sides.

> **Review Video: How to Find the Area and Perimeter of a Parallelogram**
> Visit mometrix.com/academy and enter code: 718313

RECTANGLE

A **rectangle** is a quadrilateral with four right angles. All rectangles are parallelograms and trapezoids, but not all parallelograms or trapezoids are rectangles. The diagonals of a rectangle are congruent. Rectangles have two lines of symmetry (through each pair of opposing midpoints) and 180-degree rotational symmetry about the midpoint.

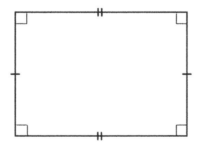

The **area of a rectangle** is found by the formula $A = lw$, where A is the area of the rectangle, l is the length (usually considered to be the longer side) and w is the width (usually considered to be the shorter side). The numbers for l and w are interchangeable.

The **perimeter of a rectangle** is found by the formula $P = 2l + 2w$ or $P = 2(l + w)$, where l is the length, and w is the width. It may be easier to add the length and width first and then double the result, as in the second formula.

RHOMBUS

A **rhombus** is a quadrilateral with four congruent sides. All rhombuses are parallelograms and kites; thus, they inherit all the properties of both types of quadrilaterals. The diagonals of a rhombus are perpendicular to each other. Rhombi have two lines of symmetry (along each of the

Copyright © Mometrix Media. You have been licensed one copy of this document for personal use only. Any other reproduction or redistribution is strictly prohibited. All rights reserved. This content is provided for test preparation purposes only and does not imply an endorsement by Mometrix of any particular political, scientific, or religious point of view.

diagonals) and 180° rotational symmetry. The **area of a rhombus** is half the product of the diagonals: $A = \frac{d_1 d_2}{2}$ and the perimeter of a rhombus is: $P = 2\sqrt{(d_1)^2 + (d_2)^2}$.

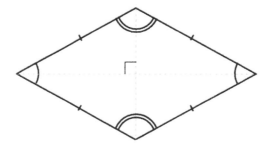

SQUARE

A **square** is a quadrilateral with four right angles and four congruent sides. Squares satisfy the criteria of all other types of quadrilaterals. The diagonals of a square are congruent and perpendicular to each other. Squares have four lines of symmetry (through each pair of opposing midpoints and along each of the diagonals) as well as 90° rotational symmetry about the midpoint.

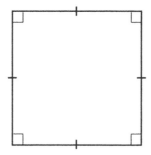

The **area of a square** is found by using the formula $A = s^2$, where s is the length of one side. The **perimeter of a square** is found by using the formula $P = 4s$, where s is the length of one side. Because all four sides are equal in a square, it is faster to multiply the length of one side by 4 than to add the same number four times. You could use the formulas for rectangles and get the same answer.

> **Review Video: Area and Perimeter of Rectangles and Squares**
> Visit mometrix.com/academy and enter code: 428109

Copyright © Mometrix Media. You have been licensed one copy of this document for personal use only. Any other reproduction or redistribution is strictly prohibited. All rights reserved.
This content is provided for test preparation purposes only and does not imply an endorsement by Mometrix of any particular political, scientific, or religious point of view.

HIERARCHY OF QUADRILATERALS

The hierarchy of quadrilaterals is as follows:

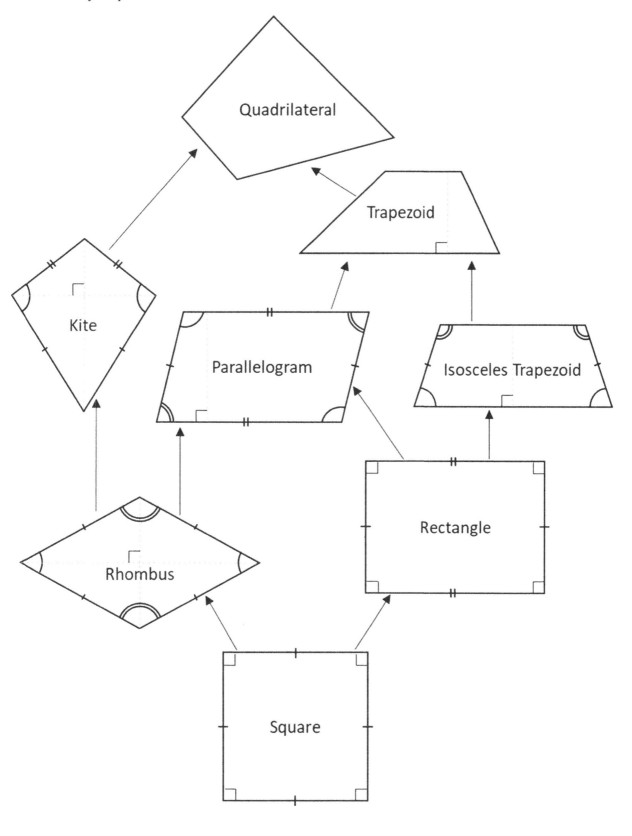

Copyright © Mometrix Media. You have been licensed one copy of this document for personal use only. Any other reproduction or redistribution is strictly prohibited. All rights reserved.
This content is provided for test preparation purposes only and does not imply an endorsement by Mometrix of any particular political, scientific, or religious point of view.

The **center** of a circle is the single point from which every point on the circle is **equidistant**. The **radius** is a line segment that joins the center of the circle and any one point on the circle. All radii of a circle are equal. Circles that have the same center but not the same length of radii are **concentric**. The **diameter** is a line segment that passes through the center of the circle and has both endpoints on the circle. The length of the diameter is exactly twice the length of the radius. Point O in the diagram below is the center of the circle, segments $\overline{OX}$, $\overline{OY}$, and $\overline{OZ}$ are radii; and segment $\overline{XZ}$ is a diameter.

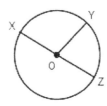

> **Review Video: Points of a Circle**
> Visit mometrix.com/academy and enter code: 420746
>
> **Review Video: The Diameter, Radius, and Circumference of Circles**
> Visit mometrix.com/academy and enter code: 448988

The **area of a circle** is found by the formula $A = \pi r^2$, where r is the length of the radius. If the diameter of the circle is given, remember to divide it in half to get the length of the radius before proceeding.

The **circumference** of a circle is found by the formula $C = 2\pi r$, where r is the radius. Again, remember to convert the diameter if you are given that measure rather than the radius.

> **Review Video: Area and Circumference of a Circle**
> Visit mometrix.com/academy and enter code: 243015

INSCRIBED AND CIRCUMSCRIBED FIGURES

These terms can both be used to describe a given arrangement of figures, depending on perspective. If each of the vertices of figure A lie on figure B, then it can be said that figure A is **inscribed** in figure B, but it can also be said that figure B is **circumscribed** about figure A. The following table and examples help to illustrate the concept. Note that the figures cannot both be circles, as they would be completely overlapping and neither would be inscribed or circumscribed.

Given	Description	Equivalent Description	Figures
Each of the sides of a pentagon is tangent to a circle	The circle is inscribed in the pentagon	The pentagon is circumscribed about the circle	
Each of the vertices of a pentagon lie on a circle	The pentagon is inscribed in the circle	The circle is circumscribed about the pentagon	

Copyright © Mometrix Media. You have been licensed one copy of this document for personal use only. Any other reproduction or redistribution is strictly prohibited. All rights reserved.
This content is provided for test preparation purposes only and does not imply an endorsement by Mometrix of any particular political, scientific, or religious point of view.

SOLIDS

The **surface area of a solid object** is the area of all sides or exterior surfaces. For objects such as prisms and pyramids, a further distinction is made between base surface area (B) and lateral surface area (LA). For a prism, the total surface area (SA) is $SA = LA + 2B$. For a pyramid or cone, the total surface area is $SA = LA + B$.

The **surface area of a sphere** can be found by the formula $A = 4\pi r^2$, where r is the radius. The volume is given by the formula $V = \frac{4}{3}\pi r^3$, where r is the radius. Both quantities are generally given in terms of π.

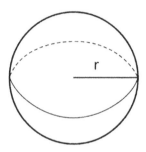

Review Video: Volume and Surface Area of a Sphere
Visit mometrix.com/academy and enter code: 786928

Review Video: How to Calculate the Volume of 3D Objects
Visit mometrix.com/academy and enter code: 163343

The **volume of any prism** is found by the formula $V = Bh$, where B is the area of the base, and h is the height (perpendicular distance between the bases). The surface area of any prism is the sum of the areas of both bases and all sides. It can be calculated as $SA = 2B + Ph$, where P is the perimeter of the base.

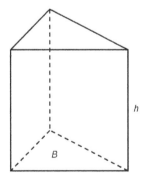

Review Video: Volume and Surface Area of a Prism
Visit mometrix.com/academy and enter code: 420158

Copyright © Mometrix Media. You have been licensed one copy of this document for personal use only. Any other reproduction or redistribution is strictly prohibited. All rights reserved.
This content is provided for test preparation purposes only and does not imply an endorsement by Mometrix of any particular political, scientific, or religious point of view.

For a **rectangular prism**, the volume can be found by the formula $V = lwh$, where V is the volume, l is the length, w is the width, and h is the height. The surface area can be calculated as $SA = 2lw + 2hl + 2wh$ or $SA = 2(lw + hl + wh)$.

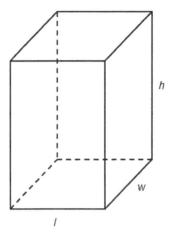

Review Video: <u>Volume and Surface Area of a Rectangular Prism</u>
Visit mometrix.com/academy and enter code: 282814

The **volume of a cube** can be found by the formula $V = s^3$, where s is the length of a side. The surface area of a cube is calculated as $SA = 6s^2$, where SA is the total surface area and s is the length of a side. These formulas are the same as the ones used for the volume and surface area of a rectangular prism, but simplified since all three quantities (length, width, and height) are the same.

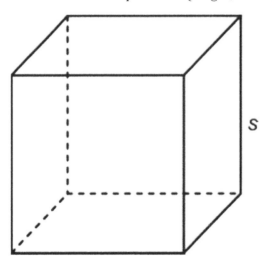

Review Video: <u>Volume and Surface Area of a Cube</u>
Visit mometrix.com/academy and enter code: 664455

The **volume of a cylinder** can be calculated by the formula $V = \pi r^2 h$, where r is the radius, and h is the height. The surface area of a cylinder can be found by the formula $SA = 2\pi r^2 + 2\pi rh$. The

Copyright © Mometrix Media. You have been licensed one copy of this document for personal use only. Any other reproduction or redistribution is strictly prohibited. All rights reserved.
This content is provided for test preparation purposes only and does not imply an endorsement by Mometrix of any particular political, scientific, or religious point of view.

first term is the base area multiplied by two, and the second term is the perimeter of the base multiplied by the height.

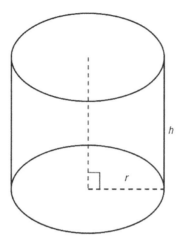

Review Video: Finding the Volume and Surface Area of a Right Circular Cylinder
Visit mometrix.com/academy and enter code: 226463

The **volume of a pyramid** is found by the formula $V = \frac{1}{3}Bh$, where B is the area of the base, and h is the height (perpendicular distance from the vertex to the base). Notice this formula is the same as $\frac{1}{3}$ times the volume of a prism. Like a prism, the base of a pyramid can be any shape.

Finding the **surface area of a pyramid** is not as simple as the other shapes we've looked at thus far. If the pyramid is a right pyramid, meaning the base is a regular polygon and the vertex is directly over the center of that polygon, the surface area can be calculated as $SA = B + \frac{1}{2}Ph_s$, where P is the perimeter of the base, and h_s is the slant height (distance from the vertex to the midpoint of one side of the base). If the pyramid is irregular, the area of each triangle side must be calculated individually and then summed, along with the base.

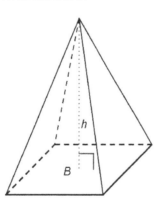

Review Video: Finding the Volume and Surface Area of a Pyramid
Visit mometrix.com/academy and enter code: 621932

Copyright © Mometrix Media. You have been licensed one copy of this document for personal use only. Any other reproduction or redistribution is strictly prohibited. All rights reserved.
This content is provided for test preparation purposes only and does not imply an endorsement by Mometrix of any particular political, scientific, or religious point of view.

The **volume of a cone** is found by the formula $V = \frac{1}{3}\pi r^2 h$, where r is the radius, and h is the height. Notice this is the same as $\frac{1}{3}$ times the volume of a cylinder. The surface area can be calculated as $SA = \pi r^2 + \pi rs$, where s is the slant height. The slant height can be calculated using the Pythagorean theorem to be $\sqrt{r^2 + h^2}$, so the surface area formula can also be written as $SA = \pi r^2 + \pi r\sqrt{r^2 + h^2}$.

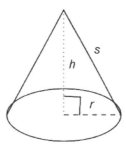

Review Video: Volume and Surface Area of a Right Circular Cone
Visit mometrix.com/academy and enter code: 573574

Probability and Statistics

FACTORIALS

The **factorial** is a function that can be performed on any **non-negative integer**. It is represented by the ! sign written after the integer on which it is being performed. The factorial of an integer is the product of all positive integers less than or equal to the number. For example, 4! (read "4 factorial") is calculated as $4 \times 3 \times 2 \times 1 = 24$.

Since 0 is not itself a positive integer, nor does it have any positive integers less than it, 0! cannot be calculated using this method. Instead, 0! is defined by convention to equal 1. This makes sense if you consider the pattern of descending factorials:

$$5! = 120$$
$$4! = \frac{5!}{5} = \frac{120}{5} = 24$$
$$3! = \frac{4!}{4} = \frac{24}{4} = 6$$
$$2! = \frac{3!}{3} = \frac{6}{3} = 2$$
$$1! = \frac{2!}{2} = \frac{2}{2} = 1$$
$$0! = \frac{1!}{1} = \frac{1}{1} = 1$$

PERMUTATIONS

For any given set of data, the individual elements in the set may be arranged in different groups containing different numbers of elements arranged in different orders. For example, given the set of integers from one to three, inclusive, the elements of the set are 1, 2, and 3: written as $\{1, 2, 3\}$. They may be arranged as follows: 1, 2, 3, 12, 21, 13, 31, 23, 32, 123, 132, 213, 231, 312, and 321. These

Copyright © Mometrix Media. You have been licensed one copy of this document for personal use only. Any other reproduction or redistribution is strictly prohibited. All rights reserved. This content is provided for test preparation purposes only and does not imply an endorsement by Mometrix of any particular political, scientific, or religious point of view.

ordered sequences of elements from the given set of data are called **permutations**. It is important to note that in permutations, the order of the elements in the sequence is important. The sequence 123 is not the same as the sequence 213. Also, no element in the given set may be used more times as an element in a permutation than it appears as an element in the original set. For example, 223 is not a permutation in the above example because the number 2 only appears one time in the given set.

To find the number of permutations of r items from a set of n items, use the formula $_nP_r = \frac{n!}{(n-r)!}$. When using this formula, each element of r must be unique. Also, this assumes that different arrangements of the same set of elements yields different outcomes. For example, 123 is not the same as 321; order is important.

A special case arises while finding the number of possible permutations of n items from a set of n items. Because $n = r$, the equation for the number of permutations becomes simply $P = n!$ The same result is true for $r = n - 1$. Both of these cases are a result of the fact that 0! and 1! are both equal to 1.

If a set contains one or more groups of **indistinguishable or interchangeable elements** (e.g., the set $\{1, 2, 3, 3\}$, which has a group of two indistinguishable 3's), there is a different formula for finding distinct permutations of all n elements. Use the formula $P = \frac{n!}{m_1!m_2!...m_k!}$, where P is the number of permutations, n is the total number of elements in the set, and m_1 through m_k are the number of identical elements in each group (e.g., for the set $\{1, 1, 2, 2, 2, 3, 3\}$, $m_1 = 2$, $m_2 = 3$, and $m_3 = 2$). It is important to note that each repeated number is counted as its own element for the purpose of defining n (e.g., for the set $\{1, 1, 2, 2, 2, 3, 3\}$, $n = 7$, not 3).

To find the number of possible permutations of **any number of elements** in a set of unique elements, you must apply the permutation formulas multiple times. For example, to find the total number of possible permutations of the set $\{1, 2, 3\}$ first apply the permutation formula for situations where $n = r$ as follows: $P = n! = 3! = 6$. This gives the number of permutations of the three elements when all three elements are used. To find the number of permutations when only two of the three elements are used, use the formula $_nP_r = \frac{n!}{(n-r)!}$, where n is 3 and r is 2.

$$_nP_r = \frac{n!}{(n-r)!} \Rightarrow {}_3P_2 = \frac{3!}{(3-2)!} = \frac{6}{1} = 6$$

To find the number of permutations when one element is used, use the formula $_nP_r = \frac{n!}{(n-r)!}$, where n is 3 and r is 1.

$$_nP_r = \frac{n!}{(n-r)!} \Rightarrow {}_3P_1 = \frac{3!}{(3-1)!} = \frac{3!}{2!} = \frac{6}{2} = 3$$

Find the sum of the three formulas: $6 + 6 + 3 = 15$ total possible permutations.

Alternatively, the general formula for total possible permutations can be written as follows:

$$P_T = \sum_{i=1}^{n} \frac{n!}{(i-1)!}$$

Copyright © Mometrix Media. You have been licensed one copy of this document for personal use only. Any other reproduction or redistribution is strictly prohibited. All rights reserved. This content is provided for test preparation purposes only and does not imply an endorsement by Mometrix of any particular political, scientific, or religious point of view.

COMBINATIONS

Combinations are essentially defined as permutations where the order in which the elements appear does not matter. Going back to the earlier example of the set {1, 2, 3}, the possible combinations that can be made from that set are 1, 2, 3, 12, 13, 23, and 123.

In a set containing n elements, the number of combinations of r items from the set can be found using the formula $_nC_r = \frac{n!}{r!(n-r)!}$. Notice the similarity to the formula for permutations. In effect, you are dividing the number of permutations by $r!$ to get the number of combinations, and the formula may be written $_nC_r = \frac{_nP_r}{r!}$. When finding the number of combinations, it is important to remember that the elements in the set must be unique (i.e., there must not be any duplicate items), and that no item may be used more than once in any given sequence.

Probability is the likelihood of a certain outcome occurring for a given event. An **event** is any situation that produces a result. It could be something as simple as flipping a coin or as complex as launching a rocket. Determining the probability of an outcome for an event can be equally simple or complex. As such, there are specific terms used in the study of probability that need to be understood:

- **Compound event**—an event that involves two or more independent events (rolling a pair of dice and taking the sum)
- **Desired outcome** (or success)—an outcome that meets a particular set of criteria (a roll of 1 or 2 if we are looking for numbers less than 3)
- **Independent events**—two or more events whose outcomes do not affect one another (two coins tossed at the same time)
- **Dependent events**—two or more events whose outcomes affect one another (two cards drawn consecutively from the same deck)
- **Certain outcome**—probability of outcome is 100% or 1
- **Impossible outcome**—probability of outcome is 0% or 0
- **Mutually exclusive outcomes**—two or more outcomes whose criteria cannot all be satisfied in a single event (a coin coming up heads and tails on the same toss)
- **Random variable**—refers to all possible outcomes of a single event which may be discrete or continuous.

Review Video: **Intro to Probability**
Visit mometrix.com/academy and enter code: 212374

SAMPLE SPACE

The total set of all possible results of a test or experiment is called a **sample space**, or sometimes a universal sample space. The sample space, represented by one of the variables S, Ω, or U (for universal sample space) has individual elements called outcomes. Other terms for outcome that may be used interchangeably include elementary outcome, simple event, or sample point. The number of outcomes in a given sample space could be infinite or finite, and some tests may yield multiple unique sample sets. For example, tests conducted by drawing playing cards from a standard deck would have one sample space of the card values, another sample space of the card suits, and a third sample space of suit-denomination combinations. For most tests, the sample spaces considered will be finite.

An **event**, represented by the variable E, is a portion of a sample space. It may be one outcome or a group of outcomes from the same sample space. If an event occurs, then the test or experiment will

Copyright © Mometrix Media. You have been licensed one copy of this document for personal use only. Any other reproduction or redistribution is strictly prohibited. All rights reserved. This content is provided for test preparation purposes only and does not imply an endorsement by Mometrix of any particular political, scientific, or religious point of view.

generate an outcome that satisfies the requirement of that event. For example, given a standard deck of 52 playing cards as the sample space, and defining the event as the collection of face cards, then the event will occur if the card drawn is a J, Q, or K. If any other card is drawn, the event is said to have not occurred.

For every sample space, each possible outcome has a specific likelihood, or probability, that it will occur. The probability measure, also called the **distribution**, is a function that assigns a real number probability, from zero to one, to each outcome. For a probability measure to be accurate, every outcome must have a real number probability measure that is greater than or equal to zero and less than or equal to one. Also, the probability measure of the sample space must equal one, and the probability measure of the union of multiple outcomes must equal the sum of the individual probability measures.

Probabilities of events are expressed as real numbers from zero to one. They give a numerical value to the chance that a particular event will occur. The probability of an event occurring is the sum of the probabilities of the individual elements of that event. For example, in a standard deck of 52 playing cards as the sample space and the collection of face cards as the event, the probability of drawing a specific face card is $\frac{1}{52} = 0.019$, but the probability of drawing any one of the twelve face cards is $12(0.019) = 0.228$. Note that rounding of numbers can generate different results. If you multiplied 12 by the fraction $\frac{1}{52}$ before converting to a decimal, you would get the answer $\frac{12}{52} = 0.231$.

THEORETICAL AND EXPERIMENTAL PROBABILITY

Theoretical probability can usually be determined without actually performing the event. The likelihood of an outcome occurring, or the probability of an outcome occurring, is given by the formula:

$$P(A) = \frac{\text{Number of acceptable outcomes}}{\text{Number of possible outcomes}}$$

Note that $P(A)$ is the probability of an outcome A occurring, and each outcome is just as likely to occur as any other outcome. If each outcome has the same probability of occurring as every other possible outcome, the outcomes are said to be equally likely to occur. The total number of acceptable outcomes must be less than or equal to the total number of possible outcomes. If the two are equal, then the outcome is certain to occur and the probability is 1. If the number of acceptable outcomes is zero, then the outcome is impossible and the probability is 0. For example, if there are 20 marbles in a bag and 5 are red, then the theoretical probability of randomly selecting a red marble is 5 out of 20, $\left(\frac{5}{20} = \frac{1}{4}, 0.25, \text{ or } 25\%\right)$.

If the theoretical probability is unknown or too complicated to calculate, it can be estimated by an experimental probability. **Experimental probability**, also called empirical probability, is an estimate of the likelihood of a certain outcome based on repeated experiments or collected data. In other words, while theoretical probability is based on what *should* happen, experimental probability is based on what *has* happened. Experimental probability is calculated in the same way as theoretical probability, except that actual outcomes are used instead of possible outcomes. The more experiments performed or datapoints gathered, the better the estimate should be.

Theoretical and experimental probability do not always line up with one another. Theoretical probability says that out of 20 coin-tosses, 10 should be heads. However, if we were actually to toss 20 coins, we might record just 5 heads. This doesn't mean that our theoretical probability is

Copyright © Mometrix Media. You have been licensed one copy of this document for personal use only. Any other reproduction or redistribution is strictly prohibited. All rights reserved. This content is provided for test preparation purposes only and does not imply an endorsement by Mometrix of any particular political, scientific, or religious point of view.

incorrect; it just means that this particular experiment had results that were different from what was predicted. A practical application of empirical probability is the insurance industry. There are no set functions that define lifespan, health, or safety. Insurance companies look at factors from hundreds of thousands of individuals to find patterns that they then use to set the formulas for insurance premiums.

> **Review Video: Empirical Probability**
> Visit mometrix.com/academy and enter code: 513468

OBJECTIVE AND SUBJECTIVE PROBABILITY

Objective probability is based on mathematical formulas and documented evidence. Examples of objective probability include raffles or lottery drawings where there is a pre-determined number of possible outcomes and a predetermined number of outcomes that correspond to an event. Other cases of objective probability include probabilities of rolling dice, flipping coins, or drawing cards. Most gambling games are based on objective probability.

In contrast, **subjective probability** is based on personal or professional feelings and judgments. Often, there is a lot of guesswork following extensive research. Areas where subjective probability is applicable include sales trends and business expenses. Attractions set admission prices based on subjective probabilities of attendance based on varying admission rates in an effort to maximize their profit.

COMPLEMENT OF AN EVENT

Sometimes it may be easier to calculate the possibility of something not happening, or the **complement of an event**. Represented by the symbol $\bar{A}$, the complement of A is the probability that event A does not happen. When you know the probability of event A occurring, you can use the formula $P(\bar{A}) = 1 - P(A)$, where $P(\bar{A})$ is the probability of event A not occurring, and $P(A)$ is the probability of event A occurring.

ADDITION RULE

The **addition rule** for probability is used for finding the probability of a compound event. Use the formula $P(A \cup B) = P(A) + P(B) - P(A \cap B)$, where $P(A \cap B)$ is the probability of both events occurring to find the probability of a compound event. The probability of both events occurring at the same time must be subtracted to eliminate any overlap in the first two probabilities.

CONDITIONAL PROBABILITY

Given two events A and B, the **conditional probability** $P(A|B)$ is the probability that event A will occur, given that event B has occurred. The conditional probability cannot be calculated simply from $P(A)$ and $P(B)$; these probabilities alone do not give sufficient information to determine the conditional probability. It can, however, be determined if you are also given the probability of the intersection of events A and B, $P(A \cap B)$, the probability that events A and B both occur. Specifically, $P(A|B) = \frac{P(A \cap B)}{P(B)}$. For instance, suppose you have a jar containing two red marbles and two blue marbles, and you draw two marbles at random. Consider event A being the event that the first marble drawn is red, and event B being the event that the second marble drawn is blue. If we want to find the probability that B occurs given that A occurred, $P(B|A)$, then we can compute it

Copyright © Mometrix Media. You have been licensed one copy of this document for personal use only. Any other reproduction or redistribution is strictly prohibited. All rights reserved.
This content is provided for test preparation purposes only and does not imply an endorsement by Mometrix of any particular political, scientific, or religious point of view.

using the fact that $P(A)$ is $\frac{1}{2}$, and $P(A \cap B)$ is $\frac{1}{3}$. (The latter may not be obvious, but may be determined by finding the product of $\frac{1}{2}$ and $\frac{2}{3}$). Therefore $P(B|A) = \frac{P(A \cap B)}{P(A)} = \frac{1/3}{1/2} = \frac{2}{3}$.

CONDITIONAL PROBABILITY IN EVERYDAY SITUATIONS

Conditional probability often arises in everyday situations in, for example, estimating the risk or benefit of certain activities. The conditional probability of having a heart attack given that you exercise daily may be smaller than the overall probability of having a heart attack. The conditional probability of having lung cancer given that you are a smoker is larger than the overall probability of having lung cancer. Note that changing the order of the conditional probability changes the meaning: the conditional probability of having lung cancer given that you are a smoker is a very different thing from the probability of being a smoker given that you have lung cancer. In an extreme case, suppose that a certain rare disease is caused only by eating a certain food, but even then, it is unlikely. Then the conditional probability of having that disease given that you eat the dangerous food is nonzero but low, but the conditional probability of having eaten that food given that you have the disease is 100%!

> **Review Video: Conditional Probability**
> Visit mometrix.com/academy and enter code: 397924

INDEPENDENCE

The conditional probability $P(A|B)$ is the probability that event A will occur given that event B occurs. If the two events are independent, we do not expect that whether or not event B occurs should have any effect on whether or not event A occurs. In other words, we expect $P(A|B) = P(A)$.

This can be proven using the usual equations for conditional probability and the joint probability of independent events. The conditional probability $P(A|B) = \frac{P(A \cap B)}{P(B)}$. If A and B are independent, then $P(A \cap B) = P(A)P(B)$. So $P(A|B) = \frac{P(A)P(B)}{P(B)} = P(A)$. By similar reasoning, if A and B are independent then $P(B|A) = P(B)$.

MULTIPLICATION RULE

The **multiplication rule** can be used to find the probability of two independent events occurring using the formula $P(A \cap B) = P(A) \times P(B)$, where $P(A \cap B)$ is the probability of two independent events occurring, $P(A)$ is the probability of the first event occurring, and $P(B)$ is the probability of the second event occurring.

The multiplication rule can also be used to find the probability of two dependent events occurring using the formula $P(A \cap B) = P(A) \times P(B|A)$, where $P(A \cap B)$ is the probability of two dependent events occurring and $P(B|A)$ is the probability of the second event occurring after the first event has already occurred.

Use a **combination of the multiplication** rule and the rule of complements to find the probability that at least one outcome of the element will occur. This is given by the general formula $P(\text{at least one event occurring}) = 1 - P(\text{no outcomes occurring})$. For example, to find the probability that at least one even number will show when a pair of dice is rolled, find the probability that two odd numbers will be rolled (no even numbers) and subtract from one. You can always use a tree diagram or make a chart to list the possible outcomes when the sample space is

Copyright © Mometrix Media. You have been licensed one copy of this document for personal use only. Any other reproduction or redistribution is strictly prohibited. All rights reserved. This content is provided for test preparation purposes only and does not imply an endorsement by Mometrix of any particular political, scientific, or religious point of view.

small, such as in the dice-rolling example, but in most cases it will be much faster to use the multiplication and complement formulas.

Review Video: Multiplication Rule
Visit mometrix.com/academy and enter code: 782598

UNION AND INTERSECTION OF TWO SETS OF OUTCOMES

If A and B are each a set of elements or outcomes from an experiment, then the **union** (symbol $\cup$) of the two sets is the set of elements found in set A or set B. For example, if $A = \{2, 3, 4\}$ and $B = \{3, 4, 5\}$, $A \cup B = \{2, 3, 4, 5\}$. Note that the outcomes 3 and 4 appear only once in the union. For statistical events, the union is equivalent to "or"; $P(A \cup B)$ is the same thing as $P(A \text{ or } B)$. The **intersection** (symbol $\cap$) of two sets is the set of outcomes common to both sets. For the above sets A and B, $A \cap B = \{3, 4\}$. For statistical events, the intersection is equivalent to "and"; $P(A \cap B)$ is the same thing as $P(A \text{ and } B)$. It is important to note that union and intersection operations commute. That is:

$$A \cup B = B \cup A \text{ and } A \cap B = B \cap A$$

When trying to calculate the probability of an event using the $\frac{\text{desired outcomes}}{\text{total outcomes}}$ formula, you may frequently find that there are too many outcomes to individually count them. **Permutation** and **combination formulas** offer a shortcut to counting outcomes. A permutation is an arrangement of a specific number of a set of objects in a specific order. The number of **permutations** of r items given a set of n items can be calculated as $_nP_r = \frac{n!}{(n-r)!}$. Combinations are similar to permutations, except there are no restrictions regarding the order of the elements. While ABC is considered a different permutation than BCA, ABC and BCA are considered the same combination. The number of **combinations** of r items given a set of n items can be calculated as $_nC_r = \frac{n!}{r!(n-r)!}$ or $_nC_r = \frac{_nP_r}{r!}$.

Suppose you want to calculate how many different 5-card hands can be drawn from a deck of 52 cards. This is a combination since the order of the cards in a hand does not matter. There are 52 cards available, and 5 to be selected. Thus, the number of different hands is $_{52}C_5 = \frac{52!}{5! \times 47!} = 2{,}598{,}960$.

Review Video: Probability - Permutation and Combination
Visit mometrix.com/academy and enter code: 907664

For a simple sample space, possible outcomes may be determined by using a **tree diagram** or an organized chart. In either case, you can easily draw or list out the possible outcomes. For example, to determine all the possible ways three objects can be ordered, you can draw a tree diagram:

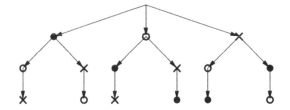

Copyright © Mometrix Media. You have been licensed one copy of this document for personal use only. Any other reproduction or redistribution is strictly prohibited. All rights reserved.
This content is provided for test preparation purposes only and does not imply an endorsement by Mometrix of any particular political, scientific, or religious point of view.

Review Video: Tree Diagrams
Visit mometrix.com/academy and enter code: 829158

You can also make a chart to list all the possibilities:

First object	Second object	Third object
●	X	O
●	O	X
O	●	X
O	X	●
X	●	O
X	O	●

Either way, you can easily see there are six possible ways the three objects can be ordered.

If two events have no outcomes in common, they are said to be **mutually exclusive**. For example, in a standard deck of 52 playing cards, the event of all card suits is mutually exclusive to the event of all card values. If two events have no bearing on each other so that one event occurring has no influence on the probability of another event occurring, the two events are said to be independent. For example, rolling a standard six-sided die multiple times does not change that probability that a particular number will be rolled from one roll to the next. If the outcome of one event does affect the probability of the second event, the two events are said to be dependent. For example, if cards are drawn from a deck, the probability of drawing an ace after an ace has been drawn is different than the probability of drawing an ace if no ace (or no other card, for that matter) has been drawn.

In probability, the **odds in favor of an event** are the number of times the event will occur compared to the number of times the event will not occur. To calculate the odds in favor of an event, use the formula $\frac{P(A)}{1-P(A)}$, where $P(A)$ is the probability that the event will occur. Many times, odds in favor is given as a ratio in the form $\frac{a}{b}$ or $a:b$, where a is the probability of the event occurring and b is the complement of the event, the probability of the event not occurring. If the odds in favor are given as 2:5, that means that you can expect the event to occur two times for every 5 times that it does not occur. In other words, the probability that the event will occur is $\frac{2}{2+5} = \frac{2}{7}$.

In probability, the **odds against an event** are the number of times the event will not occur compared to the number of times the event will occur. To calculate the odds against an event, use the formula $\frac{1-P(A)}{P(A)}$, where $P(A)$ is the probability that the event will occur. Many times, odds against is given as a ratio in the form $\frac{b}{a}$ or $b:a$, where b is the probability the event will not occur (the complement of the event) and a is the probability the event will occur. If the odds against an event are given as 3:1, that means that you can expect the event to not occur 3 times for every one time it does occur. In other words, 3 out of every 4 trials will fail.

If we have a two-way frequency table, it is generally a straightforward matter to read off the probabilities of any two events A and B, as well as the joint probability of both events occurring,

Copyright © Mometrix Media. You have been licensed one copy of this document for personal use only. Any other reproduction or redistribution is strictly prohibited. All rights reserved. This content is provided for test preparation purposes only and does not imply an endorsement by Mometrix of any particular political, scientific, or religious point of view.

$P(A \cap B)$. We can then find the conditional probability $P(A|B)$ by calculating $P(A|B) = \frac{P(A \cap B)}{P(B)}$. We could also check whether or not events are independent by verifying whether $P(A)P(B) = P(A \cap B)$.

For example, a certain store's recent T-shirt sales:

	Small	Medium	Large	Total
Blue	25	40	35	100
White	27	25	22	74
Black	8	23	15	46
Total	60	88	72	220

Suppose we want to find the conditional probability that a customer buys a black shirt (event A), given that the shirt he buys is size small (event B). From the table, the probability $P(B)$ that a customer buys a small shirt is $\frac{60}{220} = \frac{3}{11}$. The probability $P(A \cap B)$ that he buys a small, black shirt is $\frac{8}{220} = \frac{2}{55}$. The conditional probability $P(A|B)$ that he buys a black shirt, given that he buys a small shirt, is therefore $P(A|B) = \frac{2/55}{3/11} = \frac{2}{15}$.

Similarly, if we want to check whether the event a customer buys a blue shirt, A, is independent of the event that a customer buys a medium shirt, B. From the table, $P(A) = \frac{100}{220} = \frac{5}{11}$ and $P(B) = \frac{88}{220} = \frac{4}{10}$. Also, $P(A \cap B) = \frac{40}{220} = \frac{2}{11}$. Since $\left(\frac{5}{11}\right)\left(\frac{4}{10}\right) = \frac{20}{110} = \frac{2}{11}$, $P(A)P(B) = P(A \cap B)$ and these two events are indeed independent.

Statistics is the branch of mathematics that deals with collecting, recording, interpreting, illustrating, and analyzing large amounts of **data**. The following terms are often used in the discussion of data and **statistics**:

- **Data** – the collective name for pieces of information (singular is datum)
- **Quantitative data** – measurements (such as length, mass, and speed) that provide information about quantities in numbers
- **Qualitative data** – information (such as colors, scents, tastes, and shapes) that cannot be measured using numbers
- **Discrete data** – information that can be expressed only by a specific value, such as whole or half numbers. (e.g., since people can be counted only in whole numbers, a population count would be discrete data.)
- **Continuous data** – information (such as time and temperature) that can be expressed by any value within a given range
- **Primary data** – information that has been collected directly from a survey, investigation, or experiment, such as a questionnaire or the recording of daily temperatures. (Primary data that has not yet been organized or analyzed is called **raw data**.)
- **Secondary data** – information that has been collected, sorted, and processed by the researcher
- **Ordinal data** – information that can be placed in numerical order, such as age or weight
- **Nominal data** – information that *cannot* be placed in numerical order, such as names or places

Copyright © Mometrix Media. You have been licensed one copy of this document for personal use only. Any other reproduction or redistribution is strictly prohibited. All rights reserved.
This content is provided for test preparation purposes only and does not imply an endorsement by Mometrix of any particular political, scientific, or religious point of view.

DATA COLLECTION

POPULATION

In statistics, the **population** is the entire collection of people, plants, etc., that data can be collected from. For example, a study to determine how well students in local schools perform on a standardized test would have a population of all the students enrolled in those schools, although a study may include just a small sample of students from each school. A **parameter** is a numerical value that gives information about the population, such as the mean, median, mode, or standard deviation. Remember that the symbol for the mean of a population is μ and the symbol for the standard deviation of a population is σ.

SAMPLE

A **sample** is a portion of the entire population. Whereas a parameter helped describe the population, a **statistic** is a numerical value that gives information about the sample, such as mean, median, mode, or standard deviation. Keep in mind that the symbols for mean and standard deviation are different when they are referring to a sample rather than the entire population. For a sample, the symbol for mean is $\bar{x}$ and the symbol for standard deviation is s. The mean and standard deviation of a sample may or may not be identical to that of the entire population due to a sample only being a subset of the population. However, if the sample is random and large enough, statistically significant values can be attained. Samples are generally used when the population is too large to justify including every element or when acquiring data for the entire population is impossible.

INFERENTIAL STATISTICS

Inferential statistics is the branch of statistics that uses samples to make predictions about an entire population. This type of statistic is often seen in political polls, where a sample of the population is questioned about a particular topic or politician to gain an understanding of the attitudes of the entire population of the country. Often, exit polls are conducted on election days using this method. Inferential statistics can have a large margin of error if you do not have a valid sample.

SAMPLING DISTRIBUTION

Statistical values calculated from various samples of the same size make up the **sampling distribution**. For example, if several samples of identical size are randomly selected from a large population and then the mean of each sample is calculated, the distribution of values of the means would be a sampling distribution.

The **sampling distribution of the mean** is the distribution of the sample mean, $\bar{x}$, derived from random samples of a given size. It has three important characteristics. First, the mean of the sampling distribution of the mean is equal to the mean of the population that was sampled. Second, assuming the standard deviation is non-zero, the standard deviation of the sampling distribution of the mean equals the standard deviation of the sampled population divided by the square root of the sample size. This is sometimes called the standard error. Finally, as the sample size gets larger, the sampling distribution of the mean gets closer to a normal distribution via the central limit theorem.

SURVEY STUDY

A **survey study** is a method of gathering information from a small group in an attempt to gain enough information to make accurate general assumptions about the population. Once a survey study is completed, the results are then put into a summary report.

Copyright © Mometrix Media. You have been licensed one copy of this document for personal use only. Any other reproduction or redistribution is strictly prohibited. All rights reserved. This content is provided for test preparation purposes only and does not imply an endorsement by Mometrix of any particular political, scientific, or religious point of view.

Survey studies are generally in the format of surveys, interviews, or questionnaires as part of an effort to find opinions of a particular group or to find facts about a group.

It is important to note that the findings from a survey study are only as accurate as the sample chosen from the population.

CORRELATIONAL STUDIES

Correlational studies seek to determine how much one variable is affected by changes in a second variable. For example, correlational studies may look for a relationship between the amount of time a student spends studying for a test and the grade that student earned on the test or between student scores on college admissions tests and student grades in college.

It is important to note that correlational studies cannot show a cause and effect, but rather can show only that two variables are or are not potentially correlated.

EXPERIMENTAL STUDIES

Experimental studies take correlational studies one step farther, in that they attempt to prove or disprove a cause-and-effect relationship. These studies are performed by conducting a series of experiments to test the hypothesis. For a study to be scientifically accurate, it must have both an experimental group that receives the specified treatment and a control group that does not get the treatment. This is the type of study pharmaceutical companies do as part of drug trials for new medications. Experimental studies are only valid when the proper scientific method has been followed. In other words, the experiment must be well-planned and executed without bias in the testing process, all subjects must be selected at random, and the process of determining which subject is in which of the two groups must also be completely random.

OBSERVATIONAL STUDIES

Observational studies are the opposite of experimental studies. In observational studies, the tester cannot change or in any way control all of the variables in the test. For example, a study to determine which gender does better in math classes in school is strictly observational. You cannot change a person's gender, and you cannot change the subject being studied. The big downfall of observational studies is that you have no way of proving a cause-and-effect relationship because you cannot control outside influences. Events outside of school can influence a student's performance in school, and observational studies cannot take that into consideration.

RANDOM SAMPLES

For most studies, a **random sample** is necessary to produce valid results. Random samples should not have any particular influence to cause sampled subjects to behave one way or another. The goal is for the random sample to be a **representative sample**, or a sample whose characteristics give an accurate picture of the characteristics of the entire population. To accomplish this, you must make sure you have a proper **sample size**, or an appropriate number of elements in the sample.

BIASES

In statistical studies, biases must be avoided. **Bias** is an error that causes the study to favor one set of results over another. For example, if a survey to determine how the country views the president's job performance only speaks to registered voters in the president's party, the results will be skewed because a disproportionately large number of responders would tend to show approval, while a disproportionately large number of people in the opposite party would tend to express disapproval. **Extraneous variables** are, as the name implies, outside influences that can affect the outcome of a study. They are not always avoidable but could trigger bias in the result.

Copyright © Mometrix Media. You have been licensed one copy of this document for personal use only. Any other reproduction or redistribution is strictly prohibited. All rights reserved. This content is provided for test preparation purposes only and does not imply an endorsement by Mometrix of any particular political, scientific, or religious point of view.

DISPERSION

A **measure of dispersion** is a single value that helps to "interpret" the measure of central tendency by providing more information about how the data values in the set are distributed about the measure of central tendency. The measure of dispersion helps to eliminate or reduce the disadvantages of using the mean, median, or mode as a single measure of central tendency, and give a more accurate picture of the dataset as a whole. To have a measure of dispersion, you must know or calculate the range, standard deviation, or variance of the data set.

RANGE

The **range** of a set of data is the difference between the greatest and lowest values of the data in the set. To calculate the range, you must first make sure the units for all data values are the same, and then identify the greatest and lowest values. If there are multiple data values that are equal for the highest or lowest, just use one of the values in the formula. Write the answer with the same units as the data values you used to do the calculations.

> **Review Video: Statistical Range**
> Visit mometrix.com/academy and enter code: 778541

SAMPLE STANDARD DEVIATION

Standard deviation is a measure of dispersion that compares all the data values in the set to the mean of the set to give a more accurate picture. To find the **standard deviation of a sample**, use the formula

$$s = \sqrt{\frac{\sum_{i=1}^{n}(x_i - \bar{x})^2}{n-1}}$$

Note that s is the standard deviation of a sample, x_i represents the individual values in the data set, $\bar{x}$ is the mean of the data values in the set, and n is the number of data values in the set. The higher the value of the standard deviation is, the greater the variance of the data values from the mean. The units associated with the standard deviation are the same as the units of the data values.

> **Review Video: Standard Deviation**
> Visit mometrix.com/academy and enter code: 419469

SAMPLE VARIANCE

The **variance of a sample** is the square of the sample standard deviation (denoted s^2). While the mean of a set of data gives the average of the set and gives information about where a specific data value lies in relation to the average, the variance of the sample gives information about the degree to which the data values are spread out and tells you how close an individual value is to the average compared to the other values. The units associated with variance are the same as the units of the data values squared.

PERCENTILE

Percentiles and quartiles are other methods of describing data within a set. **Percentiles** tell what percentage of the data in the set fall below a specific point. For example, achievement test scores are often given in percentiles. A score at the 80th percentile is one which is equal to or higher than 80 percent of the scores in the set. In other words, 80 percent of the scores were lower than that score.

Copyright © Mometrix Media. You have been licensed one copy of this document for personal use only. Any other reproduction or redistribution is strictly prohibited. All rights reserved. This content is provided for test preparation purposes only and does not imply an endorsement by Mometrix of any particular political, scientific, or religious point of view.

Quartiles are percentile groups that make up quarter sections of the data set. The first quartile is the 25th percentile. The second quartile is the 50th percentile; this is also the median of the dataset. The third quartile is the 75th percentile.

SKEWNESS

Skewness is a way to describe the symmetry or asymmetry of the distribution of values in a dataset. If the distribution of values is symmetrical, there is no skew. In general the closer the mean of a data set is to the median of the data set, the less skew there is. Generally, if the mean is to the right of the median, the data set is *positively skewed*, or right-skewed, and if the mean is to the left of the median, the data set is *negatively skewed*, or left-skewed. However, this rule of thumb is not infallible. When the data values are graphed on a curve, a set with no skew will be a perfect bell curve.

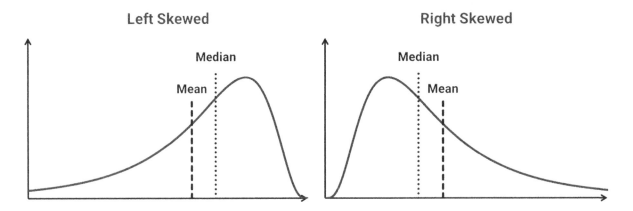

To estimate skew, use the formula:

$$\text{skew} = \frac{\sqrt{n(n-1)}}{n-2} \left(\frac{\frac{1}{n}\sum_{i=1}^{n}(x_i - \bar{x})^3}{\left(\frac{1}{n}\sum_{i=1}^{n}(x_i - \bar{x})^2\right)^{\frac{3}{2}}} \right)$$

Note that n is the datapoints in the set, x_i is the ith value in the set, and $\bar{x}$ is the mean of the set.

> **Review Video: Skew**
> Visit mometrix.com/academy and enter code: 661486

UNIMODAL VS. BIMODAL

If a distribution has a single peak, it would be considered **unimodal**. If it has two discernible peaks it would be considered **bimodal**. Bimodal distributions may be an indication that the set of data being considered is actually the combination of two sets of data with significant differences. A **uniform distribution** is a distribution in which there is *no distinct peak or variation* in the data. No values or ranges are particularly more common than any other values or ranges.

OUTLIER

An outlier is an extremely high or extremely low value in the data set. It may be the result of measurement error, in which case, the outlier is not a valid member of the data set. However, it may also be a valid member of the distribution. Unless a measurement error is identified, the experimenter cannot know for certain if an outlier is or is not a member of the distribution. There

Copyright © Mometrix Media. You have been licensed one copy of this document for personal use only. Any other reproduction or redistribution is strictly prohibited. All rights reserved. This content is provided for test preparation purposes only and does not imply an endorsement by Mometrix of any particular political, scientific, or religious point of view.

are arbitrary methods that can be employed to designate an extreme value as an outlier. One method designates an outlier (or possible outlier) to be any value less than $Q_1 - 1.5(IQR)$ or any value greater than $Q_3 + 1.5(IQR)$.

DATA ANALYSIS

SIMPLE REGRESSION

In statistics, **simple regression** is using an equation to represent a relation between independent and dependent variables. The independent variable is also referred to as the explanatory variable or the predictor and is generally represented by the variable x in the equation. The dependent variable, usually represented by the variable y, is also referred to as the response variable. The equation may be any type of function – linear, quadratic, exponential, etc. The best way to handle this task is to use the regression feature of your graphing calculator. This will easily give you the curve of best fit and provide you with the coefficients and other information you need to derive an equation.

LINE OF BEST FIT

In a scatter plot, the **line of best fit** is the line that best shows the trends of the data. The line of best fit is given by the equation $\hat{y} = ax + b$, where a and b are the regression coefficients. The regression coefficient a is also the slope of the line of best fit, and b is also the y-coordinate of the point at which the line of best fit crosses the y-axis. Not every point on the scatter plot will be on the line of best fit. The differences between the y-values of the points in the scatter plot and the corresponding y-values according to the equation of the line of best fit are the residuals. The line of best fit is also called the least-squares regression line because it is also the line that has the lowest sum of the squares of the residuals.

CORRELATION COEFFICIENT

The **correlation coefficient** is the numerical value that indicates how strong the relationship is between the two variables of a linear regression equation. A correlation coefficient of –1 is a perfect negative correlation. A correlation coefficient of +1 is a perfect positive correlation. Correlation coefficients close to –1 or +1 are very strong correlations. A correlation coefficient equal to zero indicates there is no correlation between the two variables. This test is a good indicator of whether or not the equation for the line of best fit is accurate. The formula for the correlation coefficient is

$$r = \frac{\sum_{i=1}^{n}(x_i - \bar{x})(y_i - \bar{y})}{\sqrt{\sum_{i=1}^{n}(x_i - \bar{x})^2}\sqrt{\sum_{i=1}^{n}(y_i - \bar{y})^2}}$$

where r is the correlation coefficient, n is the number of data values in the set, (x_i, y_i) is a point in the set, and $\bar{x}$ and $\bar{y}$ are the means.

Z-SCORE

A **z-score** is an indication of how many standard deviations a given value falls from the sample mean. To calculate a z-score, use the formula:

$$\frac{x - \bar{x}}{\sigma}$$

In this formula x is the data value, $\bar{x}$ is the mean of the sample data, and σ is the standard deviation of the population. If the z-score is positive, the data value lies above the mean. If the z-score is negative, the data value falls below the mean. These scores are useful in interpreting data such as standardized test scores, where every piece of data in the set has been counted, rather than just a

Copyright © Mometrix Media. You have been licensed one copy of this document for personal use only. Any other reproduction or redistribution is strictly prohibited. All rights reserved.
This content is provided for test preparation purposes only and does not imply an endorsement by Mometrix of any particular political, scientific, or religious point of view.

small random sample. In cases where standard deviations are calculated from a random sample of the set, the z-scores will not be as accurate.

CENTRAL LIMIT THEOREM

According to the **central limit theorem**, regardless of what the original distribution of a sample is, the distribution of the means tends to get closer and closer to a normal distribution as the sample size gets larger and larger (this is necessary because the sample is becoming more all-encompassing of the elements of the population). As the sample size gets larger, the distribution of the sample mean will approach a normal distribution with a mean of the population mean and a variance of the population variance divided by the sample size.

A **measure of central tendency** is a statistical value that gives a reasonable estimate for the center of a group of data. There are several different ways of describing the measure of central tendency. Each one has a unique way it is calculated, and each one gives a slightly different perspective on the data set. Whenever you give a measure of central tendency, always make sure the units are the same. If the data has different units, such as hours, minutes, and seconds, convert all the data to the same unit, and use the same unit in the measure of central tendency. If no units are given in the data, do not give units for the measure of central tendency.

MEAN

The **statistical mean** of a group of data is the same as the arithmetic average of that group. To find the mean of a set of data, first convert each value to the same units, if necessary. Then find the sum of all the values, and count the total number of data values, making sure you take into consideration each individual value. If a value appears more than once, count it more than once. Divide the sum of the values by the total number of values and apply the units, if any. Note that the mean does not have to be one of the data values in the set, and may not divide evenly.

$$\text{mean} = \frac{\text{sum of the data values}}{\text{quantity of data values}}$$

For instance, the mean of the data set {88, 72, 61, 90, 97, 68, 88, 79, 86, 93, 97, 71, 80, 84, 89} would be the sum of the fifteen numbers divided by 15:

$$\frac{88 + 72 + 61 + 90 + 97 + 68 + 88 + 79 + 86 + 93 + 97 + 71 + 80 + 84 + 89}{15} = \frac{1242}{15}$$
$$= 82.8$$

While the mean is relatively easy to calculate and averages are understood by most people, the mean can be very misleading if it is used as the sole measure of central tendency. If the data set has outliers (data values that are unusually high or unusually low compared to the rest of the data values), the mean can be very distorted, especially if the data set has a small number of values. If unusually high values are countered with unusually low values, the mean is not affected as much. For example, if five of twenty students in a class get a 100 on a test, but the other 15 students have an average of 60 on the same test, the class average would appear as 70. Whenever the mean is skewed by outliers, it is always a good idea to include the median as an alternate measure of central tendency.

A **weighted mean**, or weighted average, is a mean that uses "weighted" values. The formula is weighted mean $= \frac{w_1 x_1 + w_2 x_2 + w_3 x_3 \ldots + w_n x_n}{w_1 + w_2 + w_3 + \cdots + w_n}$. Weighted values, such as $w_1, w_2, w_3, \ldots w_n$ are assigned to

Copyright © Mometrix Media. You have been licensed one copy of this document for personal use only. Any other reproduction or redistribution is strictly prohibited. All rights reserved. This content is provided for test preparation purposes only and does not imply an endorsement by Mometrix of any particular political, scientific, or religious point of view.

each member of the set $x_1, x_2, x_3, \ldots x_n$. When calculating the weighted mean, make sure a weight value for each member of the set is used.

Review Video: All About Averages
Visit mometrix.com/academy and enter code: 176521

MEDIAN

The **statistical median** is the value in the middle of the set of data. To find the median, list all data values in order from smallest to largest or from largest to smallest. Any value that is repeated in the set must be listed the number of times it appears. If there are an odd number of data values, the median is the value in the middle of the list. If there is an even number of data values, the median is the arithmetic mean of the two middle values.

For example, the median of the data set {88, 72, 61, 90, 97, 68, 88, 79, 86, 93, 97, 71, 80, 84, 88} is 86 since the ordered set is {61, 68, 71, 72, 79, 80, 84, **86**, 88, 88, 88, 90, 93, 97, 97}.

The big disadvantage of using the median as a measure of central tendency is that is relies solely on a value's relative size as compared to the other values in the set. When the individual values in a set of data are evenly dispersed, the median can be an accurate tool. However, if there is a group of rather large values or a group of rather small values that are not offset by a different group of values, the information that can be inferred from the median may not be accurate because the distribution of values is skewed.

MODE

The **statistical mode** is the data value that occurs the greatest number of times in the data set. It is possible to have exactly one mode, more than one mode, or no mode. To find the mode of a set of data, arrange the data like you do to find the median (all values in order, listing all multiples of data values). Count the number of times each value appears in the data set. If all values appear an equal number of times, there is no mode. If one value appears more than any other value, that value is the mode. If two or more values appear the same number of times, but there are other values that appear fewer times and no values that appear more times, all of those values are the modes.

For example, the mode of the data set {**88**, 72, 61, 90, 97, 68, **88**, 79, 86, 93, 97, 71, 80, 84, **88**} is 88.

The main disadvantage of the mode is that the values of the other data in the set have no bearing on the mode. The mode may be the largest value, the smallest value, or a value anywhere in between in the set. The mode only tells which value or values, if any, occurred the greatest number of times. It does not give any suggestions about the remaining values in the set.

Review Video: Mean, Median, and Mode
Visit mometrix.com/academy and enter code: 286207

FREQUENCY TABLES

Frequency tables show how frequently each unique value appears in a set. A **relative frequency table** is one that shows the proportions of each unique value compared to the entire set. Relative frequencies are given as percentages; however, the total percent for a relative frequency table will

Copyright © Mometrix Media. You have been licensed one copy of this document for personal use only. Any other reproduction or redistribution is strictly prohibited. All rights reserved. This content is provided for test preparation purposes only and does not imply an endorsement by Mometrix of any particular political, scientific, or religious point of view.

not necessarily equal 100 percent due to rounding. An example of a frequency table with relative frequencies is below.

Favorite Color	Frequency	Relative Frequency
Blue	4	13%
Red	7	22%
Green	3	9%
Purple	6	19%
Cyan	12	38%

Review Video: Data Interpretation of Graphs
Visit mometrix.com/academy and enter code: 200439

CIRCLE GRAPHS

Circle graphs, also known as *pie charts*, provide a visual depiction of the relationship of each type of data compared to the whole set of data. The circle graph is divided into sections by drawing radii to create central angles whose percentage of the circle is equal to the individual data's percentage of the whole set. Each 1% of data is equal to 3.6° in the circle graph. Therefore, data represented by a 90° section of the circle graph makes up 25% of the whole. When complete, a circle graph often looks like a pie cut into uneven wedges. The pie chart below shows the data from the frequency table referenced earlier where people were asked their favorite color.

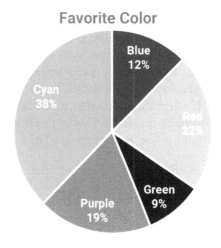

PICTOGRAPHS

A **pictograph** is a graph, generally in the horizontal orientation, that uses pictures or symbols to represent the data. Each pictograph must have a key that defines the picture or symbol and gives the quantity each picture or symbol represents. Pictures or symbols on a pictograph are not always shown as whole elements. In this case, the fraction of the picture or symbol shown represents the same fraction of the quantity a whole picture or symbol stands for. For example, a row with $3\frac{1}{2}$ ears of corn, where each ear of corn represents 100 stalks of corn in a field, would equal $3\frac{1}{2} \times 100 = 350$ stalks of corn in the field.

Review Video: Pictographs
Visit mometrix.com/academy and enter code: 147860

Copyright © Mometrix Media. You have been licensed one copy of this document for personal use only. Any other reproduction or redistribution is strictly prohibited. All rights reserved. This content is provided for test preparation purposes only and does not imply an endorsement by Mometrix of any particular political, scientific, or religious point of view.

LINE GRAPHS

Line graphs have one or more lines of varying styles (solid or broken) to show the different values for a set of data. The individual data are represented as ordered pairs, much like on a Cartesian plane. In this case, the x- and y-axes are defined in terms of their units, such as dollars or time. The individual plotted points are joined by line segments to show whether the value of the data is increasing (line sloping upward), decreasing (line sloping downward), or staying the same (horizontal line). Multiple sets of data can be graphed on the same line graph to give an easy visual comparison. An example of this would be graphing achievement test scores for different groups of students over the same time period to see which group had the greatest increase or decrease in performance from year to year (as shown below).

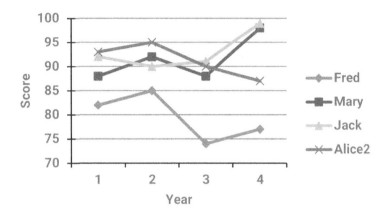

> **Review Video: How to Create a Line Graph**
> Visit mometrix.com/academy and enter code: 480147

LINE PLOTS

A **line plot**, also known as a *dot plot*, has plotted points that are not connected by line segments. In this graph, the horizontal axis lists the different possible values for the data, and the vertical axis lists the number of times the individual value occurs. A single dot is graphed for each value to show the number of times it occurs. This graph is more closely related to a bar graph than a line graph. Do not connect the dots in a line plot or it will misrepresent the data.

> **Review Video: Line Plot**
> Visit mometrix.com/academy and enter code: 754610

STEM AND LEAF PLOTS

A **stem and leaf plot** is useful for depicting groups of data that fall into a range of values. Each piece of data is separated into two parts: the first, or left, part is called the stem; the second, or right, part is called the leaf. Each stem is listed in a column from smallest to largest. Each leaf that has the common stem is listed in that stem's row from smallest to largest. For example, in a set of two-digit numbers, the digit in the tens place is the stem, and the digit in the ones place is the leaf. With a stem and leaf plot, you can easily see which subset of numbers (10s, 20s, 30s, etc.) is the largest. This information is also readily available by looking at a histogram, but a stem and leaf plot also allows you to look closer and see exactly which values fall in that range. Using a sample set of test

Copyright © Mometrix Media. You have been licensed one copy of this document for personal use only. Any other reproduction or redistribution is strictly prohibited. All rights reserved.
This content is provided for test preparation purposes only and does not imply an endorsement by Mometrix of any particular political, scientific, or religious point of view.

scores (82, 88, 92, 93, 85, 90, 92, 95, 74, 88, 90, 91, 78, 87, 98, 99), we can assemble a stem and leaf plot like the one below.

Test Scores

7	4	8						
8	2	5	7	8	8			
9	0	0	1	2	2	3	5	8	9

> **Review Video: Stem and Leaf Plots**
> Visit mometrix.com/academy and enter code: 302339

BAR GRAPHS

A **bar graph** is one of the few graphs that can be drawn correctly in two different configurations – both horizontally and vertically. A bar graph is similar to a line plot in the way the data is organized on the graph. Both axes must have their categories defined for the graph to be useful. Rather than placing a single dot to mark the point of the data's value, a bar, or thick line, is drawn from zero to the exact value of the data, whether it is a number, percentage, or other numerical value. Longer bar lengths correspond to greater data values. To read a bar graph, read the labels for the axes to find the units being reported. Then, look where the bars end in relation to the scale given on the corresponding axis and determine the associated value.

The bar chart below represents the responses from our favorite-color survey.

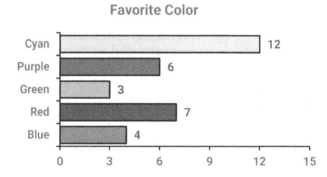

HISTOGRAMS

At first glance, a **histogram** looks like a vertical bar graph. The difference is that a bar graph has a separate bar for each piece of data and a histogram has one continuous bar for each *range* of data. For example, a histogram may have one bar for the range 0–9, one bar for 10–19, etc. While a bar graph has numerical values on one axis, a histogram has numerical values on both axes. Each range is of equal size, and they are ordered left to right from lowest to highest. The height of each column on a histogram represents the number of data values within that range. Like a stem and leaf plot, a

214

Copyright © Mometrix Media. You have been licensed one copy of this document for personal use only. Any other reproduction or redistribution is strictly prohibited. All rights reserved.
This content is provided for test preparation purposes only and does not imply an endorsement by Mometrix of any particular political, scientific, or religious point of view.

histogram makes it easy to glance at the graph and quickly determine which range has the greatest quantity of values. A simple example of a histogram is below.

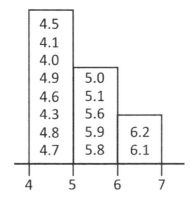

5-NUMBER SUMMARY

The **5-number summary** of a set of data gives a very informative picture of the set. The five numbers in the summary include the minimum value, maximum value, and the three quartiles. This information gives the reader the range and median of the set, as well as an indication of how the data is spread about the median.

BOX AND WHISKER PLOTS

A **box-and-whiskers plot** is a graphical representation of the 5-number summary. To draw a box-and-whiskers plot, plot the points of the 5-number summary on a number line. Draw a box whose ends are through the points for the first and third quartiles. Draw a vertical line in the box through the median to divide the box in half. Draw a line segment from the first quartile point to the minimum value, and from the third quartile point to the maximum value.

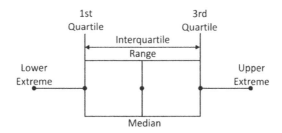

> **Review Video: Box and Whisker Plots**
> Visit mometrix.com/academy and enter code: 810817

EXAMPLE

Given the following data (32, 28, 29, 26, 35, 27, 30, 31, 27, 32), we first sort it into numerical order: 26, 27, 27, 28, 29, 30, 31, 32, 32, 35. We can then find the median. Since there are ten values, we take the average of the 5th and 6th values to get 29.5. We find the lower quartile by taking the median of the data smaller than the median. Since there are five values, we take the 3rd value, which is 27. We find the upper quartile by taking the median of the data larger than the overall median,

Copyright © Mometrix Media. You have been licensed one copy of this document for personal use only. Any other reproduction or redistribution is strictly prohibited. All rights reserved.
This content is provided for test preparation purposes only and does not imply an endorsement by Mometrix of any particular political, scientific, or religious point of view.

which is 32. Finally, we note our minimum and maximum, which are simply the smallest and largest values in the set: 26 and 35, respectively. Now we can create our box plot:

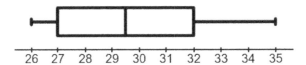

This plot is fairly "long" on the right whisker, showing one or more unusually high values (but not quite outliers). The other quartiles are similar in length, showing a fairly even distribution of data.

INTERQUARTILE RANGE

The **interquartile range, or IQR**, is the difference between the upper and lower quartiles. It measures how the data is dispersed: a high IQR means that the data is more spread out, while a low IQR means that the data is clustered more tightly around the median. To find the IQR, subtract the lower quartile value (Q_1) from the upper quartile value (Q_3).

EXAMPLE

To find the upper and lower quartiles, we first find the median and then take the median of all values above it and all values below it. In the following data set (16, 18, 13, 24, 16, 51, 32, 21, 27, 39), we first rearrange the values in numerical order: 13, 16, 16, 18, 21, 24, 27, 32, 39, 51. There are 10 values, so the median is the average of the 5th and 6th: $\frac{21+24}{2} = \frac{45}{2} = 22.5$. We do not actually need this value to find the upper and lower quartiles. We look at the set of numbers below the median: 13, 16, 16, 18, 21. There are five values, so the 3rd is the median (16), or the value of the lower quartile (Q_1). Then we look at the numbers above the median: 24, 27, 32, 39, 51. Again there are five values, so the 3rd is the median (32), or the value of the upper quartile (Q_3). We find the IQR by subtracting Q_1 from Q_3: $32 - 16 = 16$.

68-95-99.7 RULE

The **68–95–99.7 rule** describes how a normal distribution of data should appear when compared to the mean. This is also a description of a normal bell curve. According to this rule, 68 percent of the data values in a normally distributed set should fall within one standard deviation of the mean (34 percent above and 34 percent below the mean), 95 percent of the data values should fall within two standard deviations of the mean (47.5 percent above and 47.5 percent below the mean), and 99.7 percent of the data values should fall within three standard deviations of the mean, again, equally distributed on either side of the mean. This means that only 0.3 percent of all data values should fall more than three standard deviations from the mean. On the graph below, the normal

Copyright © Mometrix Media. You have been licensed one copy of this document for personal use only. Any other reproduction or redistribution is strictly prohibited. All rights reserved. This content is provided for test preparation purposes only and does not imply an endorsement by Mometrix of any particular political, scientific, or religious point of view.

curve is centered on the *y*-axis. The *x*-axis labels are how many standard deviations away from the center you are. Therefore, it is easy to see how the 68-95-99.7 rule can apply.

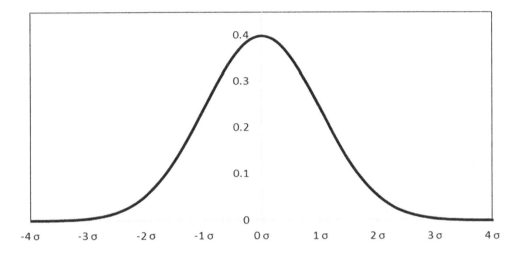

A **frequency distribution** sorts data to give a clear visual representation of the distribution. Numbers are grouped with like numbers (for instance, all numbers in their twenties may be grouped together) to measure the frequency.

EXAMPLE

We can sort the following set of numbers into a frequency distribution based on the value of the tens place: 20, 12, 37, 18, 21, 19, 32, 21, 16, and 14. To do this, we group them into sets by first digit and create a table. This can include just category and frequency, but can also include relative frequency or percentage:

Category	Frequency	Relative Frequency	Percentage
Tens	5	0.5	50%
Twenties	3	0.3	30%
Thirties	2	0.2	20%

We can see that there is a higher concentration of numbers in the tens than any other group. This means that the data will likely be skewed right, with the mean greater than the median.

CUMULATIVE FREQUENCY DISTRIBUTIONS

A **cumulative frequency distribution**, rather than showing the amount in each category, shows the *cumulative* amount. In other words, the amount for each new category is added to each of the previous amounts to show the cumulative sum. This is helpful when the goal is to compare not single groups against each other, but to look at several groups as a sample. For instance, in a cumulative frequency distribution based on employees' salaries, a person could immediately see how many employees make at or below a certain amount per year.

EXAMPLE

A teacher could create a cumulative frequency distribution out of the following test grades: 89, 76, 74, 92, 83, 86, 90, 87, 85, 82, 95, 68, 97, 94, 86, 82, 89, 81, 78, 82. The grades could be divided into

Copyright © Mometrix Media. You have been licensed one copy of this document for personal use only. Any other reproduction or redistribution is strictly prohibited. All rights reserved. This content is provided for test preparation purposes only and does not imply an endorsement by Mometrix of any particular political, scientific, or religious point of view.

groups and placed in a table, adding on each new group to the previous to find the cumulative frequency:

Limits	Frequency	Cumulative frequency
0–75	2	2
76–80	2	4
81–85	6	10
86–90	6	16
91–95	3	19
96–100	1	20

Now the teacher can easily see, for instance, that 10 of the 20 students are scoring at 85 or below.

BIVARIATE DATA

Bivariate data is simply data from two different variables. (The prefix *bi-* means *two*.) In a *scatter plot*, each value in the set of data is plotted on a grid similar to a Cartesian plane, where each axis represents one of the two variables. By looking at the pattern formed by the points on the grid, you can often determine whether or not there is a relationship between the two variables, and what that relationship is, if it exists. The variables may be directly proportionate, inversely proportionate, or show no proportion at all. It may also be possible to determine if the data is linear, and if so, to find an equation to relate the two variables. The following scatter plot shows the relationship between preference for brand "A" and the age of the consumers surveyed.

Copyright © Mometrix Media. You have been licensed one copy of this document for personal use only. Any other reproduction or redistribution is strictly prohibited. All rights reserved.
This content is provided for test preparation purposes only and does not imply an endorsement by Mometrix of any particular political, scientific, or religious point of view.

SCATTER PLOTS

Scatter plots are also useful in determining the type of function represented by the data and finding the simple regression. Linear scatter plots may be positive or negative. Nonlinear scatter plots are generally exponential or quadratic. Below are some common types of scatter plots:

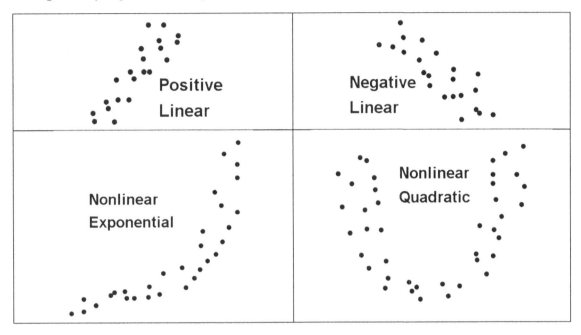

> **Review Video: What is a Scatter Plot?**
> Visit mometrix.com/academy and enter code: 596526

SET OPERATIONS WITH VENN DIAGRAMS

A Venn diagram is a useful visual tool for representing two or three sets and their common elements. Each set is drawn as a **circle**, with the different circles overlapping. Elements are placed in the circle corresponding to the appropriate set or sets—or placed outside all the circles if they belong to the universe of discourse but not to any of the sets.

For example, suppose our universe of discourse is the integers from 1 to 9, and we have the three sets $A = \{1, 2, 3, 4, 5, 6\}$, $B = \{4, 5, 6, 7\}$, and $C = \{3, 6, 9\}$. This could be illustrated with the following **Venn diagram**:

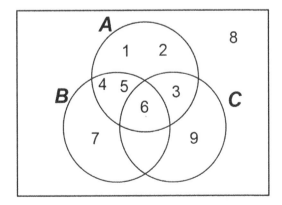

Copyright © Mometrix Media. You have been licensed one copy of this document for personal use only. Any other reproduction or redistribution is strictly prohibited. All rights reserved.
This content is provided for test preparation purposes only and does not imply an endorsement by Mometrix of any particular political, scientific, or religious point of view.

Note, for example, that 6 appears in the center of the diagram where all three circles overlap, because it is an element of all three sets. On the other hand, 8 is placed outside the three circles because it is not an element of any of the sets. Sometimes, instead of writing the elements themselves in the diagram, the total *number* of elements in each part of the Venn diagram is noted. This is especially useful for solving problems involving these numbers of elements.

USING VENN DIAGRAMS TO SOLVE PROBLEMS

Venn diagrams are useful for solving problems involving the numbers of elements in sets and in their intersections. By putting those numbers into a Venn diagram, it's simple to see how many must be in the "leftover" parts.

For example, suppose we're told that 200 voters were polled about two propositions, Proposition 1 and Proposition 2. Further, 120 support Proposition 1, 85 support Proposition 2, and 50 support both propositions. To find how many of the voters support neither proposition, we can draw a Venn diagram with a circle representing the supporters of each proposition. We know 50 voters support both propositions, so we can write a 50 in the center of the diagram.

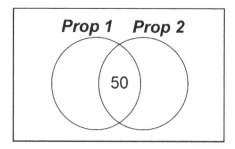

The Proposition 1 circle should contain 120 voters total, so subtracting the 50 voters in the overlap, the other section of the circle must contain $120 - 50 = 70$. Similarly, the nonoverlapping part of the Proposition 2 circle should contain $85 - 50 = 35$.

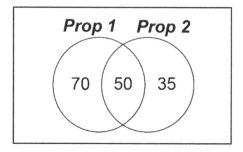

Adding all three sections, the total number of voters supporting either proposition is $70 + 50 + 35 = 155$, so there must be $200 - 155 = 45$ voters who support neither.

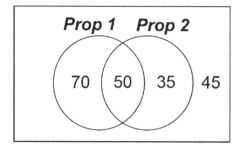

Copyright © Mometrix Media. You have been licensed one copy of this document for personal use only. Any other reproduction or redistribution is strictly prohibited. All rights reserved.
This content is provided for test preparation purposes only and does not imply an endorsement by Mometrix of any particular political, scientific, or religious point of view.

Mathematics Practice Test 1

1. Edward draws a card from a standard deck of cards, does not replace it, and then draws another card. What is the probability that he draws a heart and then a spade?

a. $\dfrac{1}{16}$

b. $\dfrac{1}{2}$

c. $\dfrac{1}{17}$

d. $\dfrac{13}{204}$

e. $\dfrac{1}{3}$

2. Given the double bar graph shown below, which of the following statements is true?

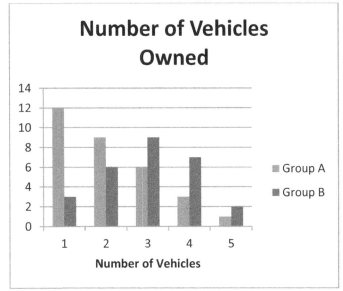

a. Group A is negatively skewed, while Group B is approximately normal.
b. Group A is positively skewed, while Group B is approximately normal.
c. Group A is positively skewed, while Group B is neutral.
d. Group A is approximately normal, while Group B is negatively skewed.
e. Group A is approximately normal, while Group B is positively skewed.

3. Identical rugs are offered for sale at two local shops and one online retailer, designated Stores A, B, and C, respectively. The rug's regular sales price is $296 at Store A, $220 at Store B, and $198.00 at Store C. Stores A and B collect 8% in sales tax on any after-discount price, while Store C collects no tax but charges a $35 shipping fee. A buyer has a 30% off coupon for Store A and a $10 off coupon for Store B. Which of these lists the stores in order of lowest to highest final sales price after all discounts, taxes, and fees are applied?

a. Store A, Store B, Store C
b. Store B, Store A, Store C
c. Store B, Store C, Store A
d. Store C, Store A, Store B
e. Store C, Store B, Store A

221

Copyright © Mometrix Media. You have been licensed one copy of this document for personal use only. Any other reproduction or redistribution is strictly prohibited. All rights reserved.
This content is provided for test preparation purposes only and does not imply an endorsement by Mometrix of any particular political, scientific, or religious point of view.

4. Which of the following values is closest to the diameter of a circle with an area of 314 square inches?

    a. 2π in

    b.   10 in

    c.   20 in

    d.   31.4 in

    e.   100 in

5. Which of the following fractions is in lowest terms?

    a. $\frac{6}{50}$

    b. $\frac{12}{100}$

    c. $\frac{3}{25}$

    d. $\frac{12}{10}$

    e. $\frac{12}{4}$

6. Natasha designs a square pyramidal tent for her children. Each of the sides of the square base measures x ft, and the tent's height is h feet. If Natasha were to increase by 1 ft the length of each side of the base, how much more interior space would the tent have?

    a. $\frac{h(x^2+2x+1)}{3}$ ft^3

    b. $\frac{h(2x+1)}{3}$ ft^3

    c. $\frac{x^2h+3}{3}$ ft^3

    d. $\frac{x^2h}{3}$ ft^3

    e. 1 ft^3

7. Identify the median for the data set {53, 81, 85, 82, 91, 72}.

    a.   81.5

    b.   81

    c.   77

    d.   38

    e.   83.5

Copyright © Mometrix Media. You have been licensed one copy of this document for personal use only. Any other reproduction or redistribution is strictly prohibited. All rights reserved.
This content is provided for test preparation purposes only and does not imply an endorsement by Mometrix of any particular political, scientific, or religious point of view.

Refer to the following for question 8:

An MP3 player is set to play songs at random from the fifteen songs it contains in memory. Any song can be played at any time, even if it is repeated. There are 5 songs by Band A, 3 songs by Band B, 2 by Band C, and 5 by Band D.

8. What is the probability that the next two songs will both be by Band B?

    a. $\dfrac{1}{25}$

    b. $\dfrac{1}{9}$

    c. $\dfrac{1}{5}$

    d. $\dfrac{1}{3}$

    e. $\dfrac{1}{2}$

9. What is 40% of 360?

    a.   90
    b.   120
    c.   144
    d.   176
    e.   270

10. Raul, Eli, Henry, and Lex all bought the same shirt from different stores for different prices. They spent $18.00, $18.50, $15.39 and $19.99 respectively. What is the average price the four men spent for the shirt?

    a. $15.97
    b. $16.97
    c. $17.97
    d. $18.97
    e. $19.97

Copyright © Mometrix Media. You have been licensed one copy of this document for personal use only. Any other reproduction or redistribution is strictly prohibited. All rights reserved. This content is provided for test preparation purposes only and does not imply an endorsement by Mometrix of any particular political, scientific, or religious point of view.

11. Forty students in a class take a test that is graded on a scale of 1 to 10. The histogram in the figure shows the grade distribution, with the x-axis representing the grades and the y-axis representing the number of students who obtain each grade. If the mean, median, and mode values are represented by n, p, and q, respectively, which of the following is true?

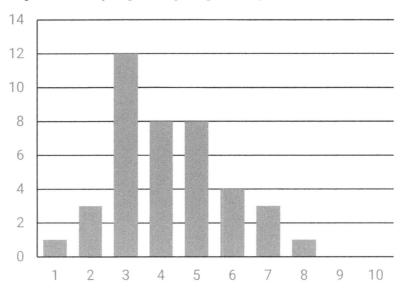

    a. $n > p > q$
    b. $n > q > p$
    c. $q > p > n$
    d. $p > q > n$
    e. $q > n > p$

12. Portia tosses a coin 1,000 times. Which of the following best represents the number of times she can expect to get tails?

    a. 350
    b. 400
    c. 450
    d. 500
    e. 1,000

13. Solve for x: $(2x - 6) + 4x = 24$

    a. 0
    b. -3
    c. 5
    d. -5
    e. 3

Copyright © Mometrix Media. You have been licensed one copy of this document for personal use only. Any other reproduction or redistribution is strictly prohibited. All rights reserved. This content is provided for test preparation purposes only and does not imply an endorsement by Mometrix of any particular political, scientific, or religious point of view.

14. On Day 1, a driver averages 60 miles per hour for 15 hours of a 2,000-mile car trip. If he maintains this average speed and duration on Day 2, how far will he be from his destination at the end of the day?

    a. 200 miles
    b. 400 miles
    c. 500 miles
    d. 700 miles
    e. 900 miles

15. What is the average of $\frac{7}{5}$ and 1.4?

    a. 1.4
    b. 2.8
    c. 4.2
    d. 5.6
    e. 7.4

16. There is a big sale taking place at the clothing store on Main Street. Everything is marked down by 33% from the original price, p. Which of the following expressions describes the sale price, S, to be paid for any item?

    a. $S = p - 0.33$
    b. $S = p - 0.33p$
    c. $S = 0.33p$
    d. $S = 0.33(1 - p)$
    e. $S = p + 0.33p$

17. A new ramp is being installed at the entrance to a building.

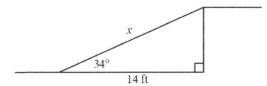

Based on the figure above, what is the length of the ramp, shown by x?

    a. $14 \cos 34°$ ft
    b. $\dfrac{14}{\cos 34°}$ ft
    c. $\dfrac{14}{\tan 34°}$ ft
    d. $\dfrac{14}{\sin 34°}$ ft
    e. $14 \sin 34°$ ft

18. Solve for y when $\frac{y}{2} - 8 = 0$.

    a. $y = 4$
    b. $y = 8$
    c. $y = 2$
    d. $y = 16$
    e. $y = 6$

Copyright © Mometrix Media. You have been licensed one copy of this document for personal use only. Any other reproduction or redistribution is strictly prohibited. All rights reserved.
This content is provided for test preparation purposes only and does not imply an endorsement by Mometrix of any particular political, scientific, or religious point of view.

19. A long-distance runner does a first lap around a track in exactly 50 seconds. As she tires, each subsequent lap takes 20% longer than the previous one. How long does she take to run 3 laps?

    a. 72 seconds
    b. 150 seconds
    c. 160 seconds
    d. 180 seconds
    e. 182 seconds

20. Which of the following choices could display data in a misleading way?

    a. Starting the y-axis at zero, even when dealing with very large numbers
    b. Listing categorical data in alphabetical order along the x-axis
    c. Choosing very small intervals for the y-axis to exaggerate differences in data
    d. Letting the number of data points determine the number of bins for a histogram
    e. Including all data collected, even if it is not consistent with the outcome you were hoping for

21. What is the probability of spinning a 2 on the first try on the spinner below?

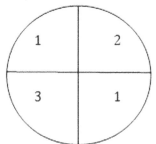

    a. $\frac{1}{2}$
    b. $\frac{1}{3}$
    c. $\frac{1}{4}$
    d. $\frac{2}{3}$
    e. $\frac{2}{4}$

22. Solve for x:

$$\frac{1}{6} \div \frac{3}{8} = x$$

    a. $x = \frac{1}{16}$
    b. $x = \frac{4}{9}$
    c. $x = 2\frac{3}{8}$
    d. $x = \frac{1}{2}$
    e. $x = 2\frac{1}{3}$

Copyright © Mometrix Media. You have been licensed one copy of this document for personal use only. Any other reproduction or redistribution is strictly prohibited. All rights reserved.
This content is provided for test preparation purposes only and does not imply an endorsement by Mometrix of any particular political, scientific, or religious point of view.

23. Simplify $8(x + 2) - 7 + 4(x - 7)$.

    a. $5x + 23$
    b. $5x - 23$
    c. $12x - 19$
    d. $12x + 19$
    e. $12x + 37$

24. What is the simplest form of $\frac{3}{8} \times \frac{3}{8}$?

    a. $\frac{3}{4}$
    b. $\frac{6}{8}$
    c. $\frac{9}{64}$
    d. 1
    e. $1\frac{1}{8}$

25. Three rectangular gardens, each with an area of 48 square feet, are created on a tract of land. Garden A measures 6 feet by 8 feet; Garden B measures 12 feet by 4 feet; Garden C measures 16 feet by 3 feet. Which garden will require the least amount of fencing to surround it?

    a. Garden A
    b. Garden B
    c. Garden C
    d. All gardens will require the same amount of fencing
    e. It cannot be determined from the information provided

26. Herbert plans to use the earnings from his lemonade stand, according to the table below, for the first month of operations. If he buys $70 worth of lemons, how much profit does he take home?

Cash Flow Item	Percentage of Total Earning Used on Item
Lemons	35%
Sugar	20%
Cups	25%
Stand improvements	5%
Profits	15%

    a. $15
    b. $20
    c. $30
    d. $35
    e. $40

Copyright © Mometrix Media. You have been licensed one copy of this document for personal use only. Any other reproduction or redistribution is strictly prohibited. All rights reserved. This content is provided for test preparation purposes only and does not imply an endorsement by Mometrix of any particular political, scientific, or religious point of view.

27. Which of the following would NOT satisfy $x \geq \frac{2}{5}$?

    a. $x = \frac{5}{11}$
    b. $x = \frac{3}{7}$
    c. $x = \frac{1}{2}$
    d. $x = \frac{1}{3}$
    e. $x = \frac{7}{15}$

28. Justin wants to re-carpet his rectangular bedroom. The bedroom has a length of 12 feet and a width of 10 feet. Which of the following measures should Justin calculate to determine the amount of carpet he will need?

    a. Justin should calculate the perimeter of his bedroom.
    b. Justin should calculate the area of the floor of his bedroom.
    c. Justin should calculate the volume of his bedroom.
    d. Justin should calculate the circumference of his bedroom.
    e. Justin should calculate the surface area of his bedroom.

29. CF is a straight line. Angle BDF measures 45°. What is the measure of angle BDC?

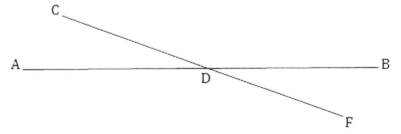

    a. 45°
    b. 135°
    c. 180°
    d. 225°
    e. 315°

30. Rachel spent $24.15 on vegetables. She bought 2 pounds of onions, 3 pounds of carrots, and $1\frac{1}{2}$ pounds of mushrooms. If the onions cost $3.69 per pound and the carrots cost $4.29 per pound, what is the price per pound of mushrooms?

    a. $2.25
    b. $2.60
    c. $2.75
    d. $2.80
    e. $3.10

Copyright © Mometrix Media. You have been licensed one copy of this document for personal use only. Any other reproduction or redistribution is strictly prohibited. All rights reserved.
This content is provided for test preparation purposes only and does not imply an endorsement by Mometrix of any particular political, scientific, or religious point of view.

31. Lauren had $80 in her savings account. When she received her paycheck, she made a deposit, which brought the balance up to $120. By what percentage did the total amount in her account increase as a result of this deposit?

a. 35%
b. 40%
c. 50%
d. 80%
e. 120%

32. An ice-cream shop offers sundaes that include a choice of an ice cream flavor, a topping, and a sauce (either hot fudge or caramel). The different ice cream flavors are chocolate, vanilla, and strawberry. The choices of toppings are sprinkles and cherries. Which of the following tree diagrams correctly shows the total number of ice-cream sundaes that could be created using one flavor of ice cream, one topping, and either hot fudge or caramel?

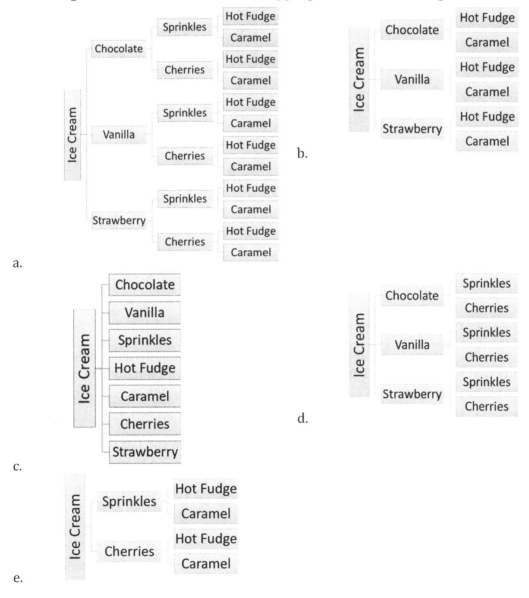

Copyright © Mometrix Media. You have been licensed one copy of this document for personal use only. Any other reproduction or redistribution is strictly prohibited. All rights reserved. This content is provided for test preparation purposes only and does not imply an endorsement by Mometrix of any particular political, scientific, or religious point of view.

33. A six-sided die is rolled one time. What is the probability of the roll yielding an odd number?

    a. 10%

    b. 20%

    c. 25%

    d. 30%

    e. 50%

34. In the figure below, ΔJKL is dilated to the image $\Delta J'K'L'$.

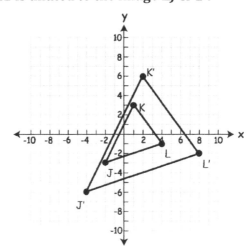

What is the scale factor of the dilation?

    a. $\frac{1}{3}$

    b. $\frac{1}{2}$

    c. 2

    d. 3

    e. $\frac{1}{4}$

Refer to the following for question 35:

Kyle bats third in the batting order for the Badgers baseball team. The table below shows the number of hits that Kyle had in each of 7 consecutive games played during one week in July.

Day	Monday	Tuesday	Wednesday	Thursday	Friday	Saturday	Sunday
Hits	1	2	3	1	1	4	2

35. What is the mean of the numbers in the distribution shown in the table?

    a. 1

    b. 2

    c. 3

    d. 4

    e. 7

Copyright © Mometrix Media. You have been licensed one copy of this document for personal use only. Any other reproduction or redistribution is strictly prohibited. All rights reserved.
This content is provided for test preparation purposes only and does not imply an endorsement by Mometrix of any particular political, scientific, or religious point of view.

36. A pair of $500 earrings is offered today at a 25% discount. If it is your birthday month, the store will take another 5% off of the discounted price. What does Mary pay for the earrings, since this is her birthday month?

    a. $250.50
    b. $300.00
    c. $356.25
    d. $405.75
    e. $400.00

37. A pump fills a cylindrical tank with water at a constant rate. The function $L(g) = 0.3g$ represents the water level of the tank (in feet) after g gallons are pumped into the tank. The function $w(t) = 1.2t$ represents the number of gallons that can be pumped into the tank in t minutes. Write a function $L(t)$ for the water level of the tank after t minutes.

    a. $L(t) = 0.25t$
    b. $L(t) = 0.36t$
    c. $L(t) = 0.9t$
    d. $L(t) = 3.6t$
    e. $L(t) = 4t$

38. Aniyah has two pairs of jeans and three shirts. How many different outfits can she create, assuming each outfit consists of one pair of jeans and a shirt?

    a. 9 outfits
    b. 5 outfits
    c. 6 outfits
    d. 8 outfits
    e. 12 outfits

39. A hotel's Internet service costs guests $3.00 for the first hour of use and $0.15 for each five minutes over that. A woman uses the service for 3 hours and 10 minutes. What will her Internet charge be?

    a. $3.90
    b. $5.60
    c. $6.90
    d. $7.20
    e. $9.30

40. Which angle measure forms a complementary angle when combined with an angle measure of 48°?

    a. 42°
    b. 48°
    c. 52°
    d. 90°
    e. 132°

Copyright © Mometrix Media. You have been licensed one copy of this document for personal use only. Any other reproduction or redistribution is strictly prohibited. All rights reserved.
This content is provided for test preparation purposes only and does not imply an endorsement by Mometrix of any particular political, scientific, or religious point of view.

41. If the two lines $2x + y = 0$ and $y = 3$ are plotted on a typical xy-coordinate grid, at which point will they intersect?

    a. $\left(-\frac{3}{2}, 0\right)$

    b. $\left(-\frac{3}{2}, 3\right)$

    c. $\left(\frac{3}{2}, 3\right)$

    d. $(4, 1)$

    e. $(4.5, 1)$

42. Which number is equivalent to 2^{-3}?

    a. $\frac{1}{2}$

    b. $\frac{1}{4}$

    c. $\frac{1}{8}$

    d. $\frac{1}{12}$

    e. $\frac{1}{16}$

43. There are 100 bacteria in a Petri dish. The number of bacteria doubles every day, so that on the first day, there are 100 bacteria; on the second, there are 200; on the third, there are 400; and so on. Write a formula for the number of bacteria on the nth day.

    a. $b(n) = 100 \times 2^{n-1}$

    b. $b(n) = 100n$

    c. $b(n) = 100n^2$

    d. $b(n) = 200(n - 1)$

    e. $b(n) = 200n^2$

44. A bag contains 5 red marbles, 4 green marbles, and 3 yellow marbles. What is the probability that Fran pulls a red marble, keeps that marble in her possession, and then pulls a green marble?

    a. $\frac{5}{36}$

    b. $\frac{1}{6}$

    c. $\frac{7}{132}$

    d. $\frac{5}{33}$

    e. $\frac{4}{11}$

Copyright © Mometrix Media. You have been licensed one copy of this document for personal use only. Any other reproduction or redistribution is strictly prohibited. All rights reserved.
This content is provided for test preparation purposes only and does not imply an endorsement by Mometrix of any particular political, scientific, or religious point of view.

45. The possible combinations of candy bars and packages of suckers that Amanda may purchase are represented by the graph shown below.

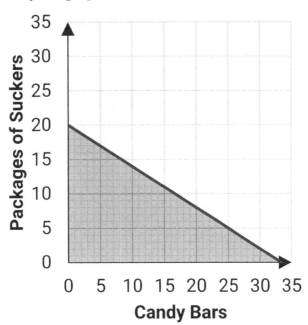

Which of the following inequalities represents the possible combinations of candy bars and packages of suckers that she may purchase?

a. $y \leq -\frac{1}{2}x + \frac{40}{3}$

b. $y \leq -\frac{2}{5}x + 20$

c. $y \leq -\frac{3}{5}x + 20$

d. $y \leq -\frac{5}{3}x + \frac{80}{3}$

e. $y \leq -\frac{2}{3}x + \frac{80}{3}$

46. Kylie describes the mode of the data set {67, 29, 57, 27, 38, 91} as zero. Which option best explains Kylie's interpretation of the data?

a. Kylie is correct because there is no value that occurs more than any other value so our mode is zero.

b. Kylie is incorrect because 27 and 29 can be averaged to find a mode of 28.

c. Kyle is correct because when we add all of our numbers and divide by 6 we get zero.

d. Kylie is incorrect because zero is not a value in the data set, therefore it cannot be the mode.

e. Kylie is incorrect because zero is never a valid mode for a data set.

Copyright © Mometrix Media. You have been licensed one copy of this document for personal use only. Any other reproduction or redistribution is strictly prohibited. All rights reserved.
This content is provided for test preparation purposes only and does not imply an endorsement by Mometrix of any particular political, scientific, or religious point of view.

47. Kendra uses the pie chart below to represent the allocation of her annual income. Her annual income is $40,000.

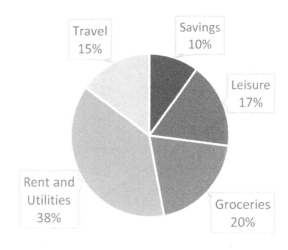

Which of the following statements is true?
   a. The amount of money she spends on travel and savings is more than $11,000.
   b. The amount of money she spends on rent and utilities is approximately $15,000.
   c. The amount of money she spends on groceries and savings is more than $13,000.
   d. The amount of money she spends on travel and leisure is more than $17,000.
   e. The amount of money she spends on leisure is less than $5,000.

48. A recipe calls for 2 cups of water for every 6 cups of flour. Josie wants to make a smaller batch using only 2 cups of flour. How much water should she use?
   a. $\frac{1}{2}$ cup
   b. 2 cups
   c. $\frac{2}{3}$ cup
   d. $2\frac{2}{3}$ cups
   e. 12 cups

Refer to the following for question 49:

An MP3 player is set to play songs at random from the fifteen songs it contains in memory. Any song can be played at any time, even if it is repeated. There are 5 songs by Band A, 3 songs by Band B, 2 by Band C, and 5 by Band D.

49. If the player has just played two songs in a row by Band D, what is the probability that the next song will also be by Band D?
   a. $\frac{1}{3}$
   b. $\frac{1}{5}$
   c. $\frac{1}{9}$
   d. $\frac{1}{15}$
   e. $\frac{1}{27}$

Copyright © Mometrix Media. You have been licensed one copy of this document for personal use only. Any other reproduction or redistribution is strictly prohibited. All rights reserved. This content is provided for test preparation purposes only and does not imply an endorsement by Mometrix of any particular political, scientific, or religious point of view.

50. Which of the following numbers is a prime number?

   a. 4
   b. 11
   c. 15
   d. 33
   e. 88

Refer to the following for question 51:

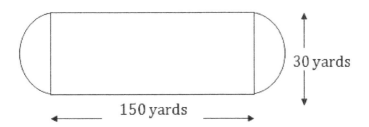

51. The diagram shows the outline of a racetrack, which consists of two long, straight sections, and two semi-circular turns. Given the dimensions shown, which of the following most closely measures the perimeter of the entire track?

   a. 180 yards
   b. 300 yards
   c. 360 yards
   d. 395 yards
   e. 425 yards

52. On a typical April day at Mayes Junior High, 8% of the 452 students who attend the school will be absent. About how many students will be absent on April 20?

   a. 36
   b. 38
   c. 40
   d. 42
   e. 44

53. Of the twenty students in the classroom, half are boys and half are girls. If all students handed in their homework, what is the probability that the top homework sheet belongs to a girl?

   a. 20%
   b. 25%
   c. 30%
   d. 40%
   e. 50%

Copyright © Mometrix Media. You have been licensed one copy of this document for personal use only. Any other reproduction or redistribution is strictly prohibited. All rights reserved.
This content is provided for test preparation purposes only and does not imply an endorsement by Mometrix of any particular political, scientific, or religious point of view.

54. If Fahrenheit, (°F) and Celsius, (°C) are related by the formula $°F = \left(\frac{9}{5}\right)°C + 32$, what is the temperature in Fahrenheit of a location with an average temperature of 20 °C?

    a. 58°
    b. 63°
    c. 68°
    d. 73°
    e. 78°

55. Marielle says the best descriptor of the data set {67, 2, 67, 73, 85, 60, 68} is the range. Choose the option that best describes Marielle's error.

    a. Marielle is incorrect because the range should never be used to describe a data set.
    b. Marielle is incorrect because this data set has an outlier.
    c. Marielle is incorrect because the mean is always the best choice for describing a data set.
    d. Marielle is incorrect because the median is best for a data set this small.
    e. Marielle is incorrect because the range for this data set is too small.

56. What is the probability of spinning a D on the spinner below?

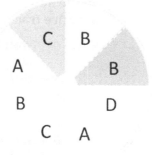

    a. $\frac{1}{8}$
    b. $\frac{1}{7}$
    c. $\frac{3}{8}$
    d. $\frac{5}{8}$
    e. $\frac{6}{7}$

Copyright © Mometrix Media. You have been licensed one copy of this document for personal use only. Any other reproduction or redistribution is strictly prohibited. All rights reserved.
This content is provided for test preparation purposes only and does not imply an endorsement by Mometrix of any particular political, scientific, or religious point of view.

Mathematics Practice Test 1 Answer Key

1. D: Since he does not replace the first card, the events are dependent. The sample space will decrease by 1 for the second draw because there will be one fewer card to choose from. Thus, the probability may be written as $P(A \text{ and } B) = \frac{13}{52} \times \frac{13}{51}$, or $P(A \text{ and } B) = \frac{169}{2,652} = \frac{13}{204}$.

2. B: Data is said to be positively skewed when there are a higher number of lower values, indicating data that is skewed right. Data is said to be negatively skewed when there are a higher number of higher values, indicating that the data is skewed left. An approximately normal distribution shows an increase in frequency, followed by a decrease in frequency, of approximately the same rate, following a general bell curve. Therefore, Group A is positively skewed, and Group B is approximately normal.

3. A: Calculate the final sales price of the rug at each store.

$$1.08(0.7 \times \$296) = \$223.78 \text{ at Store A}$$
$$1.08(\$220 - \$10) = \$226.80 \text{ at Store B}$$
$$\$198 + \$35 = \$233 \text{ at Store C}$$

Therefore, the stores in order of lowest to highest prices are Store A, Store B, Store C.

4. C: The area of a circle is given by $A = \pi \times r^2$, where r is the radius of the circle. Since π is approximately 3.14, we can solve for $r = \sqrt{\frac{A}{\pi}} = \sqrt{\frac{314 \text{ in}^2}{3.14}} = \sqrt{100 \text{ in}^2} = 10 \text{ in}$. Now, the diameter is twice the radius, or $2 \times 10 \text{ in} = 20 \text{ in}$. Therefore, the diameter is 20 inches.

5. C: Analyze each option to see if it can be further reduced. $\frac{6}{50}$ can be reduced to $\frac{3}{25}$ by dividing the numerator and denominator by 2, so it is not in lowest terms. $\frac{12}{100}$ can be reduced to $\frac{3}{25}$ by dividing the numerator and denominator by 4, so it is not in lowest terms. $\frac{12}{10}$ can be reduced to $\frac{6}{5}$ or $1\frac{1}{5}$ by dividing the numerator and denominator by 2, so it is not in lowest terms. $\frac{12}{4}$ can be rewritten as 3, so it is not in lowest terms. $\frac{3}{25}$ is the only fraction that cannot be simplified or rewritten as a mixed number, so it is the correct answer.

6. B: The volume of a square pyramid can be calculated using the formula $V = \frac{Bh}{3}$, where B is the area of the base and h is the height of the pyramid. Therefore, the volume of Natasha's tent is $\frac{x^2h}{3}$. If she were to increase by 1 ft the length of each side of the square base, the tent's volume can be calculated by substituting $x + 1$ for x in the original tent volume formula.

$$\frac{(x+1)^2h}{3} = \frac{(x^2 + 2x + 1)(h)}{3} = \frac{x^2h + 2xh + h}{3} = \frac{x^2h}{3} + \frac{2xh + h}{3}$$

Notice this is the volume of Natasha's tent, $\frac{x^2h}{3}$, increased by $\frac{2xh+h}{3}$, or $\frac{h(2x+1)}{3}$. This is how much more interior space the tent would have.

7. A: The median is the middle number of a data set when the set is listed from least to greatest. To find the median, we must first rewrite our set from least to greatest as: 53, 72, 81, 82, 85, 91.

Copyright © Mometrix Media. You have been licensed one copy of this document for personal use only. Any other reproduction or redistribution is strictly prohibited. All rights reserved. This content is provided for test preparation purposes only and does not imply an endorsement by Mometrix of any particular political, scientific, or religious point of view.

Because there are six data values, we have two numbers, 81 and 82, that can be described as the "middle numbers." To find the median of the set, we must find the mean of the two middle numbers. The mean of 81 and 82 is 81.5, so the median of our entire data set is also 81.5.

8. A: Since 3 of the 15 songs are by Band B, the probability that any one song will be by that band is $\frac{3}{15} = \frac{1}{5}$. The probability that two successive events will occur is the product of the probabilities for any one event or, in this case, $\frac{1}{5} \times \frac{1}{5} = \frac{1}{25}$.

9. C: Because 40% is the same as 0.40, multiply 360 by 0.40 to get 144.

10. C: The average is found by adding the four prices and then dividing by 4.

$$\frac{18.00 + 18.50 + 19.99 + 15.39}{4} = \frac{71.88}{4} = 17.97$$

So, the average price is $17.97.

11. A: The mean, or average, of the distribution can be computed by multiplying each grade by the number of students obtaining it, summing all products, and then dividing by the total number of students. Here, $n = 4.2$. The median is the value for which an equal number of students have received higher or lower grades. Here, $p = 4$. The mode is the most frequently obtained grade, and here $q = 3$. Thus, $n > p > q$.

12. D: The theoretical probability of getting tails is $\frac{1}{2}$. Thus, she can expect to get a total of $\frac{1}{2} \times 1,000$ tails, or 500 tails.

13. C: To solve, isolate x by rearranging the equation:

$$2x - 6 + 4x = 24$$
$$6x - 6 = 24$$
$$6x = 30$$
$$x = 5$$

14. A: Multiply 60 mph by 15 hours to find out how far he drove on Day 1:

$$60 \text{ mph} \times 15 \text{ hr} = 900 \text{ mi}$$

If he does the same on Day 2, he will have driven a total of 1,800 miles. He will have 200 miles left to go on a 2,000-mile trip.

15. A: The value of the fraction, $\frac{7}{5}$, can be evaluated by dividing 7 by 5, which yields 1.4. The average of 1.4 and 1.4 is $\frac{1.4+1.4}{2} = 1.4$.

16. B: To calculate S, first calculate the discount, and then subtract it from the original price, p. In this case, the discount is 33% of p, or $0.33p$. Thus, $S = p - 0.33p$.

17. B: Based on the location of the 34°, the 14 ft section is the adjacent leg and the ramp length is the hypotenuse of the right triangle. Therefore, in order to solve for x, it needs to be set up as $\cos 34° = \frac{\text{adjacent}}{\text{hypotenuse}}$ or $\cos 34° = \frac{14}{x}$. The value of x is found by rearranging the equation to be $x = \frac{14}{\cos 34°}$.

Copyright © Mometrix Media. You have been licensed one copy of this document for personal use only. Any other reproduction or redistribution is strictly prohibited. All rights reserved. This content is provided for test preparation purposes only and does not imply an endorsement by Mometrix of any particular political, scientific, or religious point of view.

18. D: To solve for y, we must first complete the inverse of any addition or subtraction. Here, we need to add 8 to both sides of the equation. This simplifies our equation to $\frac{y}{2} = 8$. Next, we need to complete the inverse of division, which is multiplication. When we multiply both sides of the equation by 2, we find that $y = 16$. To check our answer, we can insert 16 into our original equation. Because $\frac{16}{2} - 8 = 0$, we know we have the correct value for y.

19. E: If the first lap takes 50 seconds, the second one takes 20% more, or $T_2 = 1.2 \times T_1 = 1.2 \times 50 = 60$ seconds, where T_1 and T_2 are the times required for the first and second laps, respectively. Similarly, $T_3 = 1.2 \times T_2 = 1.2 \times 60 = 72$ seconds, the time required for the third lap. To find the total time, add the times for the three laps together: $50 + 60 + 72 = 182$ seconds.

20. C: When displaying data collected in a survey, we must always choose intervals appropriate for the data collected. This includes starting our y-axis at zero, and choosing intervals that are appropriate for the data being collected. For example, imagine we are comparing the purchase prices of homes in an area. If the homes sold for \$280,000, \$282,000, and \$284,000, most people would consider the homes to have sold for very similar prices, given that \$2,000 increments are only marginally different when describing the cost of a house. If these prices were graphed with y-axis intervals of \$10.00, the bar representing the \$284,000 house would be much higher than the bar representing the house that sold for \$282,000, even though the difference in price is only \$2,000. That graph would mislead people into thinking the houses sold for prices that were considerably different from each other, which was not the case.

21. C: There are four, equally possible places the spinner may land. The digit 2 is only present in one space, so the probability of landing there is 1 out of 4 or $\frac{1}{4}$.

22. B: To divide fractions, multiply the dividend (the first fraction) by the reciprocal (turn it upside down) of the divisor (the second fraction):

$$\frac{1}{6} \div \frac{3}{8} = \frac{1}{6} \times \frac{8}{3}$$
$$= \frac{8}{18}$$
$$= \frac{4}{9}$$

23. C: To solve, first multiply through the parentheses and then combine like terms:

$$8(x + 2) - 7 + 4(x - 7) = 8x + 16 - 7 + 4x - 28$$
$$= 12x - 19$$

24. C: Multiply the numerators by one another to get the new numerator ($3 \times 3 = 9$), and the denominators by one another to get the new denominator ($8 \times 8 = 64$). The result ($\frac{9}{16}$) is in simplest form.

Copyright © Mometrix Media. You have been licensed one copy of this document for personal use only. Any other reproduction or redistribution is strictly prohibited. All rights reserved. This content is provided for test preparation purposes only and does not imply an endorsement by Mometrix of any particular political, scientific, or religious point of view.

25. A: To solve, find the perimeter (sum of all sides) of each garden.

Garden A: 6 ft by 8 ft rectangle, 6 ft + 8 ft + 6 ft + 8 ft = 28 ft

Garden B: 12 ft by 4 ft rectangle, 12 ft + 4 ft + 12 ft + 4 ft = 32 ft

Garden C: 16 ft by 3 ft rectangle, 16 ft + 3 ft + 16 ft + 3 ft = 38 ft

The smallest perimeter, Garden A, will require the least amount of fencing.

26. C: If $70, the amount used to buy more lemons, represents 35% of Herbert's earnings, then 1% corresponds to $\frac{\$70}{35} = \$2$. To determine how much profit he takes home, multiply the dollar amount that represents 1%, which is $2, by 15 to get $2 \times 15 = \$30$. Therefore, Herbert takes home $30 in profit.

27. D: To compare fractions with unlike denominators, we can rewrite each fraction with equivalent denominators. To do so, we must first identify the least common denominator, or LCD. The LCD is the least common multiple of the denominators. Here, the LCDs between $\frac{2}{5}$ and the answer choices are 55, 35, 15, and 10. Next, we must rewrite each fraction for comparison, while maintaining equivalence. Let's start with $\frac{5}{11}$. Our new denominator, 55, is five times greater than our original denominator, 11. To maintain equivalence, we must make our new numerator five times greater than our original numerator. To do so, we multiply our original numerator, 5, by 5, which equals 25. That makes our new fraction $\frac{25}{55}$. We do the same for $\frac{2}{5} = \frac{22}{55}$, and once our denominators are equivalent, we can simply compare our numerators to determine the greater value. Because 25 is greater than 22, we know that $\frac{25}{55}$ is greater than $\frac{22}{55}$, or $\frac{5}{11} > \frac{2}{5}$. We follow the same logic to evaluate each answer choice to find that $\frac{1}{3} < \frac{2}{5}$.

28. B: Area is the measure we use to calculate the number of square units that will fit into a plane surface. To re-carpet his bedroom, Justin must calculate the total number of square feet that must be covered in order to fill the floor space. To find area, Justin should multiply the length of his bedroom, 12 feet, by the width, 10 feet. Because $12 \times 10 = 120$, Justin will need 120 square feet of carpet for his bedroom.

29. B: Since CF is a straight line, its measure is 180°. Since ∠BDF = 45°, then:

$$\angle CDB = 180° - 45° = 135°$$

30. B: To answer this question, we first determine the total cost of the onions and carrots, since these prices are given. This will equal $2 \times \$3.69 + 3 \times \$4.29 = \$20.25$. Next, this sum is subtracted from the total cost of the vegetables to determine the cost of the mushrooms: $\$24.15 - \$20.25 = \$3.90$. Finally, the cost of the mushrooms is divided by the quantity in lbs to determine the cost per lb:

$$\text{Cost per lb} = \frac{\$3.90}{1.5} = \$2.60$$

Copyright © Mometrix Media. You have been licensed one copy of this document for personal use only. Any other reproduction or redistribution is strictly prohibited. All rights reserved.
This content is provided for test preparation purposes only and does not imply an endorsement by Mometrix of any particular political, scientific, or religious point of view.

Therefore, the mushrooms cost $2.60 per pound.

31. C: To solve, use the percentage increase formula.

$$\text{Percentage Increase} = \frac{\text{new} - \text{initial}}{\text{initial}} \times 100$$

In this case, the initial value is $80, and the new value is $120.

$$\text{Percentage Increase} = \frac{120 - 80}{80} \times 100 = \frac{40}{80} \times 100 = 50\%$$

Therefore, the total amount in her account increased by 50%.

32. A: A tree diagram shows the different combinations possible by listing each option as a sort of hierarchy. To start, we list all possibilities for the first category. Here, our first category is ice cream flavor, so we need three branches to represent the three different flavors. Next, we must decide between three different toppings. Because each topping can be paired with any flavor, we need two branches coming from each flavor, to show all the flavor/topping combinations. Finally, we must decide on hot fudge or caramel. Again, each choice can be added to any of our already existing combinations, so we'll need two more branches coming from each topping choice. When finished, we can follow the branches from top to bottom to see every possible combination of ice cream sundae that can be created. So, the correct option shows every possible branch.

33. E: A die has a total of six sides, with a different number on each side. Three of these numbers are odd, and three are even. When rolling a die, the probability of rolling an odd number is 3 out of 6 or $\frac{3}{6}$. Reducing the fraction, yields a $\frac{1}{2}$ or 50% chance an odd number will be rolled.

34. C: To determine the scale factor of the dilation, compare the coordinates of $\Delta J'K'L'$ to the coordinates of ΔJKL. J is at $(-2, -3)$ and J' is at $(-4, -6)$, which means that the coordinates of J were multiplied by a scale factor of 2 to get the coordinates of J'. K is at $(1,3)$ and K' is at $(2,6)$. L is at $(4, -1)$ and L' is at $(8, -2)$. The coordinates of K and L were also multiplied by a scale factor of 2 to get to the coordinates of K' and L'. Therefore, the scale factor of the dilation is 2.

35. B: The mean, or average, is the sum of the numbers in a data set divided by the total number of items in the set. This data set has 7 items (one for each day of the week). The total number of hits that Kyle had during the week is the sum of the numbers in the right-hand column. The sum is 14, so the mean is 2 because $14 \div 7 = 2$.

36. C: This question requires two steps. The first step is to determine the discounted earring price by multiplying $500 by 0.75 (75%, the amount that isn't taken off from the discount, as a decimal).

$$\$500 \times 0.75 = \$375$$

The second step is to use the birthday discount. With the birthday discount, she will still pay 95% (100%–5%) of the discounted price, so multiply $375 by 0.95.

$$\$375 \times 0.95 = \$356.25$$

Since this is Mary's birthday month, she pays $356.25 for the pair of earrings.

37. B: The first function $L(g)$ gives the water level after g gallons are pumped into the tank. The second function $w(t)$ gives the number of gallons pumped into the tank after t minutes, which the

Copyright © Mometrix Media. You have been licensed one copy of this document for personal use only. Any other reproduction or redistribution is strictly prohibited. All rights reserved.
This content is provided for test preparation purposes only and does not imply an endorsement by Mometrix of any particular political, scientific, or religious point of view.

first function calls g. Consequently, we can have L act on w: the composition of the functions $L(w(t))$ is the water level of the tank after t minutes. Calculate $L(w(t))$.

$$L(w(t)) = 0.3 \times w(t)$$
$$L(t) = 0.3 \times 1.2t$$
$$L(t) = 0.36t$$

Thus, the function $L(t) = 0.36t$ represents the water level of the tank after t minutes.

38. C: To find the number of options Aniyah can create, we can start by making an ordered list of the different options. To start, we can assign each piece of clothing an abbreviation, such as J1 for the first pair of jeans or S1 for shirt number 1. When we list all of the different options in an organized way, we find the following combinations: J1/S1, J1/S2, J1/S3, J2/S1, J2/S2, J2/S3. We can count the numbers of combinations created to conclude that Aniyah is able to create six different outfits from two pairs of jeans and three shirts. Another way to solve this problem is to simply multiply the number of options within each category. There are two options for jeans and three options for shirts. The product of 3 and 2 is 6, again confirming that Aniyah has six possible outfit combinations.

39. C: To solve, first figure out how much she owes over the $3.00 base fee. For each five minutes, she pays an extra 15 cents. For each hour after the first one, she will pay:

$$12 \times 0.15 = \$1.80$$

She has used the service for an extra 2 hours and 10 minutes. Two hours of additional time is:

$$\$1.80 \times 2 = \$3.60$$

Ten minutes of additional time is:

$$\$0.15 \times 2 = \$0.30$$

Adding these two values gives an additional cost of $3.90. Add this to the base fee of $3 for the first hour to get a total bill of $6.90.

40. A: Complementary angles are two angles that equal 90° when added together:

$$90° - 48° = 42°$$

41. B: Since the second line, $y = 3$, is horizontal, the intersection must occur at a point where $y = 3$. Substitute $y = 3$ into the equation and solve for x.

$$2x + (3) = 0$$
$$2x = -3$$
$$x = -\frac{3}{2}$$

Therefore, the point where these two lines will intersect is at $\left(-\frac{3}{2}, 3\right)$.

42. C: According to the exponent rule $a^{-n} = \frac{1}{a^n}$, the expression 2^{-3} is equivalent to $\frac{1}{2^3}$. Since $2^3 = 2 \times 2 \times 2 = 8$, this expression is equivalent to $\frac{1}{8}$.

Copyright © Mometrix Media. You have been licensed one copy of this document for personal use only. Any other reproduction or redistribution is strictly prohibited. All rights reserved.
This content is provided for test preparation purposes only and does not imply an endorsement by Mometrix of any particular political, scientific, or religious point of view.

43. A: The number of bacteria forms a geometric sequence: 100, 200, 400, 800, 1,600, etc. Notice that, if you ignore the two zeroes, these numbers are all powers of 2 (i.e. $2^0, 2^1, 2^2, 2^3, 2^4$, etc.). In other words, they are all 100 multiplied by a power of 2, so the sequence can be written as an exponential function of the form $y = 100 \times 2^n$. However, since this sequence begins with an exponent of 0 on the first day, rather than 1, and an exponent of 1 on the second day rather than 2, you need to subtract 1 from n to get the correct power. Thus, the function $b(n) = 100 \times 2^{n-1}$ represents the number of bacteria on the nth day.

44. D: To find the probability of Fran pulling two different marbles from the bag, we must find the probability of each event occurring individually, then multiply those probabilities together. To start, we can determine that Fran's chance of pulling a red marble is $\frac{5}{12}$ because there are 5 red marbles out of a total 12 marbles. Next, we must determine that Fran has a $\frac{4}{11}$ chance of pulling a green marble because there are 4 green marbles out of a new total 11 marbles. Notice, our total must now be reduced to 11 because Fran has one marble already in her possession. When we multiply our two events, $\frac{5}{12} \times \frac{4}{11}$, we get $\frac{20}{132}$, or $\frac{5}{33}$. The chance of Fran pulling a red marble followed by a green marble is $\frac{5}{33}$.

45. C: The y-intercept of the inequality is 20. The slope can be determined by calculating the ratio of the change in y-values per change in corresponding x-values. Choose any two points to calculate the slope. For example, the points (0,20) and (25,5) can be used.

$$m = \frac{y_2 - y_1}{x_2 - x_1} = \frac{5 - 20}{25 - 0} = \frac{-15}{25} = -\frac{3}{5}$$

Therefore, the slope is –0.6. Write the inequality in slope-intercept form. Use the less than or equal to sign ($\leq$) because the line is solid and the graph is shaded below the line.

$$y \leq -\frac{3}{5}x + 20$$

46. D: In the data set {67, 29, 57, 27, 38, 91} there is no value that occurs more than any other value. However, we cannot describe the mode as "zero" because that would imply that the value "0" is part of the data set and appears more than any other value. When we have a data set without any repeating numbers, we must describe that set as having "no mode," rather than "zero."

47. B: The amount of money she spends on travel and savings is $(0.15 + 0.10) \times \$40,000 = 0.25 \times \$40,000 = \$10,000$, so choice A is false. The amount of money she spends on rent and utilities is equal to $0.38 \times \$40,000 = \$15,200$, which is approximately $15,000, so choice B is true. The amount of money she spends on groceries and savings is $(0.20 + 0.10) \times \$40,000 = 0.30 \times \$40,000 = \$12,000$, so choice C is false. The amount of money she spends on leisure is $0.17 \times \$40,000 = \$6,800$, so choices D and E are false. Therefore, choice B is the correct answer.

48. C: To start, we can write our ratio in fractional form as $\frac{2 \text{ cups of water}}{6 \text{ cups of flour}}$. We know Josie wants to lessen the flour to only 2 cups, making our proportion $\frac{2 \text{ cups of water}}{6 \text{ cups of flour}} = \frac{x \text{ cups of water}}{2 \text{ cups of flour}}$. To find the value of x, we can cross multiply the two diagonal values we know, 2 and 2, and divide their product by the remaining value, 6. $2 \times 2 = 4$, and $4 \div 6 = \frac{4}{6}$, which simplifies to $\frac{2}{3}$. This means Josie should use $\frac{2}{3}$ of a cup of water for every 2 cups of flour.

Copyright © Mometrix Media. You have been licensed one copy of this document for personal use only. Any other reproduction or redistribution is strictly prohibited. All rights reserved. This content is provided for test preparation purposes only and does not imply an endorsement by Mometrix of any particular political, scientific, or religious point of view.

49. A: The probability of playing a song by any band is proportional to the number of songs by that band over the total number of songs, or $\frac{5}{15} = \frac{1}{3}$ for Band D. The probability of playing any particular song is not affected by what has been played previously, so all 15 songs have an equal probability to be played.

50. B: A prime number is a natural, positive, non-zero number that can only be factored by itself and 1. This is the case for 11. 4 is not a prime number because 2 is a factor of 4: $2 \times 2 = 4$. 15 is not a prime number because 3 and 5 are factors of 15: $3 \times 5 = 15$. 33 is not a prime number because 3 and 11 are factors of 33: $3 \times 11 = 33$. 88 is not a prime number because 2, 4, 8, 11, 22, and 44 are factors of 88: $2 \times 44 = 88$, $4 \times 22 = 88$, and $8 \times 11 = 88$.

51. D: First, add the two straight, 150-yard portions. Also, note that the distance around the two semi-circular turns combine to form the circumference of a circle. The radius, r, of that circle is $\frac{1}{2}$ the dimension that is shown as the width of the track, or 15 yards. Now, take the formula for the circumference of a circle, $C = 2\pi r$, and add it to the length of the two straight portions of the track.

$$\text{Length} = (2\pi \times 15) + (2 \times 150) \approx 394.25$$

Therefore, the closest approximation of the perimeter is 395 yards.

52. A: To determine how many students will be absent, multiply the percentage of students who will be absent by the total number of students.

$$8\% \times 452 = 0.08 \times 452 = 36.16$$

Therefore, about 36 students will be absent on April 20.

53. E: Out of the twenty students in the classroom, half are girls. That means there is a 1 in 2, or 50%, chance that the homework handed in will belong to a girl.

54. C: To find the temperature in degrees Fahrenheit, plug 20 into the formula for degrees Celsius and solve.

$$°F = \left(\frac{9}{5}\right)(20) + 32 = 36 + 32 = 68$$

Therefore, the temperature in degrees Fahrenheit is 68°.

55. B: The data set $\{67, 2, 67, 73, 85, 60, 68\}$ contains seven numbers, six of which are within 15 units of each other. The seventh piece of data, 2, is an outlier, meaning it is much greater or smaller than the rest of the data. Using the range of this data set, 83 (because $85 - 2 = 83$), would give the impression that the entire data set greatly varies, which is not the case. For this type of data set, the median would be a better representation of the set because the outlier does not have as great an effect.

56. A: Experimental probability is a ratio of how many times the spinner will land on the specific letter to the total number of places the spinner can land. In this case, there are eight possible places where the spinner may land. The D is present only in one space, so the probability of landing there is 1 to 8 or $\frac{1}{8}$.

Copyright © Mometrix Media. You have been licensed one copy of this document for personal use only. Any other reproduction or redistribution is strictly prohibited. All rights reserved.
This content is provided for test preparation purposes only and does not imply an endorsement by Mometrix of any particular political, scientific, or religious point of view.

Mathematics Practice Test 2

Refer to the following for question 1:

Kyle bats third in the batting order for the Badgers baseball team. The table below shows the number of hits that Kyle had in each of 7 consecutive games played during one week in July.

Day	Monday	Tuesday	Wednesday	Thursday	Friday	Saturday	Sunday
Hits	1	2	3	1	1	4	2

1. What is the mode of the numbers in the distribution shown in the table?

   a. 1
   b. 2
   c. 3
   d. 4
   e. 7

2. Write $\frac{42}{7}$ as a percentage.

   a. 6%
   b. 600%
   c. 60%
   d. 0.6%
   e. 0.06%

3. Given the equation $\frac{2}{x-8} = \frac{3}{x}$, what is the value of x?

   a. 16
   b. 20
   c. 24
   d. 28
   e. 32

4. Express 18% as a decimal.

   a. 0.018
   b. 0.18
   c. 1.8
   d. 0.0018
   e. 0.108

5. Find the mean of the data set $\{76, 193, 83, 43, 105\}$.

   a. 80
   b. 83
   c. 100
   d. 150
   e. 500

Copyright © Mometrix Media. You have been licensed one copy of this document for personal use only. Any other reproduction or redistribution is strictly prohibited. All rights reserved. This content is provided for test preparation purposes only and does not imply an endorsement by Mometrix of any particular political, scientific, or religious point of view.

6. A crane raises one end of a 3,300-pound steel beam. The other end rests upon the ground. If the crane supports 30% of the beam's weight, how many pounds does it support?

    a. 330 lb
    b. 700 lb
    c. 990 lb
    d. 1,100 lb
    e. 2,310 lb

7. What is the value of x in the following equation?

$$15 - x = 78$$

    a. 5.2
    b. 63
    c. −63
    d. 93
    e. −93

8. John buys 100 shares of stock at $100 per share. The price goes up by 10%, and he sells 50 shares. Then, prices drop by 10%, and he sells his remaining 50 shares. How much did he get for the last 50 shares?

    a. $4,900
    b. $4,950
    c. $5,000
    d. $5,050
    e. $5,500

9. Brenda buys a pair of shoes for $62.00. The next day she sees that the shoes are on sale for 25% off. How much money would Brenda have saved if she had waited a day?

    a. $9.92
    b. $15.50
    c. $25.00
    d. $46.50
    e. $52.08

Refer to the following for question 10:

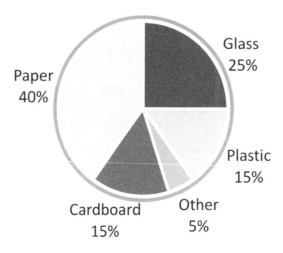

Copyright © Mometrix Media. You have been licensed one copy of this document for personal use only. Any other reproduction or redistribution is strictly prohibited. All rights reserved.
This content is provided for test preparation purposes only and does not imply an endorsement by Mometrix of any particular political, scientific, or religious point of view.

10. If there is a total of 50,000 tons of materials recycled every month, approximately how much paper is recycled every month?

    a. 15,000 tons
    b. 20,000 tons
    c. 40,000 tons
    d. 50,000 tons
    e. 60,000 tons

11. Simplify: $|7 - 5| - |5 - 7|$

    a. −4
    b. −2
    c. 0
    d. 2
    e. 4

12. Which of the following is a solution to the inequality $4x - 12 < 4$?

    a. 7
    b. 6
    c. 5
    d. 4
    e. 3

13. Three teachers from a county are chosen at random to attend a conference for high school science educators. What is the approximate probability that two women from the same department will be chosen?

	Biology	Chemistry	Physics
Women	26	31	20
Men	16	11	25

    a. 8.6%
    b. 9.6%
    c. 10.7%
    d. 11.9%
    e. 13.8%

14. Given the equation, $ax + b = c$, what is the value of x?

    a. $\frac{c+b}{a}$
    b. $\frac{ca}{b}$
    c. $c - ba$
    d. $\frac{c-b}{a}$
    e. $c + ba$

15. Put the following numbers in order from the least to greatest $2^3, 4^2, 6^0, 9, 10^1$.

    a. $2^3, 4^2, 6^0, 9, 10^1$
    b. $6^0, 9, 10^1, 2^3, 4^2$
    c. $10^1, 2^3, 6^0, 9, 4^2$
    d. $6^0, 2^3, 9, 10^1, 4^2$
    e. $2^3, 9, 10^1, 4^2, 6^0$

Copyright © Mometrix Media. You have been licensed one copy of this document for personal use only. Any other reproduction or redistribution is strictly prohibited. All rights reserved.
This content is provided for test preparation purposes only and does not imply an endorsement by Mometrix of any particular political, scientific, or religious point of view.

16. A random sample of 241 children ages 5 to 10 were asked these three questions:

Do you like baseball?
Do you like basketball?
Do you like football?

The results of the survey are shown below. If these data are representative of the population of students at the school, which of these is least probable?

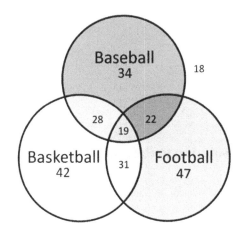

a. A child chosen at random likes football.
b. If a child chosen at random likes baseball, he also likes at least one other sport.
c. If a child chosen at random likes baseball and basketball, he also likes football.
d. A child chosen at random likes basketball and baseball.
e. A student chosen at random does not like baseball, basketball, or football.

17. A regular deck of cards has 52 cards, four of which are aces. What is the chance of drawing three aces in a row?

a. $\dfrac{1}{52}$
b. $\dfrac{1}{156}$
c. $\dfrac{1}{2,000}$
d. $\dfrac{1}{5,525}$
e. $\dfrac{1}{132,600}$

18. Consider the data set {196, 832, 736, 271, and 573}. Which of the following best describes the range of the data set?

a. 377
b. 636
c. 1,028
d. 5
e. 573

248

Copyright © Mometrix Media. You have been licensed one copy of this document for personal use only. Any other reproduction or redistribution is strictly prohibited. All rights reserved.
This content is provided for test preparation purposes only and does not imply an endorsement by Mometrix of any particular political, scientific, or religious point of view.

19. The letter H exhibits symmetry with respect to a horizontal axis, as shown in the figure, as everything below the dashed line is a mirror image of everything above it. Which of the following letters does NOT exhibit horizontal symmetry?

  a. C
  b. D
  c. E
  d. I
  e. Z

20. Mary's basketball team is losing tonight's game 42–15. Mary scores a three-point shot. How many more three-point shots will someone on her team have to score in order to tie the game?

  a. 5
  b. 6
  c. 7
  d. 8
  e. 9

21. Krystal purchased a pair of sunglasses for $19.99 and a scarf for $27.50. She paid with a $50.00 bill. How much change did she receive?

  a. $47.49
  b. $17.49
  c. $3.61
  d. $2.99
  e. $2.51

Refer to the following for question 22:

The 180 campers in Group A got to choose which kind of sandwich they wanted on the picnic. The results of the choice are given in the table below.

Sandwich	# of Campers
PB & J	60
Turkey	45
Egg salad	15
Veggie	60

22. Which expression correctly provides the ratio of campers who chose veggie sandwiches to those who chose turkey?

  a. 1 : 3
  b. 1 : 4
  c. 2 : 3
  d. 3 : 2
  e. 4 : 3

Copyright © Mometrix Media. You have been licensed one copy of this document for personal use only. Any other reproduction or redistribution is strictly prohibited. All rights reserved.
This content is provided for test preparation purposes only and does not imply an endorsement by Mometrix of any particular political, scientific, or religious point of view.

23. Which of the following could be a graph of the function $y = \frac{1}{x}$?

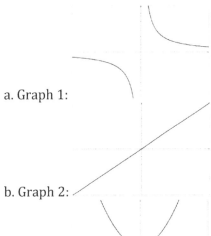

a. Graph 1:

b. Graph 2:

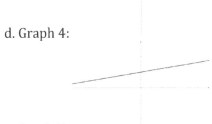

c. Graph 3:

d. Graph 4:

e. Graph 5:

24. If $10x + 2 = 7$, what is the value of $2x$?

    a.   −0.5
    b.   0.5
    c.   1
    d.   5
    e.   10

Copyright © Mometrix Media. You have been licensed one copy of this document for personal use only. Any other reproduction or redistribution is strictly prohibited. All rights reserved.
This content is provided for test preparation purposes only and does not imply an endorsement by Mometrix of any particular political, scientific, or religious point of view.

25. A rainbow pattern is designed from semi-circles as shown below.

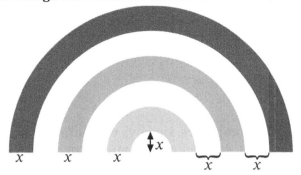

Which of the following gives the area A of the shaded region as a function of x?

    a. $A = \frac{21x^2\pi}{2}$
    b. $A = 21x^2\pi$
    c. $A = 42x^2\pi$
    d. $A = 82x^2\pi$
    e. $A = \frac{21x^2\pi}{4}$

26. What is the value of y in the following equation?
$$4y + 16 = 60$$

    a. 4
    b. 11
    c. 12
    d. 15
    e. 19

27. Mrs. Patterson's classroom has sixteen empty chairs. All of the chairs are occupied when every student is present. If $\frac{2}{5}$ of the students are absent, how many students make up her entire class?

    a. 16 students
    b. 24 students
    c. 32 students
    d. 36 students
    e. 40 students

28. Everyone in a class has blue, green, or brown eyes. 40% of the students have brown eyes and 90% of the other students have blue eyes. What can we infer from this information?

    a. We can infer that there is a majority of students with brown eyes.
    b. We can infer that there is a majority of students with blue eyes.
    c. We can infer that there is a majority of students with green eyes.
    d. We can infer that there is an equal number of students with each eye color.
    e. We cannot infer anything from this information.

Copyright © Mometrix Media. You have been licensed one copy of this document for personal use only. Any other reproduction or redistribution is strictly prohibited. All rights reserved.
This content is provided for test preparation purposes only and does not imply an endorsement by Mometrix of any particular political, scientific, or religious point of view.

29. Which of the following expressions is equivalent to the expression $(17 + 18) + 2$ according to the associative property?

    a. $35 + 2$
    b. $(18 + 17) + 2$
    c. $17 + 2(9 + 1)$
    d. $17 + (18 + 2)$
    e. $17 + 20$

30. Rafael has a business selling computers. He buys computers from the manufacturer for $450 each and sells them for $800. Each month, he must also pay fixed costs of $3,000 for rent and utilities at his store. If he sells n computers in a month, which of the following equations can be used to calculate his profit?

    a. $P = n(\$800 - \$450)$
    b. $P = n(\$800 - \$450 - \$3,000)$
    c. $P = \$3,000 \times n(\$800 - \$450)$
    d. $P = n(\$800 - \$450) - \$3,000$
    e. $P = n(\$800 - \$450) + \$3,000$

31. A television that regularly costs $400 is offered today at a price reflecting 20% off. When a customer shows a Super Saver card, another 5% is deducted at the register. What does a customer with a Super Saver card pay for the television today?

    a. $380
    b. $375
    c. $300
    d. $304
    e. $270

32. Which pair of angles is equal to 180°?

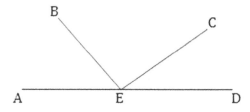

    a. $\angle AEB$ and $\angle BEC$
    b. $\angle CED$ and $\angle BEC$
    c. $\angle AEB$ and $\angle CED$
    d. $\angle AEC$ and $\angle BED$
    e. $\angle AEB$ and $\angle BED$

33. Find the mode(s) of the data set {84, 29, 84, 93, 93, 84, 39, 84, 29, 93, 93, 29}.

    a.   84
    b.   93
    c.   29
    d.   84 and 93
    e.   29, 84, and 93

Copyright © Mometrix Media. You have been licensed one copy of this document for personal use only. Any other reproduction or redistribution is strictly prohibited. All rights reserved. This content is provided for test preparation purposes only and does not imply an endorsement by Mometrix of any particular political, scientific, or religious point of view.

34. Sara and her sister Kate are standing next to one another on the beach. Kate casts a shadow that is 32 inches long. Sara's shadow is 16 inches longer than her sister's. If Kate is 40 inches tall, how tall is Sara?

a. 48 inches
b. 52 inches
c. 60 inches
d. 72 inches
e. Not enough information is given

35. The volume of a rectangular box is found by multiplying its length, width, and height. If the dimensions of a box are $\sqrt{3}$, $2\sqrt{5}$, and 4, what is its volume?

a. $2\sqrt{60}$
b. $2\sqrt{15}$
c. $4\sqrt{15}$
d. $8\sqrt{15}$
e. $24\sqrt{5}$

36. A triangle has angles measuring 40°, 100°, and 40°. Which of the following choices accurately describes the triangle?

a. It is an acute equilateral triangle.
b. It is an acute isosceles triangle.
c. It is an obtuse isosceles triangle.
d. It is an acute scalene triangle.
e. It is an obtuse scalene triangle.

37. Find and interpret the range for the data set {78, 29, 57, 10, 3, 84}.

a. The range of the data set is 6, which means that the values differ by a maximum of 6.
b. The range of the data set is 43.5, which means the average value in the set is 43.5.
c. The range of the data set is 81, which means the values of the set differ by no more than 81 units.
d. The range of the data set is 13.5, which means that the standard deviation is less than 13.5.
e. The range of the data set is 43, which means the middle number is 43.

38. Which of the following expressions is equivalent to $x^3 x^5$?

a. $2x^8$
b. x^{15}
c. x^2
d. x^8
e. $2x^{15}$

39. Simplify the expression $(10 + 4 \times 3) \div 2$.

a. 22
b. 21
c. 6
d. 20
e. 11

Copyright © Mometrix Media. You have been licensed one copy of this document for personal use only. Any other reproduction or redistribution is strictly prohibited. All rights reserved. This content is provided for test preparation purposes only and does not imply an endorsement by Mometrix of any particular political, scientific, or religious point of view.

40. Giselle is selling notebooks at the school store. She earns $45.00 for selling 30 notebooks. How much is Giselle charging for each notebook?

    a. $135.00
    b. $3.00
    c. $1.25
    d. $3.50
    e. $1.50

41. Triangle ABC below is an equilateral triangle, not drawn to scale. Which statement is true about side BC?

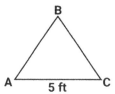

    a. It measures less than 5 ft.
    b. It measures greater than 5 ft.
    c. It measures 2.5 ft.
    d. It measures 5 ft.
    e. It measures 10 ft.

42. What is the approximate area of the shaded region between the circle and the square in the figure shown below? Use 3.14 for π.

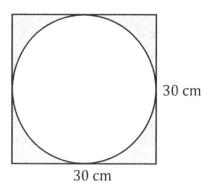

    a. 177 cm^2
    b. 181 cm^2
    c. 187 cm^2
    d. 190 cm^2
    e. 193 cm^2

43. Given the equation $\frac{3}{y-5} = \frac{15}{y+4}$, what is the value of y?

    a. $\frac{4}{45}$
    b. $\frac{4}{29}$
    c. $\frac{29}{4}$
    d. 45
    e. 54

Copyright © Mometrix Media. You have been licensed one copy of this document for personal use only. Any other reproduction or redistribution is strictly prohibited. All rights reserved.
This content is provided for test preparation purposes only and does not imply an endorsement by Mometrix of any particular political, scientific, or religious point of view.

44. A combination lock uses a three-digit code. Each digit can be any one of the ten available integers 0–9. How many different combinations are possible?

    a. 1,000
    b. 100
    c. 81
    d. 30
    e. 9

45. If $A = \begin{bmatrix} 1 & -3 \\ -4 & 2 \end{bmatrix}$ and $B = \begin{bmatrix} 1 & -3 \\ -4 & -2 \end{bmatrix}$, then what is $A - B$?

    a. $\begin{bmatrix} 2 & -6 \\ -8 & 0 \end{bmatrix}$
    b. $\begin{bmatrix} 0 & 0 \\ 0 & 0 \end{bmatrix}$
    c. $\begin{bmatrix} 0 & 0 \\ 0 & 4 \end{bmatrix}$
    d. $\begin{bmatrix} 0 & 3 \\ 4 & 2 \end{bmatrix}$
    e. $\begin{bmatrix} 0 & -6 \\ -8 & 4 \end{bmatrix}$

46. To determine a student's grade, a teacher throws out the lowest grade obtained on 5 tests, averages the remaining grades, and rounds up to the nearest integer. If Betty scored 68, 75, 88, 86, and 90 on her tests, what grade will she receive?

    a. 82
    b. 84
    c. 85
    d. 88
    e. 89

47. Which of the following expressions is equivalent to $3\left(\frac{6x-3}{3}\right) - 3(9x + 9)$?

    a. $-3(7x + 10)$
    b. $-3x + 6$
    c. $(x + 3)(x - 3)$
    d. $3x^2 - 9$
    e. $15x - 9$

48. Which of the following is true about the relationship between the two triangles shown below?

 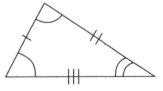

    a. The triangles are similar.
    b. The triangles are congruent.
    c. The triangles are equilateral.
    d. The triangles are both congruent and equilateral.
    e. The triangles are both similar and congruent.

Copyright © Mometrix Media. You have been licensed one copy of this document for personal use only. Any other reproduction or redistribution is strictly prohibited. All rights reserved. This content is provided for test preparation purposes only and does not imply an endorsement by Mometrix of any particular political, scientific, or religious point of view.

49. The weight in pounds of five students is 112, 112, 116, 133, and 145. What is the median weight of the group?

   a. 112 lbs
   b. 116 lbs
   c. 118.5 lbs
   d. 123.5 lbs
   e. 140 lbs

50. Given the table below, which of the following best represents the probability that a student is enrolled at TAMU or prefers lattes?

	Latte	Cappuccino	Frappuccino	Total
TAMU	350	225	175	750
NMSU	325	300	275	900
Total	675	525	450	1,650

   a. 55%
   b. 60%
   c. 65%
   d. 70%
   e. 75%

51. Express the area of the given right triangle as a function of x.

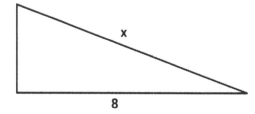

   a. $A(x) = 4x$

   b. $A(x) = \dfrac{x\sqrt{64-x^2}}{2}$

   c. $A(x) = 4\sqrt{x^2 - 64}$

   d. $A(x) = 64 - \sqrt{x^2}$

   e. $A(x) = 32 - \sqrt{\dfrac{1}{2}x^2}$

52. 30% of a woman's paycheck goes to health insurance, 15% goes to savings, and 32% goes to taxes. After these deductions, what percentage of the check is remaining?

   a. 19%
   b. 23%
   c. 38%
   d. 77%
   e. It cannot be determined from the information given.

Copyright © Mometrix Media. You have been licensed one copy of this document for personal use only. Any other reproduction or redistribution is strictly prohibited. All rights reserved. This content is provided for test preparation purposes only and does not imply an endorsement by Mometrix of any particular political, scientific, or religious point of view.

53. Solve for x: $\left(\frac{2}{5}\right) \div \left(\frac{2}{3}\right) = x$

    a. $x = \frac{1}{4}$

    b. $x = \frac{4}{15}$

    c. $x = 1\frac{2}{3}$

    d. $x = \frac{3}{5}$

    e. $x = 3\frac{1}{2}$

54. Which of the following is the largest number?

    a. 0.003

    b. 0.02

    c. 0.1

    d. 0.20

    e. 0.300

55. Solve for x:

$$(2x - 3) + 2x = 9$$

    a. 1

    b. −2

    c. 3

    d. −3

    e. 2

56. In a game of chance, 3 dice are thrown at the same time. What is the probability that all three will land on a 6?

    a. $\frac{1}{6}$

    b. $\frac{1}{18}$

    c. $\frac{1}{30}$

    d. $\frac{1}{36}$

    e. $\frac{1}{216}$

Copyright © Mometrix Media. You have been licensed one copy of this document for personal use only. Any other reproduction or redistribution is strictly prohibited. All rights reserved. This content is provided for test preparation purposes only and does not imply an endorsement by Mometrix of any particular political, scientific, or religious point of view.

Mathematics Practice Test 2 Answer Key

1. A: The mode is the number that appears most often in a set of data. If no item appears most often, then the data set has no mode. In this case, Kyle had 1 hit for a total of 3 times. There were 2 times that he had 2 hits. Also, on 1 day, he had 3 hits. Then, on another day, he had 4 hits. 1 hit happened the most times, so the mode of the data set is 1.

2. B: To solve, divide the numerator by the denominator and multiply by 100:

$$\frac{42}{7} \times 100 = 6 \times 100 = 600\%$$

3. C: To solve the equation, cross-multiply

$$\frac{2}{x-8} = \frac{3}{x}$$

$$2(x) = 3(x-8)$$

Distribute into the sets of parentheses.

$$2x = 3x - 24$$

Combine like terms by subtracting $3x$ from each side.

$$-x = -24$$

Finally, divide both sides by –1.

$$x = 24$$

4. B: To convert a percent into a decimal, change the percent sign to a decimal point and move the it two places to the left (or divide by 100).

5. C: The mean of a data set is considered a measure of center. To calculate the mean (sometimes known as the "average"), we must first find the sum of all numbers included in the data set. Here, the sum of 76, 193, 83, 43, and 105 is 500. Next, we need to divide the sum of our data set by the number of values included in the set. This data set contains 5 values, so we'll divide our sum, 500, by 5. The quotient of 500 and 5 is 100, making our mean 100.

6. C: It is helpful to recall that percentages can be converted to decimals. 30% of 3,300 is $0.3 \times 3,300 = 990$. Therefore, the crane supports 990 pounds.

7. C: The equation can be rearranged and simplified as follows:

$$15 - x = 78$$
$$15 - 78 = x$$
$$-63 = x$$

258

Copyright © Mometrix Media. You have been licensed one copy of this document for personal use only. Any other reproduction or redistribution is strictly prohibited. All rights reserved. This content is provided for test preparation purposes only and does not imply an endorsement by Mometrix of any particular political, scientific, or religious point of view.

8. B: The stock first increased by 10%, or $10 (10% of $100), to $110 per share. Then, the price decreased by $11 (10% of $110), so that the sell price was $110 − $11 = $99 per share, and the sell price for 50 shares was 99 × $50 = $4,950.

9. B: To determine how much Brenda would have saved, first find out the sale price of the shoes and then subtract this price from the amount Brenda paid. The sale price of the shoes is:

$$\$62 \times 0.75 = \$46.50$$

Then, subtract this amount from the amount Brenda paid:

$$\$62 - \$46.50 = \$15.50$$

Brenda would have saved $15.50 if she had waited a day.

10. B: The chart indicates that 40% of the total recycled material is paper. Since 50,000 tons of materials are recycled every month, the total amount of paper will be 40% of 50,000 tons, or $\frac{40}{100} \times 50{,}000 = 20{,}000$. Therefore, there are approximately 20,000 tons of paper recycled every month.

11. C: The vertical operators indicate absolute values, which are always positive. Start by simplifying the expressions inside the absolute value bars.

$$|7 - 5| - |5 - 7|$$

$$|2| - |-2|$$

Then, evaluate the absolute values and subtract. Since absolute value is always positive, both $|2|$ and $|-2|$ are equal to 2.

$$2 - 2 = 0$$

12. E: Manipulate the inequality to isolate the variable. Start by adding 12 to each side.

$$4x - 12 < 4$$
$$4x - 12 + 12 < 4 + 12$$
$$4x < 16$$

Then divide both sides by 4.

$$\frac{4x}{4} < \frac{16}{4}$$
$$x < 4$$

Since x must be less than and not equal to 4, the only correct answer choice is 3.

13. D: There are three ways in which two women from the same department can be selected: two women can be selected from Biology, two women can be selected from Chemistry, or two women can be selected from Physics. Since the events of choosing one woman and then another are both independent events, multiply the two probabilities together to get the probability of choosing two women from the same department.

| **Biology** | **Chemistry** | **Physics** |

Copyright © Mometrix Media. You have been licensed one copy of this document for personal use only. Any other reproduction or redistribution is strictly prohibited. All rights reserved. This content is provided for test preparation purposes only and does not imply an endorsement by Mometrix of any particular political, scientific, or religious point of view.

Since any of these is a distinct possible outcome, the probability that two men will be selected from the same department is the sum of these outcomes.

$$\frac{650}{16,512} + \frac{930}{16,512} + \frac{380}{16,512} = \frac{1,960}{16,512} \approx 0.119 = 11.9\%$$

14. D: The equation may be solved for x by first subtracting b from both sides of the equation. Doing so gives $ax = c - b$. Dividing both sides of the equation by a gives $x = \frac{c-b}{a}$. Therefore, the value of x is $\frac{c-b}{a}$.

15. D: When a number is raised to a power, you multiply the number by itself by the number of times of the power. For example, $2^3 = 2 \times 2 \times 2 = 8$. A number raised to the power of 0 is always equal to 1. So, 6^0 is the smallest number shown. Similarly, for the other numbers:

$$9 = 9; 10^1 = 10; 4^2 = 4 \times 4 = 16$$

Since $1 < 8 < 9 < 10 < 16$, we can write the order as $6^0, 2^3, 9, 10^1, 4^2$.

16. E: Determine the probability of each option (if s = likes baseball, b = likes basketball, and f = likes football).

For choice A, this is the total number of students in the football circle of the Venn diagram divided by the total number of students surveyed:

$$P(f) = \frac{47 + 22 + 19 + 31}{241} = \frac{119}{241} \approx 49.4\%$$

For choice B, this is the total number of students in the baseball circle and also in at least one other circle divided by the total number in the baseball circle:

$$P(s \cup f | b) = \frac{28 + 19 + 22}{28 + 19 + 22 + 34} = \frac{69}{103} \approx 67.0\%$$

For choice C, this is the number of students in the intersection of all three circles divided by the total number in the overlap of the baseball and basketball circles:

$$P(s | b \cap f) = \frac{19}{19 + 28} = \frac{19}{47} \approx 40.4\%$$

For choice D, this is the number of students in the intersection of the basketball circle and the baseball circle.

$$P(s \cap b) = \frac{28 + 19}{241} = \frac{47}{241} \approx 19.5\%$$

Copyright © Mometrix Media. You have been licensed one copy of this document for personal use only. Any other reproduction or redistribution is strictly prohibited. All rights reserved. This content is provided for test preparation purposes only and does not imply an endorsement by Mometrix of any particular political, scientific, or religious point of view.

For choice E, this is the number of students outside of all the circles divided by the total number of students surveyed:

$$P([c \cup b \cup f]') = \frac{18}{241} \approx 7.5\%$$

Since Choice E has the lowest probability, it is the correct answer.

17. D: The probability of getting three aces in a row is the product of the probabilities for each draw. For the first ace that is $\frac{4}{52}$, since there are 4 aces in a deck of 52 cards. For the second, it is $\frac{3}{51}$, since 3 aces and 51 cards remain. And for the third, it is $\frac{2}{50}$. So, the overall probability is $P = \frac{4}{52} \times \frac{3}{51} \times \frac{2}{50} \times \frac{24}{132,600} \times \frac{1}{5,525}$.

18. B: To calculate the range of any data set, we must find the difference between the largest value (known as the maximum) and the smallest value (known as the minimum). In this data set, our maximum is 832, while our minimum is 196. The difference of 832 and 196 is 636, so the range of the data set is also 636.

19. E: All of the other capital letters shown are symmetrical with respect to a horizontal axis drawn through the middle, as in the H shown in the figure. Only Z is not symmetrical in this respect.

20. D: To solve, first add Mary's shot to the score: 42–18. Subtract the figures to see how many points still need to be scored: $42 - 18 = 24$. Divide by three, since three points are attained with each shot: $24 \div 3 = 8$.

21. E: First, we must determine the total amount of money Krystal spent. To do so, we must add the cost of the sunglasses, $19.99, and the scarf, $27.50. To add decimals, we stack the numbers so that the decimal points are directly on top of one another. Then, we add using the traditional algorithm, bringing the decimal point straight down into our sum. This gives us a total cost of $47.49. To determine Krystal's change, we must subtract our total, $47.49, from $50.00. Again, we must be sure to stack our decimal points directly on top of one another. Then we subtract as normal, bringing our decimal point straight down into our answer. We need to be careful that we borrow when necessary. The difference of $50.00 and $47.49 is $2.51. Krystal will receive change in the amount of $2.51.

22. E: The ratio indicates the number of people who chose veggie (60) to the number of people who chose turkey (45). Write the ratio 60 : 45 and then reduce it by dividing both parts by 15 so that it becomes 4 : 3.

23. A: This is a typical plot of an inverse variation where the product of the dependent and independent variables, x and y, is always equal to the same value. In this case, the product is always equal to 1. So, the plot is in the first and third quadrants of the coordinate plane. As x increases and goes to infinity, y decreases and goes to zero while keeping the constant product. In contrast, graph 2 is a linear plot for an equation of the form $y = x$. Graph 3 is a quadratic plot for the equation $y = x^2$. Graph 4 is an exponential plot for the equation $y = 2^x$. And, Graph 5 is another linear plot corresponding to $y = \frac{x}{4} + 1$.

24. C: To determine this, first solve for x. Start by subtracting 2 from both sides.

$$10x + 2 = 7$$

Copyright © Mometrix Media. You have been licensed one copy of this document for personal use only. Any other reproduction or redistribution is strictly prohibited. All rights reserved. This content is provided for test preparation purposes only and does not imply an endorsement by Mometrix of any particular political, scientific, or religious point of view.

$$10x = 5$$

Then, divide both sides by 10.

$$x = \frac{5}{10} = \frac{1}{2}$$

Since $x = \frac{1}{2}$, multiply this by 2 to find that $2x = 2\left(\frac{1}{2}\right) = 1$.

25. A The area of a circle is πr^2, so the area of a semicircle is $\frac{\pi r^2}{2}$. Illustrated below is a method which can be used to find the area of the shaded region.

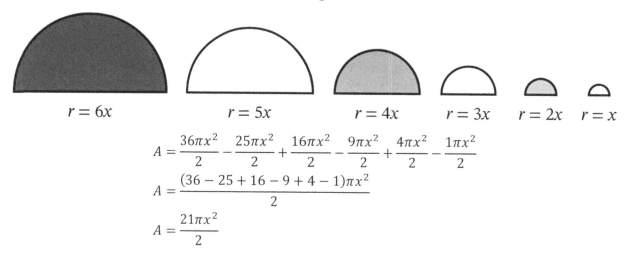

$$A = \frac{36\pi x^2}{2} - \frac{25\pi x^2}{2} + \frac{16\pi x^2}{2} - \frac{9\pi x^2}{2} + \frac{4\pi x^2}{2} - \frac{1\pi x^2}{2}$$

$$A = \frac{(36 - 25 + 16 - 9 + 4 - 1)\pi x^2}{2}$$

$$A = \frac{21\pi x^2}{2}$$

26. B: To solve, isolate y on one side of the equation:

$$4y = 60 - 16$$
$$4y = 44$$
$$y = 11$$

27. E: There are 16 empty chairs. This gives $\frac{2}{5}$ of the total enrollment. So, the full class must be:

$$\text{Class} = \frac{5}{2} \times 16 = 40 \text{ students}$$

Another option is to use proportions.

$$\frac{2}{5} = \frac{16}{x}$$

First, cross multiply to get: $2x = 80$. Then, divide each side by 2 to solve for x. So, $x = 40$, which means there are 40 students in the entire class.

28. B: Regardless of the exact number of students, we can determine the relative percentages of each eye color. We are given that 40% of the total have brown eyes, which means that $100\% - 40\%$ or 60% of the students have either blue or green eyes. Since 90% of those have blue eyes, we know that 10% of those 60% have green eyes, or 6% of the students have green eyes. Now, 90% of 60% can be found by converting both percentages to decimals and multiplying them. $(0.9) \times (0.6) =$

Copyright © Mometrix Media. You have been licensed one copy of this document for personal use only. Any other reproduction or redistribution is strictly prohibited. All rights reserved.
This content is provided for test preparation purposes only and does not imply an endorsement by Mometrix of any particular political, scientific, or religious point of view.

0.54, which is equivalent to 54%. So, in total, 40% have brown eyes, 54% have blue eyes, and 6% have green eyes. Therefore, we can definitively say that blue eyed students are the majority.

29. D: The associative property states that moving the parentheses when adding or multiplying a string of numbers will not affect the sum or product. The associative property is often used to group compatible numbers in an effort to assist with mental math. By rewriting the problem as $17 + (18 + 2)$, we have grouped our compatible numbers, 18 and 2. These are considered compatible numbers because they have a sum of 20, which is an easy number to calculate mentally. Once we have the sum of 20 we can include our final addend, 17, to arrive at our total of 37.

30. D: Rafael's profit on each computer is given by the difference between the price he pays and the price he charges his customer, or $\$800 - \$450$. If he sells n computers in a month, his total profit will be n times this difference, or $n(\$800 - \$450)$. However, it is necessary to subtract his fixed costs of $\$3,000$ from this to compute his final profit per month. This gives the complete equation:

$$P = n(\$800 - \$450) - \$3,000$$

31. D: To solve, first subtract the 20% discount ($\$400 \times 0.20 = \$80$) from the original price:

$$\$400 - \$80 = \$320$$

Then take the 5% discount ($\$320 \times 0.05 = \$16$) from the total:

$$\$320 - \$16 = \$304$$

32. E: Choose two angles that take up the entire line, since a straight line has a measure of $180°$.

33. D: The mode of any data set is the value(s) that appears most often. Here, we have two values, 84 and 93, that both occur four times. No other value occurs more than four times so we can say that we have two modes: 84 and 93.

34. C: The relationship between Kate and her shadow is the same as the relationship between Sara and her shadow; that is, $\frac{Kate}{Kate's\ shadow} = \frac{Sara}{Sara's\ shadow}$. If Sara's shadow is 16 inches longer than Kate's, it is 48 inches long.

$$\frac{x}{48} = \frac{40}{32}$$
$$32x = 48(40)$$
$$x = \frac{1920}{32}$$
$$x = 60$$

35. D: The volume of the box is the product of $\sqrt{3}$, $2\sqrt{5}$, and 4. To multiply two or more square root radicals, multiply the coefficients and then multiply the radicands.

$$\sqrt{3} \times 2\sqrt{5} \times 4 = 8\sqrt{3}\sqrt{5} = 8\sqrt{15}$$

Then, simplify the radicand if possible by factoring out any squares. Since 15 cannot be factored into any square factors, it cannot be simplified further.

36. C: Any triangle with an angle measuring over $90°$ is considered an obtuse triangle. Because this triangle has an angle measuring $100°$, we must classify it as obtuse. Since we have two 40-degree angles, we know that the sides opposite those angles must be the same length. A triangle with two

Copyright © Mometrix Media. You have been licensed one copy of this document for personal use only. Any other reproduction or redistribution is strictly prohibited. All rights reserved. This content is provided for test preparation purposes only and does not imply an endorsement by Mometrix of any particular political, scientific, or religious point of view.

equivalent sides is described as an isosceles triangle. This triangle must be described as an obtuse isosceles triangle.

37. C: We calculate the range of any data set by subtracting the smallest value from the largest value, or the maximum – the minimum. Here, our maximum is 84, while our minimum is 3. Because $84 - 3 = 81$, our range is 81. The range tells us how "spread out" our data is. Having a range of 81 means that our data is spread out by no more than 81 units.

38. D: In order to multiply two powers that have the same base, add their exponents because of the exponent rule $a^m \times a^n = a^{m+n}$. Therefore, $x^3 x^5 = x^{3+5} = x^8$.

39. E: When there are two operations within our parentheses, we must follow the order of operations *within* the parentheses as well. Because multiplication comes before addition, we must start by finding the product of 4 and 3, which is 12. Next, we add 10 and 12 to get 22. Finally, we can divide 22 by 2 to arrive at our final answer, 11.

40. E: Each notebook costs $1.50. To find the cost of each notebook, we must divide the total amount of money earned, $45.00, by the number of notebooks sold, 30. When we divide 45 by 30, we know that 30 can "fit" into 45 one time, with a remainder of 15. We can turn our remainder into a fraction by making our remainder the numerator and our divisor the denominator, creating the fraction $\frac{15}{30}$, or $\frac{1}{2}$. When working with money, 1 whole and $\frac{1}{2}$ represents one and a half dollars, or $1.50. Giselle charged $1.50 for each notebook.

41. D: An equilateral triangle means that all sides are the same length.

42. E: The area of the square is $A = s^2 = (30 \text{ cm})^2 = 900 \text{ cm}^2$. The area of the circle is $A = \pi r^2 = (3.14)(15 \text{ cm})^2 \approx 707 \text{ cm}^2$. The area of the shaded region is equal to the difference between the area of the square and the area of the circle, or $900 \text{ cm}^2 - 707 \text{ cm}^2$, which equals 193 cm^2.

43. C: Solve this equation by first using cross multiplication.

$$3(y + 4) = 15(y - 5)$$

From here, distribute on both sides.

$$3y + 12 = 15y - 75$$

Subtract $3y$ from both sides.

$$12 = 12y - 75$$

Add 75 to both sides of the equation.

$$87 = 12y$$

Finally, divide both sides by 12 and simplify the fraction.

$$\frac{87}{12} = \frac{29}{4} = y$$

Copyright © Mometrix Media. You have been licensed one copy of this document for personal use only. Any other reproduction or redistribution is strictly prohibited. All rights reserved. This content is provided for test preparation purposes only and does not imply an endorsement by Mometrix of any particular political, scientific, or religious point of view.

44. A: In this probability problem, there are three independent events (each digit of the code), each with ten possible outcomes (the numerals 0–9). Since the events are independent, the total number of possible outcomes equals the product of the possible outcomes for each of the three events.

$$P = P_1 \times P_2 \times P_3 = 10 \times 10 \times 10 = 1,000$$

This result makes sense when we consider trying every possible code in sequence, beginning with the combinations 0-0-0, 0-0-1, 0-0-2, etc. In ascending order, the last three-digit combination would be 9-9-9. Although it may seem that there would be 999 possible combinations, there are in fact 1,000 when we include the initial combination, 0-0-0.

45. C: When subtracting A from B, the difference matrix can be written as $\begin{bmatrix} 1-1 & -3-(-3) \\ -4-(-4) & 2-(-2) \end{bmatrix}$, which reduces to $\begin{bmatrix} 0 & 0 \\ 0 & 4 \end{bmatrix}$.

46. C: The lowest score, 68, is eliminated. The average of the remaining four grades is:

$$\text{Avg} = \frac{75 + 88 + 86 + 90}{4} = 84.75$$

Rounding up to the nearest integer gives a final grade of 85.

47. A: To simplify the expression, start by distributing the 3s.

$$3\left(\frac{6x-3}{3}\right) - 3(9x + 9)$$

$$6x - 3 - 27x - 27$$

Then, combine like terms.

$$(6x - 27x) + (-3 - 27)$$

$$-21x - 30$$

Since this isn't one of the answer choices, manipulate it to match one of the choices given. Factor out a –3 from each term.

$$-3(7x + 10)$$

48. E: Since the two triangles have all three corresponding pairs of sides and corresponding pairs of angles marked congruent, then the two triangles are congruent. Similar triangles are the same shape but not necessarily the same size; they have congruent angles. All congruent triangles are similar triangles, so the correct choice is that the triangles are both similar and congruent. An equilateral triangle has three congruent sides and angles measuring 60° each, so these triangles are not equilateral.

49. B: The median is the value in a group of numbers that separates the upper-half from the lower-half, so that there are an equal number of values above and below it. Order the numbers from least to greatest.

$$112, 112, 116, 133, 145$$

Copyright © Mometrix Media. You have been licensed one copy of this document for personal use only. Any other reproduction or redistribution is strictly prohibited. All rights reserved. This content is provided for test preparation purposes only and does not imply an endorsement by Mometrix of any particular political, scientific, or religious point of view.

In this distribution, there are two values greater than 116, and two values below it, so 116 is the median.

50. C: To find the probability that a student is enrolled at TAMU or that a student prefers lattes, the addition rule needs to be used. The addition rule adds the probabilities of two independent events and subtracts the probability that both events are true to avoid double counting. The probability may be written as $P(A \text{ or } B) = \frac{750}{1,650} + \frac{675}{1,650} - \frac{350}{1,650}$, which simplifies to $P(A \text{ or } B) = \frac{1,075}{1,650} \approx 65\%$. Therefore, the probability is approximately 65%.

51. C: The area of a triangle is $A = \frac{1}{2}bh$, where b and h are the lengths of the triangle's base and height, respectively. The base of the given triangle is 8, but the height is not given. Since the triangle is a right triangle and the hypotenuse is given, the triangle's height can be found using the Pythagorean theorem.

$$8^2 + h^2 = x^2$$
$$h^2 = x^2 - 64$$
$$h = \sqrt{x^2 - 64}$$

To find the area of the triangle in terms of x, substitute $\sqrt{x^2 - 64}$ for the height and 8 for the base of the triangle into the area formula, $A = \frac{1}{2}bh$.

$$A(x) = \frac{1}{2}(8)(\sqrt{x^2 - 64})$$
$$A(x) = 4\sqrt{x^2 - 64}$$

52. B: To solve, first find what percent of the paycheck is taken out: $30\% + 15\% + 32\% = 77\%$. Subtract this number from 100% to find out the amount of her paycheck that is remaining: 23%.

53. D: To divide fractions, multiply the divisor (the second fraction) by its reciprocal (turn it upside down). Then, reduce or simplify the fraction:

$$\frac{2}{5} \times \frac{3}{2} = \frac{6}{10} = \frac{3}{5}$$

54. E: A is a number in the thousandths; B is a number in the hundredths. C, D, and E are in tenths. Three-tenths (0.300) is the largest of these choices.

55. C: To solve, rearrange the equation and simplify by combining like terms:

$$(2x - 3) + 2x = 9$$
$$2x - 3 + 2x = 9$$
$$4x - 3 = 9$$
$$4x = 12$$
$$x = 3$$

56. E: For each die there is a $\frac{1}{6}$ chance that a 6 will be on top because a die has 6 sides. The probability that a 6 will show for each die is not affected by the results from another roll of the die. In other words, these probabilities are independent. So, the overall probability of throwing 3 sixes

Copyright © Mometrix Media. You have been licensed one copy of this document for personal use only. Any other reproduction or redistribution is strictly prohibited. All rights reserved. This content is provided for test preparation purposes only and does not imply an endorsement by Mometrix of any particular political, scientific, or religious point of view.

is the product of the individual probabilities: $P = \frac{1}{6} \times \frac{1}{6} \times \frac{1}{6} = \frac{1}{6^3} = \frac{1}{216}$. Therefore, the probability that all three dice will land on a 6 is $\frac{1}{216}$.

Copyright © Mometrix Media. You have been licensed one copy of this document for personal use only. Any other reproduction or redistribution is strictly prohibited. All rights reserved.
This content is provided for test preparation purposes only and does not imply an endorsement by Mometrix of any particular political, scientific, or religious point of view.

Clerical Section

A great number of civil service positions are clerical in nature, and the exams usually reflect that by testing for clerical skills. The term "clerical" has the same root as the word "clerk," and employees who do these kinds of jobs used to be widely known as clerks. These days people tend to associate the term "clerk" with "cashier," and most people doing clerical work are now referred to as office workers, support staff, or some similar term. In most cases, a college degree is not required to be eligible for clerical positions. A high school diploma or general equivalency diploma will usually meet the educational requirement for applicants.

Clerical jobs can involve a wide variety of tasks. Some of the most common job duties for clerical workers are scheduling appointments, answering phones, keeping records, light bookkeeping, making copies, filing, sorting, word processing (what used to be called typing), and data entry. In many cases, one of these tasks will be the primary function of the employee. In other positions, a clerical worker will be more of a jack-of-all-trades, who may perform all of the tasks mentioned above on a regular basis, as well as others. Examples of clerical workers include secretaries and administrative assistants, who typically have a wide range of duties.

Until about 1980, most of these jobs were done the old-fashioned way, using pencil and paper, mimeographs, file cabinets, etc. Mimeographs are a thing of the past, of course, and while file cabinets, pencils, and paper are still found in offices, nearly all clerical work is now done with computers, printers, scanners, and other high-tech machines. In order to qualify for these jobs, you'll need to know at least the basics of operating a computer: working with documents, shortcuts like copying and pasting, saving files, etc. For some positions, you'll need extensive experience using common software programs for word processing, data management, creating charts, and more. If advanced skills are required, the civil service job listing will say so. Make sure to read job postings carefully so you don't waste time and expense, applying and testing for a job you aren't qualified for.

COMMON CLERICAL CIVIL SERVICE JOBS

FILE CLERKS

Keeping records is an important and time-consuming task in every government agency and department in the country. Without proper record keeping, it would be impossible for a government agency to properly serve the public, and it would be equally impossible for citizens to trust the agency. File clerks perform this vital function, and must do it accurately and efficiently. Some government departments are now paperless, meaning that all records and files are stored, updated, organized, and revised by electronic means only. In a paperless office, file clerks will do all of their work on computers. Most departments have not made the full transition to being paperless yet, however. In these jobs, much of the work will be done on computers, but since paper files are still in use, some of them will be stored in actual file cabinets. Some clerks may do only electronic filing or only paper filing, while some will do both.

INFORMATION CLERKS AND RECEPTIONISTS

There is a lot of overlap in the job descriptions of information clerks and receptionists, and oftentimes the titles are basically interchangeable. When you enter an office building and a person behind a desk greets and assists you, you're interacting with a receptionist. Generally speaking, receptionist jobs also involve answering phones and screening and directing calls. These activities take up most of a receptionist's day.

Copyright © Mometrix Media. You have been licensed one copy of this document for personal use only. Any other reproduction or redistribution is strictly prohibited. All rights reserved. This content is provided for test preparation purposes only and does not imply an endorsement by Mometrix of any particular political, scientific, or religious point of view.

Information clerks often perform these same functions, but in many cases, they also interact with other employees, providing support in a variety of ways. They may look up needed information for a higher-level employee, for example. They may also do a fair amount of "gofer" tasks, which involve running errands or delivering work material from one employee to another. These employees tend to work with members of the public less often than receptionists do.

Since these two job titles are often used interchangeably, don't read too much into a job description on a civil service posting for a receptionist or information clerk position. If you qualify for one position, you'll probably qualify for the other, and the exams will almost certainly be very similar. The biggest difference between the two kinds of jobs is how much time an employee spends interacting with members of the public compared to the amount of time spent helping coworkers.

INFORMATION PROCESSING CLERKS

There are usually many jobs for information processing clerks in every government department. These positions fall into two main categories—word processing and data entry. Word processing used to be called typing, and being good at typing is still one of the main qualifications for these jobs. Both speed and accuracy are required; often the job listing will specify how fast an accurate you need to be in order to qualify. If so, you will need to pass a separate typing test. In addition, many of these positions require proficiency in Microsoft Word™, because it is the most common word processing software.

Data entry clerks work with numbers instead of words, and they may be referred to as accounting clerks or bookkeeping clerks. These employees use the numerical keypad on a regular keyboard, or a stand-alone device, known as a ten-key or a number pad (AKA numpad). Some jobs will require applicants to pass a test demonstrating that they have the necessary speed and accuracy on a ten-key pad.

CLERICAL PRACTICE TESTS

One thing all clerical positions have in common is that attention to detail is extremely important. Because of this, civil service exams for clerical positions have a lot of content designed to test for speed and accuracy at completing forms, coding, and spotting discrepancies between two sets of information. If you're considering applying for a clerical position, this section of the guide will help you get up to speed for this part of the civil service exam.

SECRET #1: SPEED

Practice at a higher rate of speed than your normal comfort level. This will increase your pace by the time of the exam. Your ability and tolerance for speed will increase after repeated practice. Remember to keep the accuracy ratio high. You must be fast but accurate.

SECRET #2: PREPARATION IS AN ADVANTAGE

Unlike others you will be prepared and know what is coming throughout the testing period. This should give you a level of comfort and confidence that will help you achieve a higher score.

SECRET #3: CHECK ANSWERS IF TIME ALLOWS

If you finish early, check your answers. Make sure that the answer for #4 is marked on the answer sheet as #4. Check any addresses that you were unsure of.

Copyright © Mometrix Media. You have been licensed one copy of this document for personal use only. Any other reproduction or redistribution is strictly prohibited. All rights reserved. This content is provided for test preparation purposes only and does not imply an endorsement by Mometrix of any particular political, scientific, or religious point of view.

SECRET #4: DO NOT GUESS ON THIS SECTION

For most clerical exercises on a civil service exam, wrong answers will count against you in the scoring procedure. Your score will be reduced if you guess incorrectly instead of leaving a question blank.

FORMS COMPLETION

COMPLETING FORMS

This is a test of your ability to identify information needed to complete forms like those used by many delivery companies, which are similar to many departmental forms in government agencies. You will be shown several forms on this test, along with several items about what information is required to complete each form. Each part of the form is labeled (for example, 7 and 7a).

REDUCING ERRORS

Here are suggestions to help you reduce errors on Completing Tasks:

- Study each form carefully. Each of the forms in this test section is different and calls for different information in the various sections. You should take time to study the forms carefully before responding to the items to be sure that you know what information is desired.
- Consider answering items you're sure of, and then come back and answer other items later. If you return to an item, take extreme care to make sure that you are marking the correct answer on your answer sheet. It is easy to lose your place and darken the wrong circle.

FORMS COMPLETION SAMPLE QUESTIONS

Look at the sample form and questions shown below. Please study the form and complete the sample questions. Mark your answers in the *Sample Answer Grid*.

Sample Form

1. Last Name		2. First Name	
3. Street Address			
4. City	5. State	6. ZIP Code	
7. Date 7a. Month 7b. Day 7c. Year		8. Amount Paid $	

S1. Where should the last name be entered on this form?

- A. Box 1
- B. Box 2
- C. Box 3
- D. Box 4

Copyright © Mometrix Media. You have been licensed one copy of this document for personal use only. Any other reproduction or redistribution is strictly prohibited. All rights reserved. This content is provided for test preparation purposes only and does not imply an endorsement by Mometrix of any particular political, scientific, or religious point of view.

S2. Which of these is a correct entry for Line 7a?

    A. $62.30

    B. 2005

    C. August

    D. 70455

Sample Answer Grid	
S1.	Ⓐ Ⓑ Ⓒ Ⓓ
S2.	Ⓐ Ⓑ Ⓒ Ⓓ

Completed Sample Answer Grid	
S1.	● Ⓑ Ⓒ Ⓓ
S2.	Ⓐ Ⓑ ● Ⓓ

In the **Sample Form**, Box 1 is labeled "Last Name." Therefore, the correct answer is A. In the **Sample Form**, Line 7a asks for a month, and August is the only month among the answer choices. Therefore, C is the correct answer. Notice that the **Completed Sample Answer Grid** on the right side of the page shows the correct responses filled in.

Copyright © Mometrix Media. You have been licensed one copy of this document for personal use only. Any other reproduction or redistribution is strictly prohibited. All rights reserved. This content is provided for test preparation purposes only and does not imply an endorsement by Mometrix of any particular political, scientific, or religious point of view.

FORMS COMPLETION EXERCISE

Give yourself 7 minutes to complete this exercise. While this test part is designed to allow sufficient time to read and review each form, it is important to practice responding to the items within a reasonable time period.

Read each form and answer the items based upon the information provided.

Sample Form 1

Attempted Delivery Notice	
1. Today's Date	3a. Sender's Name
2. Date Item(s) Sent	3b. Sender's Address
4. [] If checked, someone must be present at the time of delivery to sign for item(s)	
5. Enter number of each 5a. ____ Letter 5b. ____ Magazine/Catalog 5c. ____ Large envelope 5d. ____ Box	6. Postage 6a. [] If checked, there is postage due on the item(s) 6b. _____ Amount due
7. Delivery 7a. [] Item(s) will be redelivered tomorrow 7b. [] Please pick up the item(s) at your local Post Office. The item(s) will be available after: 7c. Date _____ 7d. Time _____	

1. Where would you enter the sender's address?

- A. Box 1
- B. Box 2
- C. Box 3a
- D. Box 3b

2. Which of these would be a correct entry for Box 2?

- A. A check mark
- B. 11/12/04
- C. 4
- D. Renae Smith

3. You could enter a date in each of the following boxes EXCEPT which?

- A. Box 1
- B. Box 2
- C. Line 5a
- D. Line 7c

4. Which of these would be a correct entry for Line 7d?

- A. PO Box 454 Robert, LA 70455
- B. A check mark
- C. 03/15/05
- D. 10:00 a.m.

Copyright © Mometrix Media. You have been licensed one copy of this document for personal use only. Any other reproduction or redistribution is strictly prohibited. All rights reserved.
This content is provided for test preparation purposes only and does not imply an endorsement by Mometrix of any particular political, scientific, or religious point of view.

5. Where would you indicate that the customer must pick up the item at the Post Office?

   A. Box 43a
   B. Box 5a
   C. Box 6b
   D. Box 7b

6. Which of these would be a correct entry for Box 3a?

   A. Lydia Traylor
   B. A check mark
   C. 5453 Essen Lane Baton Rouge, LA 70809
   D. $5.08

7. How would you indicate that there are two boxes to be delivered?

   A. Enter "2" in Line 5a
   B. Enter "2" in Line 5b
   C. Enter "2" in Line 5c
   D. Enter "2" in Line 5d

Sample Form 2

Mass Mailing Receipt	
1. Date	4. Name of Permit Holder
2. Post Office ZIP Code	5. Address of Permit Holder
3. 5-digit Permit Number	6. Telephone Number of Permit Holder
7. Processing Category (check one)	8. Total Number of Pieces
7a. [] Letters	9. Total Weight
7b. [] Flats	9a. ___ pounds 9b. ___ ounces
7c. [] Automation Flats	10. 2-digit Cost Code
7d. [] Parcels	11. Total Paid
	$ _____

8. Luke Strait holds the mass mailing permit. Where would you indicate this?

   A. Box 3
   B. Box 4
   C. Box 5
   D. Box 6

9. Where would you indicate that 75,000 pieces were sent?

   A. Box 3
   B. Box 8
   C. Line 7a
   D. Line 10

10. How would you indicate that the processing category is "Automation Flats"?

   A. Put a check mark in Box 7a
   B. Put a check mark in Box 7b
   C. Put a check mark in Box 7c
   D. Put a check mark in Box 7d

Copyright © Mometrix Media. You have been licensed one copy of this document for personal use only. Any other reproduction or redistribution is strictly prohibited. All rights reserved. This content is provided for test preparation purposes only and does not imply an endorsement by Mometrix of any particular political, scientific, or religious point of view.

11. The total paid was $407.59. Where would you indicate this?

    A. Box 6

    B. Line 9a

    C. Box 10

    D. Line 11

12. Which of these would be a correct entry for Box 5?

    A. 111 Lake Front Drive Miramar Beach FL 32550

    B. Berry Town Candies

    C. 2/10/04

    D. A check mark

13. Which of these would be a correct entry for Box 10?

    A. 30454

    B. 901-866-5243

    C. 30

    D. 70005-6320

14. The Post Office ZIP Code is 77706. Where would you indicate this?

    A. Box 1

    B. Box 2

    C. Box 3

    D. Box 9

15. A number would be a correct entry for every box EXCEPT which?

    A. Box 3

    B. Box 4

    C. Box 8

    D. Line 11

Copyright © Mometrix Media. You have been licensed one copy of this document for personal use only. Any other reproduction or redistribution is strictly prohibited. All rights reserved.
This content is provided for test preparation purposes only and does not imply an endorsement by Mometrix of any particular political, scientific, or religious point of view.

FORMS COMPLETION ANSWER KEY

1. D

2. B

3. C

4. D

5. D

6. A

7. D

8. B

9. B

10. C

11. D

12. A

13. C

14. B

15. B

Copyright © Mometrix Media. You have been licensed one copy of this document for personal use only. Any other reproduction or redistribution is strictly prohibited. All rights reserved. This content is provided for test preparation purposes only and does not imply an endorsement by Mometrix of any particular political, scientific, or religious point of view.

CODING AND MEMORY

This practice test consists of two sections. The Coding section tests your ability to use codes quickly and accurately, using a coding guide for reference. The Memory section tests your ability to complete the same task, but without the benefit of referring to the coding guide. Instead, you must recall the coding guide from memory.

These tests usually follow the same format. In most cases, you will be shown a coding guide, along with several items that must be assigned a code. You must look up the correct code for each item and write your response on the answer sheet accurately and quickly. During the first section of the test part, you will be allowed to look at the coding guide while you assign codes. During the second section of the test part, you must assign codes based on your memory of the same coding guide. While the coding guide is visible, try to memorize as many of the codes as you can. These are the same codes that will be used in the memory section.

Note: During the actual test:

- You are not allowed to look at the codes when answering the items in the Memory section.
- You are not allowed to write down any addresses during the memorization period.

Memory for addresses questions are often considered one of the hardest parts of the exam. You will be given a set of boxes, each of which will contain addresses. After memorizing the content in the boxes, you will have to recall in which box each appeared.

SECRET #1: MEMORIZE HORIZONTALLY

Memorize the addresses horizontally, not vertically. This is more natural and will flow more easily for you.

SECRET #2: ANSWER THE QUESTIONS IN THIS SECTION IN ORDER

Answer all questions in order. Do not attempt to go through this section twice. There is not enough time for you to answer the ones that you think are easy and then attempt to go back and answer the others.

SECRET #3: SPEED

Practice at a higher rate of speed than your normal comfort level. This will increase your pace by the time of the exam. Your ability and tolerance for speed will increase after repeated practice. Remember to keep the accuracy ratio high. You must be fast but accurate.

SCORING ANSWERS

Typically, your score on this part of the civil service exam is based on the number of items that you answer correctly minus 1/3 of the number of items you answer incorrectly. In both sections of this test part, your score depends on how many items you can correctly assign a code in the time allowed. You may not be able to assign a code to all of the items before time runs out, but you should do your best to assign as many as you can with a high degree of accuracy. There is a penalty for guessing on this test. It won't be to your advantage to guess randomly. However, if you can see that one or more responses is clearly incorrect, it will generally be to your advantage to guess from among the remaining responses.

REDUCING ERRORS

On the test, you have several opportunities to work with the coding guide and practice memorizing the codes for each range of addresses before answering items on them based upon memory. Listen

Copyright © Mometrix Media. You have been licensed one copy of this document for personal use only. Any other reproduction or redistribution is strictly prohibited. All rights reserved.
This content is provided for test preparation purposes only and does not imply an endorsement by Mometrix of any particular political, scientific, or religious point of view.

to the administrator's instructions. Do not become frustrated or discouraged; remain focused. Here are more suggestions to help you reduce errors on this portion of the test:

- Answer items you know and answer other items later. Remember that you have a time limit.
- As time permits, go back and attempt to answer the more difficult items. If you have narrowed a difficult item down to one or two choices, make an educated guess. If you return to an item, take care to make sure that you are marking the correct answer on your answer sheet. It is easy to lose your place and mark the wrong circle.
- Arbitrarily guessing will probably not help your score. If you can eliminate one or more of the answers, it may be to your advantage to guess.
- Work as quickly and accurately as possible. You are not expected to answer all items in the time allowed.
- Fully use the practice opportunities and memorization periods you are given to practice memorizing the codes.

Copyright © Mometrix Media. You have been licensed one copy of this document for personal use only. Any other reproduction or redistribution is strictly prohibited. All rights reserved.
This content is provided for test preparation purposes only and does not imply an endorsement by Mometrix of any particular political, scientific, or religious point of view.

COMPLETING EXERCISE: CODING

Move through items 1 through 15 and assign codes to each based upon the Coding Guide. Work as quickly and as accurately as possible.

Time yourself on this exercise. You should stop after 2 minutes. You may not be able to finish all of the items in this exercise in that time, but practicing with a time limit will give you a better feel for taking the actual test.

When you finish the exercise set, check your answers.

Exercise: Coding

CODING GUIDE		
Address Range		Delivery Route
1 – 99 Richoux Rd. 10 – 200 Hoffman Ave. 5 – 15 E 6th Street		A
100 – 200 Richoux Rd. 16 – 30 E 6th Street		B
10000 – 12000 Byers Lane. 1 – 10 Rural Route 1 201 – 1500 Hoffman Ave.		C
All mail that doesn't fall in one of the address ranges listed above		D
blank	Address	Delivery Route
1.	7 Richoux Rd.	A B C D
2.	102 Norwood Ave.	A B C D
3.	23 E 6th Street	A B C D
4.	16 E 6th Street	A B C D
5.	29 Richoux Rd.	A B C D
6.	8 Rural Route 1	A B C D
7.	1308 Hoffman Ave.	A B C D
8.	5 Rural Route 11	A B C D
9.	10191 Byers Lane	A B C D
10.	8 E 6th Street	A B C D
11.	183 Ridgeline Rd.	A B C D
12.	12050 Byers Lane	A B C D
13.	8 E 6th Street	A B C D
14.	1043 Hoffman Ave.	A B C D
15.	105 Richoux Rd.	A B C D
blank	blank	Blank

Copyright © Mometrix Media. You have been licensed one copy of this document for personal use only. Any other reproduction or redistribution is strictly prohibited. All rights reserved. This content is provided for test preparation purposes only and does not imply an endorsement by Mometrix of any particular political, scientific, or religious point of view.

Coding: Answer Key

1. A

2. D

3. B

4. B

5. A

6. C

7. C

8. D

9. C

10. A

11. D

12. D

13. A

14. C

15. B

Copyright © Mometrix Media. You have been licensed one copy of this document for personal use only. Any other reproduction or redistribution is strictly prohibited. All rights reserved.
This content is provided for test preparation purposes only and does not imply an endorsement by Mometrix of any particular political, scientific, or religious point of view.

COMPLETING EXERCISE: MEMORY

In this section of the test, you will assign codes based on your memory of the Coding Guide. You will use the same Coding Guide you have been using throughout this exercise.

- Take 3 minutes to memorize the Coding Guide.
- You should not take any notes when memorizing the Coding Guide, but you may write in the test booklet while you are answering the items.
- Move through the items and assign codes to each based upon your memory of the Coding Guide. Do NOT refer to the Coding Guide as you work through this exercise. Work as quickly and as accurately as possible.
- You should not be able to see the Coding Guide during the exercise, and you should not turn back to an earlier page to look at it.
- Time yourself on this exercise. You should stop after 3 minutes. You may not be able to finish all of the items in this exercise in that time, but practicing with a time limit will give you a better feel for taking the actual test.
- When you finish the exercise, check your answers against the correct ones.

Exercise: Memory

blank	Address	Delivery Route
16.	12 E. 6th Street	A B C D
17.	1494 Hoffman Ave.	A B C D
18.	255 Richoux Rd.	A B C D
19.	165 Richoux Rd.	A B C D
20.	7 Rural Route 1	A B C D
21.	17 Rural Route 1	A B C D
22.	28 E 6th Street	A B C D
23.	14 E 6th Street	A B C D
24.	4500 Byers Lane	A B C D
25.	5 N 6th Street	A B C D
26.	39 Richoux Rd.	A B C D
27.	151 Richoux Rd.	A B C D
28.	8 E 6th Street	A B C D
29.	205 Hoffman Ave.	A B C D
30.	11001 Byers Lane	A B C D

Copyright © Mometrix Media. You have been licensed one copy of this document for personal use only. Any other reproduction or redistribution is strictly prohibited. All rights reserved. This content is provided for test preparation purposes only and does not imply an endorsement by Mometrix of any particular political, scientific, or religious point of view.

Memory: Answer Key

16. A

17. C

18. D

19. B

20. C

21. D

22. B

23. A

24. D

25. D

26. A

27. B

28. A

29. C

30. C

Copyright © Mometrix Media. You have been licensed one copy of this document for personal use only. Any other reproduction or redistribution is strictly prohibited. All rights reserved.
This content is provided for test preparation purposes only and does not imply an endorsement by Mometrix of any particular political, scientific, or religious point of view.

How to Overcome Test Anxiety

Just the thought of taking a test is enough to make most people a little nervous. A test is an important event that can have a long-term impact on your future, so it's important to take it seriously and it's natural to feel anxious about performing well. But just because anxiety is normal, that doesn't mean that it's helpful in test taking, or that you should simply accept it as part of your life. Anxiety can have a variety of effects. These effects can be mild, like making you feel slightly nervous, or severe, like blocking your ability to focus or remember even a simple detail.

If you experience test anxiety—whether severe or mild—it's important to know how to beat it. To discover this, first you need to understand what causes test anxiety.

Causes of Test Anxiety

While we often think of anxiety as an uncontrollable emotional state, it can actually be caused by simple, practical things. One of the most common causes of test anxiety is that a person does not feel adequately prepared for their test. This feeling can be the result of many different issues such as poor study habits or lack of organization, but the most common culprit is time management. Starting to study too late, failing to organize your study time to cover all of the material, or being distracted while you study will mean that you're not well prepared for the test. This may lead to cramming the night before, which will cause you to be physically and mentally exhausted for the test. Poor time management also contributes to feelings of stress, fear, and hopelessness as you realize you are not well prepared but don't know what to do about it.

Other times, test anxiety is not related to your preparation for the test but comes from unresolved fear. This may be a past failure on a test, or poor performance on tests in general. It may come from comparing yourself to others who seem to be performing better or from the stress of living up to expectations. Anxiety may be driven by fears of the future—how failure on this test would affect your educational and career goals. These fears are often completely irrational, but they can still negatively impact your test performance.

Elements of Test Anxiety

As mentioned earlier, test anxiety is considered to be an emotional state, but it has physical and mental components as well. Sometimes you may not even realize that you are suffering from test anxiety until you notice the physical symptoms. These can include trembling hands, rapid heartbeat, sweating, nausea, and tense muscles. Extreme anxiety may lead to fainting or vomiting. Obviously, any of these symptoms can have a negative impact on testing. It is important to recognize them as soon as they begin to occur so that you can address the problem before it damages your performance.

The mental components of test anxiety include trouble focusing and inability to remember learned information. During a test, your mind is on high alert, which can help you recall information and stay focused for an extended period of time. However, anxiety interferes with your mind's natural processes, causing you to blank out, even on the questions you know well. The strain of testing during anxiety makes it difficult to stay focused, especially on a test that may take several hours. Extreme anxiety can take a huge mental toll, making it difficult not only to recall test information but even to understand the test questions or pull your thoughts together.

Copyright © Mometrix Media. You have been licensed one copy of this document for personal use only. Any other reproduction or redistribution is strictly prohibited. All rights reserved. This content is provided for test preparation purposes only and does not imply an endorsement by Mometrix of any particular political, scientific, or religious point of view.

Effects of Test Anxiety

Test anxiety is like a disease—if left untreated, it will get progressively worse. Anxiety leads to poor performance, and this reinforces the feelings of fear and failure, which in turn lead to poor performances on subsequent tests. It can grow from a mild nervousness to a crippling condition. If allowed to progress, test anxiety can have a big impact on your schooling, and consequently on your future.

Test anxiety can spread to other parts of your life. Anxiety on tests can become anxiety in any stressful situation, and blanking on a test can turn into panicking in a job situation. But fortunately, you don't have to let anxiety rule your testing and determine your grades. There are a number of relatively simple steps you can take to move past anxiety and function normally on a test and in the rest of life.

Physical Steps for Beating Test Anxiety

While test anxiety is a serious problem, the good news is that it can be overcome. It doesn't have to control your ability to think and remember information. While it may take time, you can begin taking steps today to beat anxiety.

Just as your first hint that you may be struggling with anxiety comes from the physical symptoms, the first step to treating it is also physical. Rest is crucial for having a clear, strong mind. If you are tired, it is much easier to give in to anxiety. But if you establish good sleep habits, your body and mind will be ready to perform optimally, without the strain of exhaustion. Additionally, sleeping well helps you to retain information better, so you're more likely to recall the answers when you see the test questions.

Getting good sleep means more than going to bed on time. It's important to allow your brain time to relax. Take study breaks from time to time so it doesn't get overworked, and don't study right before bed. Take time to rest your mind before trying to rest your body, or you may find it difficult to fall asleep.

Along with sleep, other aspects of physical health are important in preparing for a test. Good nutrition is vital for good brain function. Sugary foods and drinks may give a burst of energy but this burst is followed by a crash, both physically and emotionally. Instead, fuel your body with protein and vitamin-rich foods.

Also, drink plenty of water. Dehydration can lead to headaches and exhaustion, especially if your brain is already under stress from the rigors of the test. Particularly if your test is a long one, drink water during the breaks. And if possible, take an energy-boosting snack to eat between sections.

Along with sleep and diet, a third important part of physical health is exercise. Maintaining a steady workout schedule is helpful, but even taking 5-minute study breaks to walk can help get your blood pumping faster and clear your head. Exercise also releases endorphins, which contribute to a positive feeling and can help combat test anxiety.

When you nurture your physical health, you are also contributing to your mental health. If your body is healthy, your mind is much more likely to be healthy as well. So take time to rest, nourish your body with healthy food and water, and get moving as much as possible. Taking these physical steps will make you stronger and more able to take the mental steps necessary to overcome test anxiety.

Copyright © Mometrix Media. You have been licensed one copy of this document for personal use only. Any other reproduction or redistribution is strictly prohibited. All rights reserved. This content is provided for test preparation purposes only and does not imply an endorsement by Mometrix of any particular political, scientific, or religious point of view.

Mental Steps for Beating Test Anxiety

Working on the mental side of test anxiety can be more challenging, but as with the physical side, there are clear steps you can take to overcome it. As mentioned earlier, test anxiety often stems from lack of preparation, so the obvious solution is to prepare for the test. Effective studying may be the most important weapon you have for beating test anxiety, but you can and should employ several other mental tools to combat fear.

First, boost your confidence by reminding yourself of past success—tests or projects that you aced. If you're putting as much effort into preparing for this test as you did for those, there's no reason you should expect to fail here. Work hard to prepare; then trust your preparation.

Second, surround yourself with encouraging people. It can be helpful to find a study group, but be sure that the people you're around will encourage a positive attitude. If you spend time with others who are anxious or cynical, this will only contribute to your own anxiety. Look for others who are motivated to study hard from a desire to succeed, not from a fear of failure.

Third, reward yourself. A test is physically and mentally tiring, even without anxiety, and it can be helpful to have something to look forward to. Plan an activity following the test, regardless of the outcome, such as going to a movie or getting ice cream.

When you are taking the test, if you find yourself beginning to feel anxious, remind yourself that you know the material. Visualize successfully completing the test. Then take a few deep, relaxing breaths and return to it. Work through the questions carefully but with confidence, knowing that you are capable of succeeding.

Developing a healthy mental approach to test taking will also aid in other areas of life. Test anxiety affects more than just the actual test—it can be damaging to your mental health and even contribute to depression. It's important to beat test anxiety before it becomes a problem for more than testing.

Study Strategy

Being prepared for the test is necessary to combat anxiety, but what does being prepared look like? You may study for hours on end and still not feel prepared. What you need is a strategy for test prep. The next few pages outline our recommended steps to help you plan out and conquer the challenge of preparation.

STEP 1: SCOPE OUT THE TEST

Learn everything you can about the format (multiple choice, essay, etc.) and what will be on the test. Gather any study materials, course outlines, or sample exams that may be available. Not only will this help you to prepare, but knowing what to expect can help to alleviate test anxiety.

STEP 2: MAP OUT THE MATERIAL

Look through the textbook or study guide and make note of how many chapters or sections it has. Then divide these over the time you have. For example, if a book has 15 chapters and you have five days to study, you need to cover three chapters each day. Even better, if you have the time, leave an extra day at the end for overall review after you have gone through the material in depth.

If time is limited, you may need to prioritize the material. Look through it and make note of which sections you think you already have a good grasp on, and which need review. While you are studying, skim quickly through the familiar sections and take more time on the challenging parts.

Copyright © Mometrix Media. You have been licensed one copy of this document for personal use only. Any other reproduction or redistribution is strictly prohibited. All rights reserved. This content is provided for test preparation purposes only and does not imply an endorsement by Mometrix of any particular political, scientific, or religious point of view.

Write out your plan so you don't get lost as you go. Having a written plan also helps you feel more in control of the study, so anxiety is less likely to arise from feeling overwhelmed at the amount to cover.

STEP 3: GATHER YOUR TOOLS

Decide what study method works best for you. Do you prefer to highlight in the book as you study and then go back over the highlighted portions? Or do you type out notes of the important information? Or is it helpful to make flashcards that you can carry with you? Assemble the pens, index cards, highlighters, post-it notes, and any other materials you may need so you won't be distracted by getting up to find things while you study.

If you're having a hard time retaining the information or organizing your notes, experiment with different methods. For example, try color-coding by subject with colored pens, highlighters, or post-it notes. If you learn better by hearing, try recording yourself reading your notes so you can listen while in the car, working out, or simply sitting at your desk. Ask a friend to quiz you from your flashcards, or try teaching someone the material to solidify it in your mind.

STEP 4: CREATE YOUR ENVIRONMENT

It's important to avoid distractions while you study. This includes both the obvious distractions like visitors and the subtle distractions like an uncomfortable chair (or a too-comfortable couch that makes you want to fall asleep). Set up the best study environment possible: good lighting and a comfortable work area. If background music helps you focus, you may want to turn it on, but otherwise keep the room quiet. If you are using a computer to take notes, be sure you don't have any other windows open, especially applications like social media, games, or anything else that could distract you. Silence your phone and turn off notifications. Be sure to keep water close by so you stay hydrated while you study (but avoid unhealthy drinks and snacks).

Also, take into account the best time of day to study. Are you freshest first thing in the morning? Try to set aside some time then to work through the material. Is your mind clearer in the afternoon or evening? Schedule your study session then. Another method is to study at the same time of day that you will take the test, so that your brain gets used to working on the material at that time and will be ready to focus at test time.

STEP 5: STUDY!

Once you have done all the study preparation, it's time to settle into the actual studying. Sit down, take a few moments to settle your mind so you can focus, and begin to follow your study plan. Don't give in to distractions or let yourself procrastinate. This is your time to prepare so you'll be ready to fearlessly approach the test. Make the most of the time and stay focused.

Of course, you don't want to burn out. If you study too long you may find that you're not retaining the information very well. Take regular study breaks. For example, taking five minutes out of every hour to walk briskly, breathing deeply and swinging your arms, can help your mind stay fresh.

As you get to the end of each chapter or section, it's a good idea to do a quick review. Remind yourself of what you learned and work on any difficult parts. When you feel that you've mastered the material, move on to the next part. At the end of your study session, briefly skim through your notes again.

But while review is helpful, cramming last minute is NOT. If at all possible, work ahead so that you won't need to fit all your study into the last day. Cramming overloads your brain with more information than it can process and retain, and your tired mind may struggle to recall even

Copyright © Mometrix Media. You have been licensed one copy of this document for personal use only. Any other reproduction or redistribution is strictly prohibited. All rights reserved.
This content is provided for test preparation purposes only and does not imply an endorsement by Mometrix of any particular political, scientific, or religious point of view.

previously learned information when it is overwhelmed with last-minute study. Also, the urgent nature of cramming and the stress placed on your brain contribute to anxiety. You'll be more likely to go to the test feeling unprepared and having trouble thinking clearly.

So don't cram, and don't stay up late before the test, even just to review your notes at a leisurely pace. Your brain needs rest more than it needs to go over the information again. In fact, plan to finish your studies by noon or early afternoon the day before the test. Give your brain the rest of the day to relax or focus on other things, and get a good night's sleep. Then you will be fresh for the test and better able to recall what you've studied.

STEP 6: TAKE A PRACTICE TEST

Many courses offer sample tests, either online or in the study materials. This is an excellent resource to check whether you have mastered the material, as well as to prepare for the test format and environment.

Check the test format ahead of time: the number of questions, the type (multiple choice, free response, etc.), and the time limit. Then create a plan for working through them. For example, if you have 30 minutes to take a 60-question test, your limit is 30 seconds per question. Spend less time on the questions you know well so that you can take more time on the difficult ones.

If you have time to take several practice tests, take the first one open book, with no time limit. Work through the questions at your own pace and make sure you fully understand them. Gradually work up to taking a test under test conditions: sit at a desk with all study materials put away and set a timer. Pace yourself to make sure you finish the test with time to spare and go back to check your answers if you have time.

After each test, check your answers. On the questions you missed, be sure you understand why you missed them. Did you misread the question (tests can use tricky wording)? Did you forget the information? Or was it something you hadn't learned? Go back and study any shaky areas that the practice tests reveal.

Taking these tests not only helps with your grade, but also aids in combating test anxiety. If you're already used to the test conditions, you're less likely to worry about it, and working through tests until you're scoring well gives you a confidence boost. Go through the practice tests until you feel comfortable, and then you can go into the test knowing that you're ready for it.

Test Tips

On test day, you should be confident, knowing that you've prepared well and are ready to answer the questions. But aside from preparation, there are several test day strategies you can employ to maximize your performance.

First, as stated before, get a good night's sleep the night before the test (and for several nights before that, if possible). Go into the test with a fresh, alert mind rather than staying up late to study.

Try not to change too much about your normal routine on the day of the test. It's important to eat a nutritious breakfast, but if you normally don't eat breakfast at all, consider eating just a protein bar. If you're a coffee drinker, go ahead and have your normal coffee. Just make sure you time it so that the caffeine doesn't wear off right in the middle of your test. Avoid sugary beverages, and drink enough water to stay hydrated but not so much that you need a restroom break 10 minutes into the

Copyright © Mometrix Media. You have been licensed one copy of this document for personal use only. Any other reproduction or redistribution is strictly prohibited. All rights reserved. This content is provided for test preparation purposes only and does not imply an endorsement by Mometrix of any particular political, scientific, or religious point of view.

test. If your test isn't first thing in the morning, consider going for a walk or doing a light workout before the test to get your blood flowing.

Allow yourself enough time to get ready, and leave for the test with plenty of time to spare so you won't have the anxiety of scrambling to arrive in time. Another reason to be early is to select a good seat. It's helpful to sit away from doors and windows, which can be distracting. Find a good seat, get out your supplies, and settle your mind before the test begins.

When the test begins, start by going over the instructions carefully, even if you already know what to expect. Make sure you avoid any careless mistakes by following the directions.

Then begin working through the questions, pacing yourself as you've practiced. If you're not sure on an answer, don't spend too much time on it, and don't let it shake your confidence. Either skip it and come back later, or eliminate as many wrong answers as possible and guess among the remaining ones. Don't dwell on these questions as you continue—put them out of your mind and focus on what lies ahead.

Be sure to read all of the answer choices, even if you're sure the first one is the right answer. Sometimes you'll find a better one if you keep reading. But don't second-guess yourself if you do immediately know the answer. Your gut instinct is usually right. Don't let test anxiety rob you of the information you know.

If you have time at the end of the test (and if the test format allows), go back and review your answers. Be cautious about changing any, since your first instinct tends to be correct, but make sure you didn't misread any of the questions or accidentally mark the wrong answer choice. Look over any you skipped and make an educated guess.

At the end, leave the test feeling confident. You've done your best, so don't waste time worrying about your performance or wishing you could change anything. Instead, celebrate the successful completion of this test. And finally, use this test to learn how to deal with anxiety even better next time.

> **Review Video: Test Anxiety**
> Visit mometrix.com/academy and enter code: 100340

Important Qualification

Not all anxiety is created equal. If your test anxiety is causing major issues in your life beyond the classroom or testing center, or if you are experiencing troubling physical symptoms related to your anxiety, it may be a sign of a serious physiological or psychological condition. If this sounds like your situation, we strongly encourage you to seek professional help.

Copyright © Mometrix Media. You have been licensed one copy of this document for personal use only. Any other reproduction or redistribution is strictly prohibited. All rights reserved. This content is provided for test preparation purposes only and does not imply an endorsement by Mometrix of any particular political, scientific, or religious point of view.

Additional Bonus Material

Due to our efforts to try to keep this book to a manageable length, we've created a link that will give you access to all of your additional bonus material:

mometrix.com/bonus948/civilservice

Copyright © Mometrix Media. You have been licensed one copy of this document for personal use only. Any other reproduction or redistribution is strictly prohibited. All rights reserved. This content is provided for test preparation purposes only and does not imply an endorsement by Mometrix of any particular political, scientific, or religious point of view.

Made in United States
North Haven, CT
23 August 2024

56467922R00163